D1265741

PUBLICATION DESIGN

Samir Husni
6A University Terrace
Columbia, Mo. 65201

PUBLICATION

SECOND EDITION

Wm. C. Brown Company Publishers

Dubuque, Iowa

DESIGN *Roy Paul Nelson*

Copyright © 1972, 1978 by Wm. C. Brown Company Publishers

Library of Congress Card Number: 78-50177

ISBN 0–697–04324–X

Designer: Roy Paul Nelson

Second Edition

Second Printing, 1979

Printed in the United States of America

By Roy Paul Nelson

Publication Design
The Design of Advertising
Comic Art and Caricature
Articles and Features
Cartooning
The Fourth Estate (with John L. Hulteng)
Visits with 30 Magazine Art Directors
Fell's Guide to Commercial Art (with Byron Ferris)
Fell's Guide to the Art of Cartooning

Preface

Publication Design deals with a continuing problem in journalism: how to coordinate art and typography with content. Through text and illustration, the book suggests ways to make pages and spreads in magazines, newspapers, books, and other publications attractive and easy to read. As a book of techniques, it directs itself to potential and practicing art directors and designers and to editors who do their own designing.

It also directs itself to journalists in general, trying to build in them an appreciation for good graphic design. While these journalists may not be called upon to actually design and lay out pages, they may have the responsibility for hiring designers and approving their work. A goal of this book is to help editor and art director work together more harmoniously. Friction exists between the two on many publications: the editor suspects that art and distinctive typography detract from articles and stories; the art director thinks of the editor as a visual illiterate.

The first edition of the book noted a scarcity of material on publication design and especially magazine design, but soon afterwards several excellent books appeared on the market. One came out just before this one and, by coincidence, bore the same title. The bibliographies at the ends of the chapters list those books along with the scores of books on narrower aspects of design, such as typography and letterform. (See especially the bibliography at the end of chapter 5.)

This book differs from other books on publication design and layout in that it concerns itself as much with editing as with design matters.

As a textbook, it documents its information, where possible, and tries to keep in check its author's biases. Where the author lays down rules, he tries to offer reasons. But the rules of design in the 1970s become harder and harder to defend as art directors experiment, apparently successfully, with exciting new arrangements and styles.

While the emphasis in this new edition continues to be on magazines, the book deals at some length with newspapers and books, also; and a new chapter deals with infrequently issued publications, low-budget and odd-format publications, and pieces of printing that fall under the heading of direct-mail advertising. The reader will find that the information and advice throughout the book apply in some ways to all publications.

To distinguish between person and artifact, the book occasionally relies on the generic "he" in preference to the less precise "they" or the cumbersome "he or she," but readers will understand that graphic design as a career today recognizes no difference between the sexes.

Publication Design serves as a textbook or supplemental reading for students in such courses as Publication Design and Production, Graphic Design, Graphic Arts, Typography, Magazine Editing, Newspaper Editing, Picture Editing, Book Publishing, Publishing Procedures, Business and Industrial Journalism, and Supervision of School Publications.

Instructors who have used the book as a textbook will notice in this new edition necessary updating and rearranging of material and the introduction of new material. Illustrations that served well in the first edition remain, but many new illustrations appear in every chapter. The book now is much more generously illustrated.

Since the publication of the first edition in 1972, the author has conducted a monthly column on design for *IABC News*, a publication of the International Association of Business Communicators. An occasional section in this new edition draws from material appearing in that column. Also, as was true of the first edition, this one in its opening chapters relies in part on some informal research conducted under a grant from the Magazine Publishers Association.

—RPN

University of Oregon

Contents

Chapter 1

Emergence of magazine design

Books produced in fifteenth-century Italy, after movable type was perfected by Johann Gutenberg in Germany, are prized today by museums and collectors as art of a high order. Bibliophiles see in these books a design and printing quality not found in latter-day publications. Their excellence is all the more remarkable when you consider that the men of incunabula had to design their own types, cut them, make their own inks and in some instances their own papers, write their own books and do their own translating of the classics, set their own type, do their own printing, and sell their own product.

Or maybe that explains the excellence. With so proprietary an interest in the product, fifteenth-century artisans gave appearance and readability all necessary attention. But when the demand for printing grew, printers found it expedient to subdivide the work. Some designed and cut types—exclusively. Others set type—exclusively. Others ran presses—exclusively. Others wrote and edited copy, while still others took care of business matters. Specialization set in, and, inevitably, quality deteriorated.

By the time periodicals took their place alongside books as products of the press, page design was all but forgotten. Nobody elected to stay with the product through its various stages to see to it that it had, overall, the beauty and readability of earlier products of the press.

Then came photography and photoengraving—in the nineteenth century. As art was combined with type on the page, the need for coordination of these elements became apparent. Because art, when it was used, tended to dominate the page, the people responsible for fitting type and art together became known, first, as art editors and, later, as art directors.

The first magazine art director

No one can say who functioned as the first art editor or art director of a periodical. One of the first in this country, certainly, was Charles Parsons of the Harper & Brothers organization (now Harper & Row), publishers of books and magazines. It was Parsons who conceived the idea of gathering together a group of illustrators and schooling them in the needs of a publishing concern, and working with other artists on the outside as need for art increased at certain times of the year. He became a director of art.

Himself an illustrator of note, Parsons joined the staff at Harper's in 1863, serving twenty-six years. He directed artists for both the book- and magazine-publishing divisions of the company. Among his staffers were Winslow Homer, Thomas Nast, Edwin A. Abbey, and W. A. Rogers. Of Parsons, Rogers wrote: "Thanks to the clear vision and good common sense of wise old Charles Parsons, every man who came to Franklin Square [where the firm had offices]—and it was the Mecca of illustrators in those days—was encouraged to be true to his own ideas, to develop his own style."[1]

So great was Parsons's influence on commercial art of the late nineteenth century that artists referred to his department as "The Franklin Square School." As many as eight artists worked full time. Freelancers, including Frederic Remington and Howard Pyle, took on special assignments.

1. Quoted by Eugene Exman in *The House of Harper*, Harper & Row, Publishers, New York, 1967, p. 107.

The Cosmopolitan *of May 1895 was a far cry from the Helen Gurley Brown's* Cosmopolitan *of the 1970s. Here's a spread from an article on "The Pleasant Occupation of Tending Bees." You see square-finish and vignette halftones, each with an all-cap caption. The two-column format was standard for 6 × 9 magazines.*

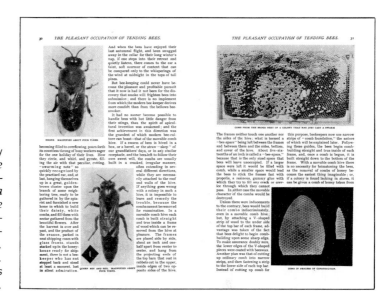

By the 1880s, Parsons was able to pay freelancers an average of $75 per illustration. For some works, he paid $150 or more.

Nearly all the illustrations had to be hand engraved on wood. It was after Parsons resigned in 1889 that photoengraving became a reality and illustration—including photos—became a vital part of most magazines. *Harper's Weekly* and *Harper's Magazine* were no longer alone as vehicles for illustrations. Every publication could run them.

Still, no one apparently thought to coordinate art with type to achieve real design in magazines.

The pioneering fashion magazines

The magazines that, as a group, pioneered in good design were, understandably, the fashion books—especially *Harper's Bazaar.*[2] It was in 1913, after it had been purchased by William Randolph Hearst, that the Russian-born Erté, a designer for the theater, joined the staff. An illustrator in the manner of Aubrey Beardsley, Erté introduced an entirely new visual sensibility to the magazine.[3]

In 1934 another Russian-born designer, Alexey Brodovitch, became the art director, a position he held until 1958. He sought to give the magazine what *Print* magazine called "a musical feeling, a rhythm resulting from the interaction of space and time—he wanted the magazine to read like a sheet of music. He and [editor] Carmel Snow would dance around the pages spread before them on the floor, trying to pick up the rhythm."

Brodovitch introduced to magazines the use of large blocks of white. For freshness, he used accomplished artists and photographers for kinds of work they had not tried before. At *Harper's Bazaar* he got Cartier-Bresson, Dali, Man Ray, and Richard Avedon to do fashions.

According to *Print*, Brodovitch "kept apprentices at his side much like an Old World master painter." He became famous not only as a designer but also as a photographer. He began teaching at the Philadelphia Museum in 1930, and among his students were Otto Storch, Henry Wolf, Samuel Antupit, and the photographer Irving Penn. Penn said: "All photographers are students of Brodovitch, whether they know it or not." Allen Hurlburt, formerly director of design for Cowles Communications, added:

By the turn of the century, magazines were able to reproduce both line and halftone art, but real flair in design had not yet taken hold. This page from the April 1903 issue of The Century Magazine *was typical. The look is more that of a book than a magazine. One article ends on this right-hand page, another begins. The only art is an ending decoration and an embellished initial letter.*

2. Some of what follows in this chapter and some of chapter 2 appeared in a different form in the author's *Visits with 30 Magazine Art Directors*, published by the Education Committee of the Magazine Publishers Association, New York. Copyright 1969 by the Magazine Publishers Association. Reprinted by permission.

3. See "Harper's Bazaar at 100," *Print*, September-October 1967, pp. 42-49.

"This also applies to graphic designers."

"This disarming, glum, elegant, shy, incredibly tough artist made an impact on the design of this country that eludes description to this day," says a writer for *U&lc.* "Measured on the quality of his graphic performances and his contributions to the modern magazine alone, he must be ranked as the towering giant of our time. . . ." He was "the master craftsman who began it all."[4]

Another leader in magazine design was Dr. M. F. Agha, who became art director of *Vanity Fair* in 1929. Hurlburt has said this of Dr. Agha: "He entered areas of editorial judgment long denied to artists and created a magazine that brought typography, illustration, photography, and page design into a cohesion that has rarely been equalled. After exposure to the severe test of more than thirty of the fastest changing years in history, the pages of *Vanity Fair* remain surprisingly fresh and exciting."[5] Hurlburt gives much credit, too, to Editor Frank Crowninshield for his "rare discernment and good taste."

Unfortunately, *Vanity Fair* became a Depression victim; but Dr. Agha continued his association with the Condé Nast organization until 1942 as art director of *Vogue* and *House and Garden.* Many of today's top designers trained under Dr. Agha.

Changes in the 1930s

Still, the well-designed magazine was an exception. Well into the 1930s, most American magazines fitted themselves together, newspaper-style; when there was a column that didn't quite reach the bottom of the page, the editor simply threw in a filler. If a visually oriented person was around, his job was primarily to buy illustrations, especially for the cover, and maybe to retouch photographs.

Two early-1930s books on magazine editing gave scant attention to art direction. John Bakeless in *Magazine Making* (Viking Press, New York, 1931) carried a six-page appendix on "Methods of Lay-Out." In it Bakeless discussed briefly a travel magazine that used "the daring device of running a picture across all of one page and part of another." The book itself mentioned "art editor" twice and recommended at least one such person for "a large, illustrated periodical." Bakeless said that magazines using no pictures "obviously do not require an art editor."

4. Jack Anson Finke, "Pro-File: Alexey Brodovitch," *U&lc.*, March 1977, p. 9. *U&lc.* beginning with this issue ran a series on famous designers and art directors.

5. Quoted from *Magazines:USA*, The American Institute of Graphic Arts, New York, 1965. See Cleveland Amory and Frederic Bradlee (Editors), *Vanity Fair: A Cavalcade of the 1920s and 1930s*, Viking Press, New York, 1970.

Here she is: The Gibson Girl of an earlier era, admired, desired, and, by a jealous few, despised. The magazine illustrator and cartoonist, Charles Dana Gibson, through the magazines made her one of the nation's most known symbols. This pen and ink sketch is from the old Life.

Lenox R. Lohr in *Magazine Publishing* (Williams & Wilkins Company, Baltimore, 1932) devoted a chapter to illustrations and another to "Mechanics of Editing'" but in them he gave only six pages to "Make-Up of an Issue."

One of the first non-fashion magazines to be fully designed was *Fortune*, introduced in February 1930 at a bold one dollar per copy. The designer was T. M. Cleland, who later set the format for the experimental newspaper *PM*. And *Esquire*, when it started in 1933, started right out with an art director. But he was a cartoonist, John Groth, who filled a good part of the first issue with his own cartoons.

Several designers from the Bauhaus in Germany, fleeing Hitler, arrived in America in the early 1930s and influenced not only magazines but also advertising design. The Bauhaus emphasis was on the functional in design. The look was one of order and precision.

Among native Americans, Paul Rand, with *Apparel Arts*, and Bradbury Thompson, with *Mademoiselle* and several other magazines, were standouts as magazine designers.

And since the 1930s

In the 1940s Alexey Brodovitch designed a magazine that, with breathtaking beauty, showed other art directors what a well-designed magazine could be. Called *Portfolio*, it lasted three issues. That it was "ahead of its time" is probably an appropriate appraisal. In the late 1940s and early 1950s *Flair* (Louis-Marie Eude and later Hershel Bramson, art directors), although not universally admired by other art directors, encouraged format experimentation. It also was short-lived. In the early 1960s *Show*, with Henry Wolf as art director, shook up magazine design thinking. Allen Hurlburt observed: "[Wolf's] imaginative cover ideas and the precise simplicity of his pages have begun to influence a new generation of designers." *Show* soon died, too.

Stimulated by these thrusts, the well-established magazines began paying more attention to design. Allen Hurlburt took over as *Look's* art director in 1953 and gradually built the magazine, from a design standpoint, into one of the most admired in America. After the mid-1950s and "Togetherness," Herbert Mayes, the new editor of *McCall's*, let his art director, Otto Storch, have a free hand: what Storch did with types and pictures prompted all magazines to make themselves more exciting visually. Prodded by what Arthur Paul was doing in design with the upstart *Playboy, Esquire* redesigned itself.

Allen Hurlburt has noted a change in the art director's function with the coming of television. Before TV, the function of the art director, in an agency or on a magazine, was simply "arranging things that were handed him." With story boards for TV, the art director provided ideas, and the copywriter filled in with words. The art director became more important. As his status improved in advertising agencies, it improved on magazines.

One of the important influences on magazine design in the 1960s in America was Push Pin Studios, New York. (A founder of Push Pin, Milton Glaser, was until 1977 design director of *New York.*) The organization was described by a magazine for the book trade as "one of the pioneering forces in developing an imaginative contemporary style that has had a major influence on the direction of current visual communications on an international scale."[6] The same magazine quoted the late Jerome Snyder, then art director of *Scientific American,* as saying that if imitation or plagiarism is any indication of flattery Push Pin "is by far the most flattered group in contemporary graphics."[7] "The growing reputation has allowed Push Pin the luxury of a healthy snobbishness in their acceptance of assignments, and potential clients have been conditioned into calling on Push Pin only when they were ready to accept the excellence of their work without too many suggestions for 'improvement,' " Henry Wolf wrote in the Foreword to *The Push Pin Style.*[8]

Since 1957 Push Pin has published *The Push Pin Graphic,* described by a writer for *The New York Times Magazine* as "one of the least known periodicals of its time." In 1977 the magazine was making a modest bid to widen its audience.

Also wielding important influence on magazine design in the 1960s were two magazines in Europe, *Tuyonne* and *Twen,* art-directed by Willie Fleckhaus. Art directors on American magazines drew considerable inspiration from these and several

6. "Louvre Holds Retrospective of Push Pin Studios' Graphics," *Publishers' Weekly,* April 13, 1970, p. 70.
7. *Ibid.,* p. 72.
8. Published by Communication Arts, Palo Alto, California, 1970.

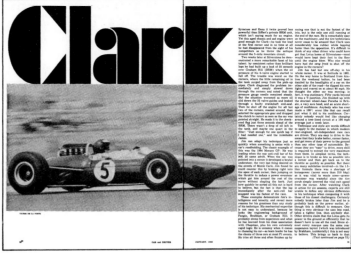

other European magazines, including some published in Great Britain. It may be true that European art direction has lagged behind American art direction where advertising is concerned, but in the case of magazine art direction, it could be argued that Europe has been more innovative than America.

Magazines of the 1970s

In the 1960s magazine design had been dazzling and spectacular, but it seemed *fitted on* rather than incorporated into the content. *Print* called the look "stupifyingly shallow." In the 1970s, magazines seemed to enter a new era: the emphasis was on content.

Communication Arts and *Print* in 1970 both put out special issues on magazine design. Both were critical of what they had seen in the 1960s. The magazine industry, they agreed, was in a bad way because it had not adjusted to the times—not in content, not in design. Both agreed that flashy graphics often covered up for lack of any really meaningful content. Nor were the graphics of a kind to delight the eye.

The chief problems were those of slickness and sameness. *Print* said major magazines look alike because their art directors play musical chairs, moving from magazine to magazine, "spreading their best ideas and perpetuating their worst mistakes." Dugald Stermer, ex-art director for *Ramparts*, was quoted as saying, 'This makes magazines very inbred, almost incestuous."

The hope of the 1970s seemed to lie with specialized publications.

". . . The magazines that are doing well (and a surprising number are doing very well indeed) are the ones that don't try to

A still contemporary layout from a 1966 issue of Car and Driver *(Gene Butera, art director). The title, "Jim Clark," in heavy, stenciled letters, starts on one page and continues on the next two pages, carrying the reader with it. The top of the x-height of the title on the inside two pages aligns with the tops of the columns of text. The article begins in one size type, then—newspaper style— it breaks down into two columns set in a smaller size.*

be all things to all people—that have well defined subject matter along with a well defined audience," said the editors of *Print*.[9]

In an interview conducted by Dick Coyne for *Communication Arts*, Henry Wolf described magazine design in this way: "There hasn't been anything really new in the past twenty years. Most of the magazines are very professional, very slick, and you can hardly tell which one you're looking at."

Allen Hurlburt was somewhat encouraged by what he saw in lesser publications. "There is something that started with the underground press and then got picked up in *Rolling Stone*. . . . This kind of brutalist, rough paper, rough printing, roughly expressed thing is as close as you can get to a trend in the physical appearance of magazines. Is this only happening because those magazines can't afford anything else? Do they dream of the day when they will be slick?"

Richard Hess, of Hess and/or Antupit, answered: "Unfortunately, too many of them do. And the terrible thing is that, when they round off the rough edges, all of that vitality seems to leak out."[10]

Writing in *Print*, Samuel Antupit also liked *Rolling Stone* ("It is designed and written by people it aims at. . . . The format is large and the design is loose."). The only other magazine he praised was *Harper's*. He noted its "gimmick-less layout, well-thought-out typography and photographs that are few but aptly chosen, used large and with great effect."[11]

Specialized magazines

Part of the impetus for better publication design today comes from small magazines, especially the new ones. Their editors, realizing that their readers are accustomed to exciting visuals from sources other than magazines, attempt to make their magazines just as exciting to look at as the new films, the new products, the new paintings. These editors don't have to buck tradition. They serve homogeneous audiences. They have less to lose.

One specialized magazine that proved to be a trend setter was *Psychology Today*. In an early issue (January 1968) Nicolas H. Charney, editor and publisher, credited the magazine's "lively new look in graphic design" to its then art director, Donald K. Wright. "We think he was born with that bemused and faraway look. . . . He has an incredible mental file of graphic oddities. . . . And he is an unbudgeable perfectionist in seeking

9. "Magazines After McLuhan," *Print*, July/August 1970, p. 19
10. "Magazines," *Communication Arts*, vol. 12, no. 4, 1970, p. 27.
11. Samuel N. Antupit, "Understanding Magazines," *Print*, July/August 1970, p. 23.

the precise scene to illustrate every article." By the time the magazine was eight issues old, the art director had (1) tranquilized rabbits to make them better models for the photographer, (2) traveled to Mexico to find some chessmen for special faces, (3) packed in to the desert, climbed mountains, traveled 100 miles along the railroad tracks "to find the necessary open land for just one photograph."

One of the most exciting groups of magazines to watch are the company magazines—sometimes called "house organs." Some of the very best graphic design is found in this group—and some of the very worst. In one respect, these magazines are an art director's dream. They carry no advertising around which editorial matter must wrap. The design theme can run through without interruption. That it does not do so in many house organs can be laid to the fact that their budgets preclude hiring an art director; they remain undesigned. And many others are designed in outside shops, inhibiting thorough integration of design and editorial matter.

Of all magazine groups, the trade journals—or "businesspapers" as they are sometimes called—are probably the least design conscious. Excepting those going to physicians, architects, and similar professional groups, these magazines—especially the smaller ones—are "laid out" by editors rather than designed by art directors. These editors are newspaper-oriented in their choice of typefaces, arrangement of headlines, and use of photographs. Exceptions include McGraw-Hill's *Fleet Owner.*

"For many years publishers have used the words 'trade journals' as an excuse for poor taste and bad design," observes Bud Clarke, art editor of *Fleet Owner.*

The art editor or art director of these publications was either using the position as a stepping stone to consumer books or semi-retirement. And in many cases the editor wore two hats. . . . [The position of] art director was an unnecessary expense.

Now, however, times are changing. Our readers have more demands placed upon their "free" time, i.e., TV. The reading they do must be selective, interesting, and suited to their particular way of life.

This basically is why there is a small, but rapidly growing interest in design for the specialized reader. Many designers and art directors today feel that trade publications are a rewarding end in themselves rather than the means. Budgets and, of course, salaries are growing along with this interest, and a new era of good taste and design is emerging.[12]

A one-page feature from Fleet Owner *(Bud Clarke, art editor). The right edge of the first line of the title lines up with the right edge of the photo; the left edge of the last word in the title lines up with the left edge of the photo. Paragraphing is accomplished by means of small boxes inside the text. The boxes relate to the boxed photo. In all, a strongly unified page. (With permission from* Fleet Owner. *Copyright 1970 by McGraw-Hill, Inc. All rights reserved.)*

12. Letter to the author from Bud Clarke, Aug. 17, 1970.

Suggested further reading

BARTHES, ROLAND, *Erté*, Franco Maria Ricci, Publisher, Parma, Italy, 1972.

BOJKO, SZYMON, *New Graphic Design in Revolutionary Russia*, Praeger Publishers, New York, 1972. (Examples from the 1920s and 1930s.)

CHAPPELL, WARREN, *A Short History of the Printed Word*, Alfred A. Knopf, Inc., New York, 1970.

FEREBEE, ANN, *A History of Design*, Van Nostrand Reinhold Company, New York, 1970. (Covers Victorian, Art Nouveau, and Modern styles.)

HAMILTON, EDWARD A., *Graphic Design for the Computer Age: Visual Communication for All Media*, Van Nostrand Reinhold Company, New York, 1970. (By the art director of Time-Life Books.)

MULLER-BROCKMANN, JOSEF, *The Development of Commercial Art*, Hastings House, Publishers, New York, 1968.

NIECE, ROBERT CLEMENS, *Art in Commerce and Industry*, Wm. C. Brown Company Publishers, Dubuque, Iowa, 1968.

REED, WALT, ed., *The Illustrator in America, 1900-1960s*, Reinhold Publishing Corporation, New York, 1967.

SPENCER, CHARLES, *Erté*, Clarkson N. Potter, Inc., New York, 1970.

The Push Pin Style, Communication Arts Magazine, Palo Alto, California, 1970.

Art Direction, New York. (Monthly.)

Communication Arts, Palo Alto, California. (Bi-monthly.)

Print, Washington, D.C. (Bi-monthly.)

Chapter 2

The magazine art director

Bob Graf, editor of *Portrait* magazine published by General Telephone Company of California, has said: "[Magazines] are not just read, they are in a sense beheld; they are enjoyed beyond the power of the information they contain to cause enjoyment, and when they finally are discarded, it is with a sort of reluctance, as there is when you reach the end of a good book." If that is true, the art directors of these publications deserve much of the credit.

This chapter, based in part on the author's interviews with magazine art directors on magazines in New York, Washington, San Francisco, Oakland, and Los Angeles, explores the role of art directors on American magazines. Whether you plan to design your own magazine or employ an art director to do it for you, you need to better understand and appreciate that role.

By any other name

As art directors have risen on magazine mastheads—in some cases to a spot just below that of the editor—they have become vaguely dissatisfied with their titles. No one has yet come up with a title that fully describes the art director's several functions: to buy and edit illustrations and photographs, choose typefaces, make production decisions, and design and lay out the magazine. Titles in use include *art editor, designer, design editor, design director, design consultant, type director, production editor, picture editor. Art director* remains the most common title.

But *art director* does not connote concern with type and design. *Art editor*, the preferred title of the 1930s and 1940s, is worse: it brings to mind a person who runs a section of the

The industrial revolution brought the machine to typography and design, and pages began to look less decorative and more sterile. Eduard Bendemann in Germany was one designer who kept romanticism alive on pages he controlled. He designed this one in 1840. Observe how he has taken the basic design of his text or blackletter type (known as Old English) and applied it to the art and border elements on the page. This is a beautifully unified page. The decorative initial M, which juts up above the first line of body copy rather than down into the paragraph, is drawn in outline form to match the heading in the box under the figures.

magazine devoted to a discussion of painting and other of the fine arts. The old terms no longer seem adequate, especially now that some art directors are making editorial and management decisions.

Perhaps a magazine should have two chief editors: a *verbal editor* and a *visual editor.* Maybe *editorial director* and *design director,* used on some magazines, represent the best combination of titles.

Some art directors are flirting with the term "communicator." And not necessarily "visual communicator." The word "visual" in some art directors' circles is outmoded. On some magazines, the job is more than "visual." Art directors are interested in bringing *all* the senses into play—not just the sense of sight. The *feel* of the paper, for instance, is part of it. So are smells. A magazine—or a book for children—may want to make use of encapsulated fragrances.

One for every magazine

Ideally, every magazine should have an art director. If he is not employed full time, he can be employed part time. If he isn't part of the magazine's own staff, he can be a freelancer or a designer attached to a design studio.

James W. O'Bryan, art director of *National Review,* runs a design studio in the building and treats the magazine as one client, although a very special one.

William Delorme handled *Los Angeles* from his studio miles away from the magazine's editorial offices. The magazine took 70 percent of his "working" time. He spent the other 30 percent on other graphic design assignments and on fine arts painting. "I put 'working' in quotes . . . because at least three weeks out of the month my time is my own. . . . The magazine work can be done at home in the evenings or on weekends. One week out of the month is practically round-the-clock labor on the magazine in order to meet printing deadlines." He visited the magazine for editorial conferences and to present his rough ideas and finished layouts. He saw photographers and illustrators in his studio.

Many company magazines are designed in this way, if not by studio designers, then by advertising agency art directors. But what about the small magazine that can't afford this help? And what if the editor doesn't want to—or can't—do his own designing?

Samuel Antupit, then with *Esquire,* said that if a magazine cannot afford an art director, it cannot afford to publish. Bernard Quint, then with *Life,* was less acrimonious. He suggested that an imaginative printer can do a lot for a magazine. Perhaps more than other magazines, the small magazine should hunt out such a printer and pay a little more for printing, if necessary.

Quint felt that too many small publications are printed by printers who cut too many corners, making already dull periodicals even duller.

If a magazine cannot afford an art director, it should hire a designer temporarily to set a simple, standard format that an editor can follow. At the least, an editor without design expertise or without an art director should avoid oddball typography, tricks with photographs, and complicated layouts. Some of the best-designed magazines are the simplest.

The art director's background

Schools do not offer adequate training programs for magazine art directors. The art schools—the commercial schools—are mostly advertising-oriented. The fine arts schools seem mostly interested in developing painters. The journalism schools—many of them—still think in terms of newspaper makeup.

So art directors come to magazines by circuitous routes. In the early history of magazine art direction, when the job involved primarily the purchasing of art work, they came largely from the ranks of illustrators. Even when type direction became a more important part of the job, the illustrator's background served him well. A good illustrator is as interested in the design of his painting as in the draftsmanship. The feel for design can be transferred from the canvas board to the printed page.

But today art directors increasingly come to magazines with backgrounds other than in illustration. They come with a more thorough knowledge of typography than their predecessors. Many neither draw nor paint. A few feel that a background in illustration would prejudice them in their art buying.

Advertising agency art direction provides a major training ground for magazine art directors. Art directors today move freely from agency to magazine jobs. This is surprising when you consider the unlikelihood of an advertising copywriter moving into a magazine editorial slot.

On small magazines, art directors may even find themselves assigned the job of designing ads for small firms who don't have their ads prepared by or placed through advertising agencies.

But the two jobs—magazine art direction and advertising art direction—are quite different. The magazine art director sees his mistakes in one issue, works to correct them in the next. He continues to polish a lasting product. His improvements are cumulative. The advertising designer, on the other hand, deals essentially with one-shots. And he has clients as well as readers to please. Henry Wolf, once an *Esquire* art director, told why magazine work had it over advertising work:

In a time when most activities are dictated by ulterior motives, designing a magazine provides a happy, if outmoded, thrill: to do something for its own sake and run out on a limb with it, waving.

In every age designers have played with type to make illustrative art of it. In this example, from the year 1886, Walter Crane takes the first letter of the book title he is working with and makes it a unit in his drawing of a house.

The art director's nature

Society has always regarded the artist with some suspicion. Even the art director—an artist gone businesslike—has a reputation for being "different." A *National Observer* article about art directors had Jo Foxworth, vice-president and creative director for Calkins & Holden advertising agency, saying this: "I know a $20,000-a-year art director who gleefully ragpicks his way through every secondhand clothing store on the Lower East Side, hunting for such treasures as pants with buttons instead of zippers and Army shirts from World War I. The other day when I had occasion to visit his agency, I couldn't tell what he had worn to work that day, because he was sitting cross-legged on his window sill, totally cocooned in an old Indian blanket that looked like a leftover from Custer's last stand. He said he was cold. And I'm sure he was; he was sitting on the air-conditioning outlet."

There is probably less of the bizarre among magazine art directors than among advertising agency art directors. On magazines, routine is more pronounced, deadlines more regular.

Still, an art director is an art director.

In *New York* magazine, Linda Abrams considered the implications of "Living with a Fussy Man."[1] "Living with an art director isn't easy," she reported, and she listed a series of complaints from various women who had experimented with so precarious an arrangement.

The basic problem, it turned out, had to do with decor. An art director is "obsessively involved with his environment." The non-art director in any kind of a living arrangement ends up, as one wife expressed it, "feel[ing] like a guest in my own home." One complainant said that whenever she arranged some flowers, her art director husband would walk into the room and promptly rearrange them.

George Lois, the advertising executive who used to design the *Esquire* covers, is quoted as saying: "When I come home from work, the first thing I do is hug my wife and the second thing I do is go around the apartment and rearrange everything so that it is placed perfectly, the way I want it."

"The home to an art director is a giant layout with endless possibilities," Abrams wrote. "Not only is he interested in what the furniture looks like, but also the shower curtains, picture frames, door knobs, dishes, Christmas cards (an important symbol of taste that everyone sees), and appliances.

"Better a toaster should be a Braun than a G.E.—the G.E. may be more functional, but the Braun is better designed."

She added: "Dining room tables look like they've been set

In the 1920s the Bauhaus in Germany was establishing the principle that design should be simple, geometric, and above all functional. Still, some important designers of that period continued to bring to design the decorative quality of an earlier era. This is a Paul Renner book cover, so rich in personality and texture that the designer was allowed to sign it.

PAUL RENNER

1. Linda Abrams, "Living with a Fussy Man," *New York*, October 8, 1973, pp. 37-51.

with a T-square and every corner is a still life waiting to be photographed."

Words used to describe art directors in Abrams's article seemed to fall mostly in the "egotistical," "rigid," and "meticulous" categories. About all that emerged on the credit side of living with an art director was that at least he "will never leave his socks on the living room floor."

Visit an art director's studio and you will see what Abrams is driving at. There you will see the usual Eames chair, and never mind that it was designed for a five-foot-eighter rather than the six-footer who bought it. Who needs support for the back of his neck as he lounges? Ask the art director the time, and watch him study carefully his Movado "museum timepiece" with its plain black face interrupted only by a small gold ball where the "12" is supposed to be. Breathtaking in its stark beauty is that watch, but all the art director can tell you is that it is before—or is it after?—noon. His fountain pen is a chrome-and-black marvel, almost impossible to hold onto as he writes because of the cone-shaped tip and because two metal clips there that hold the cap in place dig into his fingers, causing him pain.

J. B. Handelsman, the cartoonist, showed what he thought of art directors (had one redesigned a magazine and closed out the gag cartoons?) with a picture of St. Peter standing at the gates of heaven talking to a worried-looking man on the outside. In back of St. Peter was an art director (you could tell he was an art director by his hair style and mod clothes). St. Peter was telling the man outside: "I'm terribly sorry. The art director thinks your ears are too big."

Beyond page layout

Magazine art directors, like other journalists, have taken sides in the struggle for social, economic, and political changes. The art director for *National Review*, James W. O'Bryan, worked free at first because he shared the philosophy of the *Review's* ultra-conservative publisher, William F. Buckley, Jr. Dugald Stermer played the important role he did on *Ramparts* because he believed in the leftist causes of that magazine. For the cover of one of its issues—in 1967—Stermer arranged for a photograph of four hands holding up burning draft cards. One of the hands was Stermer's. "If you're looking for an editorial in the usual place this month," said the magazine, "forget it. It's on the cover." The partners at Hess and/or Antupit, besides designing magazines and advertising and corporate pieces, handled a number of causes gratis or for low fees.

One thing becomes clear as you talk to art directors: they no longer are content merely to lay out pages. They argue—and the logic here is inescapable—that for a magazine to be effective both verbally and visually, its art director must be involved in the planning as well as the production stages. Art directors on some of the magazines, major and minor, regard themselves as operating on the same level as their editors. Some art directors say that if they didn't have a say about the policy their magazines adopt and the articles and stories their magazines accept, they would resign.

Richard Gangel, as art director of *Sports Illustrated,* was part of a triumvirate which decided policy. He saw his role as primarily journalistic. Dugald Stermer, when he was art director of *Ramparts,* said he wouldn't be content to be "just an art director." He estimated that 80 percent of his time on the magazine

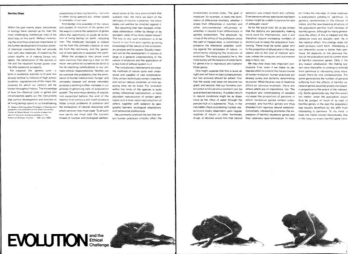

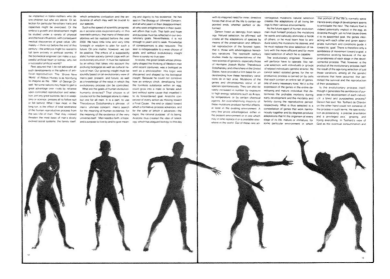

was spent on editorial matters, including fund raising. Kenneth Stuart, as art editor of *Reader's Digest,* checked articles before they were digested and suggested that certain sections be left in because they were illustrateable. Samuel Antupit on *Esquire* took an active role in accepting or rejecting manuscripts for publication.

Of course, someone has to have the final say, and that someone must be the editor. When Michael Parrish resigned in 1975 as editor of the weekly *City Magazine* of San Francisco, the San Francisco *Sunday Examiner and Chronicle* quoted a pleased art director Mike Salisbury as saying, "It's a really beautiful thing. We are all taking pictures, writing articles, and contributing in

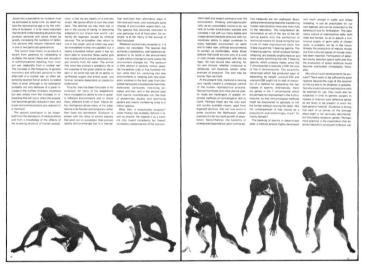

University Review, published by the State University of New York, was one of the best-designed alumni magazines in the country in the 1960s. For this August 1969 issue, designer Richard Danne reuses on the cover a portion of some inside art to create a tie-in of the cover with a lead article. The cover is in dark blue and light green. The inside pages are in stark black and white. The bottom of the copy block area remains constant while the art goes through an evolution right before the readers' eyes. Photographer was Herman Bachmann.

By Frank J. Weinstock, M.D.

blackout

The eyes are really rather fantastic organs. They each receive an image, turn it upside down, flip it back over again, perceive, and combine the images—in color in daytime, black and white when it's dark—all, literally, in less than a blink of an eye! It's not surprising, therefore, that occasionally the system malfunctions. While a sudden loss of vision may not actually stem from the eyes themselves, it's frequently the first manifestation of a change there or somewhere else.

Sound complicated? It is, of course. But really, there's often quite a lot you can do to minimize the visual loss—and sometimes reverse it altogether—if you handle the problem quickly and correctly. And if there's nothing that can or/continued

23

A dramatic and powerful spread from Emergency Medicine *making use of a large face in full color. The face is large enough and cropped close enough to run across the gutter. The size was necessary to make the fogged over eyes readable. The article starts out as reverse copy. Because this is an opening article occuring in the magazine after several pages of advertising, the editors run a small logo at the top.*

various ways. We don't have the traditional editorial hierarchy anymore." *City Magazine* didn't last long.

Life with freelancers

Among his other jobs, the art director acts as an art broker. It is up to him to find the right illustrator or photographer for every cover, article, and story. In most cases, he must deal with talent outside the organization.

The art director often finds the photographer more difficult than the illustrator to deal with. One reason may be that the art director does not recognize the photographer as an artist, and the photographer resents it. The art director is much more likely to edit the product of the photographer. He will crop a photo to fit the available space. He will even have it retouched. An illustration is different.

Mike Salisbury, when he was art director of *West*, late Sunday magazine of the Los Angeles *Times*, thought photos were easy to edit and often exercised his right to edit them. But he thought illustrations shouldn't be changed. Nor did he request an illustrator to make changes once he had submitted the work.

If the illustrator is sufficiently dependable, the art director does not even ask to see roughs first. Frank Kilker, former art editor of *The Saturday Evening Post*, told the story of his acceptance of an illustration from a regular contributor, painted to fit a large area set aside for it in one of the layouts. But clearly, the illustration was not up to that artist's standard. Rather than throw it out, Kilker revamped the layout to make the illustration occupy a smaller space in the spread.

When an art director assigns a job to an illustrator, he often specifies a size and shape to fit an already existing layout. Seldom does the illustrator play a role in the selection of the typeface for the story title or in the placement of the title and body type on the page with his illustration. But of course art directors work differently with each of the various illustrators. An illustrator like Al Parker might well design the page or pages on which his illustration appears and incorporate the title into his painting. In vol. 2, no. 4, issue 8 (1967) of the quarterly *Lithopinion* (no longer published), Parker tried his hand at redesigning the covers of eight leading magazines. Herbert R. Mayes, a magazine editor, evaluated the experimental covers: "When I had my first glimpse of these covers, my reaction was that my old and dear friend Al Parker had gone completely off his nut. At the end of two hours, my reaction was that my young-thinking friend Al Parker had done something that, in the years ahead, may knock the stuffings out of the traditional approach."

Life with the editor

It is understandable that the relationship between the editor and his art director is sometimes strained. The one is word-oriented, the other visual-oriented, and the two orientations are not necessarily compatible. The editor may actually consider display typography and pictures an *intrusion* on the text. Or the editor may expect the impossible of his art director, asking him to fit a particular story and set of photos together in too tight a space. The art director, on the other hand, may be more interested in showing off his tricks with type than in making his magazine readable. Or he may resort to the tired ways of laying out his pages while his editor is trying to move his magazine in some new direction.

The editor may think that his art director looks upon the job as one of solving design problems rather than of putting out a magazine to serve readers. He may put his art director in a class with the writer for *Architecture/West* who, in an article on the population explosion, wrote that if the present 2 percent per year increase continues, in 650 years "there will be merely one foot of space per person—a situation presenting unusual design problems." (*The New Yorker* picked up the quote and ran it under a "Department of Understatement" heading.)

Ideally, the editor and his art director should work as equal or near-equal members of a team, with the art director not only designing the magazine but also helping to make the decisions on editorial policy and content.

Art directors seem unimpressed by, if not hostile to, editors who have design backgrounds. Samuel Antupit thinks such editors, because their knowledge of design is likely to be superficial, are harder to work with than editors who know nothing about design and admit it. Editors who know design know only design clichés, he says.

Herb Lubalin agrees. Lubalin is an art director who will not take dictates from the editor on graphic matters. But neither does he interfere with strictly editorial decisions. Some of Lubalin's best work—and it's been masterful—has been done for the somewhat sleazy publications of Ralph Ginzburg: *Eros, Fact, Avant Garde,* and the currently published *Moneysworth* and *Extra!* He said once that "maybe the graphic excellence will rub off on editorial." He likes working with Ginzburg because Ginzburg gives him a free hand to do what he likes.

Lubalin doesn't think editors, even on smaller magazines, should do their own designing. 'They are bad enough as editors."

The art director and the writer

When freelance writers submit articles for publication in small magazines they often submit photographs, too. The photographs may be of only routine quality. It is up to the art director to pick those that are usable and perhaps to ask that others be retaken. Sometimes the art director can improve the composition of the photographs by cropping them. Sometimes he can turn the photographs over to illustrators to use as guides for

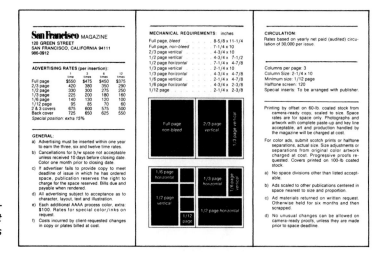

Inside panels of a San Francisco *rate card designed by art director Dan Marr. Note his helpful diagrams of ad sizes.*

paintings or drawings.

But freelance writers almost never have anything to do with the way their articles are laid out. Perhaps magazines should make more of an effort to cooperate with writers on design matters. In gathering examples of page design to be included in this book, this author found it necessary to write to another author to get reprint permission, even though the article would be reproduced in a size too small to read. It was a routine matter. But this is the note that came back: "I hope you don't think me a prig, but I must refuse your request. Each to his own taste—I happen to think the layout for my article . . . was an abomination. Title (not mine), blurb, pictures, and layout all worked together to violate the theme of my article. I cannot separate the layout from its purpose, and its purpose clearly was at odds with the text it supposedly was working with."

The realities of the job

On some magazines, the art director does not control the appearance of all the pages. James W. O'Bryan, for instance, used to do only the cover and the more important spreads for *National Review*. Recent art directors at *Esquire* did not do the covers: George Lois, an advertising art director and agency executive, did them. At *Newsweek*, art director Fred Lowry did not control the cover or the inside color section. When he was at *True*, Norman P. Schoenfeld left back-of-the-book makeup to the back shop, a practice common among magazines. In a way, you could say the whole of *The New Yorker* is put together in this way.

When a magazine sees the need for a thorough revamping of its format, it is likely to call in an outsider to confer with its art director. Herb Lubalin twice in the 1960s came to the rescue of *The Saturday Evening Post* with ideas for revamping, but that was not enough to save the magazine.[2]

Raymond Waites, Jr., the innovative art director of the *United Church Herald* and later *A.D.*, finds it necessary to include in his publication Polaroid shots taken by near amateurs, yet manages to keep the pages attractive.

That he does not oversee *all* the pages; that he gives up control of the most important page of all, the cover; that he is willing to accept art and photography he knows to be inferior; that when redesign is considered it is some outsider who gets to remake the magazine—all this is rough on an art director's ego. That he is willing to live with these conditions is a tribute to his devotion to his magazine. Or maybe it means that, like most of us, he's concerned about job security.

2. Of course, the magazine came back later under new management.

Tenure for the art director

All too many magazine art directors lack a feeling of job security. Between the time the author conducted his research into the role of art directors on American magazines and published his report with the Magazine Publishers Association, a two-year period, at least seven of the thirty art directors he interviewed had moved. *Art Direction* in an October 1969 editorial noted "a flurry of job changes by ADs of top consumer magazines" giving the magazine art director "all the stability and dignity of a major league baseball manager."

Some of the changes obviously were forced by top management people looking for scapegoats for dwindling circulations and loss of advertising revenue. But *Art Direction* admitted part of the problem lay with the art directors themselves. It recognized few great art directors compared to the late 1950s and early 1960s. It concluded that perhaps the top talent had been siphoned off into the film industry and TV.

"Today's magazines—with few exceptions—seem less exciting in content and appearance," *Art Direction* said.

Size of the art staff

On most magazines the art director is not so much a director as a doer. He is a one-person department.

On large magazines, the art director employs several assistants. When he was at *Life*, Bernard Quint had a staff of about twenty, not counting the picture editors. That *Life* came out weekly made so large an art staff necessary. Several persons were there to carry out the rough sketches of the art director, others to do keylines and assembly, others to handle production matters. *Look*, the biweekly, had about fifteen. The big monthlies operate with smaller staffs. Herb Bleiweiss, *Ladies' Home Journal*, had four assistants, but he used them in a way different from most art directors: he let each assistant handle all the details for a single article or story. It made for unity within a feature, but meant that the magazine lacked some unity overall.

Samuel Antupit, on his first stint with *Esquire*, had two assistants and a secretary. In his opinion, "the smaller the staff the better." (These figures do not include artists and designers in the advertising and promotion departments.)

Emergency Medicine, one of the best-designed professional journals in the country, uses only two designers for its 240 to 250 pages per issue. Art director Ira Silberlicht says it can be done because the magazine is a "formatted book. There are a couple of typefaces that we use . . . we don't sit and design headlines in beautiful type and go crazy. The aesthetics and excitement comes [sic] from the theme art. It looks alike from month to month because you are competing with a couple of hundred medical magazines in the field." He wants a stay-the-same look each month to help readers recognize the magazine.[3]

The magazine art director

23

Bringing in a consultant

It was a single-sentence letter: "How much would you charge us to review the last 10 issues of _____ and then meet with us to make recommendations for improving our design and format?" "The trouble with you, Ron," the designer wrote back (he happened to know the editor), "is that you beat around the bush. I had to read through your entire salutation before I came to the meat of your letter. . . ."

A pleasant enough start for a consulting job, and as it turned out, the results pleased all persons involved. The editor changed a few things, and the designer had the satisfaction of seeing the changes come about. But consulting jobs, both from the editor's and from the designer's standpoint, don't always work out as the principals hope.

No doubt editors who have used design consultants can catalog any number of complaints against them. Whether consultants are worth what they cost, in money and in the morale of the in-house designer, is subject to debate. But consultants have gripes, too. Among them, these:

1. The editor calls in the consultant, not because the editor really wants fresh ideas, but because he wants to substantiate his own.

2. The magazine is in desperate circumstances, and the editor knows—he just knows—that redesign can work a miracle.

3. The editor has read a book about design. Or he has heard a lecture by someone like Herb Lubalin or Samuel Antupit. And now the editor knows what's "in."

4. He has just seen a magazine whose looks he likes. Can the consultant duplicate those looks?

5. The editor doesn't really want to change the appearance of the magazine, a look traditional if not outdated, but he would like to try a type like Avant Garde Gothic (with alternate characters) for the headline schedule or titles.

6. Finally, the editor buys a handsome, well thought out format along with elaborate instructions about what to do in every conceivable situation, and he accepts the new design enthusiastically. Within a couple of months, though, he adds a different display face for a new standing column, say, and drops some italic in favor of boldface and decides he would like to try initial letters for some of the articles. What happens then to the look of the magazine is similar to what happens to the appearance of a new, well-designed building when somebody

3. John Peter, "The Top Ten Business Magazines," *Folio,* August 1976, p. 77.

starts placing crude, hand-painted signs above doorways and in windows.

When an editor pays for a new design program he ought to stick to it, and when changes have to be made check back with the designer. Anyway, a design program submitted by an outsider should provide for future adjustments.

Editors of magazines bring in consultants to (1) do a hit-and-run job involving a study of past issues and come up with advice for basic changes to be made by the editor or an in-house designer, (2) do a full-service job, involving the selecting of types and the setting up of a basic design pattern or grid for the editor or in-house art director to follow, or (3) do the actual issue-by-issue design and layout of the magazine. In this final instance, the consultant becomes the art director, working for the editor on a freelance basis.

Freelance art directing

When the editor works with a freelance art director, as on a company magazine, frequent conferences may be necessary not only to alert the art director to editorial complications but also to solicit his advice. Art directors like to be involved in the editorial process. They do not want to be thought of as visual persons only.

But a lot of the contact, typically, comes by phone. The art director may call in the middle of a pasteup to suggest a paragraph cut to make an article fit. This author, acting as a freelance art director, for some years designed a magazine 120 miles away from the editorial offices. Copy and photographs went back and forth by mail and Greyhound Express.

Lionel L. Fisher, editor of *Boise Cascade Paper Times*, has such a good relationship with his freelance art director, Joe Erceg of Portland, Oregon, that he doesn't even ask for thumbnails or roughs before final pasteup begins.

Some art directors carry the work to only a rough-layout, comprehensive, or rough-pasteup stage, leaving the final pasteup to a pasteup artist or to the printer. Whoever does the pasteup, then, simply follows directions. Perhaps the rough that this pasteup artist works from has all kinds of measurements and arrows and instructions marked in the margins. On the other hand, some rough pasteups are so neatly done they could almost stand in as camera-ready copy. They do not need instructions marked in the margins.

At any rate somewhere along the line, *somebody* has to bother with exact fitting of lines of type and headlines and art onto the page. If the art director really cares about the product, he may insist on doing this final pasteup himself. There are always some last-minute, precise fitting decisions to be made.

To a real art director, a half a point of space wrongly placed can ruin an otherwise good day.

The magazine art director

25

The art director as illustrator

The smaller the magazine, the more likely the art director is to do his own illustration. Raymond Waites, Jr., does many of the illustrations for his magazine. Dugald Stermer did some illustrations for *Ramparts* while he was art director, causing Norman Rockwell to remark: "I didn't know he was a painter as well as an art editor. Boy, he has it both ways." In the 1970s Stermer did cover paintings for *Time.*

And for those who cannot draw, there is the camera. It was natural that the art director, working closely with the photographer, should take up the tool himself and do his own shooting. Perhaps the photographer missed a deadline. Perhaps the art director realized he had a better feel for proportion than the photographer had. Otto Storch became so intrigued with the camera that he gave up his job at *McCall's* to go into film work. The startling photo of a woman's thighs on the February, 1970, cover of *Harper's* and a number of other magazine cover and interior shots have been taken by that former magazine art director Henry Wolf.

Some art directors arrived on magazines by way of careers as illustrators. Kenneth Stuart, former art editor of *The Saturday Evening Post,* later art editor of *Reader's Digest,* was one. But Stuart as art editor did not employ Stuart as illustrator. Those who use their own art in magazines have some misgivings about it; but for some magazines, there is no budget for outside work. The art directors do what they must do.

But most art directors can't draw or paint well enough for publication. Samuel Antupit certainly does not consider himself an illustrator. "And I'm afraid to learn. I might be tempted to pick out people who did my kind of illustrating," he says.

Some art directors don't even design. They do only what their titles suggest: they direct. They feel their time is better spent working out solutions than actually executing them.

The art director as inventor

The best of the art directors develop a mechanical aptitude as well as a design sense. Sometimes the effect the art director wants can't be had with ordinary photographs of ordinary props.

For the first issue of the now-defunct *Careers Today,* published by *Psychology Today,* art director Don Wright, to illustrate "The University Womb," cut a womb-shaped hole in a piece of plywood; put supports under the plywood to bring it up from the floor; nailed sheets of clear mylar around the hole to form a well; filled the well with water; put a nude, sandled male in the well; and photographed the setup from the top.

The influence of advertising

Magazine art directors take some inspiration from their colleagues in advertising art direction. Henry Wolf, who left magazine art direction to become a principal in an advertising agency, thinks the best design these days can be found in the ads. Peter Palazzo, who designed *New York* when it was part of the New York *Herald Tribune*, thinks advertising has the best possibilities for graphic excellence.

Bernard Quint, formerly art director for *Life* and *McCall's*, thinks advertising design has had too much effect on magazine design. "The use of design for its own sake has increased in contemporary magazines in direct ratio to the lack of content."

When he was art editor of *The Saturday Evening Post*, Frank Kilker reported that whether or not an art director was acceptable to the advertising fraternity weighed heavily in the consideration of the editor who was about to hire him.

Most art directors interviewed for the author's *Visits with 30 Magazine Art Directors* felt that advertising was setting the trends; magazine design was following. Herb Bleiweiss, of *Ladies' Home Journal*, thought otherwise. Mike Salisbury, of *West*, suggested that the trend-setting function moves back and forth between advertising and magazines, and that magazines would once again be in the forefront.

One thing all agreed on: advertising art directors are better paid. But in the opinion of Roger Waterman, who art directed *Kaiser News* and later *Chevron USA*, advertising art directors are under more pressure and so *should* be better paid.

Attitudes toward magazine design

Art directors are quick to defend certain magazines that appear to have no design. They consider *The New Yorker*, for instance, handsome enough, although it doesn't even have an art director. Its visual excitement comes partly from its cartoons and spot drawings but mostly from the beautiful advertising it carries.

Art directors like a magazine to be unpretentious. A magazine, they feel, should be what it must be, and nothing more. The clean, no-nonsense, almost monotonous look of *Scientific American* under the art direction of Jerome Snyder was much admired by Herb Lubalin, who said of the magazine: "It makes no pretense at great design. But its design really works!"

The younger art directors are particularly outspoken about

the necessity for honesty in design. One of them, Charles Rosner, whose experience has been mostly in design for social causes, has even criticized Herb Lubalin for work that is "over designed."[4]

Major art directors were especially critical of trade journals and, among general-circulation magazines, the publications of Time, Inc. The late Jerome Snyder, speaking at the University of Oregon, invited students to compare *Life* with *Paris Match.* *Paris Match*, he said, was what *Life* could be. (A dissenter was Mike Salisbury, who greatly admired *Life* when Bernard Quint was art director. "I sent him a fan letter once," he told this author.)

4. Vance Johnson, "Charles Rosner," *Communication Arts*, vol. 12, no. 4, 1970, p. 75.

John Whorrall, illustrator and art director for the California Dental Association Journal, *uses the technique of Vincent Van Gogh to imitate a famous self-portrait, but with a slight change. Van Gogh is carrying dental tools on his pallet. The full-cover painting was used both on the cover and as a full page inside to illustrate an article by Woody Allen: "If the Impressionists Had Been Dentists," taken from the book,* Without Feathers. *From one of the "letters" to Theo: ". . . I asked Cezanne if he would share an office with me, but he is old and infirm and unable to hold the instruments and they must be tied to his wrists but then he lacks accuracy and once inside a mouth, he knocks out more teeth than he saves. What to do?"*

Henry Wolf said: "Mass magazines today don't take time for aesthetics. Instead of real design they offer typographic gags. . . ." Remembering the 1950s as the golden age of magazine design, he adds, "There is less freedom now on magazines."

Samuel Antupit thought magazines were being hurt by "screaming graphics," used by people who have nothing to say. Design should be clean and uncluttered. Pages should have the fewest possible distracting elements. And that includes illustrations used solely to break up columns of gray type.

"It bugs hell out of me to see a cartoon in the middle of a serious article in *Harper's*," he told *Newsweek*. [5]

If a magazine is beautiful, says Antupit, you can bet that either the magazine has no content or the magazine is about to die. "If meaningful photography, art and design are ever to become a part of American magazines," he has written,

the editors must reorient themselves. I do not know a single editor of any national magazine who does not view artwork either with genial contempt or as a threat. [6]

"Our magazines are over-designed and under-art directed," he observed.

Antupit drew a distinction between a designer and an art director.

An art director, to distinguish him from a designer, must concern himself with converting the verbal into the visual by exploring and controlling the use of photography, drawing, painting, and typography within a magazine. By developing these elements he becomes a visual editor, interpreting and expressing the message of the magazine in visual terms. A designer is an arranger. He makes beautiful (if he's good) layouts which incorporate these elements. A designer's ultimate criteria, unfortunately, are the looks, not the meaning. A good art director may intentionally give the editor an ugly page if it best represents and expresses the material. [7]

Type preferences

The various art styles—the realistic, the stylized, the psychedelic, etc.—all find a place in American magazines. Some art directors prefer one style over another, but art directors are not united on what style is best.

They can better agree on what type styles are best. On almost every art director's list of beautiful and readable types is Times Roman, the face designed by Stanley Morison for the *Times* of

5. "Magazine Doctor," *Newsweek*, December 2, 1968, p. 56.
6. Samuel N. Antupit, "Laid Out and Laid Waste: On the Visual Violation of American Magazines," *The Antioch Review*, Spring 1969, p. 59.
7. *Ibid.*, p. 62.

London in the early 1930s and now generally available everywhere. It would be interesting to conduct a survey on the most used body type among the well-designed magazines; Times Roman would surely be at or near the top.

And almost all art directors appreciate the beauty of the newer sans serifs or gothics. There is disagreement over the readability of these in large blocks, but for article and story titles, the faces are greatly admired, provided the settings are tightly spaced.

One gets the impression, too, that art directors as a rule prefer the old style romans to the moderns.

Art directors, of course, see great differences between types that ordinary editors or laymen would miss. *Life* in the front of the book used to make extensive use of a face that looked a lot like Ultra Bodoni Italic—but call it that and art director Bernard Quint would have thrown you out of his office. The type was Normande, and indeed, on close inspection, you could see subtle differences between the two.

For all that, art directors are not very good on names of faces. This is especially true now that so many of the types are ordered in photolettering under new names. James W. O'Bryan was asked what face he used for the logo for *National Review,* and he had to look it up. It turned out to be Albertus Titling.

The exercise of taste

When a new art director takes over a magazine, he immediately makes changes. What to the casual reader would seem unimportant might greatly disturb an art director: length of ruled lines, choice of body type, the logo, placement of captions, etc. "A change of editor or art director is reflected instantly in . . . [a magazine's] pages," Henry Wolf points out. "A magazine is still largely the extension of an individual idea, a peculiar personal vision."

While they would be slow to admit it, art directors in their choice of type and art and in their arrangement of these elements on a page lean heavily on what is fashionable. For a time the Bauhaus-inspired sans serifs are "in"; then the Swiss-inspired sans serifs. Everybody bleeds photographs for a time; then suddenly, everybody wants generous white margins around pictures. Letterspacing is thought to "open up" the typography, making it more pleasant to read; then close fitting of letters takes hold, to make it possible for the reader to grasp whole words rather than individual letters. For a time, all space divisions are planned so they'll be unequal; then spaces are divided equally, and new magazines come out in a square format rather than a golden proportion size. For a few years, the look is austere, simple, straight; then swash caps and column rules and gingerbread

The inside front cover and page of the January-February 1977 issue of Bell Telephone Magazine, published by AT&T. "Priority," the feature at the left, which spills over onto the table of contents page, is reserved each issue for editorial comment by Bell System people, non-Bell System people, management, and non-management. Note the nicely-designed table of contents with its lightface sans serif numbers at the left, boldface roman titles at the right. The lineup of editors and company officers appears immediately below. An illustration, part of a larger one on an inside page, completes the unit. Design of the magazine is by Eichinger Inc.

prevail. It is the rare art director who can resist adapting current art trends to his design: witness the psychedelic look on magazine pages at the end of the 1960s. A few art directors break away, rediscover old styles, come up with unused ones; and they become the leaders. In a few months, others are following.

"Let us . . . not delude ourselves that we are lastingly right," cautions Henry Wolf.

Once in a while an art director decides to go with the banal, the obvious, or the discarded. An illustrator has passed his prime, his style outmoded. Very well, bring him back. He's the kind of an illustrator who would never have appeared in that magazine even when he was on top. But that makes him all the more appealing now. His shock value is worth a lot to the art director.

Or the art director picks one of the typefaces that, even when it was first released, was dismissed as gauche by discerning designers. He uses it now, smugly, cynically even.

A little of this goes a long way. The trouble with some magazines today is that their art directors, caught up in the revolutionary mood of the country, are breaking all the rules of typography and design. They insist on doing their own thing. Some of their experiments succeed, and less self-indulgent art directors probably will incorporate them into magazines of the future. But most of the experiments fail. They fail because the experimenters do not recognize *readability* as the one overriding requirement of magazine design.

Evans, Helen Marie, *Man the Designer,* The Macmillan Company, New York, 1973.

Glaser, Milton, *Milton Glaser: Graphic Design,* Overlook Press (Viking), New York, 1973.

Hillebrand, Henri,ed., *Graphic Designers in the U.S.A.,* Universe Books, New York, 1972-73. (Four volumes.)

———, ed., *Graphic Designers in Europe,* Universe Books, New York, 1972-73. (Four volumes.)

Nelson, George, *How to See: Visual Adventures in a World God Never Made,* Little, Brown and Company, Boston, 1977.

Nelson, Roy Paul, *Visits with 30 Magazine Art Directors,* Magazine Publishers Association, New York, 1969.

Chapter 3

Formula and format

So much for the preliminaries.

This chapter and the chapters that follow will get to fundamentals: how to make a given magazine attractive and, more than that, readable. But before the designer can accomplish these objectives, he must first understand and appreciate the nature of his magazine.

The magazine's formula

Every magazine has its unique mixture of articles and stories. We call this its *formula.*

Most editors do not put their formulas down in words, but they and their staff members have a general understanding of what kind of material the magazine should run.

A prime consideration is: what is the purpose of the magazine? Does the magazine, like *Ladies' Home Journal* or *Iron Age*, exist to make money? Does it, like *The New Republic* or *National Review*, exist to spread ideas? Does it, like *Ford Times* or *Friends*, exist to do a public relations job? Does it, like *The Rotarian* or *Junior League Magazine*, exist to serve members of an organization?

Keeping the purpose in mind, the editor of any magazine works out a formula that best serves his intended audience. Or, if he's opinionated enough for it, or idealistic enough, he works out a formula that pleases him and hopes his audience will like it, too.

The bigger the magazine is to be and the more that is invested in it, the more likely the editor is to rely on opinion research of his intended audience when he works out his formula. The object is to win as many readers as possible within the area the magazine has staked out for itself.

Since the advent of television, magazines by and large have given up the idea of serving large, general audiences and moved into areas of specialization. It is hard to think of any interest area that is not served by a magazine or a set of magazines. David Z. Orlow, in a satire in *Folio* on the trend to put together magazines to appeal to ever more specialized audiences, suggests *Death*, "the magazine of the inevitable." As a character in Orlow's story explains it, it would be a picture magazine "featuring the most dramatic aspects of the subject—obscure diseases, dramatic accidents, berserk assassins, disasters, wars, and things like that." The magazine would be "absolutely lurid with respect to photography while at the same time absolutely non-emotional with respect to copy." A magazine to appeal to a generation brought up on media violence.

"True enough, the reader time per copy may be only three minutes due to reaction to some of the better pictures, but word-of-mouth will make it the best pass-along book since the advent of beauty parlor magazines."[1] Not long after he wrote the article *Assassin* appeared on the newsstands, and it was for real.

Even magazines that operate in the same area have subtle differences that distinguish their formulas from one another. *Life* placed heavier emphasis on the sciences than *Look*, which was more interested in the social sciences. *Harper's* is more politically oriented than *The Atlantic; The Atlantic* is stronger in literature. *Time* and *Newsweek* are more liberal, less business-oriented than *U.S. News & World Report*, but *New Times* is the most radical of the newsmagazines, appealing more to

1. David Z. Orlow, "The Magazine of the Inevitable," *Folio,* January 1977, pp. 22, 23.

4

Ordinarily content would dictate design, but sometimes you have to do designing first. Here is one of several spreads designed by the author for a new magazine to help the editor decide on a format before material for his first issue was completed. This article was to be about a fish hatchery, but the title and blurb were not yet written, and photographs were not yet available. At least placement, margins, and sizes could be indicated. And a few strokes from a felt marker if nothing else could show where photos (one square, one widely horizontal) would go. Because the letters in "HATCHERY" were to be so large, the designer lined up the tail of the Y—not the Y itself—with the right-hand margin of the far-right column. Note that the initial letter is in the same face as the title letters, but smaller. Those are captions at the lower left.

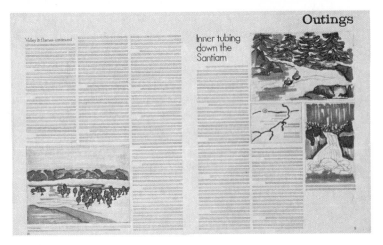

A two-page spread, part of a magazine tabloid designed by student Chris Barnes for a daily newspaper. The left page carries the conclusion of an article on field burning; the right page begins a regular feature called "Outings." As Barnes conceived the design, the regular heading each week would be large; the pertinent headline ("Inner Tubing Down the Santiam") would be smaller. She used three-column format throughout. She chose to cluster her right page photographs (which she indicated with gray felt markers) rather than scatter them. The single caption covering the three photographs when finally written no doubt would take more space than is shown here.

youthful readers and serving more as a *feature* than a *news* publication.

When rock music lost some of its fascination, *Rolling Stone*, its bible, changed editorial direction somewhat, going more for articles dealing with politics, culture, and lifestyles. It also sought to erase its earlier anti-establishment image. "We have never been an underground publication," editor Jann S. Wenner is quoted as having said. "We have always said we wanted to make money."

The New Yorker worked out a formula that puts it into a unique category: humor mixed with social consciousness; great reporting done in a casual and sometimes rambling style; stories that have no endings; and, of course, the best gag cartoons anywhere. *New York,* a new magazine some people have compared to *The New Yorker,* really has quite a different formula: a merging of the so-called "new journalism" with helpful advice on how to survive in Manhattan.

Reader's Digest is another magazine with a unique formula: dogmatism, conservatism, optimism—and, some would say, simplistic solutions to complicated problems. It is among the most consistent of magazines. Its formula has not changed basically since it was started in the early 1920s, nor, with the largest circulation of any magazine in the world, is it likely to.

The Number 2 magazine in any field is the one most likely to change its formula. When *Playboy* outstripped *Esquire* in the mid- to late-fifties, *Esquire* dropped the nudes and turned to more serious matters. When the women's magazines were locked in a death struggle in the mid-1950s, *McCall's*, second to *Ladies' Home Journal*, tried to spread out to include the entire family, calling itself a magazine of "Togetherness." The formula didn't work, and today *McCall's* and *Ladies' Home Journal* are very close again in formula, with *McCall's* perhaps the more cerebral.

The formula stays pretty much the same from issue to issue. If a magazine feels it is losing its audience or if it wants to reach out for a new audience, it changes its formula. Sometimes the change is gradual. Sometimes—especially if the magazine is desperate—the change is sudden.

The magazine's format

When a magazine changes its formula it also usually changes its *format*. The format is the *looks* of the publication: its size, its shape, its arrangement of copy and pictures on the page. Format includes design.

Sometimes a magazine changes its format, or at least its design, without changing its formula.

Settling on a format

Ruari McLean makes two major points in *Magazine Design* (Oxford University Press, 1969). One is that it is more important to be noticeable than to be clean and dignified. The other is that it doesn't matter what the magazine looks like if its contents are not worth printing in the first place.

The second point seems obvious enough. The first point is arguable. It all depends on what kind of a magazine you are putting out and what kind of an audience you are serving.

Some magazines are best suited to visual excitement and novelty. Others are best suited to visual order.

Which means that magazine design boils down to two main schools, both with respected followings. The visually exciting magazines are represented, among others, by *McCall's* and the now-defunct *Look*, both pioneers in that kind of design. The highly ordered magazines are represented by *Sports Illustrated* and *Scientific American*. This does not mean that a magazine needs to belong exclusively to one school or the other. *Sports Illustrated*, for instance, within its ordered format, has much excitement in art and photography. It does mean that a magazine should be mostly one, or mostly the other. (More about this in chapter 5.)

The first thing an editor and art director must decide, then, is What kind of a look are we after? The purpose of the magazine should have something to do with the kind of look they settle for.

A magazine published to make a profit must lure and hold the reader with visually exciting pages. Illustrations are a must. These days such a magazine almost has to use color.

A magazine published to disseminate ideas can exist with a

When *Northwest*, *magazine section of* The Oregonian, *was a letterpress operation, editor Joe Bianco had to settle for bold, flat colors and a poster format. This example shows that the poster approach to covers can result in excellent design. The artist: E. Bruce Dauner.*

more austere format as, for example, *Foreign Affairs*. Its readers already believe; they don't have to be pampered. Such magazines generally will settle for a coarse, sometimes cheap paper stock and pages unrelieved by illustrations.

A magazine published to do a public relations job needs a glossy appearance, if it is to go to outsiders; if it is an internal publication, it can be more homey.

A magazine published to serve members of an organization must watch closely what it spends. If the members of the organization pay fees to belong, they are not likely to appreciate getting an overly pretentious publication. The author once served as editor/art director of a magazine for members of a tight-fisted trade organization; his biggest challenge was to make the magazine look good without making it look expensive.

The Visiting Fireman, *published biweekly by Fireman's Fund Insurance Companies, San Francisco, uses the one-extra-fold tabloid format. You see here the 7 1/2 × 11 front page along with the 11 × 15 second front page. The first one acts more like a magazine cover, the second more like a newspaper front page. As you unfold to the second front page, of course, you turn the publication forty-five degrees. The original comes in black plus a second color. Note the thin lines that separate each line of the headlines. Ken Borger, a freelancer, is the designer.*

But purpose is only one factor in deciding format. Policy is another. Two magazines have as their policy the spreading of ideas: the one is leftist and activist; the other is moderately Republican. Will the same format serve both? Possibly. But if the tone of the articles is different, it seems reasonable to expect a difference, too, in the setting in which these articles are presented. Are there angry, vitriolic typefaces available for headlines? There are. And what about artwork: are some drawing styles more militant than others? See the work that appeared in the 1930s in *New Masses*.[2]

2. A source is Joseph North, ed., *New Masses: An Anthology of the Rebel Thirties*, International Publishers, New York, 1969.

In an interview in *Alma Mater* (April-June 1969), William Hamilton Jones, editor of the *Yale Alumni Magazine*, explains how he designs his magazine to make it appropriate to the university that publishes it. He makes two observations about Yale: (1) it is the second oldest American university and (2) it is exciting, creative, and innovative.

> I . . . [want] to capture in the design this kind of tension between the old and the new, the traditional and the innovative. The way we have ended up doing it, for the most part, is using a very traditional typeface, Garamond, and doing some very untraditional things with it, like using a ragged setting and using white space in a way that it's not often used in magazines.

While opinion research may dictate in part a magazine's formula, it has little to do with deciding a magazine's format. Format is still largely a matter of personal preference, taste, and intuition; and that's what makes format so challenging a topic.

Basic formats

Publications appear in a variety of formats, the most common of which are these:

1. Magazines, consisting of a series of bound pages that have been printed in multiples of four, eight, sixteen, or thirty-two (these are called "signatures"), then folded down to size and trimmed.

2. Newspapers, consisting of a series of oversize sheets folded down the middle to make four pages. Each set of four-pages loosely houses another, which loosely houses still another, etc. An occasional loose sheet is included. A newspaper that is bulky enough divides its sets of pages into sections. The pages are so large that, for delivery, the entire newspaper has to be folded once and then opened up when the reader gets to it.

3. Tabloids, consisting of a series of unbound oversize pages that are about half the size of regular newspaper pages.

Tabloids earned a bad name some years back when sensational newspapers appealing to evening subway riders adopted the format to make reading easier when the reader was using one hand to hold onto a strap or when he didn't have enough room at his seat to turn the pages of a newspaper published in the traditional size. With the popularity of the tabloid as a format for company publications, the name "magapaper" emerged, signaling that the format was oversize but that the design thinking was magazine-like. And certainly sex and violence were not part of the content.

The tabloid *Rolling Stone* used to give itself one extra fold to appear as an 8 1/2 × 11 magazine on the newsstand, but by 1973 the publication had become too thick to take the folding. From then on it appeared as a regular tabloid. But the idea

The Illuminator, *published monthly for employees of Appalachian Power Company and Kingsport Power Company, comes in a tabloid format, but with a difference: its main pages consist of three unequal-width columns. On this front page, an obit takes a narrow measure, an unillustrated story (center) takes a wide measure, and a captioned photo and a story on national energy policy take a still wider measure. The body type runs with unjustified right-hand margins. The nameplate, designed in letters that suggest a neon sign, and the center story both appear in wine-colored ink. Note the use of heavy bars to underline last lines of the all-cap headlines. This is a device seen on all the pages, helping to unite them.*

School of Journalism, University of Oregon | December 1967

**ALUMNI
NEWSLETTER**

The newsletter is the simplest and least expensive of the formats. No photos or drawings are needed to make it inviting, provided the designer uses enough white space and plans carefully the placing of his headings. The front page sets the style. Note that for this one the news items are blocked off into two-column rectangular units. The format works for either a printed or a duplicated piece. (Designed by the author.)

Cargill News, *an 8 1/2 × 11 slick-paper bimonthly published for employees of Cargill, Minneapolis, uses a uniformly deep sink (white space at the top) for all its pages, with the result that the "live area" of each page becomes a square. A sample spread is shown. The left page gives over the entire "live area" to a photo and caption; the right page uses the "live area" for a smaller photo and caption, a title, and three columns of text. Column rules are part of the regular format.*

caught the fancy of other editors, especially editors of company and alumni tabloids, and the Rolling Stone fold has become almost a generic term. In this format, a tabloid shows a large picture and a logo on the folded down page. As the reader unfolds, he turns the publication, too, and then faces a large page with a newspaper look. The logo usually repeats on this first full page.

4. Newsletters, consisting often, but not always, of 8 1/2 × 11 sheets printed inexpensively and stapled at the top or side. Related to this format are all the formats that have been developed over the years by direct-mail advertisers.

The newsletter, newspaper, and tabloid formats will get special attention in later chapters. For now, the book will concentrate on the magazine format.

Anything goes

Conditions beyond the control of the designer may dictate the choice of format. When a strike in 1964 made a regular magazine impossible for Vail-Ballou Press, Inc., Binghamton, New York, a printing and manufacturing firm for the book trade, it brought out its house organ in galley proof form as an emergency measure. The "publication" was 5 × 21, single column. The format seemed particularly appropriate for this particular company. The circulation, after all, was only 600.

Editor L. Jeanette Clarke said at the time: "No company should feel that if it can't have a breath-taking, expensive magazine, newsletter or tabloid it should have none at all. To a large extent employees are captive readers." She said that because her readers are curious, they don't have to be lured by fancy trimmings.

Another strange format was introduced by *Datebook,* a teenyboppers' magazine, now defunct. To create the effect of two magazines in one, *Datebook* carried a front cover at both

COWBOY'S EYEBALL, *each animal every day, watching for illness or injury. These are at Lenli, KS.*

**CAPROCK FEEDLOTS AND FOLKS
GROW QUALITY BEEF**

ends. The teen-age reader worked her way through half the magazine, came to an upside-down page, closed the magazine and turned to the other cover, and worked her way through that half.

Format innovation was one of the selling points of *Flair* when it was being published in the early 1950s. The editors constantly titillated readers with die-cut covers, inserts of sizes different from the page size, sections inside the book printed on unusual paper stocks, and so on. These practices live on in other magazines, but the editor who resorts to them is advised to check first with the post office, where regulations change frequently on what is allowed under second-class and bulk-rate mailing permits.

The role of design

The history of journalism records the names of a number of editors who were able to build and hold audiences for publications that, from a design standpoint, had the grace of a row of neon signs or, at best, no design at all. One remembers Lyle Stuart's *Expose* and *Independent*, George Seldes's *In Fact*, and I. F. Stone's newsletter. One thinks of the typical cheap-paper journal of opinion. These are often radical sheets; yet their editors hold design views that can only be considered as reactionary. Northwestern University's Emeritus Professor Curtis D. MacDougall, who could identify with many of the causes of these publications, said that "Strong editorial material can overcome bad design. On the other hand, bad design can't kill good contents."

But why give editorial matter the additional burden of bad design? The job of communicating is already difficult enough. Readers may not complain about bad design. They may not recognize it when they see it. But surely they are not wholly comfortable with it.

Good design, by itself, can't make a publication useful or important, but combined with well-conceived, well-reasoned, and well-written content, it can make the printed page a joy rather than a chore.

And what is good design?

The answer is important. *Good design is design that is readable*. The key word is *readable*. Not *unique*, not *compelling*, not even *beautiful*, although all these qualities can play a part—but *readable*.

Some editors look upon design as a magic ingredient to be applied to an ailing publication, and Presto!—the publication's problems are solved. "A . . . reason for the confusion about design is the prevailing notion that it is a kind of frosting, an aesthetic overlay that makes humdrum objects more appetizing," says the eminent designer George Nelson. "No responsible designer believes this. In nature, organic design (our best models) never show decoration that isn't functional, never show the slightest concern for aesthetics, and always try to match the organism with its environment so that it will survive."[3]

"Some publications work backwards, tailoring the editorial content to fit the graphics, but they won't live very long," adds design consultant Jan V. White. "They may make a big splash when they first appear because they are undoubtedly interesting to *look* at, but being nice to look at is not enough; if the shallowness of the content leads to reader dissatisfaction (as it must, when it becomes obvious) then the publication is on the road to oblivion."[4]

The rules of design

If ever there were rules to guide the designer in putting out a magazine or any printed piece, they were only vaguely agreed to by some of those who did the work; and in the 1970s, with the changes in other aspects of our lives, the rules for design become even harder to lay down. What once struck many purists in design as abominable today seems to fit right in with what editors, art directors, and even readers want. Consider, for instance, the helter-skelter, patched, mortised look of *House & Garden* and even *Vogue* during the last half of the 1970s.

"There are no 'don'ts' that cannot be abridged, nor any design laws that are absolute," said Allen Hurlburt. "However, a designer should understand the nature of order and have some awareness of the framework from which h∩ is departing."[5]

Hurlburt added: "Many of the most successful designs for the printed page violate all rules of order and logic. In spite of this, the skilled designer is usually familiar with the principles guiding page design and aware of the pitfalls that lurk in the path of contrived and self-indulgent results."[6]

Design and personality

How a publication looks should not be dictated by taste alone but by a knowledge of the personalities of typefaces and an understanding of how, when they are combined with the other elements on a page, they affect the mood and "color" of the page.

3. George Nelson, "We Are Here by Design," *Harper's*, April 1975, p. 3.
4. Jan V. White, *Designing for Magazines*, R. R. Bowker Company, New York, 1976, p. x.
5. Allen Hurlburt, *Publication Design*, Van Nostrand Reinhold Company, New York, 1971, p. 26.
6. *Ibid.*, p. 42.

Here are some moods an editor might want and some suggestions on how an art director can achieve them:

1. *Dignity.* Use old roman typefaces, centered headings and
art, generous amounts of white space, medium-size photos or
paintings, or drawings made to resemble woodcuts.

2. *Power.* Use bold sans serif typefaces, boldface body copy,
flush-left headings, large, black photos or drawings made with
lithographic crayons.

3. *Grace.* Use italic with swash caps or script types, light-face
body copy with unjustified (ragged edge) right-hand margins,
carefully composed photographs or wash drawings, an un-
crowded look.

4. *Excitement.* Use a mixture of typefaces, color, close cropping of pictures, an unbalanced and crowded page.

5. *Precision.* Use the newer sans serifs or a slab serif for
headings and body copy, sharp-focus photos or tight line drawings, horizontal or vertical ruled lines, highly organized design
based on a grid system.

These are only suggestions, timidly advanced. Obviously they
may not always work; and as a designer you will discover other
ways of creating similar moods on the page. For instance, you
may develop a way of taking an old roman face, with its built-in
dignity and grace, and enlist it to establish a mood of excitement
or even power. What is being said in headline or copy is always
more important than the type chosen to deliver it or the art
chosen to amplify or surround it.

Magazine page sizes

Phil Douglis, photographer and columnist, thinks the magazine
format's chief advantage over the newspaper, newsletter, and
magapaper format is "the ability to relate pictures to each other
as a sequence over a series of pages, alternately withholding
them from our view and then revealing them, carrying the
reader through a visual process not unlike the frame-by-frame
and scene-by-scene method of cinema."[7]
Magazines come in three basic sizes:

1. *Ebony*-size, roughly 10 1/2 × 13.
2. *Time*-size, roughly 8 1/2 × 11.
3. *Reader's Digest*-size, roughly 5 1/2 × 7 1/2.

By far the most popular size is 8 1/2 × 11. Most house
organs, trade journals, and many slicks come in this size.

These three sizes aren't the only ones. A company magazine
might come in a 6 × 9, 7 1/2 × 9 1/2, 7 × 10, 8 1/2 × 13, or
a 9 × 12 size, for instance. The size would depend upon the

7. Phil Douglis, "How Magazine Pages Help Sequence Pictures," *IABC News,*
October 1976, p. 3.

equipment the printer uses and the availability of paper stock.

The economics of magazine publishing forced *Esquire, McCall's, Vogue, Town & Country, House & Garden,* and other oversize magazines in the 1970s to go down to the 8 1/2 × 11 or near-8 1/2 × 11 size. For art directors, the changes meant considerable rethinking of design. "It takes a lot more thinking to keep the magazine elegant in a smaller size," said Linda Stillman, art director of *Town & Country*. "Proportions have to be exactly right if we are to maintain a consistent image . . . . The magazine contains a larger volume of material now, but with less room on a given page, design is tighter, more precise than ever."

Miki Denhof, associate editor of *House & Garden*, liked the change to a smaller size. "This is a more workable size. Suddenly, we can do a double spread of one picture; before, it would have been too overwhelming."

To meet the demands of its smaller size, *Esquire* simplified its pages, showed less white space, bled more pictures, and, in 1977, went almost exclusively to photography for its art, even art used for fiction.[8]

Magazines almost always choose a page size with a width-depth ratio that approximates the "golden mean," or roughly 3:5 (the author in this book will always mention width first). And the page almost always is vertical. (A magazine not dependent upon advertising should consider the novelty and even the design advantages of a 5:3 page. Opened out, the magazine would be unusually horizontal.)

A few magazines in recent years, along with some books—particularly art books—have gone for a square format. *Avant Garde*, an 11 × 11 publication, was one. But a square format can mean paper waste. If a magazine is big enough, it can special order paper to size. If not, it can do what *Avant Garde* did: use the paper waste—the odd-cut sheets—for direct-mail advertising campaigns.

One of the most handsome of the square-format publications is the recently redesigned *New York Times Book Review* with its horizontal rules and generous use of art.

Some editors like the square-format look because they think it says "contemporary." You can achieve the square look in an 8 1/2 × 11 magazine by adopting a consistent deep sink on the pages. That means making the "live area" of the pages—the part that does not include the margins—start low on the page. Instead of a one-inch sink, for instance, your magazine could carry a two- or three-inch sink. That does not keep you from printing anything above the sink. An occasional title may fit in that space. Or a piece of art may jut into it. Even a caption might ap-

The square—or near-square—format is popular with many editors. Here's a beautifully simple brown and yellow cover for the square-format magazine Lines, *published by Reliance Insurance Companies. An explanatory note inside the front cover explains: "The inflationary 'dragon' is still lurking nearby—preying upon the homes and businesses of underinsured policyholders. The story on page 2 explains what Reliance is doing to help its agents 'slay the dragon.' "*

---

8. "Fitting New Formats," *Art Direction,* March 1977, pp. 46-52.

pear there. But body copy would always stay confined to the square or near-square grid that you have adopted.

Whatever size page a magazine adopts, if it contains advertising, it should provide column widths and lengths that are compatible with other magazines in the field. An advertising agency doesn't like to custom design each ad for every magazine scheduled to run it. The reason *Media/Scope* went to an oversize format in the late 1960s was probably to make it easier for the advertiser who would buy *Advertising Age* to also buy equivalent space in *Media/Scope* without need for redesigning. Unfortunately, the change in size was not enough to save *Media/Scope*.

Lithopinion, the defunct graphic arts and public affairs quarterly of Local One, Amalgamated Lithographers of America, used to change its format from issue to issue to "illuminate the versatility of lithography by example." Vol. 1, No. 4 (1966), for example, was 7 × 12, with one column of copy per page set off with wide margins of white. On the other hand, about the *only thing* that stayed the same for *Kaiser News* was the page size: 8 1/2 × 11. It constantly changed design, frequency of publication, and printers. "What we are striving for is continuity through change," said Editor Don Fabun.[9]

The page size, of course, seriously affects the design. Most art directors feel that an *Ebony*-size book is easier to design than a *Time*-size book. Certainly a *Life* or *Time* page is easier to design than a *Reader's Digest* page. Ralph Hudgins, art director of *Westward* (5 1/2 × 7 1/2), found his pages rather difficult to work with, but he said that he gets satisfaction in coming up with effective layouts within the limitations of the format. His pages were sometimes crammed, but there was an excitement about them.

An advantage of the *Digest* size is that it is close to book format, and readers have more of a tendency to save the magazine. Portability, too, is an important consideration. The *Digest* size was adopted by magazines originally, of course, to fit the pocket.

With the paper shortages and postal-rate increases of the 1970s, many magazines dropped down one page size. Very few magazines any longer were larger than *Time*-size.

The grid

For any kind of a format some kind of a grid is almost mandatory. A grid, made up of vertical and horizontal lines, sets the limits of printing areas. It is usually a printed two-page spread

9. Don Fabun, "Dedicated to Human Questions," *DA: The Paper Quarterly for the Graphic Arts*, Second Quarter, 1970, p. 8.

with lines ruled in to show the edges of the pages, edges on the outside of the pages to indicate bleeds, the place for folios, and columns for body copy. The columns are often prepared with a series of ruled lines, one for the bottom of each line of type.

The art director draws up a master grid in India ink, and the printer runs enough of them, in a light blue or gray ink, to last a year or two. The printed grids can be used for both rough layouts and finished pasteups.

For a more formal looking publication, with highly organized pages, a more detailed grid is called for. It is calibrated not only in columns and lines for copy but also in areas for pictures and headings. Areas for pictures are marked off in dotted lines to distinguish them from type areas.

Many art directors enjoy working with a fully developed grid that establishes boundaries for every possibility. Within the restrictions of such a grid lie all kinds of challenges. The possibilities for variety in type and picture arrangements are still enormous. The grid no more spoils creativity than a net spoils the pleasure of a tennis game.

One grid system involves the dividing of the pages into squares, which in the design can be gathered into quarters, thirds, or halves of pages. Under this system, all headings rest on a line in the grid, and all photos and columns of copy occupy one or more squares.

Width of the columns

How wide should a column of type be?

Well, any width, really. Just remember: the wider the column, the bigger the type should be.

An oft-stated rule for length of line is 1 1/2 alphabets of lowercase letters, or 39 characters. The rule is too restrictive. George A. Stevenson in *Graphic Arts Encyclopedia* (McGraw-Hill, 1968) lays down the 39-character rule and in a column of type which is itself more than 60 characters wide!

A column can be a little less than 39 characters wide, as in a newspaper, or even more than 60, as in some books. It depends to some extent on the age of the reader. It depends also on the mood the magazine is trying to create.

If the magazine wants to create a mood of urgency, narrow, 39-character columns are best. Narrow columns with column rules say "News!" Wider columns suggest dignity and stability.

There is no reason why a magazine can't have some narrow-column pages and some wide-column pages. A *Time*-size magazine, for instance, can run two columns per page for part of the book, and three columns per page for the remainder. Nor is there any reason an article can't start out at one width and, on another page, narrow down to another.

The second two pages of an eight-page article in Forces, *Montreal, Quebec, Canada (Issue No. 34–35, 1976). The 3 1/4″ sink remains constant throughout the 9 × 12 magazine, with the occasional jutting of photos, titles, and copy blocks. The beautifully designed and printed magazine obviously follows a carefully worked out grid.*

Two pages from another article, same issue, where the sink is ignored, but the basic three-column format holds steady. Note that this spread, although it occurs after an opening spread, starts with a column of white space to set off the one column of art. A deep vertical contrasts with a wide horizontal here. The horizontal photograph is airbrushed at the top to make a vignette out of it. The boldface subhead consists of three lines, the first one indented.

One more variation of the Forces *grid. Again: a spread from Issue No. 34–35, 1976. We are inside another article. The photograph at the left establishes the sink; the one at the right redefines it. The photos also share a common bottom axis. The copy in* Forces, *set in an unjustified sans-serif type, occasionally extends up into the sink area.*

Body copy is easier to read, ordinarily, when it is leaded one or two points. Leading depends upon the typeface used. Types with large x-heights need more leading than types with small x-heights. (More about this in chapter 6.)

The lineup of magazine pages

The magazine designer arranges his articles and stories a little like a baseball manager arranges his batting lineup. In baseball, the lineup has traditionally started off with a man who gets singles consistently. The second one up is a good bunter; the third one another consistent hitter, but one who more often gets extra-base hits; the fourth one a home-run king; and so on.

The lead-off article in a magazine may not be the blockbuster; it may be a more routine kind of an article. The second piece might be entertaining. The third piece might be cerebral. And so on. The editor—and his art director—strive for change of pace from feature to feature.

When magazine articles and stories are not arranged by kind in the magazine proper, the arranging is usually done in the table of contents at the front of the book. There all the articles are grouped together; all the short stories are grouped together; all the regular departments or columns are grouped together. Some magazines even carry a separate table of contents of advertisements listed alphabetically at the back of the book.

Editors—and advertisers—know that most readers read magazines front to back, but others—especially the browsers—read them from back to front. So far as advertisers are concerned, the best display impact is found in the first part of the magazine on right-hand pages; the best impact for the last part of the magazine, especially if it is side-stitched, is found on the left-hand pages. Most advertisers consider the first part of the magazine more important than the last half, and right-hand pages for them are highly desirable. They often accompany their insertion orders with the note: "Up-front, right-hand placement urgently requested." They don't always get it.

Convinced that many readers work through the magazine from back to front, some editors start editorials or articles on a back page and continue them on preceding pages. *U.S. News & World Report*, when it ran its long editorials by David Lawrence, did this. So does one of the hunting and fishing magazines. *Esquire* followed a maddening practice of starting articles or stories in the middle or back part of the book and continuing them on pages near the front.

Some of *The New Yorker's* best articles start in the last half of the magazine.

But articles and stories in most magazines begin in the first half of the book. Most editors and art directors, given a choice,

The front page of a news-magazine tabloid published by West High School, Iowa City, Iowa. That's the logo at the upper right, with the dateline and other information at the upper left. The article's title is below, hooked up with the art. The uncluttered look continues inside.

would prefer a spread (two facing pages) for each opening, but this is not always possible. When they start a feature on just the right-hand page, they favor giving a rather gray appearance to the tail end of the article before it. This assures the new opening more impact.

Page numbering

The reader will thank the art director for leaving room on every page for page numbers. The art director will make exceptions only for full-page bleed photos or advertisements. Even then, the reader would prefer the numbers. Right-hand pages are always odd-numbered, of course; left-hand pages are even-numbered.

When the art director has a last-minute signature to insert and the other pages are already printed with numbers, he can number the insert pages with letters. For instance: if the last numbered page in the signature before the new one is 48, the first page of the new signature would be 48a, the next page 48b, and so on. You see this numbering system used in the slicks.

Some magazines, embarrassed because of the thinness of the issues and not wanting the reader to realize they are only 24- or 36- or 48-page magazines, start numbering the pages from the first issue of the year and carry through the numbering until the last issue of the year. The reader can pick up an issue in July, for instance, and find himself at the beginning of the issue with, say, page 172. Some of the opinion magazines use this system. They might argue that they do it because the issues are part of a volume, and such numbering is an aid to the researcher.

Page numbering for some magazines starts on the cover and for other magazines on the first right-hand page after the cover. It is the embarrassingly thin magazine that considers its cover Page 1.

A magazine's thickness

Most magazines let the amount of advertising dictate the number of pages of any particular issue. The more ads the magazine gets, the more pages it runs. Its thickest issues are in late fall, before Christmas. Its thinnest issues are right after the first of the year and in the middle of the summer. The ratio of ad space to editorial space, ideally, runs 70:30. For some magazines, it runs closer to 50:50 or even 40:60. When the ratio gets that low, the magazine is in trouble.

A few magazines, *Newsweek* among them, offer readers the same amount of editorial matter issue after issue. Only the amount of advertising changes. A magazine as departmentalized as *Newsweek* almost has to operate like that.

Another front page for West Side Story, *three issues later. The style remains, but this time reverse type on a black page with rules and plenty of "black space" are art enough. The black is appropriate to the subject.*

Magazines that do not contain advertising often run the same number of pages issue after issue. House organs fall into this category. And, because they contain so little advertising, so do opinion magazines.

The number of pages for most magazines runs to 32—two 16-page signatures. A signature is a collection of pages printed on one large sheet of paper. After the printing, the sheet is folded down to page size and trimmed. Signatures come in multiples of four, or eight, or sixteen, or thirty-two, depending upon the size of the page and the size of the press used to print the magazine.

If a magazine has a cover on a heavier stock—a separate cover—that's another four-page signature. Wrap it around two 16-page signatures and you have a 36-page magazine.

The back of the book

Every editor and art director is concerned about the back of the book and how to make it as attractive as the front.

Jan V. White, a magazine design consultant, notes that the "compulsion to make columnar matter have the same exciting flavor as feature matter seems irresistible . . . even though it is like shooting at hummingbirds with howitzers." He says:

> Mr. Editor, you work too hard. You believe the same approaches will solve all problems, dissimilar though the problems be. Thus you force yourself to apply to minor items in fractional pages the same journalistic flair appropriate to major feature stories, and you get frustrated when you don't succeed.[10]

So White recommends pigeonholing back-of-the-book items to make them easy for the reader to find. Organize the material into "simple patterns easily discerned. And in the front and back of the book it is even more essential . . . to make . . . editorial matter stand away from the ads."[11]

Handling advertisements

One problem the art director of most magazines faces will probably never be solved. That is the problem of ads and their intrusion into the editorial portion of the magazine. Advertisers do not have enough confidence in their ads to let them stand on their own merit. They do not want them buried in a sea of advertising. They insist that, instead, their ads be placed next to "reading matter" so that readers who otherwise would ignore the ads will wander into them, if only by mistake.

This means that only a few pages in each magazine are free of

10. Jan V. White, "Theory of the Dinner Jackets," *Better Editing,* Winter 1967, p. 19.
11. *Ibid.,* p. 20.

advertising. These are the pages the designer concentrates on. Here he has room to innovate. Here he applies the principles of design to solve visual problems. The other areas to be designed are nothing more than bands of white separating and breaking up the ads. On some magazines, ads are allowed to float in the middle of the pages. There is not much the designer can do to enliven such pages. If the art director were to succeed, he would detract from the advertising.

William Fadiman in an essay in "Phoenix Nest," a column in the *Saturday Review* for February 22, 1969, shows what it's like to begin a short story in a magazine and follow it through the ads. From his first paragraph:

Halfway up the steps . . . established since 1848 . . . he stopped to think of her . . . rugged endurance, dependable performance, and low operating costs. He finally knocked at the door determined to . . . ask for it by name. She opened the door slowly . . . and could not help admiring his manly form . . . built of mahogany and reinforced at the corners.

It was amusing comment on the design of American magazines made all the more striking by *Saturday Review* itself which, unintentionally, stuck a full-page ad in the middle of it, with this result: "Darling, he interrupted with a . . . Color Slide Art Lecture in Your Home for $1."

Floating ads, as *The Saturday Evening Post* has run, and checkerboard ads, as *Esquire* has run, and other odd shapes or placement make back-of-the-book design even more difficult. The magazine that accepts such ads risks criticism that it does not treat with proper respect the material its editorial staff has so carefully developed.

Because of their smaller page sizes and limited number of columns per page, magazines have not had to put up with the step-up half pyramid of ads that newspapers put on their inside pages. At least designers of back-of-the-book material in magazines have rectangles to work with.

It is important for art directors to make editorial matter look different from advertising matter. This is why most magazines let the advertisers have all the display—the art, the color, the big type—on the back pages and content themselves with solid, gray type broken up by quiet subheadings and column headings. This is why publications run the slug line, "An Advertisement," over any ad designed to look like an editorial page. The reader deserves the warning.

The advertisements themselves, of course, are designed not by the magazine art director but by art directors in advertising agencies. The ads then come to the magazine as self-contained units. The magazine's advertising department—not the magazine's art director—decides where in the magazine they will go, although sometimes the editor and art director prevail on the advertising staff to move ads around when they interfere with points being made in nearby articles. On small magazines, sometimes, art directors *do* help with advertising design. An advertiser may be too small to utilize the services of an agency.

Advertising can be rejected by a magazine for a variety of reasons, even for aesthetic reasons.

Magazine bindings

By definition, a magazine is a bound publication of eight or more pages issued on a regular basis more often than once a year. Not all publications are bound. Newspapers consist of un-bound sheets of paper folded and wrapped loosely around other folded sheets. Sometimes a newspaper carries a single sheet, printed on both sides, slipped inside one of the four-page "signatures."

At the least pretentious level a publication may consist of a single folded sheet of four pages. Or it may consist of a single sheet, unfolded, printed on both sides. Or it may consist of several sheets held together by a staple in one corner or by a couple of staples at the side.

There are several kinds of bindings, but only two really work for most magazines—saddle stapling (or saddle stitching) and side stapling (or side stitching).

The big advantage of saddle stitching is that the magazine opens up easily and lies flat on the table or desk. Readers can tear out pages they want to save.

And a saddle-stitched magazine may be easier to design. For instance, you can more easily run pictures and type across the gutter. When *Harper's* went from side stitching to saddle stitching, it said, in its announcement, it was doing it for design reasons. *The Atlantic* soon followed with a saddle-stitched format.

Side stitching, on the other hand, makes for a more permanent binding. It suggests to the reader: this magazine ought to be kept. If the editor wants to make it easy for his reader to tear out articles, he can have the pages perforated. Side stitching is especially recommended for magazines of many pages. Any reader can testify that the December issues of magazines like *Playboy*, *The New Yorker*, and *Sunset*, swollen with advertising, soon come apart in their hands.

After World War II *Reader's Digest* experimented with perfect binding—binding without staples—and today the *Digest* and several other major magazines are bound in this way.

CLICK, J. W., and BAIRD, RUSSELL N., *Magazine Editing and Production*, Wm. C. Brown Company Publishers, Dubuque, Iowa, 1974.

DARROW, RALPH C., *House Journal Editing*, Interstate Printers & Publishers, Danville, Illinois, 1974.

EDITORS OF FOLIO, *Magazine Publishing Management*, Folio Magazine Publishing Corporation, New Canaan, Connecticut, 1977.

FERGUSON, ROWENA, *Editing the Small Magazine*, Columbia University Press, New York, 1976. (Second Edition.)

PETERSON, THEODORE, *Magazines in the Twentieth Century*, University of Illinois Press, Urbana, 1964. (Second Edition.)

ROOT, ROBERT, *Modern Magazine Editing*, Wm. C. Brown Company Publishers, Dubuque, Iowa, 1966.

WOLSELEY, ROLAND, *Understanding Magazines*, Iowa State University Press, Ames, Iowa, 1965.

Magazine Profiles: Studies of Magazines Today, Medill School of Journalism, Northwestern University, Evanston, Illinois, 1974.

Chapter 4

Production

"You don't simply read *Aspen* . . . ," said one of its early promotion pieces, "you hear it, hang it, feel it, fly it, sniff it, play with it." *Aspen* was "the magazine in a box," a collection of odds and ends that portended the end to magazines as we had known them: the simple flat, two-dimensional storehouses of printed information, opinion, entertainment, and advertisements. But it was *Aspen* that expired. Traditional-format magazines lived on, in spite of the fact that Marshall McLuhan, in the 1960s, forecast their demise. A number of them died, that is true; they tried to serve audiences too diverse, audiences television could better accommodate. But those that narrowed their focus found receptive audiences and advertisers willing to spend money on their pages.

Despite some widely heralded improvements in technology—even in printing technology—the actual job of producing magazines remains pretty much unchanged.

This chapter deals with production: the activity necessary after editors have done their editing and art directors have laid out the pages. Defined broadly enough "production" includes the laying out of the pages (but not the actual designing of the magazine).

Art directors need a knowledge of production in order to (1) get the effects they want and (2) cut down on costs. Most magazines have a production director or editor who acts as a sort of middleman between the art director and the printer.

The main consideration in production is printing.

Gutenberg and before

Johann Gutenberg in Germany did not invent printing; the Chinese beat him to it. He did not invent movable type; the Koreans beat him to that. But, unaware of what Koreans had done, Gutenberg worked out his own system and introduced it to the Western world. He designed his types, taking as his model the black, close-fitting, angular calligraphy of the lowlands; carved them; punched them into metal to make molds; and cast them. The characters could be stored in individual compartments and used over and over again. Until then, printing had to be done from wood blocks into which characters were carved, in relief. Once used, the characters served no further purpose.

Before printing of any kind, there were the scribes, working alone, who copied manuscripts by hand. When many copies were needed, a group of scribes would sit together in a semicircle around a reader. The scribes wrote while the reader dictated. This produced several copies of a manuscript at a time. This was Middle Ages mass production.

Printing processes

The printing process Gutenberg used is still very much alive. We call it *letterpress:* printing from a raised surface. It is the process used by many—but not most—daily newspapers and by some large magazines, like *Time, Newsweek, U.S. News & World Report, Ladies' Home Journal,* and *McCall's.* Other processes are *offset lithography* (printing from a flat surface) and *gravure* (printing from tiny wells incised in a metal plate). Offset is the almost universal printing process for company magazines and specialized magazines; gravure—or rotogravure—is the process for large, generously illustrated magazines like *Seventeen* and the syndicated Sunday supplements like *Parade* and *Family Weekly.* If you want to know what printing process a magazine uses, look it up in *Consumer Magazine and Farm Publication Rates and Data* or *Business Publication Rates and Data,* monthly publications of Standard Rate & Data Service, Inc. Under Entry 15 for each magazine you will find mechanical requirements and printing process listed.

Some printers insist that the newer processes can't match letterpress for quality, especially if a coated paper stock is used. In letterpress, halftones can be beautifully crisp, type can be remarkably defined.

A disadvantage of letterpress is the high cost of photoengraving. If a magazine is heavy on art and the press run is small, it is likely to find that offset lithography is a more appropriate printing process. So far as small magazines are concerned, letterpress is competitive only when pages are made up mostly of type.

The type most often used in letterpress printing is set by one of the "hot type" composition systems: foundry (the system Gutenberg used), Ludlow (used primarily for headlines), Linotype and Intertype systems (used for body copy), and Monotype (used for high-quality letterpress printing). All of these systems can be used for offset lithography, too, after a first

Before the turn of the century, the process of engraving for reproduction in magazines involved enough hand work—enough artistry—to merit two signatures or credit lines: one for the illustrator, one for engraver. This illustration appeared in Frank Leslie's Popular Monthly Magazine.

"printing" is made (after a repro proof is pulled), but offset lithography has the additional advantage over letterpress of being able to use any of the "cold type" composition systems besides: hand lettering, hand "setting" of paper type, typewriter composition, photolettering, and phototypesetting. Before cold type composition can be used in letterpress, it must first be converted to a photoengraving.

A big advantage of offset, especially for newspapers, is its ability to reproduce photographs—especially color photographs—clearly, even on poorer quality paper. But that advantage can be a disadvantage if you don't have good photographs to start out with. One fuzzy photograph shown on a page with several outstanding ones will look out of place. Letterpress on newsprint tends to bring all photos down to an average level, so the poor photograph is not so disturbing.

Magazine art directors prefer offset lithography to letterpress because with offset lithography they have firm control over the precise placement of each element on the page. In letterpress, the printer uses the art director's *rough sketch* or *rough pasteup* only as a guide. In offset the printer takes the art director's *finished pasteup* (also called *camera-ready copy*, or *the mechanical*) and actually photographs it. (Everything in offset is photographed, including the type.)

But this means that someone on the magazine—the art director himself, his assistant, or the production man—has to do a finished pasteup: a tedious, demanding, time-consuming job. (Gravure requires a finished pasteup, too.)

What the magazine turns over to the printer is what the printer prints, exactly—crooked lines and columns, uneven impressions on the repros, smudges, and all. It is safe to say that the editor of an offset magazine has more production headaches than the editor of a letterpress magazine.

It is, of course, possible to make an arrangement with the printer so that he will make up the magazine on the stone, as he would a letterpress magazine, and make repro proofs of each full page. That, then, is "camera-ready" copy, but the job costs more. It also means that the editor and his art director give up some of their control on spacing.

Art, provided it is actual size and does not require screening, can be pasted into place with the repros. So far as the printer is concerned, it is all line art anyway.

A study of offset magazines, especially the smaller house organs, suggests that editors do not know how to take advantage of the flexibility of the process. They either treat their magazines as though they were produced by letterpress, and as a result their magazines look stilted—or they overreact: tilting pictures, cutting them into strange shapes, drawing unnecessary

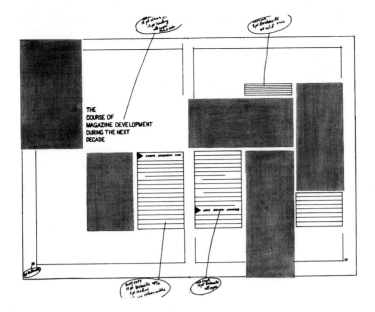

Early in the term of his Publication Design and Production course at the University of Illinois, Prof. Glenn Hanson distributes copies of manuscripts and asks students to copyfit them and incorporate them into page design. This is a first effort by student Ralph Sullivan: a spread involving five photos. The student writes notes in the margins to indicate his preferences in type styles and sizes. This is a rough layout. For a more comprehensive layout, he would be expected to omit the black outlines around the copy blocks and, using the drawing tools available to him, make the rectangles of gray actually look like photographs.

lines around them, fitting crude cartoons onto the page, and in general making their magazines look like the work of amateurs.

Getting along with the printer

Understanding the printing processes will keep the art director from asking the impossible of his printer. It will also open his eyes to printing's possibilities.

But Alfred Lowry, art director of *Newsweek,* thinks there is such a thing as knowing *too much* about printing. If you think an effect can't be had, you won't ask for it.

Every art director should know at least enough about printing and production to be able to converse intelligently with his printer.

On any magazine, the printer and art director must reconcile differences resulting from a pragmatic approach to the job on the one hand and a visionary's approach on the other. Frequent consultation is necessary.

If the printer and the editor and his staff sit down and reason with each other, explain to each other their needs and limitations, and talk frankly about costs, and if each side is willing to compromise, the relationship between editor and printer can be pleasant enough. Too many editors (and art directors) arrive at some arbitrary effect or size and hold out for it, despite the fact that with slight modification, the time involved in production (and hence the cost) could be greatly reduced.

Ideally, printing offices and editorial offices should be in the same city, but for reasons of economy, publications tend to let out contracts to printers in other parts of the country. For instance, many of the magazines edited on both the East and West Coasts are printed in the Middle West.

In seeking out a printer it is important to find one interested in innovation. Settling for the printer who comes in with the lowest bid may not be the most economical way of publishing a magazine.

Every printer has his strengths and idiosyncrasies. Every printer has his preferred ways for the editor to mark and prepare copy. An unhurried discussion at the start and frequent conferrals with the printer over the year will do much to ease production problems on the magazine.

Printing's own revolution

Carroll Streeter of *Farm Journal* sees the day when his magazine will custom build each copy to fit the special needs of each subscriber: what that subscriber wants will be recorded on electronic tape, and a computerized bindery will pick up only materials that interest him.

Less dramatic changes in format have taken place already. Printing and typesetting technology has brought great fidelity to the printed page, better color, more flexibility. Some of the newest magazines are coming out in a square rather than in the usual rectangular format. Gatefold covers and center foldouts and booklets bound within magazines are commonplace. *Venture* used three-dimensional color photographs on its covers. *Aspen* put itself in a box. *American Heritage* wrapped itself in hard covers. *Evergreen Review* made plans in 1971 to come out as a "video magazine" to take advantage of the video cassette and cartridge market.

In a 1966 article[1] *Newsweek* pointed to experiments in the graphic arts that attempted to

1. put 100,000 pages on one photosensitive crystal,

2. develop a lensless photographic system for three-dimensional home TV, and

3. develop a no-contact, no-pressure printing technique that could "print a message on a pizza and put a trademark on a raw egg yolk."

Newsweek saw these developments as part of a new industry that threatened what was then a ten-billion-dollar communications industry.

The new technology was made necessary, *Newsweek* said, by rising costs of traditional printing processes and by the increased amount of information that had to be recorded. The cost of composition was particularly prohibitive. By 1966 many U.S.

---

1. "Good-by to Gutenberg," *Newsweek*, January 24, 1966, pp. 85-87.

dailies had gone to computer composition. Computers produced tape that was fed into linecasting machines, quadrupling the speed of setting.

And computer editing was at hand. That was a system whereby copy was first typed into a computer, which hyphenated it, justified it, and fitted it into a layout. The layout was presented to the editor as a TV image. The editor used an electronic pointer and a keyboard to rewrite and rearrange the material.

The system moved to actual type after the editing was done, thereby eliminating any resetting. And if offset lithography was the printing process, hot type composition was eliminated altogether. Under the system, pages could be transmitted instantaneously via facsimile to regional printing plants.

Charles W. Lake, Jr., president of R. R. Donnelley & Sons

Roger Waterman's full-color comprehensive rough layout of a spread for Chevron USA *(top) along with the two pages as they actually appeared in the magazine. The typed note pasted down at an angle on the right-hand page is a reminder to the designer to make some adjustments: "HAWAII" is to be smaller and in heavier type. And "Motorambling in" is to be bigger. The reproduction does not show it clearly, but the smaller photo is marked to be recropped and lifted slightly on the page. Note the finished look of this rough. Most magazines do not require so high a degree of finish.*

Company, one of the nation's great printers of magazines, admitted that

a lot of revolutionary methods for putting images on paper have been coming off the drawing boards, and our research and development people are constantly evaluating every new approach. Some day, perhaps, one of these new processes will find its application in the magazine field, but it's going to take a long time and tremendous investments before any of the presently conceived new approaches can reach the quality, speed, and economy of today's basic printing processes.[2]

But by 1970 *Life* was using an Editorial Layout Display System (ELDS).[3] ELDS is a 7,000-pound electromechanical optical system with a screen, a table-top instrument panel, and some powerful transistorized equipment. Using projectors and computers, it "edits, records and prints layouts on demand."[4] It gives the art director immediate visualization of various layout ideas, in full color and in actual size.

It works this way: the art director mounts all elements in the layout on 35 mm slides and slips them into the machine. The machine holds ninety-nine of them, plus a basic library of typefaces and a layout grid.

Using the instrument panel, the art director can call any combination of elements into position, enlarge any of them, crop any of them—and work anywhere on the spread. Operators can be trained to use the machine in about two hours.

Irwin Glusker, as art director at *Life*, saw many advantages, including "happy accidents" that occur while the machine is being manipulated.

In 1977 *Reader's Digest* went to a computerized system that had the magazine's staff perform some functions normally associated with a typesetting house. *Digest* personnel put text material on computer tapes in binary coding suitable for driving the phototypesetters at York Graphic Services, where the type was set and typeset page negatives made.

Edward M. Gottschall sees the day when design formats will be programmed for computers, and all you will have to do, if you don't need customized design, is to press a button for the desired format and you will have it.

It's all rather breathtaking to contemplate. Still, the beauty of the printed page, even with all this sophisticated equipment, stems as always from the good taste and sound judgment of the art director.[5]

2. In a talk to the Magazine Publishers Association Conference on Color, New York, November. 18, 1965.
3. "Art Direction Enters New Age as LIFE Begins Layout by Machine," *Publishers' Weekly*, July 6, 1970, pp. 28, 29.
4. *Ibid.*, p. 28.
5. Prof. Harold Wilson of the University of Minnesota has put together an excellent collection of slides on *The New Technology of Print Media*, available from National Scholastic Press Association, 720 Washington Ave., S.E., Number 205, Minneapolis, Minnesota, 55414.

Four considerations should guide the editor and art director in their choice of paper for a magazine.

1. *The look of the paper.* How does its brightness, color, and texture match the mood of the magazine? Offset papers as chosen by editors of magazines are usually washday white, but they don't have to be. An off-white or even a light cream-colored stock has a richer appearance.

If the magazine is chiefly a picture book, whiteness of the paper *is* important. You want as much contrast as possible between the ink and the paper.

For special issues or for special sections, a colored stock can be arresting. It is cheaper than using a second color in printing, but with pure white gone, the art director faces a problem in giving his photographs their best display.

As for texture, glossy or smooth papers best display photographs; coarse paper best displays type.

Some editors and art directors change stock from issue to issue and even use more than one stock in a single issue.

Some editors like a paper stock with a noticeable pattern in it: like a stipple. Those editors should remember that the texture stays constant as the size of the sheet increases or decreases. The pattern may look innocuous enough on a large-size sheet, but when the sheet is cut down to page size, it may be too intrusive. Such a pattern would be better in an *Ebony*-size magazine than in a *Reader's Digest*-size magazine. Better to avoid it altogether.

2. *The feel of the paper.* Does the editor want a rough feel or a smooth one, a soft feel or a hard one (a paper can be both rough and soft, or smooth and hard), a thick sheet or a thin one?

An interesting fact about roughness: it can carry the feel of cheapness, as in the paper that was used by the old pulp magazines, or the feel of quality, as in an Alfred A. Knopf book printed on antique paper. The feel of the paper does tell the reader something about quality.

On the matter of thickness: an editor may prefer a thicker sheet so that his magazine will appear heftier. The name for such a sheet: high-bulk paper. A 60-pound sheet in one paper may be thicker than a 60-pound sheet in another simply because the one has been bulked.[6]

Most people like the feel of coated or polished stock, and that may be reason enough for editors to choose it—if they can afford it.

3. *The suitability of the paper.* Is the paper heavy enough to stand the strain of continued use? Ordinarily, the editor chooses for the cover a stock that is heavier than for the inside pages.

---

6. A paper's pound designation is determined by taking 500 sheets in the manufacturer's basic size—25 $\times$ 38 for book papers—and weighing them.

Is the paper permanent? A newspaper, quickly discarded, can go with newsprint. A scholarly quarterly, which will be bound and used for years by researchers, needs a longer lasting stock.

Is the paper suitable for the printing process? Papers manufactured for letterpress equipment will not work for offset. Offset needs a paper stock that can adapt to the dampness of the process and that will not cause lint problems. Letterpress needs a paper stock that isn't too crisp. This does not mean that the various textures, smooth and rough, aren't available in both letterpress and offset stock.

What typefaces should be used? Old style romans call for an antique stock, modern romans a glossy or polished stock. But most papers offered for magazine printing are versatile enough so that, within reason, any type can be used.

Does the editor need a paper with high opacity, or can he settle for one that is more transparent? If photographs are a consideration, or if masses of dark inks will be used, he'll have to have an opaque paper.

For good reproduction of photographs magazines should use at least a 40-pound stock, but to fight rising costs, some have gone to lighter papers. To save postage, *Life* in its last years used a 34-pound stock. "Every time postage goes up, the quality of paper and reproduction goes down," said Clay Felker, then editor of *New York*, speaking of magazines in general.[7]

It is possible that as an editor you would want your paper stock to look inexpensive. If your publication goes to members of an organization or to the public supporting you through taxes, you might not want to convey the feel of quality and expense. When a school district at Springfield, Oregon in 1977 went to a slick stock for its *What's Going on Here* publication to teachers and other employees, editor Don Wilt felt obliged to include a brief story explaining that "The switch [from newsprint] to a better grade of paper became necessary when the decision was made to begin printing the magazine in the district printing department. District 19's presses cannot run newsprint paper.

"However, by eliminating the cost of paying an outside printer for the press run, a higher quality stock can be used without creating additional cost, and in most instances, printing costs have been reduced by going 'in house.' "

The short news item told readers that each copy of the eight-page unbound 9 × 12 publication cost six cents.

4. *The cost of the paper*. It always boils down to this, doesn't it? Paper cost represents a major production cost to a magazine, which uses so much of it. The Magazine Publishers Association estimates that for a small magazine, paper represents 18 percent

7. Quoted by Charles R. Reynolds, Jr., "Magazines: Dead or Alive (Part II), " *Infinity*, December 1969, p. 21.

of operating costs; for a large magazine, 30 percent. The cost of the paper itself is only part of it. The cost of mailing comes into the picture, too. The heavier the paper, the more it will cost to mail copies of the magazine. A slight reduction in paper weight can mean thousands of dollars difference over a period of a year in mailing costs. If an editor is choosing between two papers, he should have his printer make up dummies of each to take to the post office for a consultation.

A magazine doesn't have to use high-quality paper to look well designed. First, *Rolling Stone* proved that; then, *Rags* (no longer published). Using newsprint, *Rags* in 1970 was able to print and mail copies at less than 10 cents each.[8]

The Economist, published in London, uses a Bible paper, at least for its U.S. edition, presumably to cut postage costs but perhaps for prestige reasons, too.

The publication using the most unusual stock in the late 1960s was a daily newspaper in Italy, *Giornale di Pavia,* with its bright color photographs printed on polyethylene. You could read this paper in the pouring rain, and when you were through you could shake it out, fold it up like a handkerchief, and put it in your pocket.

Color in magazines

From the time it was possible, color in printing has played an important role in the growth of many general-circulation and specialized magazines. The magazine world's initial interest in color was spurred in the 1960s with the coming of color to televi-

"Responding to the new lights and nuances of the late seventies," Time *in 1977 stepped up its use of full-color photography. One way of checking slides is to put them out on a light table and look at them through a magnifying glass. Considering a selection here are Mary Themo, picture color projects reporter/researcher; Arnold Drapkin, color editor; and John Durniak, picture editor. (Photo by Seldon Dix. Courtesy of* Time *Magazine.)*

8. Cummings Walker, "Rags," *Communication Arts,* vol. 12, no. 4, 1970, p. 63.

The social sun shines on in Saratoga Springs each August. Joan Shipman Payson turns her binoculars from the pitching mound to the starting gate. John Galbreath trots out his racing stable. And Sonny and Mary Lou open up Cady Hill to the very blue of blood. Over at the Gideon, folks are paying $75 per for the colonial atmosphere and mineral water, and the robust ghosts of Nick the Greek, Diamond Jim Brady and Polly Adler and friends frolic about the elegant lobby.

SARATOGA SPRINGS: ONCE MORE, WITH BREEDING

By JOE FLAHERTY

The town of Saratoga Springs is about 200 miles and a century removed from New York City. It is also the last civilized place in North America to drop out—if you're over 30. As the urbane critic George Jean Nathan noted, men after surviving three decades should have the common sense to pace their pleasures.

Saratoga is fringed with the proper touch of decadence. In fact, the leisurely vice is medicinal, prudently dispensed in living spoonfuls.

And, of course, like all great places, Saratoga evokes a woman. New York City is an unkempt slattern, San Francisco a frontier broad opting for class and Los Angeles is a mid-America burg who went West and "made it" as a carhop.

But Saratoga is a dowager Queen, a grand, sprawling mistress opulently exuding fatty, pleasurable promise. A woman who is capable of an operatic ending in her last great moment on the stage, unable to move not because of body-wracking disease, but from an overabundance of cholesterol. And like all women of pleasure, she has a past. A history as saucy as a harlot's appointment book and just as exclusive, since she only takes action once each year — in August.

August—its once pleasurable name now evokes such sinister phrases as "a long, hot summer." But such phrases here would be interpreted thankfully as a good run at the betting windows. At Saratoga there is a different interpretation given to social consciousness. And perhaps at a time when the other 11 months are chronicles of disaster, the one remaining should be set aside for unthinking pleasure. A clandestine whorehouse of the mind.

For a century the rich have come to the spa to play and, in the best democratic tradition, have allowed the less fortunate to put their noses to the window to watch. Over the years the tradition has been upheld—if somewhat diluted.

Gone are the days of Diamond Jim Brady, Lillian Russell, Commodore Vanderbilt, Nick the Greek and Polly Adler, who one season lost her entire two-legged stable to a group of amorous jockeys, or Berry Wall and White Hat McCarthy. Wall, who once succeeded in registering his mistress at the United States Hotel as "Wall and valet"—a feat as difficult to pull off as the Triple Crown. It moved McCarthy, who made millions at the betting windows, to up the ante and register his lady as "McCarthy and valise."

With them went the fleshy era of the grand elephantine hotels, the United States and the Grand Union, whose grounds each covered seven acres with piazzas and corridors measured in miles and dining rooms that served 1,400 at a sitting. (Their memory is preserved in Hollywood's version of Edna Ferber's *Saratoga Trunk*, with Ingrid Bergman and Gary Cooper.)

But on a warm afternoon at the racetrack, one can still with a turn of the head see Joan Shipman Payson, the mistress of the Mets, the grand lady whose face evokes "The Great Man" sitting among a scattered bouquet of highball glasses with her ever-present companion, her brother John Hay Whitney, owner of the now-dead New York *Herald-Tribune* and master of Greentree Stud. He is often described as the last of the great international sportsmen.

Within a wallet's throw are the possessors of such royal bloodlines as John Galbreath, who has cashed the enviable parlay of the Kentucky Derby and the World Series with Chateaugay and the Pittsburgh Pirates; Mrs. Alfred Gwynne Vanderbilt of Native Dancer fame; Captain Harry Guggenheim, former owner of *Newsday* and commander of the Cain Hoy Stable (Bald Eagle and Never Bend); the great horseman George D. Widener, honorary chairman of the Jockey Club, whose promising two year old, Pontifex, won the Flash Stakes and Saratoga Special last year; Colonel and Mrs. Cloyce Tippett (the former Liz Whitney), owners of California's Llangollen Farms; Mrs. Richard duPont, whose nonpareil Kelso like Old Man River just kept rolling along for eight seasons; Ogden Phipps, scion of the Wheatley Stables which each August trots out Bold Ruler's progeny hopeful that the grand old sire has done it again (last year he had, with Irish Castle winning the prophetic Hopeful Stakes); and the current superlatives of the Super Set, Sonny and Mary Lou Whitney.

When Mary Lou's jewels were stolen from their Saratoga showplace, Cady Hill (she made wearing artistic fake emeralds and diamonds respectable after the theft), legend has it that the police asked her if she knew anyone who lived well and had no money, since they suspected the thief was someone within the Whitney social circle. "Everyone," she replied. "Just take my address book and go right through it."

But with the advent of motels (though most of the swells still reside in their ancestral homes), the money has become a little more modern, too. Sonny Werblin, former head of the Music Corporation of America and former owner of football's most lovable so and sos, the American Football League's New York Jets, was overheard chatting with Ralph S. Wilson Jr., the owner of the Buffalo Bills who recently had been squeezed dry in contract negotiations with O. J. Simpson. "I don't have to deal with pro football players," Sonny said, "so I can afford to buy yearlings." Werblin's Silent Screen, purchased last year at Saratoga, won the money-loaded Arlington-Washington Futurity in a runaway in September.

And vigorously bidding for a Nashua colt at the yearling sales was John C. Mabee from San Diego, owner of the Big Bear supermarket chain. The thought of a grocer from some god-forsaken place named San Diego bidding for a son of Nashua who is out of the Aga Khan's great sire, Nasrullah, probably set Lady Astor shing-a-linging in her grave. Nonetheless, Mabee laid out $43,000 and took home the groceries.

The one new thing the rich can accept is cash, especially if it comes in quantities. Which brings us to oilman Frank McMahon, who sprung for $250,000 for Derby and Preakness winner Majestic Prince at the Keeneland Sales in 1966 and was expected and failed to show at Saratoga. His wide open checkbook was badly missed at this year's lethargic yearling sales. One must understand about crass "new money." After some handling, it becomes respectably "old."

Though one never penetrates the inner circle of Saratoga, money may be able to buy a well-bred horse even if one can't purchase "a family." So it is the old names that set the tone for the season. They carry on their tippling and whatever else the rich do at the exclusive Saratoga Golf Club and at historic Canfield's Casino (the once opulent gambling palace that is now a museum). Security against crashers at both places has Gibraltarian formidability. One *must* take precautions against lesser bloods. So if one's racing silks are not enshrined in the National Museum of Racing (you are almost moved to genuflect when passing Calumet's fabled devil red and blue), he will never blend, only clash with this tapestry of horsey aristocracy.

But for everyone, the pulse of life in Saratoga is the racetrack located on Union Avenue. The proper way to get to the races (since, sadly, there are no longer horsedrawn carriages) is a brisk, 15 minute walk from downtown. The thought of driving some foul-smelling steel contraption called a Camaro or a Fury onto this ground of hallowed hooves is a sacrilege not to be considered. And to thoroughly enjoy the setting, one should leave his bustle city matters behind with his machine, slow down and become gentried.

After years of contributing to the betterment of the breed at city tracks, one is taken back by Saratoga's racing fans. I have watched such sights as a grown man who would stand at the rail waiting for the horses to enter the stretch, then—whipping himself on the buttocks—race the horse he had bet to the wire. The tragedy was that he always won.

I also had an Italian friend who believed in the cosmic luck of the Chinese. Whenever he'd spot one at the track, he would stalk him to the windows to see what number he was buying. After about four races, the poor Chinese thought my friend was a button man from Chairman Mao.

But the last word on the manners of city horseplayers was passed on to me by a friend. Since he also has been a cornucopia of bum tips in the past, the validity of his story is not official. But he claims that on a sweltering day in July, a gentleman (whom age should have taught better) was jumping up and down as he cheered his horse through the stretch, but the excitement was too much for him, and he dropped dead. At this point, two angels of mercy stepped up on his chest to get a better view of the race, while a third who completed the unholy trinity asked: "Did anyone check his pocket to see if he had the winner?"

At Saratoga, the exotic types are gentler and perhaps more fraudulent. But that is part of the town's charm—you never question a cad with a large bankroll and a sketchy background who claims to be a gentleman.

This season, I ran into one Jack Redding, a spry gent with a button nose, blue eyes and a yearling crop of gray whiskers that left you wondering if he was growing a beard or merely had forgotten to shave. He wore the perfect clothes for a Saratoga con. They were so damn offbeat in modern colors and square cut, you didn't know whether he was a rich eccentric or had just heisted a Goodwill basket for his wardrobe.

But the impressive thing was that he was a two rubberband man—one for his stack of mutuel tickets and the other for his bankroll. And, of course, according to him, his address was the famed Gideon Putnam Hotel located on the grounds of the Spa.

The Gideon, for $75 a day, offers its guests unrivaled elegance under its colonial roof, along with health baths, golf, tennis, mineral water (a healthy gas when mixed with whiskey) and solitude from the less fortunate. Its grounds look like an Antonioni landscape with endless, peopleless plains interrupted by neo-Roman bathhouses and fountains and pools. One expects to find Dali's limp watches languidly scattered about the timeless landscape.

Redding is a world follower of action. "I've seen 'em run in Egypt, son, and next I'm off to Moscow, Russia. Where did you say you were from? Brooklyn. I love Brooklyn boys, they're great fighters. Not mean, just great fair fighters." Then, mysteriously: "My money came from the family. Kentucky—hardboots. But I've chased them all over, son. Take it easy, you're young yet. You don't have to play every race. There'll be plenty more in your lifetime. Listen to me, son. I've chased them all over the world." Is he for real? Only those whose soul demands a sure thing would give a damn.

Perhaps it is the setting of the track that makes conscience-examining so distasteful. It is impossible to be harsh here. The colors that dominate the grandstands are a racy green and white. And in this world of grating, dull gray cement, there are acres of green turf that gently carpet the footfall. Red and white canopies and vari-colored petunias give the setting a sense of dash, and ancient elms spreading like giant parasols provide nature's roof over this very special world.

There is also the snobbery of association with all those people who gave Saratoga its character. If one has a bad betting day, why not do it in *Titanic* fashion among the Phippses, Whitneys ano bilts.

But you are not limited to hobnobbing with the beautiful people. You can rub shoulders with the equine aristocracy as well in a beautiful, landscaped paddock. Here, billionaire art patron Paul Mellon, who has Rokeby Sables, watches as Arts and Letters, the champ, is saddled. And Silent Screen, the young pretender to the crown, is led out for inspection under the elms. Where else could you make the boast you were noses apart from Arts and Letters?

And the lesser part of the couplet, the jockeys, walk right by you going to the paddock and past you (an unparalleled act of courage) again after the race. Imagine Shoemaker blowing a 4-to-5 shot at Santa Anita and walking through the crowd! A mini-crucifixion.

But to others, I suppose, August in Saratoga is more than racing. There is Yaddo, the artistic retreat created by the late Spencer Trask, where artists and writers on fellowships come to work, free from outside pressures, in the silent sanctuary. People like Aaron Copland, Truman Capote, Carson McCullers, Eudora Welty, James T. Farrell, Robert Lowell, Lionel Trilling, William Carlos Williams and Leonard Bernstein have taken advantage of the creative atmosphere.

And in the magnificent outdoor Performing Arts Center, an acoustical wonder, one can hear Eugene Ormandy conduct the Philadelphia Orchestra or watch Melissa Hayden and the New York City Ballet show off their fancy footwork.

Then there are the restaurants, especially the Chez Pierre where the chateaubriand is done to specifications of the French gourmet, Robert Courtine, "charred as black as a saint's skin outside and pink as a baby's behind on the inside."

But with all these trimmings, Saratoga is still in its

18

Mike Salisbury, art director for West, originally had full color to work with for both pages, but production changes permitted him color only for the right-hand page. No matter. He rearranged things and came up with a particularly well ordered spread. The art is by James McMullan of Visible Studio Inc., New York.

sion and with the coming in the late 1950s of Hi-Fi and later SpectaColor to newspapers.

Newspapers were fighting back with color. But with their better paper stock and less hurried production deadlines, magazines clearly had it over newspapers. And magazines, because they contracted for their printing, had more than one process to choose from.

"There are no bad processes for color printing today," Charles W. Lake, Jr., the printing executive, told a Magazine Publishers Association conference on color in the 1960s. "We got rid of the early crude processes many years ago. The past few years have seen significant improvements in each of the three basic color printing processes for magazines." He added:

> Perhaps the most important overall development has been a blending of the capabilities of letterpress, gravure, and offset. There was a day when each of the processes produced a far different result. But what may have been an advantage for one of the processes a few years back likely represents far less of a distinct superiority today. And the dividing lines keep getting finer and finer. All of which further emphasizes the need for a very careful value analysis of all the processes, even if you have considered every available process in the past.

For smaller magazines wishing to use color, the obvious choice is offset, especially when lots of art is also a consideration. With offset, some smaller magazines enjoy R-O-P (run-of-press) color. That means they don't have to plan their color only for certain pages. In 1977 the major newsmagazines—they are printed letterpress—went to R-O-P color, making it possible for them to offer full-color photographs on any page, not just on pages that were part of special sections. It was possible for the magazines, then, to wait until the last minute to work in color photographs. Before, color was planned weeks in advance.

There seems little doubt that color can increase a publication's audience. The *National Star*, right after going to full color in 1975, experienced a 12 percent rise in newsstand sales.

But cost is always a factor. A second color throughout can increase the printing bill for a publication by 25 percent. Full-color can double that. So art directors should know what they're doing when they use color. Otherwise, they should leave experimenting to others. The best advice one can give regarding color is this: Build a file of the uses of color by others. Study that file. And profit from the mistakes and successes it shows.

One thing you should remember about color: when you see it in isolation, it looks one way, when you see it next to another color, it takes on a different look. Another thing: it looks one way on antique or uncoated stock, another way on coated stock.

If you cannot afford color on a regular basis you can use it on occasion, as when you put out a special issue or special section. The use of color helps say "special."

Because of costs, color in some magazines has been more the tool of the advertising than of the editorial department. The hue and placement of color may be dependent upon decisions made by the advertising department in response to insertion order specifications from advertisers. The editorial department gets a free ride, provided it uses color only on pages in signatures carrying color advertisements.

But editors and their art directors these days are demanding more of a say about where and when to use color.

Not that editors and art directors are wholly sold on color. Some feel that the additional money spent on plates and color printing could be better spent on additional black-and-white pages for the magazine. Nor are all artists sold on color. Henri Cartier-Bresson, who with Robert Capa and others founded the Magnum photographic agency in 1947, told *Time* (February 15, 1971): "I don't like color. By the time it goes through the printer, the inks, and the paper, it has nothing to do with the emotion you had when you shot it. Black and white is a transcription of that emotion, an abstraction of it." Irving Penn, another great photographer, has said: "I don't think I have ever seen a really great color photograph." Penn's reservations about color stem from his belief in photography as an *art* form. He once told David Deutsch, vice-president and executive art director for

McCann-Erickson, that photography in its purest form must deviate from realism. And color is realism.

William Hamilton Jones, the alumni magazine editor quoted elsewhere in this book, has strong reservations about color. "My own feeling about a second color is that it's usually a waste of time and money to use it." He says people don't use a second color imaginatively. "They use it in a way that's repetitious. You know, your headline is already bigger than any other type on the page. And if you put it in red besides, you really aren't serving any useful function." Or people use a second color as a tint block behind a picture or as a duotone. "It's a cheap way to call attention to your photograph. . . . It doesn't serve any positive function."

Jones adds:

. . . We have to compete for people's time with all the mass magazines. And if we're going to get into color, we're going to have to compete with . . . [big, slick magazines] and all the people who use color beautifully. It seems to me that we're much better off using our resources to do what we can do well. And I think using really good photography in black and white is a change of pace for people.[9]

One of the problems is that the editor and art director do not plan an issue of the magazine for color. When color becomes available in one of the signatures, the art director hastily finds some way to use it. Color is *added* to a page or merely *substituted for black*. It is not integrated as part of the design. Hence the many titles in color, blurbs in color blocks, photos in duotone. In some instances, line artwork is added to a page simply to make use of the color. John Peter of John Peter Associates, Inc., magazine consulting firm, calls this the "we-got-it-why-not-use-it" approach to color, an approach that leads to results "that are usually regretted by the time the issue is off the press." He advises: "When in doubt about using color, stay with black and white."[10]

Spot color

What William Hamilton Jones means by *second color* is *spot* or *flat color:* color laid in pure, solid form somewhere on the page as an area of emphasis. It is a "second" color because it is used in association with black or some other color. It involves an additional press run (or a press capable of printing two colors at once).

Some ways the art director can use a second color:

1. *For type.* Color is better for display sizes than for body

9. William Hamilton Jones in an untitled interview, *Alma Mater,* April-June 1969, pp. 68, 69.
10. John Peter, "Second Color," *Better Editing,* Spring 1968, pp. 9, 10.

sizes. When used for type, the color should be on the dark side. A bright red is all right. Yellow does not work. Sometimes it is a good idea to run only one word in a title in color to give it emphasis.

If you reverse a title (run it in white) in a dark area, say in a black part of a photograph, you can run color in the reversed area, in which case the color can be a light color, like yellow.

2. *For photographs.* The best way to print a black-and-white photograph is in black ink on white paper. When you print a photograph in a color, say green, you diminish the tonal scale; the lighter the color, the less scale you have, and the less detailed your photograph will be. If you must print your photograph in a color, you should choose one that is close to black, like dark brown, dark blue, or dark green. If you want the photograph merely as a decorative element or as a backdrop for copy printed over it, then you can print it in a light color.

If you want the complete tonal value plus the mood of color, you can print the photograph twice, once in the color and once in black. This requires two plates printed so that the dots of the black plate register just to the side of the dots in the color plate. We call this kind of halftone a *duotone.* (Example: you might want to use a brown duotone when you have an old-time photograph to reproduce.) You can also run a black-and-white wash drawing as a duotone. And you can apply the color used in the duotone as ordinary spot color elsewhere on the page or signature.

It is possible to take an ordinary black-and-white photo and *posterize* it for a run in black and one or more spot colors. The printer shoots it for line reproduction, dropping out the middle tones. He gives it more exposure for the color plate, less for

Bell Telephone Magazine *uses a second color—baby blue— boldly here to contrast one page with the other, to make two words in a title stand out, and to unite a left-hand page with a right-hand page. The initial letter starting out the article picks up the color of the page opposite. It offers the only color on that right-hand page, making the contrast between the two pages all the more remarkable. The shadow letters in the title nicely lend themselves to this color treatment. The white space on the right-hand page is arranged to take on some of the character of the white space in the shadow letters of the title. The copy area on the right-hand page, in other words, acts as a sort of shadow for the white space.*

black. In the printing, the black covers only some of the area printed in color.

It is also possible to print part of a photograph in black, part in a second color. If you have a mug shot, for instance, you can run it as a silhouette, dropping out the background; and in that white area you can print your second color, making a regular rectangle of the photograph. You can also reverse a circle, arrow, or number on a photograph, if one of these is needed, and fill it in in color.

3. *For line art.* A drawing can be printed in the second color, or it can be printed in black with second color used to fill in certain areas.

Second color has special value in charts, graphs, maps, and tables. The color clarifies and emphasizes.

4. *For lines, boxes, and blocks.* Lines in black or in color, horizontal or vertical, help organize and departmentalize a page. Putting a box around a word in a title, or a section of an article, makes it stand out. Or you can use a box to completely surround an article or story.

A block of color can be in a solid or a tint version of that color. Over these blocks you can run titles, body copy, or even photographs. If the blocks are dark enough, you can reverse type in them. A *photograph with a tint block* is different from a *duotone* in that the dot pattern in the former is even and consistent. The photograph with a tint block doesn't have as much contrast as the duotone. It looks as if it were printed on a colored paper stock.

Spot color can involve more than a second color. It can involve all the colors, as in the Sunday comic sections of newspapers. What's needed then are separate pieces of art for each of the primary colors plus black, separate plates, and multiple printings. The art in two-, three-, or four-color spot color work in most cases requires line reproduction.

Process color

A much more expensive form of color is *process color*, necessary when the magazine has full-color paintings or photographs to reproduce. In four-color spot color, the magazine supplies separate art (called *overlays*) for each of the four plates. In process color it supplies only the one piece of art; the printer (or photoengraver) must separate the colors photographically, through use of filters, and painstakingly reconstruct them for the four negatives used to make the four plates.

For best printing results for color photographs (and you should refer to them as *color* photographs rather than *colored* photographs; the latter suggests color is added after the picture is taken, as in the tinting of photographs) you should supply your printer with transparencies. He shouldn't use color prints unless he has to. They do not reproduce as well, and the printer charges more when he has to use them.

In working with transparencies, you should use the same kind of transparency viewer at every step of the reproduction process. It is necessary that everyone who makes a judgment about the transparency make it using the same kind of viewer. To expand this advice a little: you should inspect transparencies, color prints, artwork, proofs, and press sheets under identical lighting conditions in order to maintain control of the work, especially color quality. (Printers urge that one person—preferably a production chief—have full authority on production quality control for both the editorial and advertising sides. Printers find it frustrating to get instructions from one person and final okays from another. One often does not agree with the other.)

You should not ask your printer to enlarge more than five times the original negative. A 2 1/4 × 2 1/4 camera is better for color than a 35 mm, so far as picture reproduction is concerned. A 4 × 5 or an 8 × 10 is best, but of course such cameras are too cumbersome for most publications work.

Coated, or at least a calendered, stock is best for reproducing color photos and probably black and white photos, too, especially if the printing process used is letterpress. If the magazine's process is offset, the smoothness of the stock is not so important a factor in photo reproduction.

Laying out the pages

Whether he provides camera-ready copy or merely rough layouts or pasteups, the editor or his art director will have to work out the arrangement of articles, stories, and features on the various pages of his magazine, issue after issue. We call this arrangement the *dummy*. In the next chapter we will go into design considerations of the dummy; in this chapter we shall consider only the mechanics.

The problem, of course, is to fit all the items, editorial and advertising, together, so they will look good and read easily. It is impossible to tell someone who has not done it before exactly how he should do it; fitting a magazine together is something one does by feel. No two persons do it exactly the same way. There is a good deal of trial and error to the procedure, even for professionals. The designer will try one thing, discard it, and try another. When he sees the proofs he still will not be satisfied, and he'll adjust them, even at that late date.

Almost every magazine has a two-page layout sheet, or grid, on which the editor or his art director does his layouts. These sheets can be used for both the rough dummy and the finished pasteup.

The art director can either draw in, roughly, the titles and art, or he can paste into place, also roughly, the galleys and photoprints of the art. If he uses galleys, they will be a second set, marked with numbers to show the printer from what galley forms the various articles and stories were taken. The first set is used for proofreading.

The ads are already blocked in. What's left is what a newspaper would call the "news hole," what we'll call the "editorial hole." The editorial hole consists of a number of beautifully blank spreads ready for the art director's artistry.

The main chore lies with the several major items that start in the front half of the book. The editor has set aside a certain number of pages for each item. By previous decision, some items will occupy several pages, some will have one or two. Some items are to begin on a right-hand page, and some on a left-hand page. The art director often starts with this already given.

He has a choice of three basic approaches:

1. *Start from the front.* He figures out where he wants his opening art, and how big, and where he wants his title and blurb, takes what space he needs for such display, and trails the article column by column through the remaining space. If he runs over, he asks the editor to cut. If he's under, he increases the size of the art in front or adds art to the body.

2. *Start from the back.* Assuming the editor does not use fillers, the art director starts with the tail end of an article and works forward, allowing for subheads, if that is the magazine's style. The design at first is only tentative; if galleys are used they are fastened down with small dabs of rubber cement. The amount of space between where the feature is supposed to begin and where the first paragraph happens to land is the amount of space available for title, blurb, and art. If it's not very much, the art director may use it all right there at the opening. If it is considerable, he will move part of the article forward and put additional art into the space thus opened up.

3. *Work backward and forward from the middle.* This results in a better designed feature, usually, and, more than the other two approaches, requires coordination between editor and art director. The art director is as concerned with the looks of the back half of the article as with the opening spread. Some art directors run their big art near the middle rather than at the beginning.

The art director best estimates how much space the title type will take by actually lettering it. He indicates body copy by boxes or by a series of parallel lines. How does he know exactly how many lines of type the article will take? He uses one of several copyfitting systems[11] or, better, he asks his editor to

11. See Glenn Hanson's excellent book, *How to Take the Fits Out of Copyfitting*, The Mul-T-Rul Company, Fort Morgan, Colorado, 1967.

have all manuscripts typed at preset widths on calibrated copy paper. (See illustration on this page.) On most magazines a little editing at the proof stage is necessary for a perfect fit.

Some editors and art directors, recognizing that such last-minute editing is a disservice to the writer and possibly the reader, have gone in for pages whose columns do not necessarily line up at the top or bottom.

Company magazines designed by advertising agencies or design studios and some other magazines require much more finished dummies or layouts—"comprehensive roughs" or "comps," in the language of advertising. The art directors treat their editors as though they were clients. A comp leaves little to the imagination; design that doesn't work can be corrected before type is set and pictures are taken. But comps take time, and designers who do them command high fees. Comps are out of reach of most magazine editors.

Instead of using a preprinted grid sheet, the designer doing a comp or even a carefully drawn rough layout is likely to use tissue or tracing paper. For many, many years the drawing and lettering were done in pencil and chalks; now felt-tip pens and markers are the preferred medium. These come in a wide variety of colors and in various shades of gray, both warm and cool.

Typical typing sheets used by a magazine in preparing its copy for the typesetter. One is for copy that will be set in 9-point type, the other for copy that will be set in 10-point. The typist chooses the vertical line at the right that represents the correct column width and ends each line of her typing as close to that line as possible. The numbers going down the side at the left quickly show the editor how many lines the copy will take when it is set in type, greatly simplifying his copy-fitting problems.

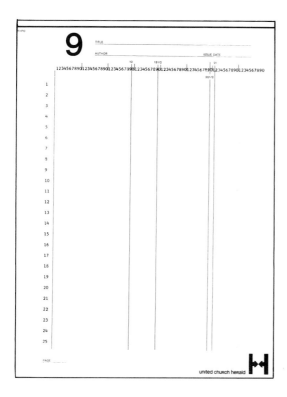

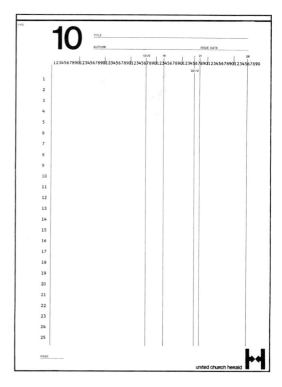

The pasteup

If the publication is printed by offset or gravure, the art director carries his layout to a higher level: the pasteup. Using rubber cement or a waxing process, the art director—or a pasteup artist under his direction—fastens everything into place: reproduction proofs of titles and text and any actual-size line art. Line art that is to be reduced and photographs and paintings are submitted to the printer separately.

Photographs can be handled in either of two ways. They can be prescreened as Velox prints and pasted down with the type as though they were pieces of line art, or they can be shot separately as halftone negatives and "stripped in." You get better fidelity, usually, using the "stripped in" process, but sometimes, as when you have many small photographs on a page, the use of Veloxes is practical. You can also easily retouch a Velox, bringing out highlights.

So far as copy is concerned, pasteup offers the desirable restriction of no last-minute partial leading between lines to even out a column. It is a lot of trouble for a pasteup artist to cut lines

A typical magazine layout sheet or grid presenting two facing pages in actual size. Each page can accommodate either a three- or four-column format. The tiny marks at the bottom left and right are for page numbers. The white lines in the grayed area are the edges for bleed pictures. This sheet can be used for both the rough layout and the pasteup. Some magazines design their layout sheets to show number of lines per column.

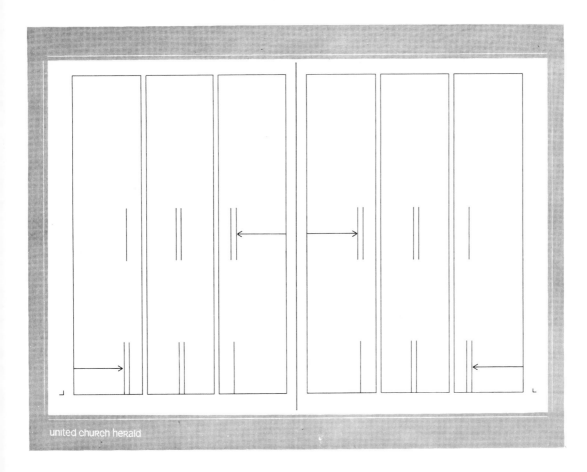

united church herald

apart and respace them. (By contrast, it is a simple matter through leads between hot-type lines to extend a story.) That you can't lead at the last minute means that you don't have unequally leaded stories side-by-side in the publication, and that makes for consistency of pattern—a good thing in design.

Wrapping it up

The production phase ends with the magazine's being readied for distribution to the reader.

The magazine that goes to the reader via the mails often goes in a wrapper of some kind: a paper sleeve, an envelope, even a box.

A sleeve might fully cover the face of the magazine, as for a thick saddle- or side-stitched magazine, or it might cover only a part of the magazine, as for a thin one that is folded vertically down the middle before the sleeve is fitted on. Some magazines, mailed flat, go out in transparent full wrappers that protect copies from rain and also allow subscribers to recognize their magazines at once when they arrive. A few magazines wrap themselves in extra covers, perhaps of kraft paper, which as four-page extra signatures are saddle-stitched on. They carry the address label, and they can be torn off when the magazines arrive to allow subscribers to fully appreciate well-designed front covers unmarred by stickers or rough handling in the mails.

Too often the wrapper is overlooked by the art director. He should be as concerned about its design—about its form and typography—as he is about the magazine itself. The wrapper is the reader's first contact with each issue as it arrives.

Suggested further reading

ARNOLD, EDMUND C., *Ink on Paper 2*, Harper & Row, Publishers, New York, 1972.

ALLEN, EDWARD M., *Harper's Dictionary of the Graphic Arts*, Harper & Row, Publishers, New York, 1964.

BALLINGER, RAYMOND A., Graphic Reproduction Techniques, Van Nostrand Reinhold, New York, 1976.

BENEVENTO, FRANK S., and others, *Art and Copy Preparation, with an Introduction to Phototypesetting*, Graphic Arts Technical Foundation, Pittsburgh, 1976.

BERG, N. EDWARD, *Electronic Composition: A Guide to the Revolution in Typesetting*, Graphic Arts Technical Foundation, Pittsburgh, 1976.

BIRREN, FABER, *Color: A Survey in Words and Pictures*, University Books, Inc., New Hyde Park, New York, 1963.

BOROWSKY, IRVIN J., *Handbook for Color Printing*, North American Publishing Company, Philadelphia, 1977. (Revised Edition. Charts showing combinations in two-color printing.)

BRUNNER, FELIX, *Handbook of Graphic Reproduction Processes*, Hastings House, Publishers, New York, 1962.

CARDAMONE, TOM, *Advertising Agency and Studio Skills: A Guide to the Preparation of Art and Mechanicals for Reproduction*, Watson-Guptill Publications, New York, 1970. (Revised Edition.)

COGOLI, JOHN, *Everything to Know About Photo-Offset*, North American Publishing Company, Philadelphia, 1973.

COLLINS, FREDERICK, HOWARD, *Authors and Printers Dictionary*, Oxford University Press, London, 1973.

COOKE, DONALD E., *Dramatic Color by Overprinting*, North American Publishing Company, Philadelphia, 1974.

CRAIG, JAMES, *Production for the Graphic Designer*, Watson-Guptill Publications, New York, 1974.

CROY, PETER, *Graphic Design and Reproduction Techniques*, Hastings House, Publishers, New York, 1967.

GARDINER, A. W., *Typewriting and Office Duplicating Processes*, Hastings House, Publishers, New York, 1968.

GARLAND, KEN, *Graphics Handbook*, Reinhold Publishing Corporation, New York, 1966.

GRAHAM, WALTER B., *Complete Guide to Pasteup*, North American Publishing Company, Philadelphia, 1975.

HUTCHINS, MICHAEL, *Typographics: A Designer's Handbook of Printing Techniques*, Van Nostrand Reinhold Company, New York, 1969.

KENT, RUTH, *The Language of Journalism*, Kent State University Press, Kent, Ohio, 1970.

KLEPER, MICHAEL L., *Understanding Phototypesetting*, North American Publishing Company, Philadelphia, 1976.

KRAMPEN, MARTIN, AND SEITZ, PETER, *Design and Planning 2: Computers in Design and Communication*, Hastings House, Publishers, New York, 1967.

KUPPERS, HARALD, *Color: Origins, Systems, Uses*, Van Nostrand Reinhold Company, New York, 1973.

LEVITAN, ELI L., *Electronic Imaging Techniques*, Van Nostrand Reinhold Company, New York, 1977.

LEWIS, JOHN, *The Anatomy of Printing: The Influence of Art and History on its Design*, Watson-Guptill Publications, New York, 1970.

MELCHER, DANIEL, AND LARRICK, NANCY, *Printing and Promotion Handbook: How to Plan, Produce and Use Printing*, McGraw-Hill Book Company, 1966. (Third Edition.)

Moran, James, *Printing in the Twentieth Century: A Penrose Anthology*, Hastings House, Publishers, New York, 1974.

Proudfoot, W. B., *The Origin of Stencil Duplicating*, R. Fenton, Publisher, New York, 1973.

Sharpe, Deborah T., *The Psychology of Color and Design*, Nelson-Hall Co., Chicago, 1974.

Silver, Gerald A., *Modern Graphic Arts Paste-up*, American Technical Society, Chicago, 1966.

Sloan, Patricia, *Color: Basic Principles and New Directions*, Reinhold Publishing Corporation, New York, 1968.

Stevenson, George A., *Graphic Arts Encyclopedia*, McGraw-Hill Book Company, New York, 1968.

Strauss, Victor, *The Printing Industry: An Introduction to its Many Branches, Processes and Products*, R. R. Bowker Company, New York, 1967.

Turnbull, Arthur T., and Baird, Russell N., *The Graphics of Communication*, Holt, Rinehart & Winston, Inc., New York, 1975. (Third Edition.)

Van Uchelen, Rod, *Paste-up: Production Techniques and New Applications*, Van Nostrand Reinhold, New York, 1976.

Yule, John A. C., *Principles of Color Reproduction*, John Wiley & Sons, New York, 1967.

Graphics Master 2, Dean Lem Associates, P.O. Box 46086, Los Angeles, California, 90046, 1977. (Expensive all-purpose reference book on production, printing, color, typesetting, copyfitting.)

Halftone Reproduction Guide, Halftone Reproduction Guide, P.O. Box 212, Great Neck, New York 11022, 1975. (More than 1,200 different effects using two-color printing.)

Paste-up Guide, Portage, P.O. Box 5500, Akron, Ohio, 1976.

Pocket Pal: A Graphic Arts Digest for Printers and Advertising Production Managers, International Paper Company, New York.

The Fundamentals of Photoengraving, American Photoengravers Association, Chicago, 1966.

Chapter 5

The approach to design

Designers come to magazines from different backgrounds. Some are ex-illustrators. Some are typographers. Some are editorial people doubling up on duties. Some get their experience with advertising agencies; some are more oriented to the fine arts. Most are neat and orderly, but some are as undisciplined as the most unkempt of the freelancers they buy from. They have their good days and their bad. A few get along splendidly with their editors; they have mastered the art of compromise.

Compromise is important because design is largely a matter of reconciling editorial needs with visual needs, statement with white space, type with art. A series of compromises helps unify the magazine.

Unity is one of the universal principles of design.

There are at least five others.

We shall deal now with those principles, especially as they apply to magazines.

The principles of magazine design

1. *Balance.* We start with the principle most respected by those who are unsure of themselves in the area of graphic design. The most obvious of the principles—and the least important—it states, simply, that what is put on the left half of the page must "weigh" as much as what is put on the right half of the page. Or: what is put on one page of a spread must "weigh" as much as what is put on the facing page.

The designer who is overconscientious about this principle can take the easy way out: he can *center* everything: the heading, the photo, the text matter. If a spread is involved, he can run the heading across the gutter so half is on each side. He puts a picture on the left page and a picture of equal size across from it on the right page. If he runs two columns of copy under one picture, he runs two columns of copy under the other. The balance is bisymmetric.

For some articles, for some magazines, that solution may be a good one. Usually it is not.

The designer, with a little more effort, can achieve balance that is asymmetric and therefore more interesting. He puts a big picture on one page near the gutter and manages to balance it with a smaller picture at the outside of the other page. It is the principle of balance involved when a parent and child use a teeter-totter; the heavier parent sits close to the fulcrum; the child sits way out on the end.

The balance becomes more complicated as graphic elements are added. We shall not take the space here to consider the possibilities. Balance comes naturally enough as the designer moves elements around and pulls white space into concentrated masses. He "feels" the balance; and his intuition is all that is needed. Not confident, he may hold his design up to a mirror and check it in its reverse flow; this will quickly dramatize any lack of balance.

The designer, then, works with optical weights. He knows from experience that big items weigh more than little ones, dark more than light, color more than black and white, unusual shapes more than usual shapes. He knows, too, that a concentration of white space, because it is unusual, can itself be "heavy."

2. *Proportion.* Good proportion comes about less naturally. The beginning designer is inclined to put equal space between the heading and the picture and the picture and the copy, and the copy and the edge of the page. His margins are monotonously the same.

Better proportion comes from Nature. The circumference of the tree trunk supersedes the circumference of the branch. The distance between the tip of the finger and the first joint is different from the distance between the first joint and the second joint.

We have the inspiration of Nature in the "golden section" (or "golden mean") of the fine arts. It provides that the lesser dimension in a plane figure is to the greater as the greater is to the sum of both; or, the dimensions are in a 0.616 to 1.000 ratio. Roughly 3 to 5. We base page size—of typing sheets, of books, of magazines—on this ratio. We find the ratio more interesting, less tiresome, less obvious than a simple 1 to 1. We avoid 2 to 1, 3 to 1, and 4 to 2 ratios, because they are merely variations of 1 to 1. They divide into equal portions. We avoid cutting pages into halves or quarters. We avoid running pictures that are perfectly square because the ratio of width to depth is 1 to 1.

In most well-designed magazines, the pages are rectangular,

You get a good idea of what makes for a set of pleasing proportions by observing the ruled lines, provided by the author, in the margins of this decorative title page designed near the turn of the century by Charles Ricketts at the Vale Press.

A page of short items, united with strong ruled lines. The column heading art is appropriate to the magazine: Fleet Owner. *Note that for headings within the column, the editor has simply put first words in boldface type. (With permission from* Fleet Owner. *Copyright 1970 by McGraw-Hill, Inc. All rights reserved.)*

the pictures are rectangular (vertical and/or horizontal), and distances between elements are only subtly related.

But with the varying proportions, the designer maintains consistent spacing throughout the book where elements are *meant* to be equal, as in the separation of subheads from the body of the article and captions from their pictures.

The page margin for many magazines is narrowest between inside edge of copy and gutter, wider between top of copy and top of page, wider still between outside edge of copy and outside edge of page, and widest between bottom of copy and bottom of page. (This book uses a different margin arrangement for style reasons and to save the reader from having to fight the gutter to read the long columns of copy.)

Total picture area takes up more space than non-picture area; or it takes up less space. The ratio is never 1 to 1.

3. *Sequence.* First things first. The designer does not leave to chance the order in which the reader takes in the items on a page or spread. He knows the reader ordinarily starts at the top left of a page or spread and works his way to the bottom right. Arranging the elements so they read from left to right and from top to bottom is easy enough; but it limits design flexibility.

The reader also has a tendency to move from big items to smaller items, from black to white, from color to noncolor, from unusual shape to usual shape. The designer finds it possible, then, to begin his design *anywhere*, directing the reader to the left, the right, the top, the bottom—in a circular motion, diagonally, whatever way he wishes. Diminishing visual impact does the job.

The designer directs the reader, too, through the use of lines, real or implied, which carry the eye as tracks carry a train. The pictures themselves have direction or facing; as surely as if they were arrows, they point the way. This is why you would always arrange a major mug shot so that the subject looks into the text.

The designer tries to arrange photographs so that an edge or a force from one photograph flows into an adjoining one. The curve of an arm, for instance, if carried over to the next paragraph would merge into the roll of a hill. This happens without regard to what may be the outer dimensions of the photographs; one photograph might be considerably larger than the other and not aligned with it.

Or: taking a line from within the picture—say the edge of a building—the designer extends it (without actually drawing it) and fits against it another item—say a block of copy. Or: taking the hard edge of a picture and extending it, he fits another picture against it somewhere across the page.

And do not discount the possibility of actually *numbering* the pictures. If chronological order is all-important, as for a step-by-step illustrated article on how to build a guest house, the designer may not find a better way for handling sequence.

Developing sequence from spread to spread is also part of the assignment. Which leads to another principle.

4. *Unity.* The typeface must look as if it were designed to fit the style of the illustration. It must fit the mood of the piece. The overall effect of the spread, of the entire article or story, of the entire magazine must be one of unity, of harmony. The pieces, the pages belong together.

Ideally, all typefaces in a magazine come from the same family. Ideally, all art is furnished by the same artist or photographer.

Heavy rules or borders ordinarily call for boldface sans serifs. Bold sans serifs call for line drawings with plenty of solid blacks.

Thick and thin rules call for modern romans. Modern romans call for well-ordered photographs, or clean line drawings, arranged in severe horizontal and vertical patterns.

And pattern concerns the designer. Stepping back, the designer contemplates the overall effect. No longer looking for

No medication is foolproof, but taken with your doctor's advice…

THE
PILL
IS
SAFE

ONLY ONE birth-control measure is safer or more effective than the pill—total sexual abstinence. And that has never been too popular a choice. Any other method—rhythm, diaphragm, condom, foam, intra-uterine device (IUD)—is either less effective or not as safe as the ubiquitous tablet more than eight million women swallow daily.

Unfortunately, the pill's benefits have been blackened, and its evils—real and imagined—have been magnified at the recent Senate subcommittee hearings chaired by Sen. Gaylord Nelson (D., Wis.). Contrary to newspaper and television reports, the hearings did not uncover new dangers in the pill but merely repeated old stories that had already been carefully weighed by responsible medical authorities.

So sensational were the charges, however, that a public-opinion poll suggests that more than a million women have been too frightened to continue using the oral contraceptive, although 87 out of 100 women said they previously were satisfied with it. Planned or not, the anti-pill hysteria has panicked these women into making—on their own—a complicated medical decision that demands a physician's guidance.

Dire predictions of death from blood clots and cancer frightened the women away. While the blood-clot danger is statistically small but real, the cancer scare is neither statistical nor real; it is simply conjectural.

Two years ago, a British survey showed that death from blood

Since 1956, Dr. Tyler has played a major role in developing and testing the pill. An associate clinical professor of obstetrics and gynecology at UCLA, he is also medical director of the Family Planning Centers of Greater Los Angeles.

BY EDWARD T. TYLER, M.D.,
WITH ROLAND H. BERG

clots occurred nearly seven times more often among pill-users than among similar-aged women not on the pill. A smaller United States survey found that the risk was about four times greater. Seven or four, even the smaller number is significant and must not be ignored. Any woman taking the pill should be aware that there is the danger of blood clots.

Although the risk is real, it is equally important for every woman to know what the added danger actually means. The British study revealed that three women out of every 100,000 taking the pill died from blood clots. The toll involved was no greater than that among women who are killed while riding in cars or crossing the street. Certainly, such accidental deaths are deplorable, but no one suggests that the risk is so great women should stop riding in automobiles.

It is even more significant that pregnancy entails harsh risks of its own. Actually, the chance of death associated with pregnancy is 17 times greater than with pill-taking. Thus, the million or more women who reportedly abandoned the pill in fear because of the hearings may find their lives in greater jeopardy should they become pregnant as a consequence.

Although the blood-clot problem is relatively recent, hints of it appeared eight years ago. As an editorial consultant to the *Journal* of the American Medical Association, I recommended in 1962 that the *Journal* publish a report by a clinician linking the occurrence of blood clots with oral contracep-

tives. The *Journal* did so, and also asked me to write an editorial calling for definitive research on the how and why of the relationship.

To this date, no definitive research has been done.

One reason may be the near-impossible task of evaluating the pill's role, when the basic mechanism of blood clotting is largely a mystery to scientists. Another is the unresolved argument over who should foot the bill for the research. Is it the drug companies' responsibility, because they stand to profit from the sale of oral contraceptives? Or should it be the Government's concern because, with eight million users, the pill has become a public-health problem?

During the Washington hearings, several witnesses advocated that women switch from the pill to one of the many intrauterine devices available. (One witness who was the pill's severest critic is the developer of an IUD that is now being manufactured and sold.) An IUD is a piece of plastic or metal (a coil, spiral, loop, etc.) that is inserted by a physician into a woman's uterus and left there. How it prevents pregnancy, no one knows.

With oral contraceptives, however, there are no doubts. The pill prevents conception by tricking the body into believing it is already pregnant. The pill accomplishes this with its two chemical ingredients that mimic the action of the female sex hormones—estrogen and progestogen.

One pill—the sequential type—consists of a synthetic estrogen tablet taken daily for two weeks, followed for one week by a daily tablet containing both synthetic hormones. The other—the combination type—contains both hormones in a single tablet that is taken daily for three weeks.

As each menstrual cycle rolls around, the pills' cumulative effect

continued

LOOK 6-30-70 **65**

All the principles of design described in this chapter are incorporated by Don Menell, assistant art director of Look, in this single page. It is the opening page of a two-page article that starts on a right-hand page and ends on the (next) left-hand page. Menell combines roman display type with sans serif body type, adds column rules, and carefully fits the type around the illustration. The illustration ties in beautifully with the title, carrying the reader down into the article and dividing the page pleasingly. Note that the hand both holds a pill and forms into the symbol for "okay." The ring on the finger, faintly seen, is a nice added touch. (Reproduced by courtesy of the editors. From the June 30, 1970, issue of Look magazine. Copyright 1970 by Cowles Communications, Inc.)

individual trees, he surveys the forest. Does it all seem to fit together?

The pattern may be loose, tight, bulky, smooth, rugged, soft, loud, dark, light, hard, straight, rolling, changing, any number of things—but the pattern is unmistakably there.

The designer takes a major step toward unity when he pushes his white space to the outside edges of his spreads. This teams photographs with other elements so that they work together. When large amounts of white space seep into the center, there is an explosion, sending the elements off in all directions. White space on the outside edges should be there in unequal concentrations, in conformance with the principle of pleasing proportion.

5. *Simplicity*. Here we come to a design principle not so universal as the others. Graphic design accommodates to trends in fashion, architecture, the fine arts, the political climate, culture in general. What strikes us as a good magazine page now might not strike us that way ten years from now, or even next year. At times in the history of the graphic arts, a cluttered, busy, crowded page, overly decorated, has impressed designers if not readers. Even today, such a page is good, under certain conditions, simply because it is different from others. The principle of contrast—contrast with other designs—gives the page respectability.

But the main thrust of design today is toward simplicity. The reader simply does not have time to browse and hunt.

So the magazine designer gives him as few elements per page or spread as he can. Instead of many small pictures—two or three large ones. Instead of three columns to the page—two or one. Instead of a multi-decked heading—a single title. Instead of a three-line title—a title in a single line.

Even when the designer has a half dozen or more photographs

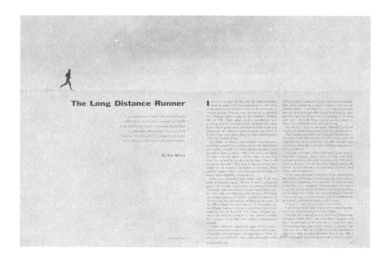

to work into the design, he can organize them into one mass, butting them together so they make either a true rectangle or a square.

Some designers organize all the elements so that they will form three basic areas of unequal size separated from each other by unequal distances.

6. *Contrast.* Put negatively, the principle is Contrast. Put positively, it is Emphasis. Either way, something on the page or on the spread stands out from all else. What stands out is probably the most important item on the page. It is probably the item the reader sees first.

The designer achieves contrast or gives an item emphasis by making it bigger than anything else there—blacker, more colorful, or more unusually shaped. Or he gets it by causing all other items to point to the item or by putting it in a different setting, giving it different texture, or otherwise making it seem out of place.

This is important: only *one* item—or one cluster of items—dominates. When the designer gives graphic emphasis to several items, they all compete for attention, frustrating the reader, causing him to bring down his gavel and declare an adjournment.

The principles in perspective

Two men seated together on a plane trip enter into a discussion about the pollution problem. One says to the other: "I-I-I th-th-thi, I-I think . . . we, we, we ought to, uh, . . . I think we ought to c-c-clean up the air and w-w-w-water." And the other one answers: "That's easy enough for you to say!"

And so are these principles. If they sound glib, that's because

This two-spread, four-page article from Old Oregon, *an alumni magazine, is held together by a single photograph, full bleed on all pages. The designer, Stan Bettis, who took the picture, uses part of it for one spread, part for another. He runs the photo in a light tone so he can surprint the title and body copy. Note how the runner and the title move the reader to the initial letter that begins the article. The horizon line in the photo carries the reader from the first spread to the second.*

The ups and downs of camera movements

... ON SEESAWS, SWINGS, AND SLIDES

BY BOB DUNCAN

PHOTOGRAPHS BY HARVEY V. FONDILLER

Playground seesaw becomes moving platform from which to shoot action scene of person on the other end.

Mention camera movements to the man who has just lovingly unpacked and is in the process of loading his sleek new super 8, and chances are he'll react as he would to a word-association test. "Green" equals grass. "Fat" signifies mother-in-law. And "camera movement" implies panning. If he has given the instruction book or a how-do-to-it article a superficial going-over, he'll probably snarl at the very thought. Only a fathead, not in the know, would jeopardize precious footage by panning.

The other extreme is, sad to say, less far-fetched. Possibly our amateur film maker has never heard that the pan, like strychnine for the heart, is a valuable aid when used in moderation, but certain death if used to excess. That, or he simply cannot resist the temptation. So off he goes, as though armed with a flamethrower, never dreaming how it can backfire. Maybe he has had basic training with an enamel spray can, and is a master of the long, sweeping stroke. But if he has a strain of mercy in his makeup (and his self-preservation instinct is in good working order), he'll lay in a supply of tranquilizers prior to screening time.

Who—or which—is right? Obviously neither, and not only in the flat rejection or warm embrace of the pan shot, for camera movement is by no means synonymous with, nor restricted to, panning. Let's look into some of the other methods of putting the motion picture camera into motion, any of which can enhance your movies if, like the pan, they are used with some degree of discretion.

Before making a few observations on the pan, here is a significant statistic: an overwhelming percentage (maybe up to 95 percent) of home movie footage is shot from eye level. This makes for monotony, no matter how ingenious your variation of pace.

medium, and close shots, and no matter which of the camera movement devices suggested below you decide to experiment with.

If you pan you must (and there are times when this is called for, especially when following a moving object), try a low level. Let's say you are filming running or toddling feet as your youngster moves across the lawn. Since it is feet that you want on film, lower the tripod and camera to their level, and see what a dramatic difference this take makes when cut in with other shots of the action. Now that you've gone low, try going high. Position yourself on a ladder with the tripod legs together and braced between your feet, or lashed to the ladder. Or, shoot from the porch roof or a second-floor window. Keep your pan short, first holding it on the subject for about three seconds before the action starts, then framing just ahead, allowing face room. Then end and hold as your subject moves off the movie screen.

Surrounded by tall buildings or tall trees? Here is another camera motion "additive," again in the panning department. First, select your shooting location. The most effective one quite likely will be somewhere near dead center. Set up and tilt up, scanning through the viewfinder for the most effective angle. Do a 360-degree dry run, revolving the camera slowly. One building or a treetop may be a bit taller than its neighbors, and depending upon how much sky area your framing calls for, adjust the tilt accordingly. Then shoot at a happy medium between a dizzying revolution and a leisurely, overlong pan. (N.B.: A fast, "dizzying" pan might just possibly prove useful as a special effect intending to convey exactly that sensation and might come in handy if it fits into your present or a future movie script.)

How to be a real swinger: grip camera firmly while swinging back and forth, thus producing a point-of-view shot.

So far, so good. You have already simulated two kinds of effects presumably reserved for Hollywood sets and enormously expensive gizmos such as the crane. But you have been limited to the pan. What about the so-called tracking shot, in which the camera moves parallel with the moving subject, and the dolly shot, in which the camera moves in upon or retreats from the target? Let's investigate the latter, which is more familiar. Well, it is and it isn't equivalent. True, the camera appears to move in and out when you zoom in and out. But there is a basic difference between zooming and dollying. At the beginning of a zoom-in, the lens shows about a forty-degree background area ... but when it's in telephoto position, it covers no more than about ten degrees. In dolly shots, the angle covered remains the same—a factor that is often highly desirable, especially if you want to retain, not diminish, a significant background.

How to get that dolly effect without liquidating your next year's film budget? You guessed it—use a caster-equipped platform dolly, which can be either bought or built. If you can

handle a screwdriver, you're in business. Put a slab of ¾" plywood on a set of casters, or wheels from a baby carriage, or old roller skate, and your dolly is practically a reality. And for that matter, you may well ask yourself, why not use a baby buggy or a roller skate? No reason why not, though as in the case of whatever improvised dolly you may decide upon, you'll need some form of camera mount. If it's a flat-platform furniture dolly, a low tripod or an angle-iron will do the trick. With the baby buggy, use a tripod or strap. The latter will work if you use a roller skate. Guide the skate with an attached pole such as a broomstick. Or, as in the case with the furniture dolly (provided you haven't rigged it up with a rigid pushing-type handle) get a couple of assistants who can haul it with ropes or wires stretched at such an angle that they won't get in the way of the lens.

The supermarket buggy, the Red Racer rubber-tire wagon, borrowed, rented, or just plain expropriated from Junior or the Little Woman, will provide you with an efficient tracking or in-and-out dolly. And that's only the beginning, really. Try using the family car, with tires slightly deflated to minimize bumps, and the camera hand-held (the body serves as a shock-absorber). In fact, almost anything on wheels, even a wheelbarrow, can serve the purpose. Needless to say, pitted terrain or a pot-holed road should be avoided, even as a sway-backed beach. Bumpy sidewalks, especially the single-slab variety which have a grievous tendency to tilt askew, are a hazard. And a neighbor of ours, who gave no heed to his wife's protests over the molehills in their lawn, became a reformed character when he experimented with a kid-wagon dolly and realized they were indeed, (continued on page 113)

Poised for descent at top of slide (left), the cameraman starts the shot, which continues while he slides (right). A fast camera speed, such as 36 fps, will produce a slow-motion effect.

110

111

Popular Photography combines three same-size pictures and one big one, all in square format, with some column rules for an opening spread in the back of the book. The main picture is cropped to lead the reader down the teeter-totter to the beginning of the article's title. Note that art director George N. Soppelsa was able to retain formally balanced sections (the title and the right-hand page) in an informally balanced context.

they are. Designing a magazine is not so simple as all that.

Nor do practicing designers pay a great deal of attention to these principles. Perhaps they could not state them if asked. Certainly they would not give them exactly as they are given here.

Still it is a worthwhile list to contemplate. The amateur designer, or the editor who has the design job by default, especially, should give the principles his attention.

They represent a starting point.

It may have occurred to you that the principles are contradictory. How can you have unity, for instance, when you insist on setting up one item to contrast with others? And doesn't use of unequal space divisions break up the sequence?

The challenge in the list lies in knowing when to stress one principle, when to stress another. Obviously they can't all be applied in equal measure. When one does not seem appropriate, the designer should not hesitate to abandon it.

Two basic approaches

A magazine designer takes one of two basic approaches to magazine design. The first approach goes like this: Each picture, each caption, each title, each block of copy falls into a consistent pattern to unify the book. The book is orderly. The reader feels secure. He knows what to expect.

The second approach provides great variety, page after page. The reader prepares himself for a series of surprises. The art director worries about unity, but only within a given article or story. He believes that the nature of the article or story should dictate the choice of typeface and illustration.

One writer characterized the two styles as Bauhaus/Swiss Design and Push Pin. Bauhaus/Swiss Design, as he saw it, was spare, functional, austere, uncluttered. It made use of a grid. It seemed particularly appropriate for corporate publications. The second style, popularized by Push Pin Studios, was more inventive, combining many styles, including decorative. In the Push Pin style there was often a touch of humor, a whiff of nostalgia. It seemed particularly appropriate to magazine covers, posters, and advertising.[1]

A magazine may have elements of both approaches, but one approach should predominate. One may be more appropriate than the other for a given magazine, but properly handled, either approach can work, regardless of magazine content.

1. *The ordered approach.* Herb Lubalin has called *Scientific American* "the best designed magazine in America." *Sports Illustrated* impresses many art directors as a magazine of great beauty. The magazines have this in common: they are highly organized, almost predictable in their approach to design. Each uses a single typeface for all major titles. Each makes limited use of ruled lines to set off some of the type, but otherwise, each avoids typographic frills. The art directors frame their pictures nicely in white. They avoid crowding. A look of quiet luxury results. More important, readers can get through their articles, look at their pictures, unhampered by visual pyrotechnics.

Don't be misled by the simplicity of the look. The subtle relationship of spaces is not easy to duplicate. Still, of the two basic approaches, this one is the approach that should be used by the editor-without-an-art-director. Ideally he should call in a consulting art director and have him set up a format, choose the types, and draw up a set of instructions and diagrams on how to handle special features and standing departments.

Two other magazines stand out as unique examples of the ordered approach. *The New Republic* from 1959 to 1967 was about as ordered as any magazine can get, and handsome for it. Noel Martin, brought in as a consultant for a complete format redesign, chose a roman typeface, Palatino, designed in 1950 by Hermann Zapf. Looking very contemporary, Palatino nevertheless draws its inspiration from the early Venetian types. It suggests a happy blend of tradition and progress. Martin used it not only for main titles but for subtitles, credit lines, body copy,

1. Harold T. P. Hayes, "The Push Pin Conspiracy," *The New York Times Magazine,* March 6, 1977, pp. 19-22.

This single-page article from Destination: Philadelphia, *the publication of the Philadelphia Port Corporation, shows that a title and subtitle, a little white space, a byline, and a mug shot can combine to make a decent visual impact at the beginning of nearly three columns of solid copy. These items cluster in one corner; they don't spread out over the page. This gives them more impact. Note the small silhouetted ship signaling the article's end. All articles of this publication end with that device. It has more character than an ordinary black or hollowed out small box.*

the logo—everything. He permitted typographic variety only through varying the sizes and combining uprights with italics. The editors never varied Martin's simple two-column pattern until someone there, unfortunately, decided to jazz up the magazine with boldface versions of the type (most type designs lose their beauty when their strokes are thickened) and with an angular script that for some column headings occasionally ran on a diagonal.

The New Yorker's design is so ordered as to be nonexistent. A cartoonist back in the early 1920s, when it was founded, designed its display face, and the magazine has never changed it. It uses a few spot drawings and, of course, those celebrated gag cartoons to provide occasional graphic oases, but otherwise its "designer" simply pours the editorial material into the holes left over by the advertising. There is no opening display for any of the articles or stories. The advertisers love it, because it makes their insertions, always well designed anyway, striking by comparison.

2. *The diversified approach.* Whereas the ordered approach virtually guarantees reasonably good design, even for magazines with limited resources, the diversified approach works only when directed by a professional designer. Its success depends to a considerable extent on violations of traditional principles of design.

In the diversified approach, the designer may arrange elements to create a large void on one side of a page. He purposely disturbs the reader in order to focus his attention on an article which deals, let us say, with student unrest. Out goes balance.

Or the designer uses square- rather than rectangular-shaped photographs. His reason may be that for this particular set of

The last two pages of a four-page "Commentary" article in Bell Telephone Magazine. *The title is "On Regulation," as the folio line at the top reminds readers. The folio line and the two initial letters are in red, forming a triangle of color. The spread features both initial letters and a blurb, plus a photograph, to keep the design active. The initial letters take scattered placement: one is low on its page, the other one is high; one is in a middle column, the other in a left-hand column. Each of the pages in the article is surrounded by a thin-line box, and each of the columns is fenced in by the same thin lines. The heavier bars, used above and below the blurb, take their thickness from the black box that signals the article's end. The top bar lines up with the top of the photograph, helping to unify the two elements. A pleasantly organized spread, even though it's crowded. It takes a no-nonsense approach to design.*

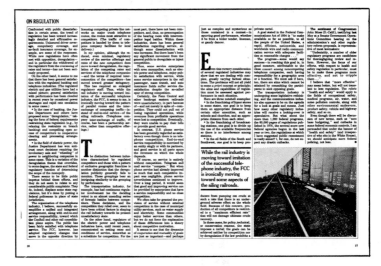

photographs, cropping to squares brings out the best composition. Or he chooses a permanent square page format, as Herb Lubalin did for *Avant Garde,* to make the magazine stand out from all others. Out goes standard proportion.

Or the designer doesn't care in which direction the reader goes. The designer scrambles the pictures because there is no correct order. The effect need not be cumulative for the article: it is no how-to-do-it. Out goes sequence.

Or the designer wants to show the complicated strategy of a single football play, as *Esquire* did in September 1968. In this case Samuel Antupit ran a chart showing all players on both sides, officials and coaches, fans in the stands, the press corps, the stadium and scoreboard, with labels and captions and directional lines and boxes fighting for attention with the article itself and its title. Out goes simplicity.

Or the designer is dealing with an article that makes five or six main points, equally important. No one item should stand out. So the designer decides on a series of equal-size pictures. Out goes contrast.

And yet in each case the designer maintains a semblance of each of the design principles. The concentration of white space is itself "heavy," and tends to counterbalance the dark elements on the other side of the page. Square-shaped photographs appear on a rectangular page. Scrambled pictures precede a column of type that moves in the conventional way from top to bottom. Visual confusion is confined only to the display types. One cluttered article fits into an issue filled otherwise with pages stark and clean. Even-size pictures, no one of them standing out from the others, form one large mass that overpowers a smaller copy block, providing contrast to the page after all.

It would be more accurate to say that the designer using the diversified approach does not so much ignore design principles as emphasize one over the others.

The diversified approach is the experimental approach. And experiment is best conducted by those who are grounded in the fundamentals.

Two of the most honored practitioners of the diversified approach were Allen Hurlburt of *Look* and Otto Storch of *McCall's. Look's* imaginative handling of photographs in sequence caused *Life* to revitalize its appearance. *McCall's* brought new life to the women's magazines.

"It is more interesting for the reader if the visual pace of the magazine varies," Storch said. "Some pages can be quiet and others bold, some restful and others exciting, some with pictures dominating the layout and others with no pictures at all."

Some observers feel the diversified approach makes things difficult for the reader. A writer in *Columbia Journalism Review* in 1974 thought that *Rolling Stone* was confusing because of its informal design. ". . . you never quite know what kind of a story is going to hit you next as you turn the pages. The makeup is often so sloppy that you can't tell where a story starts and stops—or tell the difference between an editorial page and an advertising page. And page after page of solid text gives an impenetrable appearance—although they are often worth reading."[2]

The diversified approach works best for large-format publications. The *Digest* size of some magazines tends to cramp the style of the freewheeling designer.

Visualization

As a designer taking on a magazine assignment, you would first make a decision on format (chapter 3). Then you would decide which of the two basic approaches to design to take: the ordered or diversified.

Already, you have placed some limitations on yourself. Additional limitations may come from the editor. You get a manuscript of, say, 2,500 words, a title, and four photographs, and five pages in the magazine where you can put them. You make of this what you can, deciding which photograph to play up, how far down on the page to start the article, where subheads will go, how much white space to allow. Other articles will follow. And similar restrictions will accompany them.

In this case you are not much more than a layout artist. You get some satisfaction out of fitting these things together, but clearly, you are not fully engaged in graphic design. You are not exercising your creative talent.

Far better is the arrangement whereby you plan the issue with the editor, helping decide subject areas for articles and stories. Occasionally you may plan the art and lay out the pages before the article is written; the article then is tailored to fit.

Most important in the visualization process is the setting of the mood. You decide: photographs or drawings or no art at all? color? sans serif or roman type for the title? two-column or three-column pages? initial letters or subheads?

Realism might be better served through photography. Clarity might be better served through drawings. Color has psychological effects. Sans serifs may say "now"; romans may say "yesterday." Wide columns may suggest urgency, but narrow columns may be more immediate. Initial letters can be decorated to suggest the period of the piece.

You consider all of this, keeping in mind, always, production problems likely to result. Color adds to costs. Wide columns take more space because type has to be set larger.

2. Peter A. Janssen, "Rolling Stone's Quest for Respectability," *Columbia Journalism Review*, January/February 1974, p. 65.

Another illustration of the use of white to unite elements on a page rather than separate them. The line of white stretches straight across the top of the spread but becomes irregular at the bottom. The main title is in maroon, all else in black. The square-finish photos are in a textured screen so that the people playing the game do not become too prominent. After all, it is the game (pictured at the left) that needs to be seen. The spread is from Jordan, a quarterly published by the Jordan Information Bureau and designed by Doremus & Company, an advertising and public relations organization.

Designers faced a difficult assignment in the mid-1960s with the "Death of God" debate. Nearly every magazine dealt with the matter; the question was: how to illustrate it. Designers could run mug shots of the theologians quoted, but these would not make very good opening spreads. And photographs of God Himself were hard to come by. Most designers took this way out: beautiful display of the article titles in old roman type. This seemed appropriate to the mood. *Time* (April 8, 1966), doing a major story on the debate, settled, for the first time in its history, on an all-type cover.

Whether art follows copy or copy follows art, the two must work in harmony. An article on the hippies of the 1960s features psychedelic lettering and art. An article about the computer age appears under a title in a typeface we associate with punch cards. One on the navy appears under a title done in stencil letters. An article on the population explosion swells out to the edge of a crowded page.

The art accompanying the article should say the same thing the title says. For an article on 'The Hectic Life of the College President," for instance, you would not select a routine shot of a well-dressed executive, hands folded, behind a cleared-off desk. For fiction, you would use a drawing or painting for the opening spread; for nonfiction, photography. For fiction, you can reach deep into the story for a scene to illustrate. The scene need not be thematic. For nonfiction, the main piece of art should *typify* what's in type.

As a designer you normally would read the manuscript before it is set in type to decide what kind of typographic and illustrative treatment it should have. You may have a copy made for the illustrator and entrust the decision on illustration technique to him.

With some idea of what the picture or pictures will be, and knowing how much space the manuscript will take, you begin with a series of thumbnail sketches of the pages, toying with space divisions. When you have thumbnails that show promise, you redraw them actual size so that you can begin figuring exact dimensions.

Mike Salisbury, when he was art director of *West*, told how he did it:

> I don't rework any layouts. The first ideas I sketch out are usually the ones produced.
>
> I work very loose and spontaneously, trying to keep a good pacing of layout styles throughout the book.
>
> The less attention I give a layout's styling the better it will look.
>
> I spend more time getting the proper photos, illustrations, and research material organized. The layout is usually secondary in importance to the material used in the layout.[3]

In some cases, especially for letterpress books, you would do your designing with galley proofs and photostats of the art, cutting and pasting and moving items around until they give the fit and the look you desire. You may ask the editor to cut down or increase wordage as an aid to fitting the manuscript to the page. This is one area where the editor who serves as his own designer has an advantage; he can do the cutting and the padding exactly where he needs it, when he needs it.

Design clichés

In what may be misguided enthusiasm for one or the other of the design principles, or because of his lack of knowledge of what good design is, the amateur designer makes a number of mistakes, and makes them consistently. Perhaps he has seen a design solution, liked it, and used it himself in a new situation even if it didn't fit the problem. It probably has been used to death. Or, if his background was in the newspaper business, he may have brought with him the tired typography of that branch of publishing.

Writers have their "tired but happy"s and "last but not least"s; designers have these:

1. *Picture cutouts.* The amateur designer seems to think that pictures displayed in regular rectangle or square shapes bore the reader. They may. But only because the pictures themselves are boring. Cutting them into circles or triangles or stars or whatever will not make them better pictures. If the pictures are good to begin with, such cutting will stunt their impact, ruin their composition, and demoralize the photographer who took them.

3. Letter to the author from Mike Salisbury, November 27, 1970.

2. _Tilts_. Closely related to Cliché No. 1 is the practice of putting a picture or a headline on a diagonal. Presumably, the designer feels this will make it stand out from others. It will, but at the expense of causing the reader irritation.

The introduction of the diagonal suggests movement. The picture is falling. The reader gets caught up in this phenomenon at the expense of giving his full attention to what the picture actually says. Readability suffers.

More defensible—but just barely—is the practice of putting the entire contents of the spread on a single or on parallel diagonals. The designer should have a good reason for doing this—a reason better than "to be different."

3. _Vertical typography_. The designer has a deep vertical space left over and a title to fit in. So he runs it with the letters on top of each other in succession down the page. The title is unreadable; and the designer has probably run it in type larger than necessary.

He would save white space and make his title more readable—make it stand out better—by decreasing its size and running it in usual left-to-right form at a strategic spot near the article's beginning.

4. _Mortises_. Seeing an expanse of picture that is all sky or all foreground, some designers, prompted perhaps by a lack of space elsewhere, cut out a block and put type there. The block may be completely surrounded by photograph, or it may be at an edge or corner. Wherever the mortise is located, it usually hurts the composition of the picture and cheapens the page.

The mortise is slightly more defensible when another photograph rather than type is placed into the cut-out portion of the original photograph, providing for a picture within a picture. _Look_ used this technique effectively.

5. _Overlaps_. The designer runs his type—usually for a heading—partly in the white space next to a photograph and partly in the photograph itself. As it passes from white space to photograph, the type can remain black (surprint). Or, as it makes the crossing, it can change to white letters (reverse printing).

The designer resorts to this cliché for two reasons: (1) to save space (perhaps the heading is too wide for the space allotted to it) and (2) to draw type and picture together (the principle of unity). But he saves space at the expense of a visual interruption where the type crosses over. And he unifies type and photo at the expense of photo clarity and beauty.

The list of clichés could be expanded. For instance, it would be easy to make a case against all reverses and surprints. Designers too often resort to these—at some expense to readability.

Occasionally, a venturesome designer, sure of himself, goes slumming among the clichés, picks one out, and lends his dignity

BY JOHN MAASS

In 1834 a boy named Horatio Alger was born. He became the author of successful books for young people. The plot was always the same: a poor boy of virtue and diligence rises to riches and happiness (it is an odd fact that Alger himself was born to affluence and died poor). Four years later another boy was born whose real life followed the pattern of the Horatio Alger stories.

John Wanamaker was born in what is now the Grays Ferry neighborhood of South Philadelphia. In 1838 the neighborhood was not yet part of the City of Philadelphia though it was only a 20 minute walk to Broad and Market Streets. John was the oldest of seven children of Nelson Wanamaker who operated a small brickyard. The family was not poverty-stricken but lived modestly

in a small 2-story house. In later years John Wanamaker recalled that he began to help in the brickyard and earned his first 7¢ for turning bricks at the age of nine.

At fourteen the boy left school and went to work in the city. He walked to Philadelphia on muddy country lanes, carrying his shoes; when he reached pavement he cleaned the mud off his feet and put on the shoes.

Continued on page 22

Destination: Philadelphia March/April 1977 9

If you must tip or arch your display or play any other tricks with it, have a reason. The art director of Destination: Philadelphia _had a reason: his photograph of the inside of the John Wanamaker store featured arches, so he picked up the same roundness of those arches and used it to define the top of his photo, then fitted display type around it. He put the byline at the base of the photo, left, and the short caption at the base, right. Column rules in a second color stand in contrast to the arches. The article, which begins on a right-hand page, continues for several more pages._

The boxing of articles appeals to many art directors, just for the visual order it brings. In this right-page opener, the subject matter calls for a box—or wall; so the visual treatment is all the more appropriate. To tie the title with the initial letter, the designer uses a chiseled-out style for both. The original employs a second color, maroon, in solid and two different tints arrived at by screening. Only the area outside the box—or wall—is white. (Courtesy of Liberty, *"A Magazine of Religious Freedom.")*

to it. In good hands, even a cliché can please.

But after all is said and done, all things considered, it goes without saying that you should avoid clichés like the plague.

Rules, bars, boxes, and other delights

Sorting through typical newspapers, you can pretty much tell the modern from the old-fashioned by the lack of column rules. Get rid of column rules, editors figure, go to all-lowercase heads, and change the nameplate from Old English to, say Bodoni, or, if you are really daring, go to Helvetica, and you put your newspaper among the avant-garde.

What the newspapers throweth away, the magazines picketh up. Or: One medium's garbage is another medium's treasure.

Column rules are big news in magazine design, now that art directors have rediscovered them. And when rules are not enough, there are bars. Nice, thick bars. Some magazines combine thick bars with thin rules. The bars can be used, for instance, as horizontal underlines or overlines, the thin rules as column or story separators.

When he was art director of *New York*, Milton Glaser brought the Scotch rule back into general use. Many magazines copied the look. A Scotch rule consists of a thick line sandwiched between two thin lines.

And for many editors and art directors, the box is a staple of design, especially when several vaguely related items appear on a page or spread. Boxes may be built from single-width lines, decorative lines, or sets of parallel lines (like Scotch rules). You can also get a box by running a tint block in gray or color under a unit of type.

Lines, bars, boxes, and other typographic gimmicks can help sort things out for the reader. But they can become clichés. One day, perhaps, magazine editors and art directors will grow tired of them and toss them aside, where young newspaper art directors (or makeup people) will rediscover them, and a new trend will come to newspaper design. In fact, looking at the handsome special sections of the New York *Times* and other important newspapers, you get the impression the trend has already begun. The rules in this reincarnation run horizontally rather than vertically.

The swipe file

A cartoonist copies the cross-hatched, carefully controlled lines of David Levine, and his colleagues, if not his readers, will spot the plagiarism. An illustrator copies the delicate line, the flat colors, and the decorative look of Milton Glaser or the virile, freshly painted look of Al Parker, and his fellow painters will see at once the influence of the master. And the appropriation of another person's style or technique seldom results in work that is the equal of the original.

In the area of graphic design, lifting ideas comes easier and with less stigma attached. Nobody can successfully trace design to its source. It is the rare designer who is not influenced—and not just subconsciously—by the work of other designers. Nor is this bad. The innovators—Herb Lubalin, Henry Wolf, Peter Palazzo, Paul Rand, and the others—have doubtless had great influence on the look of magazines other than those they've designed, and they must be pleased to have played a role in upgrading the general level of graphic design; they do not have exclusive interest in any one solution, anyway. Their great satisfaction lies in moving on to unexplored design plateaus.

Even these designers maintain swipe files—printed portfolios of prize-winning work, if not the more obvious folders of clippings. Every designer and editor should build up his own collection of designs that please, inspire, and, most important, communicate clearly.

For scholastic editors who stand in awe of the job of graphic design one publisher brought out a book frankly devoted to the techniques of applying the page designs of the slick magazines to the pages of high school yearbooks.[4]

There is such a thing as creative copying. No beginning designer can get much satisfaction out of lifting a spread, whole, out of one publication and putting it down in his own magazine with a mere substitution of pictures and wording. He will try to change facings and picture sizes, adjust title length and placement, and so on; not solely to disguise the fact that he lifted the design, but to try to improve on it. He should use another's design primarily as a starting point. And he should remember that good design is tailored to the needs of a specific article or story.

A designer will draw inspiration not only from other graphic designs but from architectural structures, oil paintings (they are designed, too), and, of course, Nature's landscapes.

He may find some stimulus from that classic set of ready-made designs: the alphabet. An *L* or a *U* or an *A* or an *R*, or a number, or one of the letters turned sideways or upside-down might suggest a pattern for a page or spread. Of course the reader will not see the letter or figure. The designer will not be bound by it. He will merely use it as a beginning.

Obviously, much of magazine design springs from advertising design. Advertising designers, probably more than magazine designers, take chances with graphics. The magazine designer

A set of boxes sometimes can best organize a page of miscellaneous items. In "Futurescope," a full-color page from Johns-Manville Future, *the designer uses different typefaces for each feature and where necessary wraps copy around the art. The all-the-way-across-the-page heading, the black border, and the same-style drawings help unify the page that otherwise might have looked like a hodgepodge.*

4. James Magmer and Franklin Ronan, *Look and Life as Guides for the Successful Yearbook Editor,* Midwest Publications Company, Inc., Birmingham, Michigan, 1964.

who borrows from advertisers will at least keep abreast of graphic design trends. He should remember, though, that many of these "trends" turn out to be short-lived fads.

Redesign

This book has already made the point that the publication undertaking a revision of format and design is usually a publication worried about dwindling circulation. But not always. The New York *Times* recently updated the design of its Sunday magazine and the book review and other of its Sunday sections, notably "The Week In Review," and it made these changes while yet a leading newspaper. It was a sign of progressive spirit on the paper rather than one of desperation. When another leading newspaper, the Louisville *Courier-Journal* and its sister publication, the Louisville *Times,* changed to a better looking six-column format, *Columbia Journalism Review* (Fall 1965) commented: "Abrupt changes are common among teetering publications; it is a bold act for a prosperous organization to attempt improvements on an already successful format."

To outsiders, the reasons for changes may seem trivial. *Electronics* in the 1960s went to a bolder type for its logo and changed the beginning *E* from lower- to uppercase. The consulting art director convinced management that the new logo would be "more forceful," a quality presumably that would appeal to the electronic engineers reading the magazine.

Feeling the need of a change in format, the editor and art director may find, on getting into it, that the old way of doing things wasn't so bad after all. A case in point is *Advertising Age.* Many readers, including this author, have felt the magazine has needed a face-lifting. Its editors apparently felt the same way. In 1966 they called in John Peter to consider changing the looks of the magazine. At first, Peter offered a multiplicity of suggestions for changes. "But the more he and our editors discussed the matter, the more they all agreed that only a minimum of change should be made—that basically, the typographic dress we've been using for 15 years or more was still pretty sound," the magazine said in a 1967 statement. A weekly, the magazine is really a news magazine; and so it wants a newspaper look.

Peter did do these things:

He eliminated column rules.

He modernized the logo, using a condensed Clarendon, a better looking slab serif type than the more standard slab serif the magazine had been using.

He modernized (read that: *simplified*) the standing heads.

In 1971 *Advertising Age* made another modest change by substituting a modern sans serif for the slab serif it had been using for its heads.

Christianity and Crisis is another magazine that thought it needed a complete change, and then decided against it. The magazine gave full freedom to two designers to make major changes. The changes they recommended were trivial. They came up with a new logo and a new masthead, and that's about all. One of the designers, Robert Newman, was quoted in the May 15, 1967, issue: "While all avenues were open, we decided not to change it very much. We concluded that the magazine is what it seems to be, which is rare and a virtue in typographic design."

A redesign job, when it is attempted, usually takes a period of several months while the designer learns all about the editorial processes of the magazine (every magazine develops its own routines) and familiarizes himself with the production and printing facilities available to the magazine. Decisions must be made to cover every contingency, guidelines laid down to be followed more or less permanently by persons who may not have had a hand in the setting of the design. One of Milton Glaser's most remarkable achievements, in light of this, was his overnight redesign of *Paris Match* several years ago. When he had been called over there he thought he would have the usual time to develop a program, but he found himself facing more an emergency than a challenge.[5]

The time to redesign is when a magazine is still successful but not looking the part. Waiting until their magazines are slipping, editors may wait too long. Beautiful new design can't hide a lack of editorial vitality.

It is better, probably, for editors to change their magazines' looks gradually as the times change. Too abrupt and far-reaching changes could lose some loyal followers. Readers tend to be conservative in matters of design. They like the familiar. *The secret is to hold on to old readers with familiar typographic landmarks while luring new readers with innovation.*

When editors think Redesign, they should think beyond typefaces and uses of art. They should start with basic size and format. They should reexamine their typesetting systems, their printing processes, their paper stock. They should even rethink their magazines' purposes. After several years as a hardcover quarterly, *Horizon* in 1977 became a softcover monthly. "A new magazine with a new purpose in life," said an ad in *Advertising Age.* "The new Horizon will explore the civilized pleasures of life in America's urban centers today. It will be the national journal of the cultural diversions available in cities: theatre, music, art, dance, architecture. And also of the popular diversions: movies, sports, food, even television."

5. See Gertrude Snyder, "Pro-File: Milton Glaser," *U&lc.*, March 1977, p. 12.

One major reason for rethinking design for a consumer magazine is to influence advertising agency media buyers. These people face choices from among scores of competing magazines in any one field; obviously they can't read all the magazines thoroughly to determine editorial content and meanings. But they can *look* at the magazines. Appearance is important in selling of space to advertisers.

ADAMS, ROBERT, *Creativity in Communications*, New York Graphic Society Ltd., Greenwich, Connecticut, 1971.

ARNHEIM, RUDOLPH, *Visual Thinking*, University of California Press, Berkeley, 1969.

BALLINGER, RAYMOND A., *Layout and Graphic Design*, Van Nostrand Reinhold Company, New York, 1970. (Revised Edition.)

DAVIS, ALEC, *Graphics: Design into Production*, Pitman Publishing Corporation, New York, 1974.

DORN, RAYMOND, *How to Design & Improve Magazine Layouts*, Brookwood Publications, P.O. Box 1229, Oakbrook, Illinois, 60521, 1976.

EVANS, HAROLD, *Editing and Design: A Five Volume Manual of English, Typography, and Layout*, Heinemann, London, 1972-.

FELTON, CHARLES J., *Layout 4: Printing Design and Typography*, Charles J. Felton, St. Petersburg, Florida, 1970.

FRY, ROGER, *Vision and Design*, A Meridian Book, New American Library, New York.

GARRETT, LILLIAN, *Visual Design: A Problem Solving Approach*, Reinhold Publishing Corporation, New York, 1966.

HILL, DONALD E., *Techniques of Magazine Layout and Design*, Donald E. Hill, Huntsville, Alabama, 1970.

HOFMANN, ARMIN, *Graphic Design Manual: Principles and Practice*, Reinhold Publishing Corporation, New York, 1965.

HURLBURT, ALLEN F., *Publication Design*, Van Nostrand Reinhold Company, New York, 1976. (Second Edition.)

———, *Layout: The Design of the Printed Page*, Watson-Guptill Publications, New York, 1977.

JUSSIM, ESTELLE, *Visual Communication and the Graphic Arts*, R. R. Bowker Company, New York, 1974.

KARO, JERRY, *Graphic Design*, Van Nostrand Reinhold Company, New York, 1975.

McCONNELL, JOHN, ed., *Design and Art Direction*, Hastings House, Publishers, New York, 1974.

McLEAN, RAURI, *Magazine Design*, Oxford University Press, New York, 1969.

MULVEY, FRANK, *Graphic Perception of Space*, Van Nostrand Reinhold Company, New York, 1969.

MURGATROYD, KEITH, *Modern Graphics*, E. P. Dutton & Company, New York, 1969.

NELSON, GEORGE, *Problems of Design*, Whitney Publications, New York, 1965. (Second Edition.)

RAND, PAUL, *Thoughts on Design*, Van Nostrand Reinhold Company, New York, 1971. (Second Edition.)

SMITH, CORTLAND GRAY, *Magazine Layout: Principles, Patterns, Practices*, published by the author, Plandome, New York, 1973.

WHITE, JAN V., *Editing by Design*, R. R. Bowker Company, New York, 1974.

———, *Designing for Magazines*, R. R. Bowker Company, New York, 1976.

The Print Casebooks, Print, Washington, D.C., 1976. (Six volumes. 253 award-winning designs.)

Chapter 6

Typography

"Too much is said about good typography and not enough set," Herb Lubalin has observed. Still, for readers of this book, some additional advice on the use of types may be in order.

Readability

The point cannot be made too often: the one overriding consideration in typography is readability. If it's not readable, it's not good typography.

Type arranged in tricky formation may work for an occasional heading, but for most headings and for long columns of text matter, the traditional types, traditionally spaced, work best. The reader's reaction should be "What an interesting article!" not "What interesting typography!"

Some typographers make a point of distinguishing between readability and legibility. Legibility has to do with the ease with which the reader distinguishes one letter from another. Readability, a broader term, has to do with the ease with which the reader takes in a column or page of type. Readability also has to do with the way the story or article is written.

Readability, from a typographic standpoint, is affected by these factors:

1. *The style of the typeface.* Familiar styles are usually the most readable.

2. *The size of the typeface.* Within reason, the larger the face, the better.

3. *The length of the line.* Comfortably narrow columns are better than wide columns.

4. *The amount of leading (pronounced "ledding") between lines.* Most body sizes can use at least two points.

5. *The pattern of the column of type.* It should be even-toned.

6. *The contrast between the darkness of the type and the lightness of the paper.* The more contrast the better.

7. *The texture of the paper.* It shouldn't be intrusive.

8. *The relationship of the type to other elements on the page.* The relationship should be obvious.

9. *The suitability of type to content.* The art director should exploit the "personality" of types.

Of course, it isn't all that simple. More on readability later.

Type development

The early types were designed to approximate the handwriting—the calligraphy—of the countries in which they developed. The first German types of Gutenberg and his followers in the fifteenth century were harsh, black, and close-fitting—the German blackletter we today mistakenly refer to as "Old English." (A more accurate term for these types is "text," taken from the "texture" of the page, with its heavy, woven look.)

In Italy the faces were lighter, more delicate, after the Humanistic hand of Petrarch. These types were the forerunners of what we today call roman (small *r*) types.

The first two centuries of printing in Europe (1450-1650) saw these two faces—blackletter and roman—used extensively. One other took its place beside them. It was italic, introduced by Aldus Manutius in 1501.

The advantage of italic, as Manutius designed it, was that it was close-fitting. That meant you could get more type per page. That was important because paper was scarce. And italic looked more like handwriting, which added to its desirability. Italic became an auxiliary face to roman, borrowing its caps from roman fonts. The two together became the most popular face everywhere in Europe except for Germany.

Typesetting

The types of Gutenberg and Manutius were set by hand. Today we still set some types this way. But, thanks to Ottmar Mergenthaler's invention (1884) and some follow-up inventions in both America and Great Britain, most types are set now by machine.

Hand-set types (foundry type and Ludlow) and machine-set types (Linotype, Intertype, and Monotype) were all developed for letterpress printing. The later printing process, offset lithography, brought about new methods of typesetting. Type produced by these new methods is called "cold type."

Cold type systems, which have cut typesetting costs in some cases to one-fourth of what they would be by "hot type"

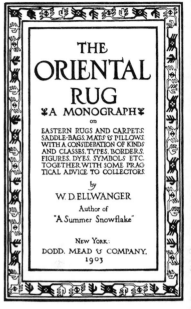

Hand lettering put inside a border that looks like the border of a fine rug makes this exquisite title page from 1903 say "rug" twice, verbally and visually.

systems, have broadened considerably the art director's choice of faces, and given him great flexibility in designing his pages. Of the cold type systems, the chief is photocomposition.

Photocomposition has these advantages over hot type:

1. The type can be blown up to several times the original size without losing its sharpness. Repros of hot type, when blown up, would show irregularities. Furthermore, the type can be expanded in width, condensed, slanted, or otherwise distorted to make it fit a given space.

2. Characters can be closely fitted. In fact, they can even be made to overlap. If the art director wants close fitting in his hot type composition, he has to ask for repro proofs, then cut and paste them together.

3. The type can be set in wider measure. Most Linotype machines go out to only 30 picas.

4. The type is cheaper.

5. A photocomposition house is likely to offer a wider selection of types than a hot type house.

As early as 1950 type houses were bringing out new faces on a trial basis on film for photocomposition before putting them on metal. The Dom Casual face was introduced in this way. Today most of the familiar types are available on photocomposition machines. In addition, photocomposition houses have brought out hundreds of faces of their own. That's why type recognition these days is so difficult.

While phototypesetting has made great gains over hot type methods of composition, it has not eliminated them. In America and Europe there is still room for both systems. But in undeveloped countries, where type composing systems start from scratch, the old, conventional systems do not have a chance. It costs a lot less money to set up photocomposition houses. And the presses are almost always likely to be offset.

Unfortunately, much of the cold type composition is, from an aesthetic standpoint, less than satisfactory. The villain has not been photocomposition. The various phototypesetters produce type every bit as good as that produced by Linotype, Intertype, and Monotype machines. The villain has been certain typewriter-like machines with their unsuitable types and their awkward spacing.

Many of the typewriter-composers produce letters designed to fit a single width or, at best, three or four widths. Letters in their ideal state occupy a great variety of widths. A typewriter composition system clearly superior to most others is IBM's Selectric Composer.

Art directors using one of the inferior typewriter systems should consider carefully the money being saved and ask if the saving is worth the loss of quality readers have to put up with. Sometimes, on close analysis, with the inconvenience of making corrections and cutting and pasting them into place, it turns out

P E O P L E

DON'T BE A STATISTIC

THEY'RE IN BUSINESS

All-cap titles or headlines showing spacing possibilities. The first uses letterspacing. The second uses normal spacing between letters. The third uses tight spacing between letters, which in most magazines these days is normal spacing. Note the tight spacing between words, too.

that "economical" typesetting systems are not so economical after all.

The availability of moderately priced electronic components make it possible now for magazines to set type "in house." But some magazines that have experimented with "in house" setting have found that it is actually cheaper to stick with regular typesetters on the outside.

That may hold true for body copy. But titles and headlines, often, can be set economically and conveniently "in house." Many designers, even for big magazines, make use of dry-transfer letters obtainable in a wide variety of faces and sizes from any large art-supply store. Others make use of photolettering machines. One useful table-top typesetter is Mergenthaler's Linocomp, which can sit adjacent to the designer's drawing table. It makes available more than 600 typefaces.

Computer typesetting

When type was set only by hand, a speed of one character per second was possible. Mechanical typesetters increased the speed to five characters per second. Photographic typesetters since World War II brought it up to 500 characters per second. By the end of the 1960s electronic-computer typesetting could reach a speed of 10,000 characters per second.[1]

Many of the new typesetters relate to computers that take care of justification and its necessary hyphenation. The new typesetters also offer kerning (fitting letters together so that their spaces overlap or, as one typographer describes it, "nesting . . . letters to avoid typographic gaposis"), hung punctuation (punctuation placed outside the edges of a copy block), and minus leading (less than normal spacing between lines). Of course they also offer the qualities standard typesetters have always offered—like letterspacing and regular leading.

Some newspapers now own typesetters that compose not just by columns but by pages. Printers of magazines are experimenting with similar typesetters. Edward M. Gottschall of International Typeface Corporation reports that the Optronics Pagitron system can "size, screen, crop, enhance, and distort halftones and line art, and position them on a page by means of video terminal controls. This system can also set type and position it accurately on the page. Such a system employs laser scanners/plotters. . . ."[2]

With computer composition, McGraw-Hill in its book-publishing operation has found it can cut production time for a book (after the manuscript has been copyedited) from a normal

1. Gerald O. Walter, "Typesetting," *Scientific American,* May 1969, p. 61.
2. Edward M. Gottschall, "Words into Type," *DA,* vol. 62, no. 4, 1976, p. 9.

seven months to a spectacular seven weeks. The savings in time come not so much from the faster typesetting as from the doing away with all the steps that follow it—especially the back and forth movement of proofs of all kinds.[3]

OCR (optical character reader) scanners can read typed manuscripts and feed what they read directly into typesetting equipment. This means no additional keyboarding, as at a Linotype machine. Direct-entry typesetters in 1977 were available at around $10,000 where earlier they cost as much as $200,000. And a secretary or office worker could operate the machines.

Computers have changed—and will change—typesetting procedures for magazines, but they won't change the basic role of the art director, which is to pick the right types and the right art and put them together to give the best possible display to editorial matter. "Computers have been called 'very fast idiots,' " says Paul J. Sampson, associate editor of *Inland Printer/American Lithographer.* "They can make it easier for the careless editor to rush into print with a poor product. They are completely neutral. It's still up to the editor to use his tools, new or old, to serve his field."

Copyfitting

Most editors find it necessary to determine, before the type is set, how much space it will take in the magazine. Essentially, copyfitting, for magazines, at least, involves these five steps:

1. Decide on the width of the columns in print.

2. Consult a character-count chart (available from your type house) to find the number of characters you can get in that line width in the typeface you want to use.

3. Set the typewriter margins for that number of characters.

4. Type your copy, going only slightly under or over that count for each line.

5. Count the lines in your typed manuscript. You will know from previous settings how many printed lines you can get in a column.

In most magazine operations, there is considerable adjusting of copy during the layout or makeup stage. Lines are added or deleted, art is enlarged or reduced—all as part of the copyfitting process. One of the pleasant outcomes of the current practice of allowing columns to run to uneven lengths on pages is that copyfitting becomes less of a problem.

Copyfitting for titles and headlines become less a problem of counting and more a problem of tracing off letters from existing

3. Leonard Shatzkin, "The Secrets of Computer Printing," *Editor's Notebook,* May-June 1970, p. 8.

alphabets and estimating space to be occupied. Increasingly, editors and art directors are asking typesetters to set to fit in the typeface chosen.

The point system

The typesetter or printer uses *points* to measure type sizes, *picas* to measure column widths. There are 72 points to an inch. There are 12 points to a pica, hence 6 picas to an inch.

The point system is not universal. America and England use it; the countries on the Continent do not. There the Didot system prevails (points are slightly bigger). Now it looks as if all of us will be moving, gradually, into the metric system for measuring type (as for measuring everything else). Already a few type manufacturers are measuring their types in centimeters.[4]

What to tell the typesetter

Sending copy to the typesetter or printer, you would in most cases specify the following:

1. Point size.
2. Name of the typeface.
3. Weight of the typeface, if other than regular (light, book, medium, bold, demibold, ultrabold, black).
4. Style, if other than upright (italic, condensed, expanded; it could be both italic *and* condensed or expanded).
5. Amount of leading between lines (the art director should specify "set solid" if no leading is desired).
6. Amount of letterspacing, if any.
7. Any special instructions on paragraph indentions and margins (flush left? flush right?).
8. Width of column (in picas).

Copyediting marks will take care of such matters as occasional use of italics, small caps, etc.

To save space this book will not reproduce the various copyreading and proofreading marks used to communicate with the typesetter and printer. These marks, basically standardized, are shown in most good dictionaries, style books, editing books, and type specimen books.

Copyediting marks are made right on the original copy, which has been double spaced—triple spaced if for a newspaper—to

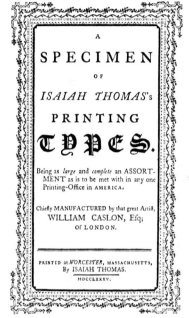

A printer or typesetting house offers customers a type specimen book to use, with available types shown in complete alphabets and in a variety of sizes. One house in New York, Photo-Lettering, Inc., shows samples of close to 10,000 faces. Typesetting houses of an earlier era, when type was all foundry type, had fewer faces to show, but those houses put out books, too. This is the title page of the book offered by Isaiah Thomas, printer at Worcester, Massachusetts. The year was 1785.

4. Sandra B. Ernst, "Measuring Column Inches in Centimeters," *Art Direction,* March 1977, pp. 68, 69. Her article contains tables showing conversion of metrics to points, points to metrics.

provide the necessary write-in area. Proofreading marks are made in the margins of galley or page proofs.

One piece of advice is in order here: Both copyreading and proofreading marks should be made with a soft pencil to facilitate erasures. The copyreader or proofreader sometimes has second thoughts about his changes.

Categories of type

There are many ways to classify type. If you were to do it from an historical standpoint you would classify them one way. If you were to do it from a utilitarian standpoint, you would do it another.

This book will classify types according to *use*.

We start by dividing types into two broad categories:

1. Body types (up to 14 points).
2. Display types (14 points and larger).

While many faces come in both body and display sizes, some come only as body types and some come only as display types. In a face designed for both categories you can detect subtle changes as it moves from the large to the small. For instance, the interior area of the loop of the "e" has to be proportionately

larger in the smaller sizes of a face. Otherwise it would fill in with ink.

The body faces are divided into *book* faces (the most common faces and the faces used for texts of magazines) and *news* faces. News faces have been especially designed for letterpress printing in small sizes on newsprint. They are bold faces, essentially, with large x-heights.[5] They do not come in display sizes.

We can break down typefaces, body and display, into several broad categories called "races." The "races" include:

1. *Roman.* These faces have two distinguishing characteristics: (a) thick and thin strokes and (b) serifs at the stroke terminals. Where the differences in the strokes are minimal and where serifs blend into the letters, the romans are "old style"; where the differences are pronounced and where the serifs appear almost tacked on as an afterthought, the romans are "modern." In-between styles are "transitional" or "traditional."[6]

2. *Sans serif.* Sans serif types came along first in the early 1800s and were revived by the Bauhaus in the 1920s. Their strokes are essentially of the same thickness. There are no serifs

An illustration from a whimsical ad sponsored by Quad Typographers, New York. The company has matched typefaces with illustration styles. These characters supposedly attended the typesetting company's "posh Fifth Anniversary Party." From left: European industrialist Claude Graphique, society columnist Lightline Gothic, impresario Futura Black, Baroness Excelsior Script, health faddist 20th Century Ultrabold, unidentified maid (her face is the company insignia), Texas tycoon Windsor Elongated, underground film star Prisma, Italian futurist designer Sig. Modern Roman No. 20, former channel swimmer Samantha Smoke, and her escort, Seventh Ave. mogul Max Balloon. Concept and design by Peter Rauch and Herb Levitt; illustration by Tim Lewis.

5. The x-height is the height of the lowercase "x."
6. The term "roman" is used by some printers to designate all upright types (as opposed to italic—or slanted—types).

at the terminals. More recent sans serifs, with slight differences in stroke thickness and with a slightly squared look, are called "gothics" or "grotesques."[7]

3. *Slab serif.* Slab or square serif types have even-thickness strokes as on the sans serif types, and serifs as on the roman types. The most beautiful of the slab serifs, because they lean toward the romans, are the Clarendons. Slab serifs were developed in England at a time when the country was taken by Egyptian culture, and the term "Egyptian," for no particular reason, was applied to them. Many of the slab serif faces are named after Egyptian cities. These faces have also been referred to as "antiques." Slab serif faces enjoyed popularity in the 1930s, but their use now is limited.

4. *Ornamental.* To keep the list workable, the author lumps a number of faces under this one category. There are the text or

---

7. The word "gothic" has been applied to many new—and hence controversial—types, including the type we know as Old English.

black letters (Old English), the scripts (which are intended to look like handwriting), and the gimmick letters (made to look like logs, pieces of furniture, etc.).

In each of the "races" are hundreds of "families"—adding up to several thousand types. For instance, in the sans serif race are such families as Franklin Gothic, Futura, Helvetica, News Gothic, Record Gothic, Spartan, Tempo, Trade Gothic, Standard, and Univers.

One of the interesting features of Univers is that the designer of the face, instead of giving the various versions descriptive names like "light" and "heavy" and "expanded," gave them numbers. He reserved odd numbers in Univers for upright letters, even numbers for italics. One of the newest families among the sans serifs is Avant Garde Gothic, designed by Herb Lubalin and Tom Carnase for International Typeface Corporation. The face is named after *Avant Garde*, drawing its character from the logo for that magazine. The face, available in several weights, is noteworthy for its close-fitting characters, its large x-height, and the unusual number of ligatures and alternate characters.[8]

Not only does the art director find it difficult to distinguish among the various families (exactly how does Granjon differ from Janson?), he also has difficulty distinguishing among variations in the same family of type. Linotype's Garamond differs from Ludlow's Garamond which differs from the Garamond issued by a foundry type manufacturer.

The Mergenthaler Linotype Corporation currently has two kinds of Garamond: regular and Garamond #3. Garamond #3 is very similar to a version of Garamond offered by Intertype, but Linotype's regular Garamond is quite different from the other two.

Some more recent faces have been designed exclusively for one company or the ot⌐ er. Caledonia is exclusively Linotype. Century Schoolbook is an Intertype exclusive.

Most families of type come in more than one weight (light, regular, bold, ultrabold) and more than one width (regular, expanded, condensed).

The italics

Although from an historical standpoint italics deserve their own category, typographers do not consider them as a "race." The reason: italics have become more a style variation than a type in their own right. Almost every face has its italic version.

For some types the italics are exactly like the uprights, but slanted. For other types, the italics are quite different—so dif-

8. A ligature is a combination of two or more characters designed in a way to make them one unit.

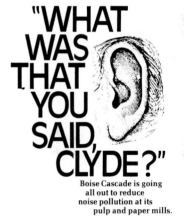

"WHAT WAS THAT YOU SAID, CLYDE?"

Boise Cascade is going all out to reduce noise pollution at its pulp and paper mills.

By Linda Miller

Sometimes an art director incorporates a piece of art with the article's title. Art director Joe Erceg does it here for Paper Times, *using some public-domain art. The title type wraps around the ear, and the blurb takes its place just below. A little extra space separates the byline from the title-blurb unit. Ragged-right and -left setting work for both title and blurb.*

ferent, in fact, that they appear to be of a different design. Many art directors prefer italics different in design from their uprights because then they are more useful as contrast types.

Italics, as conceived by Manutius, were narrower than the uprights, but in some faces today they are actually wider. In Linotype and Intertype faces they are equal in width to their uprights. That's because both the upright and the italic version of each letter are on the same mat, one underneath the other.

Because they are designed on a diagonal, italics tend to project a mood of restlessness or haste. Italics are not quite as easy to read as uprights. Art directors find italics useful for captions, for emphasis in body copy, for foreign phraseology, and for names of publications, plays, ships, and works of art. Used column after column, solid italics can be fatiguing. Nor does the reader appreciate them as occasional paragraphs in body copy; when readers move back into the uprights they get the optical illusion of reading type that bends over to the left.

Chevron USA's art director, Roger Waterman, for this right-hand page opener, was able to come up with a type-face that perfectly matched his drawing of a moose. Or maybe it was the other way around: he drew his moose to take on the look of the type.

When the editor or art director underlines a word in a manuscript, he is telling the typesetter to set the word in italics. He should make sure italics are *available* in that face; if not, the printer may set the word in boldface. It is a mistake to set names of publications in boldface. It makes them stand out unnecessarily from other words. If no italics are available, names of publications should be set in ordinary uprights.

Some magazines run the names of publications in italics but they run their own names, when they're mentioned in the copy, in caps and small caps. Like this: PUBLICATION DESIGN.

Small caps, only as tall as the x-height of the letters, are also useful for jobs ordinarily assigned to full-size caps: for instance, headlines quoted from newspapers and telegrams from letters-to-the-editor writers.

The character of types

Some types are versatile enough to be appropriate for almost any job. Others are more limited in what they can do. But all have some special qualities that set them apart. Art directors are not in agreement about these qualities, but here are a few familiar faces, along with descriptions of the moods they seem to convey:

1. *Baskerville*—beauty, quality, urbanity.
2. *Bodoni*—formality, aristocracy, modernity.
3. *Caslon*—dignity, character, maturity.
4. *Century*—elegance, clarity.
5. *Cheltenham*—honesty, reliability, awkwardness.
6. *Franklin Gothic*—urgency, bluntness.
7. *Futura*—severity, utility.
8. *Garamond*—grace, worth, fragility.
9. *Standard*—order, newness.
10. *Stymie*—precision, solidarity.
11. *Times Roman*—tradition, efficiency.

Baskerville
Bodoni
Caslon
Century
Cheltenham
Franklin Gothic
Futura
Garamond
Standard
Stymie
Times Roman

These qualities, if they come across to readers, come across only vaguely. Furthermore, a single face can have qualities that tend to cancel out each other. (Can a type be both tradition-oriented and efficient?) While the art director should be conscious of these qualities and make whatever use he can of them, he should not feel bound to any one type because of a mood he wants to convey.

Assume that he is designing a radical, militant magazine like *Ramparts*. Baskerville seems an unlikely choice for the title face. And yet Dugald Stermer used it successfully there while Kenneth Stuart was using it, also successfully, at *Reader's Digest*, a magazine near the opposite end of the political spectrum.

GREECE
JAMAICA
Ceylon
China
MEXICO
France
Tahiti
Canada
Hong Kong
Ireland
Scotland
𝕯enmark
Japan
PORTUGAL
BRITAIN

Some attempts by art directors to find typefaces or letterforms appropriate to specific countries or places. Do they work? Well, if they do, they work in some cases because art directors have used them in the past to do similar jobs. In a few cases, you could say the types are appropriate because of how they evolved. For instance: the "GREECE" imitates early Greek letters, when they were scratched with a stylus on a wax tablet; the "China" has a Chinese calligraphy look; the "Ireland" stems from Irish calligraphy (semiuncials); the "Denmark" comes in the text or blackletter that developed out of the European lowlands.

Sometimes the best answer to the question "What type to use in title display?" is to go with a stately, readable type—like Baskerville—and rely upon the *words* in the title to express the mood of the piece.

Type revivals

What may be good for one period of time in typography may not be good in another. Type preferences change. Types come and go—and come back again.

A case in point is Bookman, rediscovered in the mid-1960s as a display face. Bookman is a face adapted from an oldstyle antique face of the 1860s. It is like Clarendon, but it has more roundness.

At the turn of the century it had become so popular that a reaction set in against it. Designers began to consider it monotonous. It was kept alive by offset and gravure, because its strong lines and serifs stood up well in that kind of printing. (The old *Collier's* magazine used it.) As these processes became more sophisticated and better able to handle more fragile types, Bookman died out.

In revival, it gives display matter a solid, strong look. In its italic version, with swash caps, it has a charm that has captivated some of our leading designers. (See the *New York* logo in chapter 8.)

Other types that have made a comeback in magazine design include Cooper Black, Cheltenham, and Futura. In the 1970s Souvenir, a bowlegged roman type, came on strong, both as display and body copy. In 1977 TypeSpecta, a type-design house, introduced Souvenir Gothic (below), a san-serif version. In an advertisement to art directors, TypeSpectra said: "When you order Souvenir Gothic you are certain of getting the original . . . because months will pass before the round-cornered misaligned, pirate copies come out." The type-designing industry is plagued by imitation.

Souvenir Gothic.

The variety of typefaces

In all, you face a choice of several thousand typefaces. And if you can't find exactly what you want from one of the houses supplying photolettering, you can take a standard type and doctor it, coming up with a title like this one taken from *Pacific Powerland*, a publication of Pacific Power & Light Company,

Portland. "More dramatically than words," went the lead of the article underneath, "the parched mudflat pictured on the cover tells the story of an unprecedented six-month drought in much of the region served by Pacific Power." The texture in the letters duplicated the texture in the picture.

DROUGHT!

Eventually, you will develop strong prejudices against many typefaces, strong preferences for others. You may conclude that only a few fit your magazine. And you will change your mind from time to time as to which ones those are.

Because he worked for a magazine that ran articles on subject matter that "ranges literally from pickles to politics," Herb Bleiweiss, art director of *Ladies' Home Journal*, used a great variety of typefaces, as many as thirty in a single issue. ". . . An art director must let a natural variety develop without preconceptions which might limit effectiveness," he said.

He even tried running headlines or titles that were smaller than the body type. Once he had a heading set on a piece of acetate and frozen into a cake of ice. That was for a feature with the title: "Work Wonders with Canned and Frozen Poultry Products." Resting on top of the ice were assorted products.

An art director like Herb Bleiweiss can get away with such innovation, but the beginning art director is wise to stick with only a few faces in traditional arrangements. A magazine's pages can easily turn into what Will Burton has described as "visual riddles." The reader will not have the patience for them.

"If . . . [editors] have a good art director who can handle the new tricks [made possible with phototypesetting] with taste and punch, editors can benefit from the new freedom. If not, they may have only new ropes with which to hang themselves," says Paul J. Sampson, associate editor of *Inland Printer/American Lithographer.*

What type to use

The art director selects his types largely on the basis of personal preference. Still he has some rules to guide him.

"Objective research has produced few dramatic results," says Herbert Spencer, "but it has provided a wealth of information about factors of typography which contribute to greater reader efficiency, and it has confirmed the validity of many established typographic conventions, but not of all."[9]

9. Herbert Spencer, *The Visible Word,* Hastings House, Publishers, New York, 1969, p. 6.

Among findings verified by research are these:

1. All caps slow reading speed. They also occupy 40-50 percent more space.

2. Italics are harder to read than uprights.

3. Very short lines—and very long lines—are hard to read.

4. Unjustified lines do *not* hurt readability, especially now that we are getting used to them.

Most art directors decide on a body type and stick with it issue after issue. Occasionally an art director runs a special article in a different face. Or he uses one face for articles and another for standing features like columns and departments.

In making his original choice for body type or types, the art director takes paper stock into consideration. For instance, old style romans work better on rough paper stock; modern romans reproduce best on smooth or coated stocks.

The choice of typeface should also be influenced by the printing process to be used. Some of the Bodoni faces, because of their hairline serifs, do not show up well in offset.[10] Typefaces in gravure tend to darken; hence for a text face the art director might not want to start out with a type already boldface. That everything in gravure is screened, including the type, suggests he would want to use a face without frills.

Once the art director makes his choice of type or types for body copy, he lives with it for a period of several years, perhaps even for the duration of the magazine. Choosing type for titles, on the other hand, represents a continuing problem. Often he chooses the type to match the mood of the article.

That the display type does not match the body type shouldn't bother him. But he should see to it that the various display types for a spread come from the same family. The display types should be obviously related and perfectly matched. If that's not possible, then they should be *clearly* unrelated. The art director should not put display types together that are *almost* related. *Almost* related types create the illusion that a mistake was made in setting.

An art director could combine an old style roman with a sans serif very nicely, but he would almost never combine an old style roman with a modern roman.

The you-can't-go-wrong types

Every art director has his favorite typeface, and one favorite may differ radically from another. Most art directors, however, could agree on a half dozen or so faces that form the standards against which other types are measured. A Basic Seven, so far as

10. See the typography in the first edition of Theodore Peterson's *Magazines in the Twentieth Century*, University of Illinois Press, Urbana, 1956. The editors changed the face in the second edition, 1964.

this author is concerned, would include these:

1. *Baskerville.* This face has to rank as one of the most beautiful ever designed. It comes now in many versions, but it was originally designed by John Baskerville, a British calligrapher, around 1760. Considered a threat to Caslon when it was introduced, Baskerville represented a break with the past, a move to a more modern look. It is a transitional face, more precise than the old style romans but not so precise as Bodoni.

A "wide set" type, it needs some leading. It looks best on smooth paper.

A quirk in the design results in a lowercase *g* with an incomplete bottom loop.

2. *Bodoni.* Italian designer Giambattista Bodoni drew some inspiration from Baskerville as he created Bodoni, a beautifully balanced if severe face, with marked differences in the thicks and thins of the strokes and with clean, harsh serifs.

The face looks best on slick paper and must be properly inked and printed. It is a little difficult to read in large doses. Like most faces, its beauty is lost in its bold and ultrabold versions.

3. *Caslon.* To most printers over the years, Caslon, designed in the eighteenth century by the Englishman, William Caslon, served as the No. 1 typeface. The rule was: "When in doubt, use Caslon."

The most familiar example of old style roman, this face still enjoys wide use. It has been described variously as "honest," "unobtrusive," and "classical."

Its caps, when you study them, are surprisingly wide, and its cap *A* seems to have a chip cut out of its top. The bottom loop on the lowercase *g* seems small. Otherwise, the face has no eccentricities.

4. *Clarendon.* The Clarendon faces are a cross between slab serifs and old style romans. The serifs, heavy as in slab serif letters, are bracketed, as in roman. They merge into the main strokes.

The first Clarendons appeared in England in the middle of the nineteenth century. Two recent versions are Hermann Eidenbenz's (1952) and Freeman Craw's (1954).

5. *Garamond.* This face was named after a sixteenth-century French typefounder, Claude Garamond, but it was probably designed by Jean Jannon. Equipped with unpredictable serifs, it is, nonetheless, beautiful and readable. It is a rather narrow face with a small x-height. It can be set solid.

6. *Helvetica.* Three great gothic faces came out of Europe in 1957: Univers, from France, designed by Adrian Frutiger; Folio, from Germany, designed by Konrad Bauer and Walter Baum; and Helvetica, from Switzerland, designed by Mas Miedinger. Clean and crisp, they look very much alike.

Helvetica, introduced in America in 1963 in body and display

ABCDEFGHIJKL
MNOPQRSTUV
WXYZ
abcdefghijklmnopq
rstuvwxyz
1234567890

ABCDEFGHIJ
KLMNOPQRS
TUVWXYZ
abcdefghijklmno
pqrstuvwxyz
1234567890

ABCDEFGHIJ
KLMNOPQR
STUVWXYZ
abcdefghijklmn
opqrstuvwxyz
1234567890

ABCDEFGH
IJKLMNOP
QRSTUVW
XYZ
abcdefghijkl
mnopqrstuv
wxyz
1234567890

ABCDEFGHIJKL
MNOPQRSTUV
WXYZ
abcdefghijklmnop
qrstuvwxyz
1234567890

**ABCDEFGHIJK
LMNOPQRSTU
VWXYZ
abcdefghijklmno
pqrstuvwxyz
1234567890**

ABCDEFGHIJ
KLMNOPQRS
TUVWXYZ
abcdefghijklmno
pqrstuvwxyz
1234567890

sizes, is perhaps the most available of the three. Unlike Univers, it is a close-fitting type, even on the Linotype. Like all the newer gothics, its rounds are slightly squared, and its strokes vary just a bit in thickness. The terminals on letters such as *e* and *s* are cut on the horizontal, aiding in readability. In all a handsome, modern face.

It comes in light, regular, regular italic, medium, bold, bold compact italic, regular extended, bold extended, extra bold extended, regular condensed, bold condensed, and extra bold condensed. The example shown here is Helvetica Regular.

7. *Times Roman.* Sometimes called *New Times Roman* or *Times New Roman,* this is the face designed by Stanley Morison for *The Times* of London in 1931. It is very much a twentieth-century type, not a revival, good for all kinds of jobs, although it is more of a body than a display face. Essentially an old style roman, it could, with its sharp-cut serifs, be classified as a transitional face. A peculiarity is the rounded bottom of the *b.*

Its large x-height makes some leading necessary. With its bold look, it was first a newspaper face, becoming popular later as a magazine and book face, particularly in America.

In 1975 *The Times* discontinued its use of Times Roman as a text face. Allen Hutt says Times Roman is not always a good body face for newspapers because it requires good press work.[11]

Title display

Titles for magazine articles differ from newspaper headlines in that their shape and placement are not dictated by a *headline schedule.* Only the designer's lack of imagination limits what may be done.

Many art directors fail to take advantage of the greater flexibility magazines have over newspapers. The trade magazines, especially, seem wedded to old newspaper ideas about titles or headlines. They use the same old flush-left, multi-line settings. Even the jargon of the headlines is the same. On the other hand, some magazines resort to so much typographic and design trickery that their readers become bewildered. And that isn't good either.

Only rarely should you make a title curve, dip, slant, overlap, pile on, or turn sideways. It should remain on the horizontal. A good starting point could be to design a title that occupies a single line of type in a size only slightly larger than the body copy. Perhaps it would be set in the same face as the body copy. The reader, then, finds it possible to take the title in as a single unit, not having to jump from one line to another. The title

11. Allen Hutt, "Times Roman: A Reassessment," *The Journal of Typographic Research,* Summer 1970, pp. 259-70.

would be like a sentence taken from out of the copy and made larger for easy access.

For some magazines, this style works very well, page after page. For other magazines, a more lively arrangement would be necessary. Not only would titles be broken up into two or more lines; they would also be set in type considerably larger than and different from the body copy.

The mood of the article could dictate the choice of title typeface, and that choice might vary greatly from article to article in a single issue.

Sometimes you may choose to vary the typeface—or at least the size—*within* the title. Let's say one word in the title should stand out over the others. You can bring out its importance in many ways: by setting it in a different face, a different size, a different weight; by printing it in color; by putting a box around it or underlining it; by reversing it in a black box or a color block; by separating it from the other words with a small piece of art; by showing it in perspective; by running it out of alignment. The important thing to remember is: only that one word should get the treatment. When two different words are made to stand out they cancel each other out.

Should you want to innovate with the entire title, you can try setting it in giant letters; building it with letters cut from a photographic background; surprinting or reversing it in a photograph or tint block; wrapping it around a photograph; arranging the lines in a piggyback fashion; nesting the lines partially inside other lines; fitting them inside the text; alternating the letters in black and color; superimposing them—the list is endless.

When *Sunset* sets a title in giant letters, it screens the letters to gray to keep them from looking cheap or loud. Another idea is to set giant-size titles in lowercase. Lowercase letters are more complicated in design and hence more interesting to view in large sizes.

Titles should ordinarily be set in lowercase anyway, with only the first word and all proper nouns capitalized. Lowercase is easier to read than all caps because lowercase letters are easier to distinguish from one another. Lowercase is easier to read than caps and lowercase because caps and lowercase cause the eye to move up and down, like the springs on a car moving along a bumpy road. Besides, writing caps-and-lowercase titles takes longer than writing all-lowercase titles: the title writer faces a complicated set of rules on which words to capitalize, which ones to leave lowercase.

When you have a multi-line title to deal with, you can show it flush left, flush right, or centered. It is not a good idea to run it flush left-flush right. To make it come out even on both sides usually takes some fancy and unnatural spacing. The most in-

Publishers Weekly *for an article on university presses uses hand lettering rather than type in order to give the title a chalk-on-blackboard look.*

triguing multi-line titles are those set in a staggered pattern to form an irregular silhouette. The lines should be kept close enough together so the title reads as a unit.

In multi-line titles it is almost never desirable to single out one word for emphasis. Asking the reader to jump from line to line is interruption enough. Asking him to accept a change in type style in the middle of it is asking too much. If you *must* have one word in a multi-line title stand out, you can put it in a line by itself, and without changing the typeface. To make it stand out more, in a flush-left title, you can run it a little to the left of the axis.

In planning a multi-line title, you should pay more attention to the logic of the arrangement than its looks. It is desirable, of course, that lines be reasonably equal in length, but it is more important by far that they be easily read.

When the title comes as two sentences, you cannot very well separate them with a period (unless the magazine's style is to end titles with periods), so you have to resort to some other device. You can use a semicolon, as a newspaper would do; you can use a typographic dingbat at the beginning of each sentence; you can use some extra white space; you can change to another typeface or size for the second sentence; you can change to color; you can change the position.

Blurbs

"Blurb" is another one of those elastic words in magazinedom, taking on any number of meanings. Article titles printed on covers are "blurbs." Excerpts taken out of articles and run in larger-than-body-copy type, one or more to a spread, to (1) break up gray areas of type and (2) stop readers who maybe

An unusual way to dramatize interior blurbs within a spread. Actually, they aren't blurbs so much as parts of the article writ large. The magnifying-glass motif is set up on the opening spread (on the previous two pages) where a detective is shown, page high, inspecting the title of the article, using his glass. The title is: "Right to Privacy—at What Price?" Notice the generous amount of white space on this spread and the building of the columns from the bottom. Notice, too, that this continuation does not begin immediately in the left-hand column. It waits a column. The spread is from In-tegon Listener, published bimonthly for the employees, field representatives, and families of Integon Corporation, Winston-Salem, North Carolina.

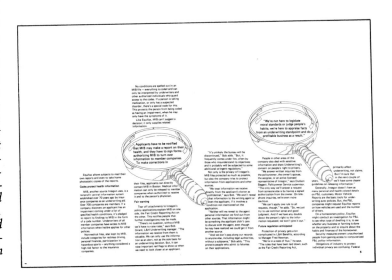

didn't stop at the article titles, are "blurbs," too. We will use the word right here to mean secondary titles adjacent to main titles of articles. Newspaper people would call them "second decks."

Magazines run them either above or below the titles, almost always in smaller type. Often they are longer than the titles, running for several sentences. They elaborate on titles, which often are more clever than illuminating.

Punctuation up large

While the editor bears the primary responsibility for punctuation, the art director should be concerned about punctuation, too, especially as he letters in the titles and headlines, where errors are most glaring. Oddly, in his haste in checking proofs, the editor often misses punctuation errors that creep into display type.

As art director you would be careful to letter in apostrophes where they're called for. The word is *it's* when *it* and *is* are contracted. Only the possessive is *its*. The possessive for *men* is *men's*, never *mens*.

When the title carries a quote, you would use double quote marks, as in the body copy, unless you're working for a newspaper. Newspapers use single quote marks to save space. If the title consists of several flush-left lines, you may elect to put the quote marks outside the line of the axis. This is called "hung punctuation," and it results in margins that appear more straightly cut. It works for body copy, too, and includes all marks of punctuation, but not many magazines and certainly few newspapers can afford the luxury of that kind of setting.

The art director must not make the mistake of using a hyphen when he needs a dash (long or short—there are two sizes). And he should avoid the cliché of using a series of periods to end a line, like this . . .

The late Carl Dair made an interesting contribution to the typography of punctuation. He introduced an upright, straight line, the height of the x-height, set off with extra white space, to help readers make a distinction between a broken word (broken because it wouldn't fit at the end of the line) and a compound word (like *world-wide*). He used the ordinary hyphen for compound words only.[12]

Another punctuation contribution comes from American Type Founders Company, which introduced the interabang, special punctuation combining both the question mark and the exclamation mark (for use in such sentences as "Are you kidding?").

12. See how the system works in his book, *Design with Type*, University of Toronto Press, Toronto, Canada, 1967.

Dog 'n pony
CASH N' CARRY
HEAT n EAT
rhythm 'n' blues
Cook'N' Clean
Sugar 'n' spice

Which of these abbreviated "and"s is correct? Only the last one. The first example leaves out the second apostrophe (you need two, because both the a and d are missing). The second example leaves off the first apostrophe. The third example doesn't carry any. The fourth example uses single quote marks rather than apostrophes. (The first mark, you can see, turns inward; that means it's not an apostrophe.) The fifth example capitalizes the N. It should not be capitalized. "Sugar 'n' spice" wins. But why not use an honest "and" and be done with all the apostrophes?

Body copy

In choosing a typeface for body copy, the art director is not quite so concerned with the beauty of the face as when he chooses display type. His primary concern should be: Is the type readable column after column? Further: What kind of pattern does the type make over a large area? The pattern should be even-textured, not spotty.

Most art directors prefer roman to sans serif faces for body copy simply because readers are used to them. Novelty hurts readability. But as sans serif finds increasing acceptance among readers of avant-garde magazines it will find increasing acceptance among readers of all magazines. As a matter of fact, sans serif has in recent years become almost commonplace as body copy for some general-circulation magazines.

One objection to sans serif used to be that it was too "vertical"; it did not have serifs to help move the reader horizontally across the line. But the newer sans serifs feature terminals that are sliced horizontally, and this tends to do the job serifs do. Also, the strokes of the newer sans serifs vary slightly in thickness, just as roman strokes do; sans serif type now is less monotonous in large doses.

Sans serifs, because of their solid character, are especially recommended where printing quality is inferior. Types with intricate serifs need superior printing in order to reproduce well.

Art directors have also changed their minds about unjustified lines. More and more magazines use them. Advertisers in their copy often get away with unjustified *left-hand* margins. Magazines avoid this. In magazine editorial matter, the lack of justification occurs on the *right*. In long blocks of copy, the reader needs a constant margin at the left to which he can return, line after line.

Some types need more space between words than others. Expanded types need more space between words than condensed types. Types with large x-heights need more space between words than those with small x-heights.

The spacing between words should never exceed the space between lines.

Copy needs extra spacing between lines when

1. the type has a large x-height;

2. the type has a pronounced vertical stress, as with Bodoni and with most of the sans serifs; and

3. the line length is longer than usual.

If copy is set in a single width, leading should be consistent throughout. It is best to specify the amount of leading before copy is set, as: "Set 10 on 12" (which means, "Set it in 10-point type on a 12-point slug."). Adding leading between lines afterwards costs more. Newspapers sometimes "lead out" the beginning or ending of a story to make it fit—a practice magazines should avoid. Leading part of a story tends to make the type in that part of the story look bigger than the remaining type.

If you want a highly contemporary, crowded look, you might consider the possibility of *minus*-leading. This means setting a point size (say 10-point) on a smaller body (say 9-point). You would do this only when you have a face with a large x-height (with short descenders). And you would do it for a minimum amount of copy because minus-leading is hard to read.

Many art directors no longer consider a widow—a less than full-length line at the top of a column in a multicolumn spread—as the typographic monstrosity it was thought to be. But when a widow consists of a single word or syllable, the left-over space is great enough to spoil the horizontal axis at the top of the columns. The art director then should do some rearranging of his lines to get rid of the widow.

But readers appreciate an occasional oasis deep into long columns of copy. Art directors supply it with subheadings or—better still—just a little extra white space. Sometimes an initial letter helps.

Subheads

Subheads—small headlines within the columns of copy—give readers a place to catch their breath. Subheads make the copy look less foreboding. They divide it into easier—shorter—takes.

They take the form usually of independent labels or sentences, summarizing what is to follow or teasing the reader to carry on. To set them apart from the body copy, you would put extra space above and below, especially above, and you would set them in boldface type, possibly in the same face and size as the body copy. Or you might set them in all caps, small caps, or italics. You could center them or run them flush left. Designing a book, you might choose to put them in the margins.

Book publishers, in contrast to magazine editors, set up a couple of levels of subheads, the more important ones appearing in a bolder type or centered in the column. The book you are now reading, however, uses a single level of subheads.

Some newspapers have adopted a style of subheads that puts the first few words of a paragraph in all-caps, boldface type. The subhead is not a separate line. A little extra space separates the subhead from the paragraph above. The advantage of this system is that you don't have to write the subhead. It is already written. The disadvantage is that you find it harder to eliminate or add subheads after the copy is set.

Where subheads go in a magazine article will probably be determined by the art director rather than the editor. The art director wants them spotted on the page to form a pleasing pattern.

Can you spot the problems with these body-copy excerpts from various publications? The first example shows too much space between words, a condition caused by justifying the copy to too narrow a measure. The type is too big for the column width. What you see are isolated words rather than flowing lines. The second example shows uneven spacing between letters. Compare "Bully" with "filled." The pattern of the setting is faulty. The third example shows a publication name in boldface type. The machine setting this type, apparently, does not have italics available. The editor underlines the name of a publication on the manuscript and gets not italics but the only alternate characters available: boldface. Should the name of a publication jump out from the page? Not unless you run a column about the media. When italics are not available you should treat names of publications as you would ordinary proper names. No underlining on the manuscript. The fourth example shows unequal spacing between two of the lines. No doubt you will see some examples in this book. The makeup artist needs to measure accurately the distance between lines when patching copy. The fifth example shows a subhead with too little space above and below. The subhead doesn't stand out enough. It is lost between the paragraphs, even though it's in boldface.

Editors who do not have a news-oriented content tend to avoid subheads, feeling they are more a part of newspapering than magazine making. In place of subheads these editors use initial letters, blurbs, or merely units of white space. Some editors feel that small photographs or art pieces strategically placed serve as subheads.

Initial letters

An oversize letter used at the beginning of an article or story and at each of its breaks can help get readers started and rekindle their interest as the story progresses. When using initial letters, you should go to the face of your title, not the face of your body copy. And if you start off with a quote mark, you should use it in the size of the initial, not in the size of the body copy. Otherwise, the quote mark will be overpowered by the initial. Some magazines leave off the beginning quote mark, feeling that the big letter can do duty both as an initial and as a quote mark. That the quotation *ends* with a quote mark is signal enough for readers.

It is called a two-, three-, four-, or five-line initial, depending upon how deep in lines it is. It can be bigger than the title-type size. You may find it desirable to help readers make the step down from the initial to the body copy by giving them the remainder of the first word and maybe another word or two in all caps or small caps. And you will probably want your body copy to fit snugly around the initial. Sometimes this takes some fancy work by the composing room.

You might want to consider using initial letters that project out or up from the body copy rather than fit down into it. You may also want to use an initial word instead of an initial letter. *Go,* the Goodyear tire-dealer magazine, doesn't use initial letters but does start its articles off with one complete line of boldface type in sans serif, where the remainder of the body copy is in roman and in a size slightly smaller than the boldface lead in. *The New Era,* a publication of The Church of Jesus Christ of Latter-day Saints, uses a small version of its cover logo as an "initial letter" for each of its major articles. It ends each article with yet a smaller version of the logo.

Initials really get interesting when you contract to have them

Some of the ways magazines handle initial letters, both at the beginnings and in the interiors of articles. The first is a two-line initial in a three-line setting. Several words in caps ease the reader from the initial into the text. The second uses boldface type to make the bridge, and carries the boldfacing all the way across the first line. The third uses an initial word. Not a bad idea, unless you happen to begin an article with "Paleontography" or something similar. The fourth, an interior initial, does not ask for any extra space between itself and the previous paragraph. Note that the copy fits around the initial. The fifth, also an interior initial, juts up from the line. There is some extra space for this one. The sixth illustrates what to do when you start out with a direct quote. You use quote marks in the initial size, not in the body-copy size. Some designers leave off the beginning quote marks in a situation like this. That works, too.

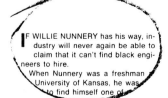

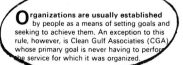

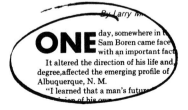

drawn to fit the mood of an article. For instance: you ask an artist to construct the initials out of cartoon figures and props, perhaps adding a second color. One of the charms of Hendrick Willem van Loon's illustrated histories published in the 1920s and 1930s were the initial letters he drew for chapter openings.

It would be foolhardy to pick one style as being superior to others, or to argue that using initial letters in the first place is preferable to bypassing them. It comes down to being a matter of one person's taste matched against another's.

One thing is certain: initial letters poorly planned look a lot worse than standard opening and white-space interior rests. And it probably is true that to work well, initial letters should work boldly.

When used in two or three places on a spread as interior rests, they should be spaced so that distances between them vary. And ordinarily, they should not line up horizontally. They should succeed in dividing the columns of a spread into unequal takes.

Having settled on the kind and placement of initial letters, you had better sit back and give the spread some study. Do the letters, by any chance, spell out some word your readers may find offensive? You may have to make some last minute changes, just as you would make if, on looking over the final page proofs, you see an ad placed right next to editorial matter that makes a contradictory point.

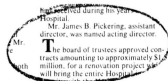

An initial letter can be more than a mere piece of type set large. This one is drawn, and it is as much a gag cartoon as an initial letter. Now as an editor all you would have to do is make sure your article on sleep starts out with a word beginning with "Z."

Article starts

Sometimes the design of a magazine page confuses readers, making it difficult for them to know where to start the article. For instance, the title may be off to the right. Do readers start right under the title, then, or do they move over to the left and start there?

If titles go right over the first column of copy, no special typographic treatment is needed. The first paragraph can be set indented to look like the other paragraphs.

But in other cases, the readers need help. One solution, of course, is to use an initial letter. Even if the spread has several, readers will pick up first the initial letter at the far-left point. Another solution is to line up the columns evenly across the top. Readers will see that the columns are related and start with the

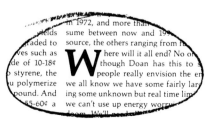

one at the extreme left. Still another solution, less often tried, is to put a small piece of art near the start, to sort of point to the beginning.

For many magazines, the best way of saying "Here is where the article starts" is to set the first paragraph without an indentation. The "indenting," which is nothing more than an arresting of reader attention, anyway, has already been done by the title, these editors feel.

If the art director feels any doubt that readers will begin articles where they should, he should redesign the page. Getting readers started is a chief function of page design.

Captions

The design has flair. And the comp is executed brilliantly. But the instructor notices something missing.

He asks the student about it.

"I didn't indicate the captions because I didn't think the pictures needed captions."

The student reflects a design attitude that seems on the upswing. In some quarters the caption has fallen from favor. The advertising-design look so prevalent in company magazines, for instance, tends to regard the caption as nothing more than visual clutter. So art directors—some of them—talk their editors out of captions.

Some photographers applaud the practice. Long have they argued that captions are redundant. Considering what some captions are made to say by editors, maybe the photographers are right.

Still, looking at the matter from a reader's standpoint, you have to conclude that the caption is necessary for a full understanding of the photograph except in those cases—rare in news oriented publications—where the photograph's purpose is merely to establish a mood. An operating rule ought to be that the editor should always include a caption unless there is a compelling reason to leave it out.

In the classroom the caption often disappears simply because the student, preoccupied with title and picture placement, forgets to plan for it.

Caption designing takes two basic approaches: either the captions appear adjacent to the pictures they describe or they gather themselves together in a group and key themselves to the various pictures in the spread. You do not necessarily have to use numbers to key the captions. You can key through description. *Integon Listener*, published by the Integon Corporation, Winston-Salem, N.C., in one issue showed photographs of a business executive alone at his desk talking into a phone, the executive shaking hands with visitors, and the executive playing shuffleboard with his family. The caption off to the side reads: "Despite his busy schedule, Ed Collette believes in making time for people, whether it's a customer or employee on the phone, a group of new fieldmen like these from Provident Life, or his own family, including wife Evelyn, daughter Gayle and twin grandsons Johnny and Jerry."

Art directors like the cluster-caption idea because it allows them to butt pictures against each other, bleed them, and in other ways better display them. Using a cluster caption, you don't have to plan for just the right space between the pictures to accommodate the various captions.

But where names are involved, at least, readers no doubt prefer captions right next to each picture for ready reference.

If your caption seems to be off to one side and not obviously connected to the photograph, your solution is *not* to include an arrow that points the reader in the right direction. Your solution is to redesign the page.

Captions right above or below photographs should appear in the same widths as the photographs—or narrower. You would not want to run them wider. Some art directors like to run captions at a standard width regardless of how wide the photographs are. This does help simplify the design and speed up the typesetting. You always know how wide to set your captions.

Some editors seem to feel that caption writers should even out the last line each time so that it is fully filled and flush with the other lines. This is folly. The time spent counting characters and rewriting to make that last line fit can be spent better on other editorial matters.

Bylines

The New Yorker places bylines at the ends of articles or stories, apparently in the belief that readers should get into editorial material without regard to who wrote it. Most magazines, if they use bylines, place them at the beginnings. *The New Republic*, for example, runs bylines well removed from the titles of articles and right next to the articles' beginnings. Because both title and byline are in boldface, the reader's eye moves from title across white space to byline—and to the beginning of the article.

Bylines are set in type smaller than that used for article or story titles but larger, usually, than type used for body copy.

Some magazines combine bylines with blurbs about the author. Example: "Mathew S. Ogawa shows how after-midnight broadcasts are reaching Japanese youth." The authors' names are set in italics, boldface, all-caps, or they are even underlined to make them stand out. Other magazines run blurbs about the authors in small type at the bottoms of article openings, sort of as footnotes. Still others, such as *Esquire,* run separate columns combining information about all the contributors.

Credit lines

Some magazines run credit lines in a box on the table of contents page or somewhere else in the magazine. It is surprising that companies granting permission to reprint photographs or other illustrations would settle for that kind of credit. Few readers study such a box to find out who took what picture.

The more common practice is to run credit lines right next to the photographs, whether they be original or borrowed. Credit-line type is usually smaller than caption type, to keep the two entirely separate; often a sans serif type is used. Some magazines run credit lines up the sides of pictures to keep the lines from interfering with captions.

Credit lines can be reversed or surprinted inside the photographs at their bottom edges.

If a magazine does not want to be bothered with separate settings for credit lines, it can run them as last lines of captions, set off by parentheses.

When one photographer takes all the pictures for a feature, he gets a byline rather than a credit line, just as illustrators get. The photographer's or illustrator's byline may be slightly smaller than the author's and placed away from the story's opening.

Typographic endings

Like a good cup of coffee after a meal, some writer has said. That's what an article's ending should be. The reader should know when he's reached the end of the article or story; he should walk away inspired, shocked, amused, instructed, perhaps even moved to some course of action.

Many editors feel that the writing alone may not be enough to signal that the encounter between the writer and reader is over. Some typographic accessory should announce, in effect: this is The End. This is especially true now that so few magazines provide a cushion of fillers at the ends of articles. They end at the bottom of pages.

The standard typographic device is the small, square box, available on any linecasting machine. Some magazines design their own end device and see that special matrices are available to the Linotype operator. *Playboy,* for instance, uses its rabbit symbol, reversed in a small black square with rounded corners. *Popular Photography* uses a stylized rendering of a lens opening. *Esquire* uses three vertical lines with a horizontal line running through them in the middle. *Sweden Now* uses a tiny, slightly altered version of its logo. *Scene,* published by South-

For a class in calligraphy, Joanne Hasegawa, student at the University of Oregon, creates an experimental design with old style roman letters in various sizes. A feel for letter-form should be part of the training of every potential magazine art director.

western Bell Telephone Company, and *Sports Illustrated*, among other magazines, use the word "End" set in tiny letters.

A book needs none of these devices to end a chapter. A little leftover space does the job.

Suggested further reading

BAIN, ERIC K., *Display Typography: Theory and Practice*, Hastings House, Publishers, New York, 1970.

BIGGS, JOHN, *Basic Typography*, Watson-Guptill Publications, New York, 1969.

BIEGELEISEN, J. I., *Art Directors' Book of Type Faces*, Arco Publishing Company, Inc., New York, 1976. (Revised and Enlarged Edition.)

CLEMENTS, BEN, AND ROSENFIELD, DAVID, *Photographic Composition*, Prentice-Hall, New York, 1974.

DAIR, CARL, *Design with Type*, University of Toronto Press, Toronto, Canada, 1967. (Revised Edition.)

FYFFE, CHARLES, *Basic Copyfitting*, Watson-Guptill Publications, New York, 1969.

GATES, DAVID, *Lettering for Reproduction*, Watson-Guptill Publications, New York, 1969.

HAAB, ARMIN, AND HAETTENSCHWEILER, WALTER, *Lettera 3*, Hastings House, Publishers, New York, 1968.

HANSON, GLENN, *How to Take the Fits Out of Copyfitting*, Mul-T-Rul Company, Ft. Morgan, Colorado, 1967.

HILL, DONALD E., *The Practice of Copyfitting*, Graphic Arts & Journalism Publishing Company, Huntsville, Alabama, 1971.

HOPKINS, RICHARD L., *Origin of the American Point System for Printers' Type Measurement*, Hill & Dale Press, Terra Alta, West Virginia, 1976.

HUTCHINGS, R. S., ed., *A Manual of Decorated Types*, Hastings House, Publishers, New York, 1965.

———, *A Manual of Script Typefaces: A Definitive Guide to Series in Current Use*, Hastings House, Publishers, New York, 1965.

———, *A Manual of Sans Serif Typefaces*, Hastings House, Publishers, New York, 1966.

KLARE, GEORGE R., *Measurement of Readability*, Iowa State University Press, Ames, Iowa, 1963.

LAMBERT, FREDERICK, *Letter Forms: Alphabets for Designers*, Hastings House, Publishers, New York, 1964.

LAWSON, ALEXANDER, *Printing Types*, Beacon Press, Boston, 1971.

———, AND PROVAN, ARCHIE, *Typography for Composition*, National Composition Association, 1730 N. Lynn St., Arlington, Virginia, 22209, 1976.

LIEBERMAN, J. BEN, *Types of Typefaces and How to Recognize Them*, Sterling Publishing Company, Inc., New York, 1967.

LONGYEAR, WILLIAM LEVWYN, *Type & Lettering*, Watson-Guptill Publications, New York, 1966. (Fourth Edition.)

MORISON, STANLEY, *A Tally of Types*, Cambridge University Press, New York, 1973. (Covering types designed by Morison.)

OGG, OSCAR, *The 26 Letters*, Thomas Y. Crowell Company, New York, 1971. (Revised Edition.)

REHE, ROLF F., *Typography: How to Make it More Legible*, Design Research Publications, Indianapolis, 1974.

ROSEN, BEN, *Type and Typography: The Designer's Notebook*, Van Nostrand Reinhold, New York, 1976. (Revised Edition.)

RUDER, EMIL, *Typography: A Manual of Design*, Hastings House, Publishers, New York, 1967.

SPENCER, HERBERT, *The Visible Word: Problems of Legibility*, Hastings House, Publishers, Inc., New York, 1969. (Second Edition.)

SUTTON, JAMES, AND BARTRAM, ALAN, *An Atlas of Typeforms*, Hastings House, Publishers, New York, 1968.

SWANN, CAL, *The Techniques of Typography*, Watson-Guptill Publications, New York, 1969.

TSCHICHOLD, JAN, *Treasury of Alphabets and Lettering*, Reinhold Publishing Corporation, New York, 1966.

ZACHRISSON, BROR, *Studies in the Legibility of Printed Text*, Almqvist and Wiksell, Stockholm, 1965.

ZAPF, HERMANN, *About Alphabets: Some Marginal Notes on Type Design*, M. I. T. Press, Cambridge, Massachusetts, 1970.

Banta Book of Typographical Tips, George Banta Company, Inc., Menasha, Wisconsin, 1969.

The Type Specimen Book, Van Nostrand Reinhold Company, New York, 1974. (544 faces, 3,000 sizes.)

Chapter 7

Art

Let's say your subject is "love," and you need an illustration. How about something like this? From Werbezeichen: An Album, *Munich, n.d.*

One of the big advantages of offset is that almost anything from almost any source can be reproduced with little or no additional expense. In fact the flexibility and adaptability of offset has tempted editors of marginal publications to steal printed photographs and artwork from the more affluent publications. The only reason these editors are not prosecuted is that their publications attract virtually no attention outside their own limited audiences. But clearly they are violating the law if the material they appropriate is copyrighted, and often it is.

There are enough low-cost art and photographic services around to make such illegal activity unnecessary, even for the most mendicant of editors.

Public-domain art

Up until 1978, any art published in books or magazines that were 56 years old or older could be clipped and used with or without credit at no cost to the user. After 56 years the original copyright (granted for a 28-year period) and the second and final copyright (granted for another 28-year period if it was applied for) had expired. The art had fallen into the public domain.

Now, because Congress changed the copyright law to make it conform to the law in other countries, things are more complicated. Editors and art directors are still free to lift material from publications whose copyrights expired before 1978. But material whose copyright periods extend beyond January 1978 and material copyrighted since then come under a different ruling: the copyrights last for the lifetime of the holders and for fifty years beyond that.

Still, plenty of material remains in the public domain. And if it is not yet there, you can always contact the owner and get permission to use it, possibly paying a small fee for the privilege. Also in the public domain are most government publications.

While the price is right for public-domain art, the dated look of much of the material may be a problem.

Stock art

If you can't find what you want from public-domain sources you can turn to any of the hundreds of picture agencies and stock-art houses, to government agencies, to chambers of commerce, to trade and professional organizations, to businesses, to libraries, to historical societies, to other publications who sell or loan prints, or to publishers who make clipbooks available.[1]

Dover Publications, 180 Varick Street, New York, New York 10014, remains a leader in this field with its Pictorial Archives Series of inexpensive collections, mostly of public-domain art. Dover does ask that you use no more than a half a dozen pieces for any one job. This is to prevent people from republishing and marketing the books. Hart Publishing Company, Inc., 15 West 4th Street, New York, New York 10012, has recently entered the field with some first-rate collections centering on, for instance, Chairs, Weather, Dining and Drinking, Trades and Professions, and Animals.

Art Direction Book Company, 19 West 44th Street, New York, New York 10036, publisher of *Art Direction* magazine, publishes and distributes a number of clipbooks of public-domain art, including the *Ron Yablon Graphic Archives* covering Nature, People, Things, and Typography & Design.

Calling itself "The World's Leading Publisher of Copyright Free Archive Material," The Dick Sutphen Studio," Box 628, Scottsdale, Arizona 85252, offers editors books of both old art and new material, including illustrative cartoons "in numerous sizes and categories."

Among organizations offering a regularly-issued clipbook service are Volk Studios, Pleasantville, New Jersey 08232, and Dynamic Graphics, Inc., 6707 N. Sheridan Road, Peoria, Illinois 61614. The work from these and similar organizations is contemporary, executed by a variety of artists in a kind of house style: adequate, slick, and not particularly exciting.

In addition to stock-art organizations you have hundreds of stock-photo organizations and agencies at your call. Some specialize; others offer a great variety of photographs. Harold M. Lambert Studios, Inc., Philadelphia, for example, has on hand some 500,000 black and white photographs and 50,000 color

A sample drawing from "Human Relations," one of scores of clip books available from Volk Studios, one of the better stock-art houses. Editors can purchase clip books by subject area for a few dollars each, and each book contains about two dozen drawings from which to choose. There are no limitations on how they are used, or on frequency of use. Of course, no editor or advertiser who uses the Volk service, or some similar service, gets exclusive rights to the material.

---

1. See listings in *Literary Market Place, Writer's Market,* and *Photographer's Market.*

transparencies. Rental fees vary, depending upon intended use. A magazine working with any of the stock-photo organizations can expect to pay from $25 per picture for one-time publication. That price can be far less than what the magazine would pay for custom work.

A stock-art house differs from a stock-photo house in that once you purchase the clipbook or service from a stock-art house you are free to use it in any way that you wish and as often as you wish. A stock-photo house ordinarily grants you one-time use.

A problem with both of these sources, of course, is that ordinarily you would not get exclusive use. You face the chance that some other publication will show the same material.

Art from within

Accessible as it is, public-domain or stock art does not often exactly fit your needs. So when possible—when you can afford it—you order art to fit. Or you go to a staff artist or photographer. Or, if you have the necessary talent, you do the work yourself.

On company magazines, especially, editors do their own photography. The favorite camera is the 35 mm, single-lens reflex with interchangeable lenses. If the camera has some automatic features, so much the better.

Mario Micossi of Italy, whose works form part of the permanent collections of at least a dozen museums in Europe and in America, frequently does his scratchboard drawings for American magazines, especially The New Yorker. *This one is from* The Reporter, *a magazine that wasn't very well designed but which featured excellent artwork.*

Most editors/photographers prefer using fast film—Tri-X—and doing their photography, even their inside photography, in natural light. Getting the subject well lighted and in focus is only part of the challenge. What really separates the amateur photographer from the professional is the composition of the photograph. It should not be necessary to improve the photograph's composition through cropping, although if the photograph can take some cropping it becomes a more versatile element in the hands of an imaginative art director looking, say, for a deep vertical or wide horizontal to add interest to the page.

Taking many more pictures than you would want, you are likely to come up with at least a few that work well. You would

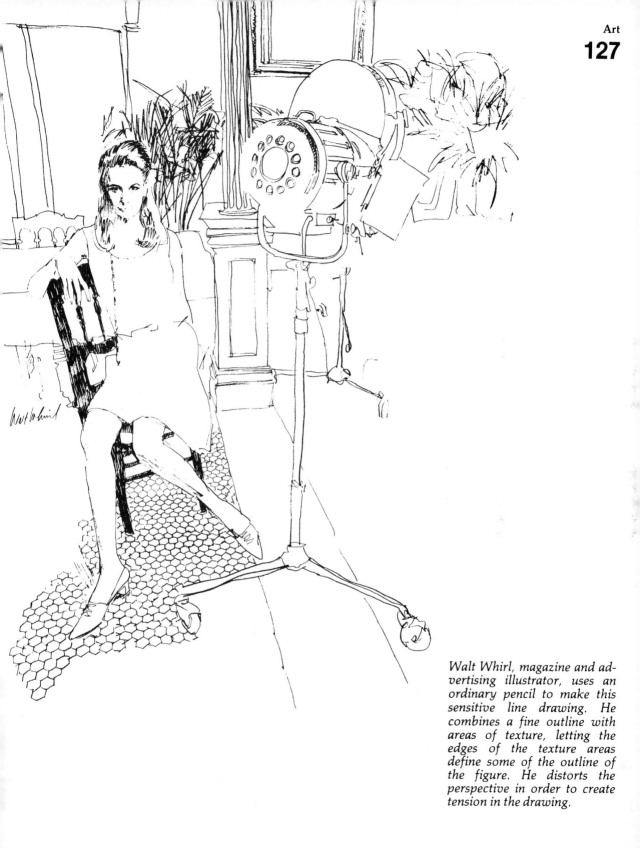

Walt Whirl, magazine and advertising illustrator, uses an ordinary pencil to make this sensitive line drawing. He combines a fine outline with areas of texture, letting the edges of the texture areas define some of the outline of the figure. He distorts the perspective in order to create tension in the drawing.

ask for contact prints from your developer and mark the promising ones for enlargement.

If you have a staff artist or photographer, you would work with him much as you would work with a freelancer. The big advantage is that the staffer will be readily available and at a comparatively modest cost. But there has to be a continuous flow of work to make such an arrangement pay off.

Art from freelancers

Many art directors feel that the ideal arrangement is to buy all art—photography and illustration—from freelancers.

Freelancers are everywhere. Once the word gets out that your magazine is in the market, you will face a steady stream of them—illustrators and photographers nervously clutching their portfolios of examples. "Sorry Mr.—what's the name again?—we really don't have many assignments that call for charcoal renderings of nudes." In case you don't find the freelancer you want, you can turn to several directories now available.

Popular in literary and book-review magazines and in newspaper "forum" sections or on op-ed pages is line art with scratchy shading and barely defined features. Such art carries the feel of sophistication. This example by Sovetskii Khudozhnik comes from Album: Fifty Years of Soviet Art: Graphic Arts, Moscow, n.d.

It is one thing to pick out prints or drawings from among those submitted on speculation. It is another to pick out a photographer or illustrator from among those available and send him off on an assignment. A person's portfolio may not be representative of what he can do under adverse conditions. Bob Pliskin, vice-president in charge of art for Benton & Bowles, the advertising agency, has a unique test for the photographer who sees him for an assignment. He has the photographer empty his pockets—the change, the handkerchief, and whatever else he may be carrying, and then asks him to arrange these things and take photos, up to fifty of them. The photographer then submits his half dozen best prints. If he can make such a collection of materials exciting and stimulating, he probably can handle any other assignment, Pliskin reasons.

Another problem has to do with deadlines. You can't be sure that a new artist will deliver his work on time. So you tend to stick to a small stable of freelancers whose work and working habits you are familiar with.

Samuel Antupit says art directors have been negligent in developing new talent. They should be willing to try the work of the lesser-knowns. Only the small specialized magazines seem willing to heed his advice, if for no other reason than that they can't afford the big names.

The big magazines have shown some interest in using name artists in unfamiliar roles. Herb Bleiweiss, when he was art director for *Ladies' Home Journal,* used photographers on assignments they had not tried before. "These people when working in a new area approach problems with a fresh eye," he said. When *LHJ* ran Truman Capote's "A Christmas Memory," Bleiweiss used a fine art painting by Andrew Wyeth to illustrate it. When *Ramparts* in May 1967 ran a cover on the controversial Bertrand Russell, the then art director, Dugald Stermer, commissioned an unlikely artist to do the portrait: the American-as-Apple-Pie illustrator Norman Rockwell.

The temperamental artist

Working with artists and photographers you are likely to face some tensions. An artist or photographer is never quite as awed by a deadline as an editor or art director is. Nor does the artist take kindly to changes in his work, however necessary they may be from an editorial standpoint. So far as the artist is concerned, the editor or art director always wants the work yesterday and seems to change his mind about what he wants after the final art is in.

Paul Hightower, a participant in a University of Iowa Visual Scholars Program, offered tongue-in-cheek definitions of editors and photographers. An *editor,* he said, "leaps tall buildings in a

A line drawing is not just a line drawing. You see here three different kinds of line drawings done by one artist, Don Thompson, for one issue of Aramco World Magazine. Each illustrated its own article. The top illustration, one of several done in that style for an article, has a sketchy look. The lines seem to be scrubbed onto the paper quickly. (You see the illustration greatly reduced.) The tightly drawn second example has a sort of Aubrey Beardsley decorative look. The third, with its calligraphic look, qualifies as a stylized drawing. It is the most abstract of the three.

Final two pages of a six-page article in San Francisco *on busing of school children. Art director Dan Marr uses Earl Thollander's line sketches—ten of them—throughout to tie the pages together and, of course, to make them visually alive. Drawings can be a refreshing change in a magazine, even for articles that seem to call for photographs.*

single bound, is more powerful than a locomotive, is faster than a speeding bullet, walks on water, dictates policy to God" while an *assistant editor* "barely clears a thatched hut, loses a tug of war with a hand car, can fire a speeding bullet, swims well, is occasionally addressed by God." A *copy editor* "makes high marks on the wall while trying to leap tall buildings. . . ." And the *photographer*?

[He] Lifts buildings and walks under them, kicks locomotives off the tracks, catches bullets in his teeth and eats them, freezes water with a single glance, *is* God.[2]

"Photographers hang their new, sensitive cameras with super lenses around their neck, a Gucci bag of light meters dangling smartly beside them," observes another artist-watcher. "Such gourds of intention.

"But the attitude! They seem to be shuttering in a museum gallery syndrome. . . as if everything they take is a masterpiece. . . . Like hairdressers, they want instant success. Unfortunately, they put too much 'me-me' in the negative, and not enough 'eye' in the take."[3]

2. Reported by *Journalism Educator*, April 1977, p. 64.
3. Robert N. Essman, "Photography and Photographers," *DA*, vol. 62, no. 4, 1976, p. 22.

In any kind of skirmish, the art director has to have the last word. He is doing the buying. This does not mean that the two—art director and artist—cannot work together harmoniously. But the art director has to be something of a public relations person and personnel director. He must put himself in the place of the artist. He may find that a photographer he's hired, for instance, has much more to offer than an ability to follow directions. A good photographer may have ideas for illustrating the story or article that the art director has not thought of. The art director should be willing to listen. And he should be willing to consider alternate shots submitted by the photographer when he submits the shots he went out of the studio to get. The photographer often finds new illustrative possibilities at the scene that neither he nor the art director envisioned when they worked out plans for photographic coverage.

The art director owes it to his photographer to explain the nature of the article or story being illustrated, the reasons for the pictures, their intended use and placement, and the nature of other art for that issue. Often the art director provides the photographer with a rough layout of the pages when the assignment is given.

Settling on rates

The staff artist or staff photographer works on a regular salary, so rates are not a problem. The freelancer works differently. His rates are negotiable.

The freelance illustrator may be attached to a studio, or he may work independently. He is often willing to accept less for his work for a magazine than for an advertising agency simply because he finds magazine work more gratifying.

The usual procedure is to give the illustrator a copy of the manuscript with the request that he submit a series of rough sketches.[4] From these the art director orders the finished drawings or paintings he wants, specifying any necessary changes. Often the magazine and the illustrator settle on a price in advance. A magazine, depending upon its size, can expect to pay anywhere from $10 or $20 to several hundred dollars per drawing or painting. Sometimes it's a matter of saying, "We have $150 to spend on a cover illustration. Interested?"

Rates vary widely. A small-town illustrator or designer with little experience may feel he's worth $5 an hour while a real professional may ask $20 or $30. One artist/designer (he shall go nameless here), when he has to set a price ahead of time, in-

". . . Each story calls for its own individual technique," says Robert Quackenbush, who did the illustration for this right-hand opener for Clipper. "For this reason, I experiment with many mediums and tools to find the 'right' technique for a story. I have worked in nearly all mediums . . . from woodcuts, to etchings, to water colors . . . even to . . . a five-cent pencil." Note how well the art is integrated with the display type: each has a bold, hand-carved look. (Reproduced by permission from Clipper Magazine, published and copyrighted by Pan American World Airways.)

---

4. Samuel Antupit suggests that the artist should have *more* than the manuscript to read; he should have the writer's research as well so that he will know more than the reader. Then the artist can really make a contribution.

evitably underestimates the time the job will take. Knowing this, he automatically doubles the figure he thinks of first. "That way I come out about right." On a job he undertook with a collaborator some years ago, neither man could figure out what to charge. So one said to the other: "Why don't you count the change in your pocket and we'll multiply that number by $10?" And that's how the job was billed.

Helping artists and designers and photographers, too, to standardize their rates are the various professional societies and guilds that have sprung up in recent years.

As a group, photographers seem to have standardized their rates more than other artists have. Still, routine photography, if you are willing to settle for it, is probably the least expensive custom art you can buy. Good photography, though, comes high. A good freelance photographer will charge a magazine $150 to $250 a day plus expenses. The rate may go higher if a large number of prints from the shooting are used. Whether the pictures and negatives afterwards belong to the magazine or to the photographer depends upon the agreement arrived at before the shooting. Many photographers feel that photographs should earn something for them each time they're used and that the price should fluctuate according to use. Photographs for promotional purposes bring more than photographs for editorial use.

Using art imaginatively

The usual procedure is to do the article or story first, then go out after the pictures to illustrate it. But sometimes it's better to do it the other way around: tell the story in pictures, using words only where facts or statistics are not clear without them.

What the art director tries to do is come up with the one visualization that will tell the story immediately and forcefully. One indication of Otto Storch's genius was the illustration he commissioned for a May 1966 *McCall's* article on infidelity: a big red apple with a couple of bites taken out of it. Nothing else.

When Herb Bleiweiss of *Ladies' Home Journal* had the job of illustrating a feature on women's nightgowns, he didn't show the girls in just typical poses; he caught them in action, including one girl being rescued from a burning building.

When *Life* for one of its last issues ran a feature on the dress styles of Pat Nixon and daughters, it showed doll-like drawings of each, with drawings of dresses alongside. The dresses had little flaps on them, the kind you find in paper doll clothes. In keeping with the illustrations, the article started out with the line: "Once upon a time. . . ." One might read into the feature the condescending attitude most of the major magazines had for the Nixons.

When *New York* ran a feature on "How Israel Got Blueprints

A right-hand page opener for an article in Bell Telephone Magazine *on government regulation. The black border is appropriate in view of the word "Strangling" in the title. Further dramatizing the concept of strangling is the twisted shape of the phone, accomplished by heating it in an oven and working it over before taking the photograph. To tell readers that the article really starts on the next page, the editor, after the italicized blurb, runs the word "continued."*

for France's Hottest Fighter Plane" (August 30, 1976) it used, as illustrations, adventure comic strips drawn by Vincente Alcazar. The strips ran across the tops of the several pages devoted to the article.

For a feature on builds of athletes, *Esquire* (October 1975) showed actual-size photos of the biceps of Arnold Schwarzenegger, the neck of Mean Joe Greene, the forearm of Rod Laver, the hand of Robyn C. Smith, and the thigh of Pele.

To accompany "The All-Purpose Manager," *Bell Telephone Magazine* (July/August 1976) reproduced with some color a photograph of one of those Swiss army knives, opened out so you could see the various tools. That was on the opening spread. On a followup spread, to illustrate the blurb, "When a multifunctional group meets a more traditional one, meshing can be difficult, but not insurmountable," the magazine showed the

West's *art director, Mike Salisbury, flew from Los Angeles to Atlanta to dig up the art for this article on Coca-Cola and its advertising gimmicks. "The signs, bottles, matchbooks, and trays—some of which are now collectors' items—are as American as . . . well . . . Coke itself,"* says the blurb. "Soda-Pop Art" was laid out to be "as documentary as possible," Salisbury reports, "—very straight." (The article is copyrighted by Lawrence Dietz. Used by permission.)

To illustrate an article on how to "deal" with customers swarming the marketplace "after a long winter's sleep," Go, the Goodyear magazine for tire dealers, came up with this photograph taken by Don Landstrom, an amateur magician. The article discussed a nationwide "Goodyear Cuts the Deck and Deals" promotion. Because few magicians or even gamblers are able to shuffle cards like this, Landstrom drilled a hole through the center of the cards and threaded them with a string to "enable the cards to follow a predetermined path from the top hand to the bottom," according to editor Larry Miller. "Landstrom tells us that this method is used by most magicians who demonstrate this trick. A black string was used against a black background with strong side lighting with the result being an almost-invisible string. Slight retouching eliminated the string entirely."

knife open, looking terribly complicated with all those prongs sticking every which way, then closed, except for one blade: neat and compact.

For an article entitled "What To Do in Case of Armed Robbery," *Go*, Goodyear's dealer magazine, showed a frightening close-up of a gun pointing straight out at the reader. No question about it: it compelled attention.

For a feature on "9 Ways to Beat Winter," *Small World*, the magazine for Volkswagen owners, showed a drawing of a VW, head on, enclosed in giant earmuffs. What better way to set the mood?

Sometimes the art stands by itself. *Minutes*, the magazine once published by Nationwide Insurance, ran two pages of pictures of manhole covers. There was no copy, there were no captions. The variety of patterns stamped on the covers was story enough.

Another idea is to concentrate on texture rather than form. If the subject is "Forests," the art director can make a rubbing or painting from a piece of bark and use it as a piece of line art. If the subject is "Accidents," he can make a rubbing or printing from a piece of bandage cloth.

But the style or technique of illustration doesn't have to have an obvious connection with the subject matter. Art Young, the socialist cartoonist, used an outdated drawing style, not unlike that of a crude woodcut, to fight capitalism and social injustice. Young considered the matter later in one of his autobiographies. "Here I was, a man commonly thought to be 'ahead of the procession' in ideas, who was for progress and change, and with little reverence for tradition, and yet my style was 'archaic,' reminiscent of the ancient past."[5]

Nor does the artist have to use traditional media. Art directors recently have encouraged their illustrators to experiment. The collage has lately become popular: the pasting together of fragments of art, already printed art, or papers and textiles. These can be used to form an abstraction or something that, viewed from a distance, looks quite representational. Some art directors are even using photographs of pieces of sculpture done especially for their magazines. For its March 15, 1971, cover on "Suburbia: A Myth Challenged," *Time* used a color photo of a needlepoint picture.

What kind of art the art director settles for depends upon what he wants his art to do. Does he want it to be informative? Then he asks for realism, either in photographs or illustrations. Does he want it to supply mood for the article or story? Then he asks for abstraction, something as simple, say, as a black border to symbolize death. Does he want it simply to decorate his page?

5. Art Young, *On My Way*, Horace Liveright, New York, 1928, p. 193.

Then he asks for ornament.

The job often requires some kind of art that suggests universality. A single individual on a cover of a recruitment piece, for instance, might suggest to the viewer that he has to fit that mold and be ruled out. So the art director works for some kind of a montage. Then the problem becomes one of quotas. Both male and female must be represented, for instance; and so must members of several races. Perhaps both young and old should be there. These days special efforts must be made, especially where the government is involved, to get members of minority groups up front.

Involving the reader

How often have we been disappointed when a radio announcer whose voice we've admired shows up on the TV screen! He doesn't look at all as we imagined. If it's possible to leave the "illustrating" to the reader, the art director should do it. Charles Schulz will never show us the inside of Snoopy's doghouse. We can be grateful. We already have our own ideas of what it looks like.

The art director can directly involve the reader in the use of illustrations. *Playboy* for February 1968 ran an article on possible winners of the 1968 presidential election. On a left-hand page was a painting of the president seated at his desk. A blank white box blocked out his head. At the right were portraits of the various candidates boxed in with dotted lines. It was a sort of do-it-yourself spread; the reader presumably was tempted to cut out one of the faces and paste it in place.

The cartoon

The cartoon continues to play an important role—sometimes diversionary, sometimes propagandistic—for many publications. Newspapers run editorial cartoons on their editorial pages to bring current events into sharp, if distorted, focus. And they give over most of a page daily to a selection of comic strips purchased from feature syndicates.

Gag cartoons are largely the province of magazines. Where editorial cartoons and comic strips are done on a salary or contract basis, gag cartoons are done on speculation by freelancers. The cartoon editors on magazines buy them occasionally and keep them ready to drop into holes in the back of the book. These cartoons are used primarily as fillers. But *The New Yorker*, the magazine that really developed this art form in America, continues to use gag cartoons as a principal element of editorial display.

The magazines published in New York have designated

Sam Berman earned a national reputation for his World War II caricatures of Nazi leaders for Collier's. *Later, as head of his own map-making firm, he created the largest global relief map ever made, copies of which sold to more than sixty-five museums and colleges. Now he combines his interest in three-dimensional art with his first love, caricature. The bust of Attorney General John Mitchell was one of a series done for* Lithopinion, *the former graphic arts and public affairs journal of Local One, Amalgamated Lithographers of America.*

Wednesday as market day for cartoonists in the area. On that day, dozens of cartoonists carry their "roughs" from magazine office to magazine office hoping to sell a few of them or at least to get some "O.K."s from editors. But cartoonists sell their work through the mails, too, especially to the smaller, specialized magazines. An editor can pick out what he wants from a batch (a batch consists of about a dozen cartoons) and send the rest back. If he wants them done in a more finished form, he can mark "O.K."s on those he likes and give the cartoonist instructions on what medium to use (ink or ink-and-wash) and indicate whether he wants verticals or horizontals. If nothing in the batch looks promising, the editor simply puts the roughs and a rejection slip into the self-addressed, stamped envelope provided by the cartoonist.

Once the editor uses gag cartoons he may find himself swamped with submissions. Cartoonists can smell a market from clear across the country. To get submissions started, the editor can have his magazine listed at no charge at the end of Jack Markow's regular column on cartooning in *Writer's Digest.*

Editors pay anywhere from $5 to $200 or more per cartoon. A common rate is $20.

Using cartoons effectively

U.S. News & World Report in its September 15, 1975 issue, to go along with an article on New York City's financial crisis, reprints three editorial cartoons under the heading, "As Other Big Cities View It . . ." The "other big cities," identified by 12-point bold all-cap sans-serif subheadings, are Chicago, Los Angeles, and Philadelphia.

The cartoon spread brings up three questions:

1. Does a lone editorial cartoonist accurately represent the "view" of an entire city, especially when, as is true of each of these cities, other editorial cartoonists are there also at work?

It turns out that none of the cartoons is controversial. So no harm done. But the *USN&WR* heading would have been more accurate if it had read: "As Cartoonists in Other Big Cities View It . . ."

2. When a cartoonist's work appears in a newspaper does he, necessarily, represent that newspaper? In the spread under discussion we have Tony Auth identified with the Philadelphia *Inquirer.* Okay. We have Paul Conrad attached to the Los Angeles *Times.* Okay again. But Jeff MacNelly with the Chicago *Tribune?* Records show that this young Pulitzer-prize winner with a wry humor and a dazzling sense of perspective is the cartoonist for the Richmond *News Leader.*

The confusion stems from the syndication of all three cartoonists. *USN&WR* editors did not see the MacNelly cartoon in his home paper, apparently, but did see it in the *Tribune* or

The last two pages of a four-page article on "Autocross: Amateur Indy," in the Second Quarter 1970 issue of The Humble Way, *a 9 × 12 external house organ published by Humble Oil & Refining Company, Houston. The opening spread features an illustration similar to those on this spread. The artwork appears in color, with a sort of 1930s-crayon-look. The copy is set to fit around the illustrations. Note the byline—at the end of the article. Design by Baxter + Korge, Inc.*

notice a Chicago Tribune-New York News Syndicate credit line.

3. Did any of these cartoons carry captions when they appeared in the newspapers? Editorial cartoonists usually—but not always—caption their work. None of the cartoons in the magazine carried a caption. Maybe the magazine just happened to pick three uncaptioned cartoons for this showing. Each reads well enough without a caption: Auth shows an arm, labeled "BEAM," holding a tin cup in which you see a collection of Manhattan buildings; Conrad shows buildings that look like dominoes falling; MacNelly shows a garbage truck, "NEW YORK SANITATION DEPT.," carrying away a skyline of buildings.

But editors are all-too-willing to tamper with a cartoonist's caption—to omit it when it may be necessary to the meaning or to change its wording. It is one thing to change a few words of a manuscript without consulting its author; it is another to change a word or two in a four- or five-word caption. A "minor" caption change may represent a 25 or even 50 percent change in the cartoonist's "manuscript." In this writer's editorial-cartoon days, editors went so far as to completely reverse the intent of the caption—from, say, something negative to something positive—without so much as giving him a chance to change the expressions on the faces. One way a cartoonist can fight this kind of editing is to change the caption to a conversation balloon and put it inside the drawing. At least that makes things more difficult for the nitpicking editor.

Editors should understand that there are two kinds of captions for editorial cartoons: those that represent further comment of the cartoonist and those that represent conversation coming from someone within the cartoon—from the one character with his mouth open. Only in the latter case should quotation marks be used.

In gag cartoons—as distinguished from editorial cartoons—the caption (or gag-line) always carries quote marks.

Captions without quote marks—descriptive captions—belong above a cartoon. Captions in quotes go below.

Other suggestions editors should consider in their use of cartoons:

1. Avoid cropping a cartoon. If it is well drawn—and why buy it if it is not?—it has been deliberately composed for a square or vertical or horizontal showing. An expanse of "unused" foreground in a farm scene, for instance, should not be an open invitation to change a vertical into a horizontal.

2. Do not reduce the cartoon to a size where the reader has to strain to get its message or enjoy its hilarity. The move to miniatures has made a mockery of the comic strips, driving Al Capp, for instance, to using ridiculously intrusive balloons in his daily strips before quitting altogether in late 1977. The move to miniatures must not happen to gag cartoons, the preserve of magazines. Better to run one or two generous-size gag cartoons than a half a dozen postage-stamp ones.

3. Don't consider the cartoon as simply a change of page-texture, a visual oasis in a landscape of body copy. Treat it as you would any other feature in your magazine. Subject it to the same rigid test of usefulness to the reader as you would a piece of copy. Thanks to paper patches and white paint, a cartoon can be corrected by its originator as easily as a piece of copy can be corrected by a writer. Of course, if you are picking up gag cartoons from a NAM clip sheet or some other stock-art source, you can't very well order the adjustments. But you have enough of a choice there to be able to find cartoons that perfectly suit you.

4. Guard against too big a dose of cartoons for a single issue. You know from your own reading of cartoon albums that after a few pages the cartoons begin to lose their punch, even when the collection is from *The New Yorker*. The magazine that brings a half a dozen gag cartoons together on a single spread or the newspaper that crowds several editorial cartoons onto the editorial page is not giving any of the cartoons much chance to make its point. You can make more of a case for bunching *illustrative* cartoons, because they often are more decorative than anything else. They do not compete with one another in the messages they bring.

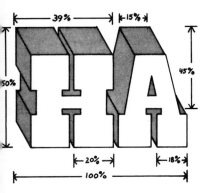

John Simon in one of his theater columns in New York *makes the point that critics should not feel obligated to report on the length or loudness of the laughter of the audience for any given play. "For that you could install laugh-and-applause meters in the theatres and publish graphs instead of reviews." To illustrate the column, Beth Charney letters a laugh complete with some imaginary measurements.*

Charts, graphs, tables, and maps

When the text matter deals with statistics, you can amplify, clarify, or summarize them with charts, graphs, or tables. Purely abstract thoughts and information already simple enough to understand do not lend themselves to charts, graphs, or tables, but almost everything else does. What you need to look for is what Matthew P. Murgio in *Communications Graphics* has described as a "visual handle."

You can use a *flow chart* to show how machinery works, an *organization chart* to show how a company functions, a *line graph* or *bar chart* to show growth in numbers over a given period of time, or a *pie chart* to show percentages of a whole.

Ordinary charts and graphs are clear enough, but an artist can heighten their impact by changing them to *pictographs*: drawings in which lines, bars, or circles have been converted to representational art shown in perspective. For instance, he can draw people in place of bars or a silver dollar in place of a pie chart. But when using pictographs you must make certain the scale is not distorted.[6]

You can make a *table* more useful by careful organization of material and skillful use of color, tint blocks, and rules. (See the tables carried in *U.S. News & World Report.*)

You can add drama to a *map* by showing it in perspective, by showing its topography as well as its outline, or by simplifying and stylizing its outline. It may even be desirable to distort a map to make a point (provided the reader understands), as one of the airlines did in its advertising in the late 1960s to dramatize the fact that its fast planes had brought Europe and America closer together.

Hendrik Hertzberg built an entire book around a single graph—page after page of dots, one million of them. "This book is a yardstick, a ruler divided into a million parts instead of a dozen," he said in his introduction. "The chief value of the book is as an aid to comprehension, and to contemplation. By riffling slowly through its pages, the reader may discover precisely what is meant by one million." At various intervals the reader finds a blank spot where a dot is supposed to be; a line runs from that blank spot out into the margin, and there the dot is reproduced with a caption. Dot No. 2, for instance, represents the "Population of the Garden of Eden," Dot No. 46,399 the "Number of times the word 'and' appears in the King James Bible," Dot No. 407,316 the number of "U.S. soldiers killed in World War II."[7]

To illustrate "What a Way to Make a Living," an article about the injuries suffered by the running backs in professional football, *Sports Illustrated* for November 16, 1970, ran a drawing of a player, standing, facing to the front. The various injuries to the players were listed at the side. Ruled lines connected the various listings to various parts of the body, allowing readers to see at a glance where the concentration of injuries was. The

6. See Darrell Huff's *How to Lie with Statistics,* W. W. Norton & Company, Inc., New York, 1954.

7. See Hendrik Hertzberg, *One Million,* Simon & Schuster, Inc., New York, 1970.

diagram in a minimum amount of space summarized information that, in ordinary prose, would have taken a lot more space and told the story a lot less vividly.

In this set of nine faces, used on the cover of a college catalog, designer Jim Bodoh of the University of Oregon was careful to pick faces to represent all classes of students. The faces started out as regular photographs, but the reproduction called for was line. Then, on his prints, Bodoh did some retouching to dramatize some of the shapes. And of course he gave careful attention to cropping in every case. Note the beautiful pattern he gets out of the face in the lower right-hand corner: the relationships between the highlighted face, the earring, and the collar.

Photographs or illustrations?

Early in this century magazine illustrators became important persons in building circulations for magazines. People became much more familiar with art in magazines than in museums. The most popular magazine artist of all, of course, was Norman Rockwell, who did a total of 317 covers for *The Saturday Evening Post.* One estimate had it that each of his covers was seen by 4,000,000 persons.

But illustrators whose work appeared *inside* the magazines became popular, too. Charles Dana Gibson, who drew for *Life, Collier's,* and *Harper's Weekly,* set the standard for the beautiful girl in America. Stephen Becker in *Comic Art in America* said that "From the early nineties to the First World War, the Gibson Girl was the American ideal: women imitated her, men desired her."

Illustrators enjoyed a "golden age" in the 1930s, 1940s, and early 1950s. But in the mid-1950s, their magazine market shriveled. Magazines were hard-hit by that new medium, television, and in their search for a new identity they turned to the camera. Fiction was no longer a major part of magazines; nonfiction seemed better served by photographs. Illustrators, if they got magazine assignments at all, had to offer something the camera could not. One illustrator, Mark English, remarked in an interview in *The National Observer:* "The camera has helped the artist see the direction he shouldn't be going in."

No doubt about it: the camera put many illustrators out of work. Art directors preferred photographs because they were more realistic, when realism was important; and they were more readily available and at less cost. Furthermore, the photographer gave the art director a choice of many poses and scenes.

But there was some evidence that the illustration had made a comeback. Donald Holden, art book editor for Watson-Guptill Publications, said that photography "is becoming a very fatiguing medium." Art directors, he observed, were constantly looking for new ways to use the camera; using it in focus, using it out of focus, changing the angle. "I sense a certain desperateness in their efforts," he said." . . . The fatigue factor may force the art director to rediscover illustration."

Fiction did not return in the 1970s but think pieces multiplied, and illustrations seem better suited to these than photographs. "Although concept photography can be employed it's usually easier to draw symbols than to photograph them," says designer John Peter.

Peter points out that the old illustration devoted itself to narrative or incident while the new devotes itself to spirit or mood.

The return of illustration was, to him, inevitable. Proliferating magazines need special identity, and they can get it more obviously with illustration than with photography. "Photography has many assets, but it takes an expert to recognize the styles of even the most distinctive photographers. To a reader a photograph is a photograph."

Peter quotes illustrator Cliff Condak as saying:

I think photography is great. But I think also there is something of an anonymous look [in photography]. I don't really mean anonymous in a derogatory way, but there is something about illustration that is warmer and individual—that a human being has done it. Maybe just from that standpoint alone people are starting to appreciate illustration again.[8]

James McMullan, a well-known illustrator with ties to Push Pin Studios and later his own organization, Visible Studio Inc., saw the field of illustration in the 1970s as "chaotic but fertile. There is an increased interest in illustration, many new players in the game, and an almost confusing assortment of new clients."

The art director plays an important role in setting standards. "Illustration can only rise to the level of taste of those that commission it," says McMullan.[9]

Unlike earlier decades, the 1970s saw many styles existing at one time. No longer did a few big general-circulation magazines set the standards. The many small, specialized magazines were willing to experiment. Some of the material was awful—James McMullan could visualize young art directors calling buddies from high school art classes to give them their chances—but some of it was great.

Illustration suffered a setback with *Esquire's* Christmas 1976 issue when the magazine, known for its imaginative use of illustrations, went to an all-photograph format. Photographs were to be used to illustrate both articles and short stories. "Illustrations created too many problems," said art director Jane Prettyman. "We wanted a more consistent look, with a stronger feeling."[10]

In his days on *Look*, Allen Hurlburt preferred photographs to illustrations, but *Look*, like *Life*, was essentially a photographic magazine. Even on *Look*, Hurlburt saw situations where illustrations were called for. For instance: carrying a camera sometimes

8. See John Peter, "The Re-emergence of the Illustrator," *Folio*, October 1976, pp. 76-83.
9. James McMullan, "Illustration's New Clientele," *DA*, vol. 62, no. 4, 1976, p. 14.
10. "Esquire Nixes Illustrations," *Art Direction*, December 1976, p. 73.

can be dangerous or even illegal, or sometimes it is difficult or impossible to gain model releases. An example of Hurlburt's imaginative approach to illustration was his commissioning of Norman Rockwell to do a series of paintings on integration. Hurlburt reasoned that because Rockwell had so long been trusted and admired by the middle class as an upholder of traditional American values, his work in this area would be all the more effective.

Now that we have some photographers who have abandoned realism for abstraction and we have some painters who have come back to realism—in some cases to hyperrealism—the line between photography and illustration is blurred. It's still the policy of most art directors to order photography for nonfiction and illustrations for fiction, but that is no hard-and-fast rule. An obvious exception is the use of cartoons to illustrate a piece of nonfiction on, say, human foibles.

So the only answer the art director can give to the question, Should we use photographs or illustrations? has to be: It depends.

Realism or abstraction?

The penchant for realism in art goes back a long way. The closer a piece of art was to real life, the better. *Time* tells the story of Zeuxis, fifth century, B.C., Greek artist, competing with another artist to see who could paint the most realistic picture. When his painting of grapes was unveiled, birds flew down and pecked at them. Surely he had won. But when the judges started to unveil the other painting, they were stunned. *The veil was the painting.* Zeuxis had fooled the birds, but his opponent had fooled the judges.

The coming of photography in the 1800s brought into question the idea that art was imitation. The camera was an instrument that could do the job better. So, many artists assumed a new role. Art became more than imitation; it became something with a value of its own.

Abstraction followed. Not that artists had not worked in abstractions before. But now abstraction became a dominant movement in art. Eventually, almost anything could pass for art: pieces of junk, objects that moved, combinations of common artifacts.

Not everyone was impressed. A writer in *True* told the story of a man who told Pablo Picasso that he didn't like modern paintings because they weren't realistic. When the man later showed Picasso a snapshot of his girl friend, Picasso asked: "My word, is she really as small as all that?"

With the Armory Show in 1913, when modern art made its debut in America, artists favoring realism as an art form went into a decline, as far as the critics were concerned. But the average person continued to admire the Norman Rockwell kind of artist. Late in his career, perhaps because Americans then enjoyed a "vogue for the old,"[11] partly because Andrew Wyeth had made realism respectable again, Rockwell staged a comeback in the magazines. And at least two major books came out offering his collected works—at premium prices. Even the critics reassessed the man.

"It is difficult for the art world to take the people's choice very seriously, almost impossible if that choice has ignored all approved innovations," wrote Thomas Buechner, director of the Brooklyn Museum. "But Rockwell is the choice. He's the best of his kind and to some of us that's what art is all about."

He added: "If the democratization of the arts is to avoid the ultimate absurdity of accepting everything and therefore nothing, it must take Rockwell into account. He has the artist's capacity to communicate with people—lots of them—rather than simply to innovate for a historically oriented elite."[12]

Art as it has appeared in magazines has been slow to give up realism. Only in recent years have magazines made the move toward abstraction. But now the leaders among them and the smaller, specialized magazines, too, seem willing to experiment with any art form that can stand up to the printing process.

It would be difficult—certainly this book will not attempt it—to make a case for one kind of art as preferable to another. There is a place for all kinds of art in American magazines. For some magazines, for some articles, for some audiences—realism would be the ideal choice. In other circumstances, abstract art would be preferable. For some magazines the art might best follow current trends. For others, the art director might encourage among his contributors a highly original approach.

All these approaches in art are defensible. What you must guard against as an art director is making decisions based entirely on your own taste of preference without regard for the needs of the article or story and the preferences of your readers.

Art teacher Marilyn McKenzie Chaffee shows how to make a realistic portrait by pasting down pieces of black paper where she wants deep shadows and pieces of printed body copy where she wants lighter shadows. The technique is particularly appropriate for this portrait: it is of Graham Greene, the writer.

The purpose of art

Art can be used merely to set a mood. It can be used merely to decorate. It can also have a more specific purpose. It can (1) restate or amplify the text or (2) "make a separate statement," to use Dugald Stermer's phrasing. He likes the "separate statement" idea. So does William Hamilton Jones, editor of the *Yale Alumni News.*

"I really think photography should give an article an addi-

11. See the December 28, 1970, issue of *Newsweek.*

12. Thomas Buechner, "If We All Like It, Is It Art?" *Life,* November 3, 1970, p. 16.

tional dimension," he says. "You can follow one line of thought in your text and you can deal with another in your visual material, and they'll reinforce each other and each will add to the dimensions of the other."

But there is a question in this approach. An illustration *illustrates*; it does not exist of itself. If it does, it is something else. Perhaps it is all a matter of placement on the page. If the illustration or photograph makes "a separate statement," the reader can, one supposes, consider it a separate feature. What we have then inside the original feature is one that is not illustrated.

And that isn't necessarily bad.

Style

Art style preferences change—for magazine art as well as gallery art. At the turn of the century the look was Art Nouveau: sinuous, decorative, curvy. In the 1920s the Bauhaus made its influence felt; the look was orderly, geometric, functional. The Bauhaus look never did die out. It took a slightly more elegant turn in the 1950s with the introduction of Swiss design: the magazine page was still tightly organized, but some of the stiffness was gone.

Art Nouveau made a comeback in the 1960s, as did almost every art style. The 1960s were a decade of revival and experimentation. Among the new styles: Op Art, with its illusions in color and shape; Pop Art, with its attachment to the comic strip and high-Camp packaging; and the psychedelic look, with its sliding blobs of color in weird combinations, its illegible typefaces expanded, condensed, and contorted to fit curved spaces. Fortunately for readers, many of these styles died young.

For their art and their design—when it comes to style it's hard to separate the two—magazine art directors in the late 1960s turned increasingly to the 1920s and 1930s for inspiration. They simplified line and form, chose pastel rather than bold colors,

An example of Art Nouveau. From The Studio.

To execute this small-town winter scene, Prof. Glenn Hanson of the University of Illinois Department of Journalism uses nylon-tip pens and, finally, some Zipatone at the top for the sky. Hanson's composition leads you right into the center of the picture. He makes use of a low horizon line to give you almost a worm's-eye view. He provides three distinct textures: the Zipatone dot-pattern, the tree-top lace-pattern, and the horizontal-line pattern for the shading on the buildings and the shadows in the snow.

arranged type and art symmetrically rather than asymmetrically. Much of the art took on a rainbow motif. Futura typefaces were back. Bevis Hillier in a book in 1968 called the look "Art Deco." (The *Deco* was short for *decoration*.)

If one had to use a single term to describe the art that came out of Push Pin Studios, the term might well be "Art Deco." Magazines that at the beginning of the 1970s had an Art Deco look included *Evergreen Review, Rags, Gentlemen's Quarterly*, and, to a lesser extent, *Avant Garde*. [13]

Technique

Preferences in technique change, too. Brush painting, pallet knife painting, wash drawing, line drawing, scratchboard drawing, pencil drawing, felt- and nylon-tip drawing: they all have a place. Some techniques require tight handling, some a loose flair. Every imaginable tool is used on every kind of surface. In the 1960s, for instance, many illustrators were working in washes on glossy paper not meant to take washes. This resulted in tones that seemed to shrivel, like water on an oily surface.

Print in the late 1960s thought illustrators were preoccupied with techniques—at the expense of content. Maybe so. But illustrators need to constantly experiment with their styles and techniques, and art directors should encourage them to do so.

Design of the art

Art directors cannot agree what style is best for magazines or what techniques best do the job. They cannot agree on whether art should be realistic or abstract. But they can agree on this: *The illustration should be well designed.* The principles of design that govern the arrangement of type and illustration on a page or spread also govern the placement of figures, props, and background within an illustration. Every illustration, from the crudest cartoon to the finest painting, should be well designed.

To most art directors, design in illustration is more important than draftsmanship.

Reproducing the art

In working with line art, you should see to it that it all takes the same reduction. This is desirable not only to save costs but also to keep consistent the strength of the artist's line. It is not a good idea to use both fine-line art and thick-line art in the same feature. This means that you must decide where you want big

One way an artist can get tone into a line drawing is by doing the art in ink on textured paper and then using a grease crayon for shading. This is Horace Greeley, drawn by the author on Glarco No. 12 paper.

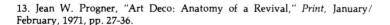

13. Jean W. Progner, "Art Deco: Anatomy of a Revival," *Print*, January/February, 1971, pp. 27-36.

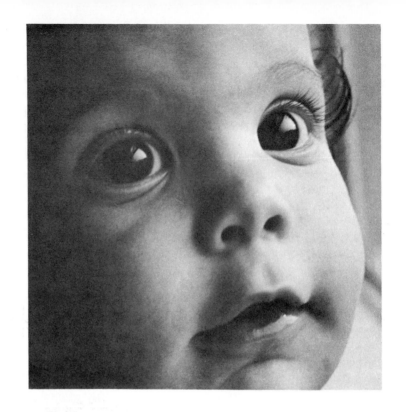

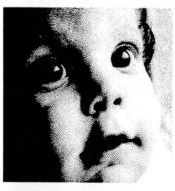

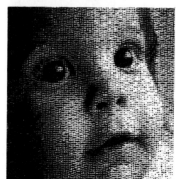

The original photograph printed as a normal-screen halftone and, in a smaller size, four line art conversions: random dot (top left), spiral (top right), mesh (bottom left), and wavy line (bottom right). (Courtesy of Line Art Unlimited, Princeton, New Jersey.)

art and where you want small art before giving out your assignments.

Line art—and halftone art, too—generally turns out best when reduced to about two-thirds of original size. The slight imperfections or irregularities are thus minimized. For a change of pace, though, you ought to try *blowing up* in size your line artwork. This adds greatly to its strength and sometimes gives the art a refreshingly crude, bold look it doesn't have in its original state.

One of the advantages of line art over halftone art is that line art, at least when it is run actual size, always comes out as the art director expects. With a halftone, you can never be quite sure.

Art directors soon learn that a photograph that has the necessary qualities to hang in an art gallery is not always the photograph that reproduces well. Some art directors feel that a photograph a little on the gray side reproduces better than one a little on the black side. Sometimes the photoengraver or offset cameraman can bring out a gray photograph by overexposing it; there is not much they can do with an already overexposed print.

You must choose your photographs not so much on the basis of how well they look in hand as on the basis of how well they will reproduce. Only long experience with photographs can really teach you this.

Art directors used to salvage unsatisfactory photographs by retouching them, but this is not done as much as formerly. Thanks to the 35 mm camera, you have many prints to choose from.

Photographs do not reproduce well in letterpress unless a fine screen is used in making the halftone and a smooth paper is used in the printing. Newspaper halftones are often inferior to magazine halftones because newspapers, at least the big ones, are printed letterpress on cheap, rough-textured newsprint. The screen used to make each plate has to be coarse; otherwise the paper stock would not be able to receive it. As a consequence, much of the detail is lost.

The ordinary newspaper halftone takes a 65-line screen, the magazine halftone a 133-line screen. Offset lithography makes possible the use of finer screens—for both newspapers and magazines.

For four-color process work, offset printers often use a 150-line screen, better than a 133-line screen but still not as fine as they can go. The new offset process can handle a 200-line screen, and art directors should ask that such a screen be used, especially if they are using coated stock.

Polaroid has made it possible for photographers working for offset publications to produce their own prescreened halftones, ready for pasteup as line art. It makes available a camera that houses its own screen in any coarseness, from 45 to 133 lines. The Polaroid camera is not an ideal camera for newspaper or magazine work—it is bulkier than a 35 mm, does not have the accessories, and the pictures it produces are sometimes flatter than those made with other cameras—but for small weekly newspapers, especially, the prescreen feature may more than compensate for these disadvantages.

While the usual halftone for both letterpress and offset appears in a dot pattern, newer developments in both photo preparation and photo reproduction make possible halftones in various line patterns and textures. *Newsweek,* when it did a cover story entitled, "Does TV Tell It Straight?" ran photographs of four TV newsmen—all in ruled-line halftones. Because the photos were cut to a shape resembling a TV screen, the pattern related the halftones even more meaningfully to the subject.

Sometimes the art director must use—may prefer to use—an already-screened halftone. If his publication is offset, he can paste the halftone repro proof in place along with the type repros, and the printer will treat it as line art.

If the screened halftone is from a newspaper, he may find the screening too coarse for his needs. He should then have the halftone reduced. This will bring the dots closer together, making the picture clearer.

If the halftone is not clear or the screening is too fine, it may be necessary to rescreen it. In rescreening, the platemaker must make sure he avoids a moire pattern—a sort of swirl—in the final print. Sometimes you get a moire pattern even when working with an original photograph, as when a figure in that photograph wears a suit or dress with a pronounced pattern. The platemaker may be able to eliminate the moire in a second

When a magazine reproduces paintings, especially fine arts paintings, it should not change their basic proportions. Nelson Gruppo, art director for Famous Artists Magazine, *faced this problem when he designed this four-page feature. He devotes one page to each of four artists, and on the first page he is able to add two paragraphs of general introduction without disturbing the organizational pattern. He is also able to combine different kinds of mug shots. Note that the second two pages repeat the title, not in the display face but in the body face, and in a size slightly smaller than body type size. Columns are unjustified.*

shooting by adjusting the angle of the screen.

Art directors have a number of ways to turn an ordinary photograph into something that looks like the work of an illustrator or painter. The most common practice—it has almost become a cliché—is to make a line reproduction from the photograph rather than a halftone reproduction. The platemaker simply handles the photograph as if it were a line drawing. He doesn't use a screen. What happens is: all the middle tones of gray drop out. You get a high-contrast print—stark, dramatic, bold. And sections of it, if desired, can easily be painted out or retouched. A variation is to take the bold line art and screen it to, say, 60 percent of black or combine it with a block of solid second color.

You can get an unusual effect, too, by ordering his halftone in a jumbo size screen, so that the dots are much larger than normal. From a distance, the art looks like a photograph. Up close, it looks like a piece of Pop Art.

Photography in magazines

The halftone was developed in the 1880s. One of the first magazines to use halftones regularly was the *National Geographic*, beginning in 1903. The photographs in this magazine even today are technically superior to those in other magazines. Interestingly enough, *National Geographic*, for all its stodginess, is remembered by some for its photographs of female breasts in an age when other magazines recoiled at such photographs. The girls of course were always dark-skinned natives of foreign countries. One writer observes,

. . . During the grim nineteen-thirties and forties, curious youth turned to *The Geographic*. Certain pictures are burned deep into the

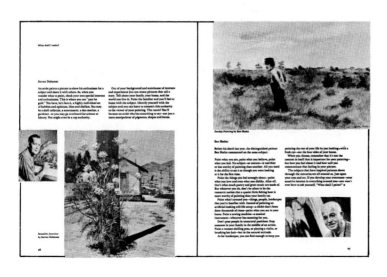

Before the square-format Lines *dropped its personals to be included in another publication, it ran a separate page—what the high school yearbooks call a "divider page"—to introduce the special section. It was a photo over which was superimposed the names of the reporters who were submitting news items from each of the branches. In its original printed state, the page was a bleed duotone. Notice how the designer has arranged his columns to follow the lines of the building.* Lines *is published by Reliance Insurance Companies.*

brain of countless thousands of men who were adolescents in those years. . . . [Some of the photographs were] the stuff of multidimensional sexual fantasy beside whom the girls in *Playboy* are poor plastic things indeed.[14]

Life's contribution to the development of photography in magazines was undoubtedly greater than *National Geographic's.* Started in 1936 as a sort of illustrated *Time, Life* gradually changed from a news magazine to a magazine of special features. More than any other publication it developed the idea of photojournalism: great photographs taken on the spot, where and when important things were happening. Sometimes the photographs merely reported, sometimes they expressed a form of opinion. Often their greatness was accidental.

Acting as moderator of a seminar sponsored by the American Society of Magazine Editors in 1969, Harold Hayes, editor of *Esquire,* noted the demise of photojournalism. TV has killed photojournalism, he said.

What's important for magazines these days, he said, is photographic *art.* Photographs shouldn't just be *shot;* they should be *arranged*—by art directors and photographers working together.

There are those who would argue with this. They point out that photographs are nothing more, nothing less, than a journalistic tool. Like written journalism, the photograph informs, expresses opinion, entertains. Let those photographers who would do their own thing or make their "statements" do it—but not for publication.

A lot of readers and some editors and art directors disapprove of some of the recent trends in photography.

The magazines' infatuation with blurred photographs in the early 1970s became the subject of some satire in *Saturday Review.* "What has happened," wrote Dereck Williamson,

. . . is that the improperly exposed and badly focused photograph has become Art. The bad picture is now good, and the good picture is bad. For amateur 35-millimeter photographers like myself, this is distressing news. For years I've been culling my slides and throwing away Art.

Many of my mistakes would now be worth big money in the modern magazine market place.

He cites a number of his culls, including "One Tennis Shoe, with Kneecap," "Child Unrolling Agfachrome at High Noon," and "Daughter's Birthday Party with Failing Flashcube." His "Giant Redwoods and Finger," had it been sent to a magazine, would have been accepted and probably captioned: "A personal statement of the photographer concerning man's ruthless attitude

14. Tom Buckley, "With the National Geographic on its Endless, Cloudless Voyage," *The New York Times Magazine,* September 6, 1970, p. 20.

Robert N. Essman, art director of *People,* notes a deterioration in photography submitted to magazines. Photographs to him these days seem too precious, as though they were taken for museum showing rather than publication. And often when the pictures are good, the focus is bad. "Why not focus clearly?" he asks. "Is there a course being given somewhere that now teaches one how to take out-of-focus pictures?"

There are still plenty of art directors who insist on sharply focused, well-lighted photographs. Editors and art directors like them because they say things that need to be said. And they are readily available. While only a few persons can turn out usable drawings or paintings, almost anyone can turn out publishable photographs, not the kind that would delight the heart of a W. Eugene Smith, perhaps, but publishable nevertheless. To many, photography represents "instant art"; and everyone can participate. Out of thousands upon thousands of routine photographs, there just have to be some that, if they don't qualify as works of art, at least have enough clarity or meaning to justify reproduction in some publication.

Among the most popular courses offered on college campuses these days—and in the high schools, too—are the courses in photography. Moholy-Nagy once said, prophetically: "The illiterate of the future will be the man who does not know how to take a photograph."

The photo essay

For many years the photograph, like the painting or drawing, was used merely to *illustrate* an article or story. It still is used that way. But in the 1930s some editors, especially those at *Life,* worked out an additional use for photographs, putting them into a spread or a series of spreads and letting them tell their own story, sometimes without captions. The photo essay was born.

Like a piece of prose, a photo essay has a story to tell or a point to make. The pictures all revolve around a central theme. They may be uniform in size, or they may vary greatly in both size and shape. There is always a key photograph for the series, but there may be a sub-key photograph for each spread, too. It is up to the art director to unify the photographs.

Any combination of pictures is likely to say something different from what each picture by itself says. The sum is different from its parts. So as an art director you must share with the photographer the responsibility for developing the theme of the essay. The order of presentation and the juxtaposition of one picture with another greatly affect what the essay says.

15. Dereck Williamson, "Shutter Shudders," Phoenix Nest column of *Saturday Review,* December 5, 1970, p. 4.

Deciding on photographs

You should make sure the photographer fully understands any assignment and knows how the pictures will be used, whether for illustration or essay purposes.

If you want to emphasize height, you should direct the photographer to take his picture from a worm's-eye angle. If you want to show an item in context with its surrounding, you may ask for a bird's-eye view.

Often a photograph does not tell the complete story unless scale is included. A photograph of a tree seedling may not mean much unless a knife or shovel or some other item whose size is understood is included in the picture. When *Posh,* the quarterly published by P & O Lines, Inc., ran an article on sculptures in miniature, the art director saw to it that photographs showed the various pieces held in hands. Closeup shots were made from different angles to heighten interest.

As art director you should insist on a wide selection of prints. Contact sheets are good enough. You can study the prints with an 8-power magnifier. You should ask for more blowups than you can use—three or four times as many—because no matter how well you read the prints, you'll see new things when they're bigger. You should have some choices at that level, too.

When *Time* decided to devote a cover story to air pollution for its January 27, 1967, issue, 23 photographers were sent out and kept shooting for three days. In all, the team shot 160 rolls of black-and-white and color film. When it was all over, when all the selections had been made, the magazine used only 13 shots, including the shot for the cover. *People,* the relatively new Time-Life publication, uses up to 100 black and white photographs an issue. They come into the magazine from all over. You can imagine how many the editors look at before settling on the 100. *Arizona Highways* works with 45 photographers every issue.

Other magazines can't afford such luxury of choice. Small magazines often settle for the single picture or two that are available. Often the art director uses a picture he knows is inferior; but it is the only one that is offered him.

Sometimes he has two or three excellent shots, but there is not much difference among them in camera angle, camera distance, or subject matter. He should resist the impulse to use them all. Redundancy spoils good photography.

There is some merit, however, in using a series of similar shots of an individual who is the subject of an interview. A series of photographs tells the reader more about the interviewee than a single photograph can. Besides, the several similar pictures give the reader a nice feel of visual continuity.

When he needs a mug shot to go with an article or story and he has several to choose from, the art director should choose the one which has an expression appropriate to the mood of the article. The reader can't help being puzzled when, while reading about someone involved in a tragedy, he sees the person with a silly grin on his face. At the least the reader should be made to realize, perhaps in the caption, that the picture was taken on some earlier occasion.

Color photography

For certain kinds of magazines—those dealing with exquisite scenery and luxurious travel, for instance—full-color photography is a must. But, as chapter 4 points out, it is expensive.

Another problem with full-color photography is that it makes *everything* look beautiful. By focusing close, the photographer makes the pattern and the splash of color more important than the content of his picture. Ugly things, like filth washing up on a river bank, become works of art to be admired. For this reason, the art director, even when he can afford color, chooses to stay with black and white for some of his features.

Photographic clichés

While any pose, from any angle, with any focus, can find a place in today's magazines, certain pictures, at least in ordinary usage, should be avoided by the art director if for no other reason than that they have been used too often. These pictures include the following poses:

1. people shaking hands during award ceremonies.
2. public officials signing proclamations and other papers.
3. people studying documents.
4. people pointing to maps, to trees, to anything.
5. committees at work.
6. public speakers at the rostrum.

But even the photographic cliché has its place in well-designed magazines. The fact that a picture may be "Camp" might be reason enough to run it. Or maybe the nature of the article calls for a photograph that, under other circumstances, would be considered as too stilted to use. Magazine art directors of the early 1970s seemed more willing than in the past to run group shots, with subjects looking straight ahead into the lens of the camera.

The Western Art Directors Club in a publicity stunt in 1970 got away with a photographic cliché when it sent out a formal group shot of newly-elected officers. All persons but one were looking straight ahead into the camera, painfully serious. One,

The accepting-the-award picture will, unfortunately, always be with us, and in many cases it will be in a form no less awkward than this.

in the middle of the front row, had his back facing the camera. He was the outgoing president.

Handling photographs

When finally laying out the pages, you work with 8 × 10 glossies. Using a grease crayon, you make your crop marks in the margin. You do not write on the backs of photos for fear of denting the front surfaces. Dents, bends, and folds show up in the final printing.

You should be particularly careful in your handling of transparencies. When a black-and-white print is lost, a new one can be made easily. But when a transparency is lost, all is lost.

In indicating sizes to the photographer or printer, you always give width first, then depth. (The British do it just the opposite.) You can make sure there is no misunderstanding when you write down a size by marking a short horizontal line above the width and a short vertical line above the depth.

Cropping photographs

Most art directors feel they can improve on the original composition of photographs, dramatize them, make them more "readable," change the emphasis, by cropping—cutting away unnecessary detail and background. This is the age of the closeup. It is also the age of the strongly vertical or the strongly horizontal shape—anything to get away from the rectangle of average proportions.

Much of this cropping is good. But some of it is unnecessary and, worse, destructive of good photography. What appears to be monotonous background or foreground may be vital to a photograph's proportion.

You must never crop a photograph of a painting. The reader assumes that when he sees one in a magazine he is seeing it in its entirety. But it is acceptable to run only a section of a painting and label it as a detail from the original.

Doctoring photographs

Inexperienced art directors often cut photographs into odd shapes because squares and rectangles are "monotonous." These art directors make the mistake of thinking that readers are more interested in shape than in content.

Nothing—nothing—beats the rectangle or square as a shape for a photograph. A circle, a triangle, a star, a free form—these may have occasional impact; but as a general rule, they should be avoided. If you want some added impact you can crop your photographs into extremely wide or tall rectangles.

Some art directors like to outline their photographs with thin black lines, but the edge formed by the photograph itself is usually best.

A silhouette halftone—the reproduction of a photograph in which a figure is outlined against a pure white background— provides an effective change of pace for the art director. The silhouette is much preferred to the photograph with doctored edges because it does not represent shape for the sake of shape; it emphasizes content. A single silhouette can be used for contrast on a spread of photographs in the usual rectangular and square shapes.

If you feel that one element in a picture should "walk out" from the rest of the picture, you can put that element—or part of it—into a silhouette and square off the rest of the picture.

When silhouetting (also referred to as outlining) a photograph, you may find it necessary to do your own cutting or opaquing. You should be sure the figure or object in the photograph is large enough to take the silhouetting. You should avoid intricate silhouettes, such as a girl with windblown hair.

Bleeding photographs

Bleeding photographs—running them off the edge of the page— tends to dramatize them and make them appear larger than they really are. Not only does a bleed picture occupy extra white space that would be used as margins; it also seems to stretch beyond the page. There is no optical fence to contain it.

Generally speaking, only large photographs should be bled. It is never advisable to bleed small mug shots. Nor is it necessary, when you use bleeds, to bleed consistently throughout the magazine. Sometimes a combination of bleed and nonbleed pictures is best.

You must order your halftones with an extra one-eighth to one-quarter inch strip (final halftone size) for each edge that bleeds. Because extra trimming may be involved and an oversize sheet must be used, the printer may charge more for bleed pages.

Art directors favor bleeding for a while, then abandon the practice, then pick it up again.

The practice of running boxes around photographs flourishes for a while, then dies out, then comes back again. In some cases, the lines are more than lines; they are bold bars, butted up against the photograph's edges. A variation is the boxing of silhouetted photographs, as practiced especially by the Sunday New York *Times* in its "Week in Review" section.

Flopping photographs

You may be tempted to flop a photograph—change its facing—if it seems to point off a page. But this is tricky business.

Flop a portrait, and the part in the hair is on the wrong side. The suit is buttoned on the wrong side. If a sign is included in the picture, it will read from right to left.

Scholastic Editor once ran a photograph of the cover of *Onondagan*, the yearbook of Syracuse University. On the yearbook's cover was a picture of a light switch turned on. The "ON" in caps showed plainly (*On* is a shortened version of the yearbook's name). But for the sake of a facing, the editor of *Scholastic Editor* flopped his photograph. And the "ON" came out reading "NO."

Arranging photos on the page

It might be useful here to consider chapter 5's design principles as they apply to the use of photographs.

To bring order to your pages, you should use fewer pictures—perhaps fewer than you would consider desirable—and you should use them in large sizes. A large photograph is many times more effective than a smaller one. The impact does not increase arithmetically; it increases by geometric progression.

Big photographs also save money. It costs as much to take a small picture as it does to take a big one. As much thinking and effort go into a small picture.

For the sake of unity, you should bring related photographs together in your layout. Organization for content is more important than organization based on the way photographs happen to face.

When you use several photographs per page or spread, you should place the closeups at the bottom because this conforms more naturally to the way we see things in perspective. You

Because this nearly full-page photograph appeared on a left-hand page of a college magazine, the editor flopped it to make it face the gutter. But in the process he made a left-hander out of singer-guitarist Ric Masten, changed the arrangement of strings on his guitar, buttoned the man's shirt the wrong way, and moved the pocket over to the other side. It would have been much better to let the picture face off the page. The flopping was made all the more ludicrous by a picture elsewhere on the spread that showed Masten playing the guitar in his normal way—from his right side.

should keep your photographs all the same size—or you should make them obviously different in size. You want to avoid making them almost—but not quite—equal. In most cases you would have some large, some middle-size, some small photographs; and you would combine squares with rectangles, and among your rectangles you would have some horizontals and some verticals.

It is not a good idea to run full-page pictures on both left- and right-hand pages, especially if they bleed on three sides and run into the gutter. The two then appear to be a single, massive, photograph. A small band of white should separate them at the gutter.

Here is a summary of techniques for combining several photographs on a page, unifying them and yet allowing them to stand separately:

1. *Run a small band of white between them.* The band may vary in width, or it can stay the same throughout the spread. Art directors used to prefer separations of no more than an eighth of an inch, but now they seem to prefer a wider band: a quarter of an inch or more.

2. *Butt the photos up against each other.* This works well if the photos are of different sizes; some of the photo edges will be printed against a field of white. Some art directors like to run a thin black line where the photographs join.

3. *Overlap the photos.* This means cutting mortises into photos and slipping portions of other photos into the holes. The overlap can fit snugly. Or it can have a small white line around it to help separate one photo from the other.

Overlapping is not always desirable because it calls attention to shape rather than content. When you overlap, you get photos

Captions under or right next to photographs make things easy for the reader, but it is sometimes necessary, from a design standpoint, to run photographs together as a unit, uninterrupted by type. These beautiful full-color photographs form one bleed unit on the right-hand page of a two-page spread; only a thin white line separates them from each other. This reproduction may not show it clearly, but the one caption for the pictures appears on the left-hand page, about in the middle of the third column, in a slightly smaller, different type, printed in blue ink. Nor was it necessary to number the photographs so the caption could point to them. The caption starts out this way: "Clockwise from upper left:." The reader has no trouble finding his way. The pages, part of a six-page article, are from Exxon USA, published by the Exxon Company, U.S.A., Houston. Downs Matthews, editor; Richard Payne, art director.

that are *L*- or *U*-shaped. This spoils the composition of the photos, even when what is mortised out appears to be unimportant foreground or sky.

The usual overlap allows only one of the photographs to print in the shared area. For an unusual effect you can print one photograph in black, one in color, without bothering to mortise; you can let them both show. Or you can print one photograph in one color, one in another, and where they overlap he will get a third color.

4. *Fit one photo inside the other.* You can do this when the center of interest of the base photograph is concentrated in one area. Your base photograph would be one you would otherwise crop. The smaller photo would fit into an internal mortise. Again it could fit snugly, or it could carry a thin white outline.

Fitting captions to pictures

You should use as much care in the placement of captions as in the placement of the photographs themselves. You can line captions up against an edge—or both edges—of the photograph, or you can line them up against an edge inside the photograph. Captions should fit up close to the photographs they describe so that the reader will have no trouble correctly associating them.

Captions give photographs an additional dimension.

They can tell what happened before the picture was taken. Or what happened afterwards.

Mug shots almost always need captions. When a magazine runs a mug shot with a standing column, the reader can't tell whether the picture is of the columnist or the person being written about unless the shot carries a caption.

West High School, Iowa City, Iowa, found it possible in an issue of its newsmagazine to fully identify all its seniors shown in a large and rather informal group shot by including a tracing with the printed photograph. A long caption referred to the numbers in the faces. The artist gave the line drawing a photographic look by using Zipatone to imitate the tones of the photographs. The line drawing ran slightly smaller and just below the photograph.

Nation's Cities uses a piece of line art to supply visual interest to a right-hand opener, and then, where the article continues, reuses part of the art to help the reader adjust to the new page. Actually, the magazine reuses two *parts of the art—the bottom five figures and two more figures ahead of them in the line. Art directors are Louise Levine and Evelyn Sanford.*

Is art necessary?

Not every article and story needs art in the traditional sense. Carefully selected display typography, tastefully arranged with generous amounts of white space, can be art enough.

Some subjects simply do not lend themselves to art. A subject can be too momentous, too tragic, too lofty. Art would be at best redundant, at worse anticlimactic.

And when an art director can't afford art or finds he has on hand for a particular feature only mediocre-quality photography, he should be willing to design his pages without art. A quiet, even stilted page is preferable to an amateurish one.

Suggested further reading

BOWMAN, WILLIAM J., *Graphic Communication*, John Wiley & Sons, Inc., New York, 1968. (How to translate ideas into "visual statements.")

CHERNOFF, GEORGE, AND SARBIN, HERSHEL, *Photography and the Law*, Chilton Book Company, Philadelphia, 1971. (Fourth Edition.)

CHERRY, DAVID, *Preparing Artwork for Reproduction*, Crown Publishers, Inc., New York, 1976. (From the standpoint of a British artist.)

CRAVEN, GEORGE M., *Object and Image: An Introduction to Photography*, Prentice-Hall, Inc., Englewood Cliffs, N.J., 1975.

CRAWFORD, TAD, *Legal Guide for the Visual Artist*, Hawthorn Books, New York, 1977.

CROY, O. R., *Croy's Camera Trickery*, Hastings House, Publishers, New York, 1977.

DAVIS, PHIL, *Photography*, Wm. C. Brown Company Publishers, Dubuque, 1975. (Second edition.)

DOUGLIS, PHIL, *Communicating with Pictures*, Lawrence Ragan Communications, Inc., Chicago, 1977.

EDOM, CLIFTON C., *Photojournalism*, Wm. C. Brown Company Publishers, Dubuque, Iowa, 1976.

FEININGER, ANDREAS, *The Color Photo Book*, Prentice-Hall, Inc., Englewood Cliffs, N.J., 1970.

GRAHAM, DONALD W., *Composing Pictures*, Van Nostrand Reinhold Company, New York, 1970.

GUITAR, MARY ANNE, *22 Famous Painters and Illustrators Tell How They Work*, David McKay Company, Inc., New York, 1964.

HERDEG, WALTER, *Graphis/Diagrams: The Graphic Visualization of Abstract Data*, Hastings House, Publishers, New York, 1975.

HESS, STEPHEN, AND KAPLAN, MILTON, *The Ungentlemanly Art*, The Macmillan Company, New York, 1968.

HILLIER, BEVIS, *Art Deco*, E. P. Dutton, New York, 1968.

HOGARTH, PAUL, *The Artist as Reporter: A Survey of Art in Journalism*, Reinhold Publishing Corporation, New York, 1967.

HURLEY, GERALD D., AND MCDOUGALL, ANGUS, *Visual Impact in Print: How to Make Pictures Communicate: A Guide for the Photographer, the Editor, the Designer*, American Publishers Press, Chicago, 1971.

HUTTER, HERIBERT, *Styles in Art*, Universe Books, New York, 1977.

JACOBS, LOU, JR., *Free Lance Magazine Photography*, Hastings House, Publishers, New York, 1970. (Revised Edition.)

KEMP, WESTON D., *Photography for Visual Communicators*, Prentice-Hall, Englewood Cliffs, New Jersey, 1973.

LINDERMAN, E. W., *Invitation to Vision: Ideas and Imaginations for Art*, Wm. C. Brown Company Publishers, Dubuque, Iowa, 1967.

MEYER, HANS, *150 Techniques in Art*, Reinhold Publishing Corporation, New York, 1963.

MILLS, JOHN FITZ-MAURICE, *Studio and Art-Room Techniques*, Pitman Publishing Corp., New York, 1965.

MURGIO, MATTHEW P., *Communications Graphics*, Van Nostrand Reinhold Company, New York, 1969. (Charts and graphs and other visual presentations.)

NELSON, ROY PAUL, *Fell's Guide to the Art of Cartooning*, Frederick Fell, Inc., New York, 1962.

———, AND FERRIS, BYRON, *Fell's Guide to Commercial Art*, Frederick Fell, Inc., New York, 1966.

———, *Cartooning*, Henry Regnery Company Publishers, Chicago, 1975.

———, *Comic Art and Caricature*, Contemporary Books, Inc., Chicago, 1978.

McDarrah, Fred W., ed., *Stock Photo and Assignment Source Book*, R. R. Bowker Company, New York, 1977. (Guide to photos available from 6,000 sources.)

Pollack, Peter, *The Picture History of Photography*, Harry N. Abrams, Inc., New York, 1970. (Revised Edition.)

Quick, John, *Artists' and Illustrators' Encyclopedia*, McGraw-Hill Book Company, New York, 1969.

Rhode, Robert B., and McCall, Floyd H., *Introduction to Photography*, Macmillan Company, New York, 1976. (Third Edition.)

Rothstein, Arthur, *Photojournalism*, Amphoto, Garden City, N.Y., 1974.

Rubin, Len S., *Editor with a Camera*, A. S. Barnes & Company, Inc., Cranbury, New Jersey, 1968.

Rodewald, Fred C., and Gottschall, Edward, *Commercial Art as a Business*, Viking Press, Inc., New York, 1970. (Second Revised Edition.)

Rothstein, Arthur, *Photojournalism*, Amphoto, Garden City, New York, 1974.

Sheppard, Julian, *Photo Design Methods*, Hastings House, Publishers, New York, 1970.

Schuneman, R. Smith, ed., *Photographic Communication: Principles, Problems, and Challenges of Photojournalism*, Hastings House, Publishers, Inc., New York, 1972.

Snyder, John, *Commercial Artists Handbook*, Watson-Guptill Publications, New York, 1973.

Snyder, Norman, ed., *The Photography Catalog: A Sourcebook of the Best Equipment, Materials, and Photographic Resources*, Harper & Row, Publishers, New York, 1976.

Sontag, Susan, *On Photography*, Farrar Straus and Giroux, Inc., 1976.

Vestal, David, *The Craft of Photography*, Harper & Row, Publishers, New York, 1975.

Chapter 8

The magazine cover

You can't judge a book by its cover, they say. And you probably can't judge a magazine by its cover, either. But a lot of readers think they can, especially if they buy the magazine on the newsstand.

No feature is so important to a magazine as its cover, no matter how the magazine is circulated.

"Every business publication has a substantial body of what might best be termed uncommitted readership—denizens of the circulation who, depending on the level of their distraction, might or might not read a given issue of the magazine," says G. Barry Kay, editor of *Canadian Paint and Finishing.*

". . . The difficulty in overcoming this preoccupation [with things other than the magazine] is compounded for you by the fact that you must wage your entire battle on the strength and appeal of one page—your cover."[1]

What the cover does

A magazine cover does these things:

1. *It identifies the magazine.* The art director tries to come up with something in the cover design to set the magazine apart from all others.

2. *It attracts attention.* The art director must stop the reader somehow—and then get him inside.

3. *It creates a suitable mood for the reader.*

And if the magazine is displayed on newsstands, the cover has one more function:

4. *It sells the magazine.* No wonder the circulation depart-

---

1. G. Barry Kay, "Your Covers," *Better Editing,* Fall 1970, p. 5.

ment takes more than a casual interest in the choice of art and the wording of titles and blurbs on the cover.

In 1976, for the first time, the top general-circulation or consumer magazines—those with circulations of 300,000 or more—sold more copies on newsstands than they circulated through the mails. With postal rates so high, magazines were making a concerted effort to sell single copies. *TV Guide* set its subscription rate higher than a year's worth of single copies would cost.

What goes on the cover takes on added importance as magazines depend more on newsstand sales than on mail circulation. A magazine's circulation then rests on impulse buying. What is shown on the cover and how the blurbs are worded become vital editorial decisions.

But covers are important for non-newsstand magazines, too. Howard Paine, chief of editorial layout for *National Geographic,* says: "We may not have to compete on the newsstand but we do have to compete on the coffee table."[2]

The art that goes on the cover—the back cover, really—of *Reader's Digest* is important enough to the editors that they commission 70 or more paintings a year and they use only 12.

What goes on the cover

The typical magazine cover carries a logo (the name set or drawn in appropriate or memorable type); date of the issue and price per copy; art; and titles of major features, with names of authors.

Sometimes the art director has additional elements to contend with. *Freedom & Union* used to run the name of the editor on the cover.

Major display on covers takes any of these forms:

1. *A photograph or illustration tied to a feature inside.*

2. *Abstract art or a photograph or illustration that stands by itself.* The art director may want to keep such art free of all type, including the logo, so it will be suitable for framing. An explanation of the art can be carried in a caption on the title page.

The cover of the *Bulletin of the Atomic Scientists* permanently accommodates a "doomsday" clock. The hands occasionally move back and forth as world conditions change. The hands, of course, are always close to midnight.

3. *Type only.* The type can be in the form of a title or two from articles inside, as in the case of opinion magazines like *The Nation;* or as a table of contents, a form *Reader's Digest* was instrumental in popularizing.

4. *The beginning of an article or editorial that continues inside. The New Republic* has used an occasional cover for this

Buildings, *the construction and building management journal, moves its logo around each issue and completely changes its cover art. For this cover, art director John E. Sirotiak uses a montage of newspaper clippings behind two figures in full color. The logo and the blurb at the bottom are in bronze. Note that the figures are arranged to match the logo in width.*

2. Quoted in *Folio,* March/April 1974, p. 58.

Newspapers and magazines with a newspaper format (like Advertising Age) use their front pages for stories. Regular 8 1/2 × 11 magazines can do this, too, as Long Lines *shows here. The story is about a first-line supervisor. The large-type lead continues on page 1 inside the magazine, then narrows down to regular-size columns. In the original, the logo appears in black, the lead in green, the silhouette art in full color. A thin line in red tops the story beginning.* Long Lines *is a slick-paper publication for the employees of the Long Lines Department of the American Telephone & Telegraph Company.*

Long Lines

AUGUST/SEPTEMBER 1975

Before his day is over, he will make 25 phone calls, answer 15 others, travel 200 miles and read scores of reports and technical materials. He'll write a dozen memos (some of them to himself) and talk with his boss five times. He'll answer a hundred questions and ask twice as many. At microwave facilities, he'll make note of weeds that need uprooting and scratch his head about a sniper who's been taking potshots at a tower beacon, youths who are jumping a fence...

(continued on page 1)

purpose. Some magazines—*Advertising Age,* for example—run several articles or stories on the cover, newspaper-style.

5. *An advertisement. Editor & Publisher* uses its cover for this purpose. A cover ad brings premium rates.

Making decisions about the cover

Covers require both a permanent decision on basic format and an issue-by-issue decision on art and typography.

For your basic format you must answer the following questions:

1. Should the cover be of the same stock as the remainder of the magazine? Or should it be of a heavier stock?

2. What process should be used to print the cover? The same as for the remainder of the magazine? Or some other?

3. What kind of a logo does the magazine need? Where

should it go on the cover? Need it stay in the same place issue after issue?

4. Does the cover need art? Photograph or illustration? Must the art have a tie with an inside feature? Or can it stand on its own, like the old Norman Rockwell covers for *The Saturday Evening Post?*

5. Does the cover need color? Spot color or process color?

6. Are titles or blurbs necessary? Where should they go on the cover?

7. Will a regular cover do? Or is a gatefold called for? Or maybe an oversize cover, like those on the pulp magazines of the 1930s?

A major decision for each issue will be the selection of the art. "Perhaps the most frequently encountered error in cover design today, according to top editors and publishers, is committed by those who go all out to get attention with abstract or other unusual art but fail to direct the attention they have captured to anything that will entice the reader inside the magazine," observed *Better Editing.* "A magnificent window display may stop the shopper but it won't get him into the store unless it offers merchandise he wants."[3]

Newsstand considerations

A magazine sold on the newsstands, in contrast to one delivered only by mail, needs to (1) sell itself to the impulse buyer and (2) identify itself for the regular buyer. Where a through-the-mail magazine can run its logo anywhere on the cover and in different typefaces from issue to issue, the newsstand magazine needs a standard logo and in a standard position.

3. "The Most Important Page," *Better Editing,* Fall 1965, p. 5.

As his model for this cover painting, Charles E. White III used an old Life *cover photograph of a Los Angeles car hop, substituting one platter for another—a record for a tray—and adding the palm trees. Art director Mike Salisbury completed the illusion by putting the illustration in an old* Life *cover setting. Salisbury's idea here was to provide "a nice surrealistic image for Sunday readers . . . and something a bit different from the very abstract album cover type of art."*

To call attention to the fact that the magazine was brand new, Crown Zellerbach Corporation wrapped its Northwest *with a narrow orange sleeve carrying the words (in black) "FIRST ISSUE." When the reader tore off the sleeve, which was lightly attached with rubber cement, he found a photo underneath with the same dimensions. This first-issue cover shows mostly solid brown ink, with the logo reversed and the photo in black and brown duotone.*

Most newsstand magazines are displayed in an upright position, often with only the left side showing. This is why many newsstand magazines have their logos crowded in the upper left. If the magazine is *Ebony*-size, it lies on its back, it stacks, often low in the stands.

What art and blurbs the art director puts on the cover seriously affect sales. "Trends in cover art change rapidly," said Norman P. Schoenfeld, when he was art director at *True*. "We have to keep close tabs on how a given cover sells on the newsstand. . . . Naturally, our circulation department takes a keen interest in our cover selection."

Timing

A magazine that features people in the news on its covers may be deeply embarrassed as news changes while the magazine is being printed and delivered.

Art director Mike Salisbury took his own photograph for this West *cover, but not on location. He took it in front of his house. He was careful to choose a pair of glasses, with blue lenses, that symbolized rebellious youth; that the glasses were broken symbolized retaliation by the Establishment. The original cover was in full color.*

The surprise victory of President Harry S Truman over Thomas E. Dewey in 1948 caught a number of editors out on a limb. An embarrassment on the cover is much more serious than an embarrassment inside. When choosing cover art you must give some thought to what a sudden turn of events might do to the message your cover art conveys. Perhaps the wording of the blurb can be adjusted to make it more flexible.

Another problem involves duplication. Editors (and art directors) come from similar backgrounds and hence tend to think alike. Often, then, they arrive at similar ideas for covers. Competing magazines like *Time* and *Newsweek* can't help but appear in the same week with the same cover themes. It is not a matter of editorial leaks—one magazine does not want to copy the other. Nor is it a matter of taking precautions to avoid the duplication. If a story is there it gets the coverage. It is a matter of staying abreast of the times.

West was not afraid to change the size of the logo from issue to issue or to move it around on the cover. For this cover promoting an article on photography as "everyman's art form," art director Mike Salisbury put his logo into a setting that approximates the Kodak logo. Photographer Ron Mesaros used a Polaroid camera to take this picture of someone taking a picture.

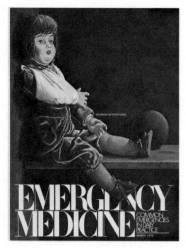

And when you see a magazine for one week moving away from serious cover art to, say, art showing a well-endowed female entertainer, you can rightly suspect it is that time in the year when the magazine is attempting to step up newsstand sales to impress advertisers or make a good showing in a circulation audit.

The prestige of a cover

The ultimate goal for some people, it seems, is to make the cover of a national magazine. Dr. Hook and the Medicine Show did a song about getting on the cover of *Rolling Stone*, and a few weeks after the song hit the Top 40, Dr. Hook made it. A few weeks after that, as the song suggested he would do, Dr. Hook

Allowing part of the cover art to hide part of the logo is common practice. Moving the logo to the bottom of the page is less common. Emergency Medicine *for this issue does both. The doll put up on the shelf to mend is a full-color painting (by Donald Hedin) rather than a photograph. Tom Lennon designed this cover; Ira Silberlicht art directed.* Emergency Magazine *long has impressed the magazine industry as a splendidly designed publication; its covers often find a place in art directors' annuals.*

With its July 1970 issue, Fleet Owner *introduced a new logo designed by Appelbaum & Curtis, New York. The logo "reflects today's fleet operation: strong, bold, modern, progressive." Note that the cover identifies the month by number rather than by name. Colors for this issue were black, blue, and red. (With permission from* Fleet Owner. *Copyright 1970 by McGraw-Hill, Inc. All rights reserved.)*

walked into the magazine's San Francisco office (it has since moved to New York), and bought five copies for his mother.[4]

The most prestigious cover spot, probably, is on the front of *Time*. Malcolm Muggeridge contemptuously called the *Time* cover spot "post-Christendom's most notable stained-glass window." At the end of each year *Time's* editors and letters-to-the-editor writers engage in a navel-contemplation maneuver as the decision is made about the "Man of the Year."

1977 saw a new low in magazine covers with the publication and national distribution of something called *Assassin*. The cover of the first issue showed a picture of President Carter with the crosshairs of a telescopic sight superimposed over his face. The blurb said: "How Would You Do It: See Special Entry Page." Inside the magazine also was information on how to blow up a car using a homemade bomb and how to build an atomic bomb.

The stock cover

Small-circulation magazines unable to afford original art and the printing of full-color covers can turn to a house that mass produces them for local imprinting. Editors simply choose from among a series of nicely produced if mundane scenes and order enough sheets to wrap around each of the copies of the magazines. Each cover acts as an extra four-page signature. The inside front cover, inside back cover, and back cover are blank. The editor works out copy for these and has his local printer run the sheets through a press to print appropriate material on the blank pages and the magazine's name over part of the full-color cover art. Monthly Cover Service, 400 North Michigan Avenue, Chicago, Illinois 60601 supplies stock covers.

What's in a name?

Picking a name for a magazine could be the single most important step a publisher or editor makes. Once decided upon, the name sticks, even when the formula for the magazine changes. That's why editors are well advised to avoid publication frequency in the name. Put *Quarterly* into the title, and what do you do when the publication becomes successful enough to go bi-monthly or monthly? What is the significance now of the *Saturday* in *Saturday Review* and *Saturday Evening Post*?

Your emphasis may seem permanent at the start, but in a few years, as times change, you may want your magazine to change. How can anyone take seriously a magazine that still goes by the name of *Playboy*?

4. Peter A. Janssen, "Rolling Stone's Quest for Respectability," *Columbia Journalism Review*, January/February 1974, p. 59.

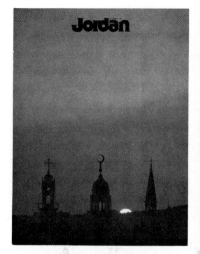

A non-newsstand magazine, especially, can afford to move the logo around on the front cover from issue to issue or change its size, as Jordan *does in these succeeding issues. In addition, the magazine, a quarterly published by the Jordan Information Bureau, Washington, D.C., changes completely the nature of the cover art: a full-color photograph, in one case; a full-color illustration (by John Trotta) in the other. The photo bleeds; the illustration does not.*

To call attention to an article on the results of an essay contest on how to run the company, Paper Times *got a machine-room oiler to sit at the desk of a company executive and pose for a cover photograph. The equipment on the desk added to the novelty of the shot.* Paper Times *ordinarily does not run cover blurbs, but one seemed appropriate for this cover (you see it at the man's left elbow). Usually the cover carries only a logo with the bleed photo. Editor Lionel L. Fisher doesn't even run a line indicating month and year. Why should he? He doesn't put his magazine on the newsstand. And the information is on the masthead inside, if anyone wants to check. The logo floats from issue to issue. Art director Joe Erceg puts it wherever it fits best, in this case at the lower left.*

You want to be clever in your name choice but appropriate, too. So how does *The Avant Gardener* strike you? Or *Statutory Rap*, a publication of the University of Dayton Law School? Or *Rider's Digest*, a publication of the Metropolitan Atlanta Rapid Transit Authority? Or *The Eggsaminer*, once published for egg producers?

In *Annie Hall*, Woody Allen came up with a name for the merger of *Dissent* with *Commentary*: the name was *Dissentary*. *Atlas*, a digest of foreign press news, features, and comment, was named after the Titan who held up the heavens. "Our own more modest purpose," said the editors, "is to hold the world up to our readers."

Magazines with long names can make references to themselves less cumbersome by going to initials. Hence, the Journal of the American Medical Association becomes *JAMA* and the Journal of the Association of Operating Room Nurses becomes the *AORN Journal*. *CA* was lucky enough in its initials that when it wanted to erase the commercial art image (it was originally called *Commercial Art*) it found its initials also stood for *Communication Arts*, the name by which it is now known. *National Review* sometimes features a big *NR* on its cover rather than its full name.

Few magazines would start off that way today, but a few of the older magazines carry their founders' name: *McCall's, Forbes, Hoard's Dairyman, Best's Insurance News.* Sometimes this causes confusion. *Moody Monthly* is not a magazine for depressed persons; it is an evangelical magazine named after Dwight L. Moody.

A modifier seems useful to some editors who put a *Modern* or *Today's* in front of the title or an *Age* or *World* behind it, but often a single, straightforward word does the job: *Banking* or *Eternity*. Of course, a single name can be jarring to someone outside the magazine's readership. The student senate of the University of Louisville School of Dentistry publishes the perfectly serious *Abscess*.

Because it appears in the West, one important consumer magazine calls itself *Sunset*.

Often it is hard to find a name because all the possibilities seem to be taken. *Esquire* editors worked with "Trend," "Stag," and "Beaut" before getting a letter addressed with the quaint "Esq." after the recipient's name, and decided to try that word spelled out.

Prison publications have shown a feel for the ironic with such choices of titles as these: *Time & Tied, The Stretch, Bars & Stripes, Detour, The New Leaf, The Key,* and (are you ready for this?) *The Prism.*

Company magazines have shown imagination in their choices of names, too. The company that makes Heath bars publishes

Sweet Talk, Blue Chip Stamps publishes Chip Chat, Gulf Oil Corp. publishes Gulf Oilmanac, Wisconsin Electric Power publishes The Outlet, and Public Service Indiana puts out, er, Watts Cookin'.

The job of the art director is to come up with the right typeface to help say visually what the title says in words. But that does not mean that Sweet Talk should be dripping in chocolate or that The Outlet has to be in a script made from an electric cord.

The logo

The logo, a typographic rendering of the magazine's name, is much like a company trademark. Its adoption is a serious matter. Once adopted, it settles in for many years of service. Its value increases to the point where its owner feels reluctant to abandon it even when its design becomes outmoded.

In designing a logo, then, you would avoid types or letterforms that soon will be out of date. Yet you would pick type that is distinctive. More important, you would pick type that is appropriate.

The Sporting News is an example of a magazine with an inappropriate logo face: Old English. The editors would argue that their weekly publication is newspaperlike in its approach, and Old English has been used, historically, for newspaper logos. But Old English has an ecclesiastical feel; it is far removed from the roughness and vitality of the sports world.

Whatever face you decide on, you would rough the idea for your logo on tissue, but because of a logo's specialized nature, its importance, and its permanence, you would call in a profes-

National Review, *even though some of its circulation comes from newsstand sales, changes back and forth from a full logo to an initials logo with the full name in small type below. Usually, art director James W. O'Bryan uses full color, but for the cover at the far right a black and white photo seemed appropriate to illustrate William F. Buckley, Jr.'s review of* Scoundrel Time *inside. The photo is from a full-page ad for a fur coat that the author of* Scoundrel Time, *Lillian Hellman, had recently posed for. Often a* National Review *cover has a small diagonal banner running across a corner as a supplemental cover blurb. (Note the Castro cover.) For the "New Party" cover, O'Bryan uses campaign pins for current parties and an egg cracking open for the new party. A rounded-corner thick blue border, often interrupted by jutting art, is a permanent cover feature.*

NewTimes

Steve Phillips, art director of the magazine, designed the New Times logo, using tightly spaced sans serifs and bringing the two words together by allowing the T to overlap the w. The T picks up the slant of the w for its left cross-bar; the right cross-bar does extra duty as the dot for the i.

Family Circle

A logo designed by Herb Lubalin for Family Circle. This was one of the first of the "nestled" logos, with letters from one line fitting snugly against letters from another. The C actually overlaps the m. "Circle" is so placed that a couple of vertical axes are formed, one with the two i's, the other with the l and r. The tail of the y is clipped to fit the tail of the r. And of course the letters are unusually close-fitting horizontally. All of which makes for a tightly knit Family Circle.

skeptic
THE MAGAZINE OF OPPOSING VIEWS

The logo for Skeptic, "the magazine of opposing views," features a question-mark in place of p. The slogan fits snugly below the logo.

sional calligrapher or letterform artist to do the finish. You should not allow your logo to be hand-lettered by just anyone who knows how to draw. Illustrators as a rule are unfamiliar with type and letterform, and many of them do a poor job of lettering.

Settling for a regularly set typeface instead of hand lettering is the best solution when professional lettering help is not available or affordable. Without much ability as a lettering artist, you can do some innovating with type yourself. You can order reproduction proofs of the type and then cut the letters apart and respace them to bring to your logo a flair ordinary typography can't supply. Because logos involve only one or two words and because readers have a chance to study them issue after issue, you can do things with spacing that you wouldn't do when working on article and story titles. For instance, you can move two capitalized words together, with no space between.

LikeThis

You can doctor some of the letters, too, so that they would be unrecognizable were they not seen in context. Herb Lubalin, who designed *Sport's* new tight-fitting all-cap logo, chopped off the bottom half of the main downstroke of the *R* and propped the letter up against the *O. Dare*, a magazine once published for barbershops, ran its logo in mirror reverse, so that it read from right to left. It was in keeping with the nature of the magazine; it "dared" to be different.

Popular Photography for its logo found it necessary to separate the word "Photography." (The "Popular" in the title is run small and up the side, an inconspicuous part of the logo.) The dictionary separates "photography" between the *g* and the *r*. But that doesn't read right. The magazine wanted "Photo" to stand out. So it went ahead and separated the word like this: "Photo-graphy," even though the separation technically is wrong.

The logo can run in a different color each issue. It can even be embossed,as for *Venture* and occasional issues of *Playboy*. But most art directors feel it should appear in the same place on the cover, issue after issue, especially if the magazine sells on the newsstands. Of course, the logo could be so unique it could be spotted by potential buyers no matter where it's placed. *Family Circle*, wholly a newsstand magazine, has that kind of a logo. *Woman's Day* moves its logo around from issue to issue, sometimes keeping it in a single line, sometimes in two lines.

Often a good idea to let the art partially hide part of the logo, to give the cover dimension. But not enough should be hid to keep the logo from being readily recognized. You can also doctor the logo slightly to make it appropriate for a special issue.

Changing the logo

There comes a time in a magazine's growth when it must—it just must—change its logo.

Some magazines change suddenly, some gradually. *Newsweek* has made its changes gradually. Entering the 1960s *Newsweek* had a slab serif logo that stretched most of the way—but not all the way—across the top, with a heavy underline that continued down the left side and across the bottom. The line formed sort of a flattened-out *C*. Then in the mid-1960s *Newsweek* dropped the left and bottom line and retained only the underline. Later the magazine dropped the underline. In

For its logo, Alma Mater, *publication for alumni directors, overlaps the two words of its name. The overlapping "ma" takes on characters of letters both at the left and at the right. The result is a logo made up of three kinds of letters. Yet the designer succeeds in making it all look like one tightly ordered unit.*

The organization publishing this bimonthly newsletter is Public Employees Retirement System, or PERS. So "Perspective" was a natural as a name. Editor Bernerd Fred Park and graphic artist Arnold Albertson got together and worked out this logo that emphasizes the PERS initials. Park feels it is "the best kind of relationship between an editor and a designer. An editor can not often be an artist, and few graphic artists seem capable of their best without the right stimulus from the editor." Studying the logo you see that the small type at the top lines up with the S in "PERS," and the State of Oregon seal is placed to act as a sort of dot for the I.

Print

Close-fitting sans serif letters make up the logo for Print. *It is always run small and to the side at the top of the cover. Note that the r and t are designed to pick up the shape of the n. And note that the cross-bar on the t is elongated to give the letter better balance in context with the other letters.*

New York's logo is adopted from an earlier one used by New York *when it was part of the* Herald Tribune. *The original was in Caslon swash. Now, in a bolder version, it combines elements of both Caslon and Bookman. Designer: Tom Carnase. Art director: Walter Bernard.*

Change
IN HIGHER EDUCATION

Change is made from a set of ligatures. This handsome type is based on a photolettering face which the magazine uses for titles inside.

1970 only the word *Newsweek* was left (with the art and cover blurb). And the slab serif letters were modernized, made more expanded than before. The logo stretched all the way across the top.

Family Circle, on the other hand, when it changed its logo, changed it suddenly and dramatically.

Perhaps the rule should be: if the logo is salvageable, change it gradually, in order to retain what recognition value the logo holds for the reader. If the resistance to change has gone on too long and the logo is hopelessly outdated, go ahead and make a clean break.

Art on the cover

The late Joe Ratner, after considering the various claims for one kind of cover over another, concluded that as far as the art was concerned, the ideal cover would show a nude woman sitting on a braided rug, with a dog at her elbow, a rose in her teeth, holding a baby, and eating apple pie.

But cover art today tends to be less predictable than in the past. It is more direct and less cluttered. Art directors of newsstand magazines think of their covers as posters to be seen from 30 feet away. They look for closeup art with a strong silhouette—art not dissimilar from the art on billboards.

Whether you should use photographs or illustrations depends again on the nature of the magazine and its audience. A journalistic magazine would normally use photographs, a literary magazine illustrations. It is probably not a good idea to switch back and forth.

Photographs have virtually replaced illustrations as cover art on magazines because photographs are more readily available on short notice and, in most cases, cheaper.

When working out your cover format you are wise to pick a square rather than a rectangular hole for the photograph. Picking a rectangle, you have to commit yourself to all horizontal or all vertical shots for your cover. Picking a square, you can, with judicious cropping, accommodate both horizontals and verticals, and of course you can run Rollei shots without any cropping. Whatever shape you choose, the photograph should dominate the page, perhaps even bleeding all around.

If you use art that ties in with something inside, you'll want to run a blurb on the cover pointing to that tie. If the art is independent, you'll have to separate the cover blurbs, if any, from the art to prevent the reader from making a wrong—and sometimes incongruous—connection.

While abstraction in cover art—both in photography and illustration—is making gains, realism still works best for certain magazines. Petersen Publications, publishers of magazines for car buffs, gun lovers, and hot rodders, has experimented with arty covers but has found they do not sell as well as covers crowded with type and illustrated with no-nonsense, sleeves-rolled-up paintings. Albert H. Isaacs, art director, would probably rather commission the arty covers, but he tries to keep his audiences in mind. Good design for such audiences is not necessarily what good design would be for other audiences.

The use of offbeat art can unsettle the reader not used to it. When *Time* for its February 16, 1968, cover ran a photograph of a papier-mache bust of Kenneth Galbraith by Gerald Scarfe, one reader wrote in: "My five-year-old son looked at the cover picture and said: 'Well, I guess they did the best they could.' "

Even realism can be overdone. The July 10, 1967, issue of *Newsweek* carried a cover showing a map of Vietnam burning on an American flag background. This angered a reader. "Did you actually burn our flag? If so, I am now making a citizen's arrest." *Newsweek* placated the letter writer by pointing out that the stars and stripes were painted on cardboard; a paper cutout of Vietnam was set afire and dropped on the cardboard, and a photographer took the picture.

Titles on the cover

Titles—or blurbs—on the cover are meant to lure the reader inside. Some magazines devote their entire cover to them. Others combine them with art. Obviously, the simpler the cover, the better. If titles and blurbs must be included, they should be held down to just a few words in two or three lines at the most.

Most annoying, from the reader's standpoint, is the practice of running a title on the cover and changing it when it appears over the article inside. Why do editors persist in doing it?

Color on the cover

If he doesn't use color anywhere else, an editor seems to feel he must use it at least on the cover. The possibilities include 3-D full color, ordinary process color, spot color, and one-color printing.

Time developed a special red as a cover border to help readers instantly identify the magazine. *National Geographic* similarly has used a bright yellow.

If the cover is printed separately from the magazine itself, color on the cover is within the budget of most magazines even when they can't afford color throughout.

Small magazines usually go the second-color route, using a bright color that will contrast with the black-and-white photography. Often the second color consists of a band or block into

For his magazine called Bird, *created for a Magazine Editing class, student William Lingle produces an all-lowercase logo with press-on Helvetica Bold letters. To make the logo appropriate to the subject matter of his magazine, he substitutes for the dot of the i a bird drawn in silhouette. It had to be a fat, squatting bird so it wouldn't be too different from the expected dot.*

"The Magazine of Winter" almost buries its logo in snow. But enough of the type shows so that the name stands out adequately on the newsstands.

Reach, *published by the Church of God, Anderson, Ind., for its logo, uses some trick typography to capture the spirit of the magazine.*

which the logo or blurbs have been surprinted or reversed.

When only a second color is available, you are unlikely to come up with a more useful and powerful color than a red that is light enough to contrast with black and dark enough to carry reverse letters. Even when you have full color available, you want to have one color predominate. Colors tend to convey certain moods, and often the subject of the cover will dictate what color you want to stand out.

Editors and art directors—and circulation managers, too—have some pretty firm ideas as to which colors work best for their magazines. *House & Garden*, for instance, finds that for its covers blue sells best, followed by green, then red.

Covers to remember

The gatefold cover continues to intrigue art directors. The folded extra sheet not only makes possible a cover with a one-two punch but also an inside cover ad that stretches over three facing pages. A classic gatefold was *The Saturday Evening Post*'s for April 28, 1962. It showed first a lineup of ball players looking pious while the "Star Spangled Banner" was being played, then a wild fight involving the players and umpires.

Another classic was *Esquire*'s cover for November 1966. Hubert Humphrey, then Vice-President, was shown saying, "I have known for 16 years his courage, his wisdom, his tact, his persuasion, his judgment, and his leadership." When you turned the page you found Humphrey was really sitting on President Johnson's lap. He was a ventriloquist's puppet! Johnson is shown saying, "You tell 'em, Hubert."

Many of *Esquire*'s covers of the 1960s and early 1970s were memorable. They were the ideas of George Lois, the advertising

executive and art director, with photography supplied by Carl Fischer—"The photographic magician," as Dugald Stermer calls him. As "concept covers," they referred to lead articles inside the magazine. Lieutenant Calley poses with children looking very Vietnamese. Muhammed Ali poses with arrows stuck in his chest. Andy Warhol drowns in a can of Campbell's tomato soup. Many of the effects resulted from doctoring photographs, but some of them resulted from celebrities' willingness to pose.

Lois said that ". . . nobody ever refused to do anything, no matter how outrageous. . . ." "So why do they put up with it?" Dugald Stermer asked Lois. "Pure ego seems to be the answer; . . . people, at least many people, suffer any indignity to have their face out there in public."[5]

Rivaling *Esquire* with the uniqueness of its covers is a younger magazine, *New York*, like *Esquire* an exponent of the "new journalism." For a cover promoting an article on ice cream, *New York* for August 3, 1970, showed a nude girl holding out two ice cream cones, placed to look at first like a bra. The title, parodying a best-selling book at the time, went: "Everything You Always Wanted to Know About Ice Cream But Were Too Fat to Ask."

In its 1970 year-end issue, *New York* gave readers a 12-page handbook for consumers, telling them, among other things, "How to Break the Supermarket Code and Guarantee Your Food Is Fresh." The cover consisted of a drawing of a box one might find in his grocery store, gaudy in color, with a sunburst saying "Special" and a band with type running diagonally across the face. The designer even uglified the logo to make it appear as

5. Quoted by Dugald Stermer, "Carl Fischer," *Communication Arts*, May/June 1975, p. 30.

The assignment: do a cover, including logo, for Ethics, *a pretend new magazine with some newsstand distribution. (There is a real quarterly called* Ethics *published by the University of Chicago.) Feature on the cover an article on "Reporting Watergate: Some Second Thoughts" by John L. Hulteng. Full-color is available. Come up with a basic design that can be utilized in follow-up issues. Here are four student solutions: by (from left) Robin Andrea Teter, Anne Mangan, Robin Perkins, and Mary Fish. Teter centers her bold logo, puts the blurb immediately below, and offers large art symbolic of the article. The colors are mostly green and brown. The strength of her design lies in the proportions. Mangan makes use of a blue border to match the extended-letter roman logo. The generous-size blurb, in red, superimposes itself over the simulated columns of a newspaper page. Perkins builds a Nixon out of newsclippings and puts a flag in full color behind. Instead of using standard type for her logo, she designs her own, coming up with letters that seem related. Note the ligature she builds out of the first three letters. Fish goes to a classic drawing from a museum collection to bring symbolism to her page. She centers her all-lowercase logo. She chooses yellow as her principle bleed color.*

though it belonged on the package. The 40¢ price for this issue was stamped on the top of the box in the familiar purple indelible ink under the printed words, "You pay only." The box carried the line, "Net weight 6 oz.," which was about what that issue weighed.

Even *The Atlantic* has become more innovative in its covers. For its October 1970 issue it ran a gatefold for the first time. It provided plenty of room to display a collage by Larry Rivers for a "Soldiers" feature. A title running across the bottom read: "The Army is the only damn thing [and then you had to turn the flap] holding this country together." To illustrate a "Trains in Trouble" blurb the August 1976 cover showed a drawing of an old fashion train engine chained to photographed railroad tracks with a circular inset of a woman in period costume, agonizing, asking "Will help arrive in time?"

It took a magazine like *Psychology Today* to give the gatefold its ultimate impact. For July 1971 the magazine ran a *six*-page gatefold cover, which featured a game readers could play and also made possible an ad that spread over four side-by-side pages inside.

National Lampoon came up with a talked about cover for January 1973 when it showed a dog with a gun pointed to its head. The blurb read: "If You Don't Buy This Magazine, We'll Kill This Dog."

Cover traditions

The New Yorker once each February reruns its first cover designed in the early 1920s by the cartoonist Rea Irwin. It shows a foppish gentleman studying a butterfly. *The Saturday Evening Post* used to devote one cover each year to Benjamin Franklin, even after historian Frank Luther Mott exposed the magazine's tie to Franklin as highly imaginary.

Many magazines like to tie their covers to the seasons of the year. *McCall's* has used the *M* and *C* of its name to spell out "Merry Christmas."

Promotional considerations

The cover is important to both the circulation and advertising departments of a magazine.

The art and the blurbs on the cover strongly affect the number of copies sold on the newsstands. Sometimes the circulation department is not content with the cover as printed; it adds some promotional literature of its own.

To sell copies or subscriptions or to urge renewals, a magazine attaches slips of paper to the cover and sews or staples notices into the binding. This practice got out of hand in the 1950s and

1960s as readers angrily ripped their magazines apart trying to dispose of all the come-ons. Now magazines show more consideration for their readers. They add stick-ons and stick-ins that, when removed, do not damage the magazine. An *Esquire* notice stuck on the cover, reminding a subscriber his subscription is about to expire, carries the note: "Pull card gently and cover will not be damaged." *Time* and other magazines include a reorder card not bound into—simply slipped into—the magazine, so that it falls out when the magazine is opened.

The stick-ons are often localized for newsstand display. They call attention to articles high in local interest. Even though the magazine puts out several regional editions, covers themselves stay the same.

But for one issue (June 1968) a new editor at *Esquire,* Harold Hayes, decided he needed seven different covers, one for most of the country, six others for selected large cities featured in an article. It was an experiment not often to be duplicated.[6] *Sunset,* which publishes four regional editions, has used two different covers for an occasional issue to better set the stage for material inside.

When a magazine offers reprints of an article, it wraps the reprint with the cover for that issue. When an advertiser requests reprints of his ad for direct-mail use, he expects the cover to accompany the reprint.

A picture of the cover may also be included in advertising directed to media buyers in advertising agencies. For that reason, the cover should be reproducible in a reduced size.

The back cover

Editors of newsstand magazines don't face the problem—the page belongs to the advertiser willing to pay a premium rate—but editors of company magazines must do something about it: the troublesome back cover.

Too often the decision about what to put there is last-minute. And that's a shame. The space is too valuable for such cavalier treatment.

On a typical 8 1/2 × 11 or 9 × 12 magazine the back cover ranks second only to the front cover in its impact on and its accessibility to the reader. It deserves the editor's thoughtful attention.

Logic suggests that the back cover be appealing—but not too appealing. It should not overshadow the front cover. The editor

For its back cover, **Soldiers,** *not bothered by advertising, promotes one of its inside features. Under this arrangement, both the front and back covers can be used to get the reader inside. Both covers for* **Soldiers** *appear in full color.*

---

6. It must have been a production and distribution nightmare. It was tried because the new editor didn't know any better. Reported the magazine: ". . . so in the end it turned out to be easier to do than to make him understand why it couldn't be done."

wants to encourage readers to start at the beginning of the magazine. Too many readers already seem inclined to start at the back and flip forward.

Whether the magazine is a self-cover or whether it wraps itself in a separate, heavy-stock, four-page signature makes a difference in the editor's plans. If the magazine is a self-cover, the editor might want to consider the back cover as just another page, as in a tabloid. An article on previous pages could carry over onto the back cover. But if it is built of firmer stock, the back cover should be a self-contained unit or at least part of a unit that is separate from the interior of the magazine.

Whether the magazine is a self-mailer with a part of the back cover reserved for addressing affects the editor's plans, too.

Here are some ways in which editors with separate-stock covers—and with self-covers, too—can solve their back-cover problems:

1. Choose horizontal art and wrap it around the spine. But make sure the art divides itself logically into two sections. The art on the back need not stretch all the way across the page.

2. Flop the front-cover art so that it reads right-to-left on the back.

3. Repeat the front-cover art, but without the logo. A variation of this has been tried by *Items*, published by the Federal Reserve Bank of Dallas. The back cover repeats the front-cover photo, but slightly cropped and in a smaller size, and includes a caption for the photo.

4. If the waste doesn't disturb you, leave the back cover blank. Or pick up one of the front cover colors and spread it across the back page.

5. Use a different photo or piece of art on the back cover from what you use on the front cover. *Reader's Digest* carries this idea to the extreme of using the *only* cover art on the back, reserving the front—or most of it—for a table of contents.

6. Put your table of contents on the back cover, as *Exxon USA* does.

7. Use public-service material, as from the Advertising Council, National Safety Council, etc. There is enough of it around to give you plenty of variety.

8. Use a company ad designed originally for consumer magazines with a "This is how we're advertising" introduction.

9. Design ads specifically for your readers. Or use material the company might also use for plant posters.

10. Give the page over to cartoons, short humor pieces, poems, or other literary or art creations.

11. Use the page for a one-page feature that differs from features inside the book. A series of personality sketches of interesting employees has worked out well for some publications.

If the magazine has a separate, different-stock cover, similar

Western World, a tabloid published by AT&T Long Lines, San Francisco, several times a year gives over its back page to a series of short items "to inform & delight our readers!" It has a lively, deep logo built appropriately from a variety of typefaces, mostly circus-like. Western World uses a three-column rather than the publication's regular four-column format here because, as editor Molly Miller explains, "the artwork [logo]—to my mind—seems to demand a three-column format." Note the blank space reserved for address labels. The masthead, held off until this page, does double duty— as a masthead and also as the return address required by the mailing permit.

problems occur for the inside-front and inside-back covers. The materials on these two covers also should be self-contained. It is not a good idea, for instance, to continue a story on the inside back cover of a separate-cover magazine. The reader will be puzzled if not disturbed by the change of stock that occurs midway in his reading.

One of the interesting back covers of the past was part of a teeny-bopper magazine. The magazine really had two covers. The front cover took care of the first half of the magazine; the back cover, run upside-down, started the reader into the last half of the magazine, with those pages printed upside down to match.

Another memorable back cover was offered by *Mad* in 1960. The day after the elections the newsstand browser was surprised to see a picture of John Kennedy, the newly elected President, and a congratulatory message. How could the magazine's production allow such planning? It was to be a close election.

The answer lay with the back cover. There the reader found a picture of Nixon, with the same congratulatory message. All the dealer needed to do, it turned out, was to make sure he had the right cover facing up when he put the magazine out on display after the election.

The spine

For a magazine that is side-stitched—and that means a magazine with many pages—the art director faces another problem: what to do with the spine? The monthly Standard Rate & Data Service publications are thick enough to sell space for advertising there.

But in most cases, designing the spine involves only coming up with type running sideways giving the name of the publication and the date. Even so, type selection and placement should be carefully worked out. It should not be a matter for the printer to decide at the last minute. Spine display is not likely to affect newsstand sales, but it does affect appearance when the magazines are shelved like books.

The final touch

The art director puts a disproportionate amount of his time on the cover. He agonizes over the art. He worries about the placement of the type. He checks the color proofs—and checks them again. Finally, it all fits. Everything is perfect. The magazine is printed. The circulation department takes over.

And what happens? The subscriber gets his magazine, and plunked down right over the type and art is a mailing sticker.

A unique case involved an early November 1969 issue of

Time, which featured a cover portrait of Vice-President Spiro T. Agnew right after his first attack on the news media. About 320,000 copies of the magazine (only part of the press run) went out with the label pasted across Agnew's mouth. A spokesman for the magazine said it was "a production error."

Suggested further reading

BUECHNER, THOMAS, *Norman Rockwell: Artist and Illustrator,* Harry N. Abrams, Inc., New York, 1970. (All 317 *Saturday Evening Post* covers plus other illustrations are reproduced.)

LOIS, GEORGE, *The Art of Advertising,* Harry N. Abrams, Inc., New York, 1977. (Some of the 92 covers he did for *Esquire* are included.)

Chapter 9

Inside pages

The reader opens up a magazine and sees a left- and right-hand page together. It is up to you as the art director to arrange these two pages to form a single unit. You must do this and at the same time make each page readable of itself. You must create design within design.

Crossing the gutter

The big problem is the gutter running between the pages of a spread, a psychological as well as a physical barrier. When left and right pages are complete in themselves, the gutter actually helps readers by acting as a separator; but for most spreads, you must build some kind of a graphic bridge to get the reader across.

You can be obvious about it, positioning a piece of art or a heading so that part is on one side of the gutter, part on another. Or you can do it with more subtlety, repeating on the right-hand page a style of art, a pattern, or a color from the left-hand page to help the reader make a visual association.

If you choose to run art across the gutter, you should do it at a natural break. If a face or figure is involved, you should not let the gutter split it in two. You should not split any art down the middle, unless you want it to stretch all the way across the spread and bleed left and right. In most cases more of the art should be put on one side of the gutter than the other.

Using art in this way puts design considerations ahead of art appreciation. Readers really don't like their art to go across the gutter. The art, somehow, seems damaged to them, bent—as indeed it is.

Unaware of production limitations, you may make the

A good way of tying two pages together is to run a photograph large enough to cover completely the pages and then to either surprint or reverse your type, both title and text. You have to be careful, of course, to pick a photograph that has the right amount of neutral area where the type can go and one that would not be bothered by a gutter running down the middle. The usual solution is to pick a scenic shot, but you can do the job as well with an informal portrait, as Profile *does here for this article beginning. The article focuses on an individual, so the art is appropriate, and it needs no caption. Notice that the art actually cradles the copy block.* Profile *is published monthly for employees of the Exxon Company, U.S.A., Houston.*

Xerox World solves the problem of showing two different-length articles on a single spread by surprinting one of them over a bleed photo that runs across the gutter and by printing the other in the white space left over. The photo chosen for the winter story is even-toned enough to allow the overprinting. The toned area nicely separates itself from the white area, but a repetition of a typeface in the two titles helps hold the pages together. The bar running across the top of the second article in a second color is a fixture in the magazine. Note how the designer handles the problem of identifying all the people in the group shot. Making a tracing of the figures in line and adding numbers is a simple enough job for anyone steady of hand.

mistake of running art across the gutter at a spot on the signature, or between signatures, where perfect alignment is impossible. It is a good idea to check with the printer to determine where across-the-gutter placement will permit the best production.

When you use a line of display type to bridge the gutter, you should use it in a large size. You should not separate the line between letters; you should separate it between words. You should also leave a little extra space at the point of separation, especially if the magazine is side stitched.

The two-openings spread

Sometimes it is necessary to run two article openers on one spread. The article on the left page is a one-pager. A new article begins on the right-hand page. Both articles contain illustra-

CZ's Clallam Managed Forest, the company's second largest Northwest timber holding

Near the top of the peninsula is CZ's Clallam Managed Forest, at 90,000 acres the company's second largest Pacific Northwest timber holding and an economic mainstay of the Sekiu-Neah Bay region. Here at the Makah Indian Reservation fishing village of Neah Bay, only a couple of miles from the most northwesterly point on the United States mainland, is CZ's Neah Bay Boom, where Clallam logs begin a voyage inland to the company's Port Angeles and Port Townsend pulp and paper mills and other regional markets along the beautiful Strait of Juan de Fuca waterway.

The logs reach Neah Bay by truck over the company's 285-mile network of logging roads through the Clallam Managed Forest, the huge western hemlock and other native species rumbling in from the sorting yard on three-trailer "mule trains."

Lifted, lowered, and maneuvered . . .

Here they are carefully lifted from the trucks by a crane capable of hoisting up to 60 tons and then gently lowered into the water, where agile, snorting little boom boats maneuver them into selected areas for temporary storage. Then they are cabled together in large tow rafts, or booms, to be towed up the choppy strait by tugboats. CZ installed the boom in 1945 to achieve more efficient, lower cost log transportation by utilizing the strait's natural waterway to reduce highway truck travel.

Staff of nine men

The Neah Bay Boom staff consists of a nine-man crew. They work mostly in cold, usually wet and often windy conditions, but they're little concerned about the climate.

"We work every day regardless,"

We work every day, regardless," said Fred Norman, boom foreman, one hand firmly gripping the bill of his hardhat to keep it from being blown off by a chill wind whipping in from the Pacific. "That is, except when one of our winter storms sends waves over the dike and raises all kinds of trouble with our boat operators. She does get rough, plenty rough, sometimes."

The only visitors, besides the truck drivers, are the seagulls that circle

almost continually overhead. For the seeker of solitude, this is the place.

Jim McLean, whose "straw boss" job title seems perfectly suited to his tough, stocky, football lineman build, has 20 years-plus of continual Neah Bay Boom service under his water safety belt.

Bill Mahone

Don Haltom   *Dean Francis   Bill Mahone*

20   21

---

tions. How do you keep them separated visually?

Some possibilities:

1. You run a wider-than-usual river of white between the two. You can, of course, separate them horizontally rather than vertically, running one across the top of the two pages, the other across the bottom.

2. If you separate the articles vertically, keeping one on the left-hand page and the other on the right-, you can hold the illustrations for the one on the right until later in the article.

3. You can make the heading of one article bigger than the other.

4. You can put one in a box or run a tint block over it.

5. You can set the articles in different types or set one in two-column format, the other in three-column format.

6. You can establish an optical gap by using and positioning artwork for both articles that pulls the reader to the outside edges.

When one of the articles or openers is to occupy more space than the other, you would want to make a special effort to close the gap at the gutter and establish a new gap between the articles. In addition to the devices already described for separating articles, you can use a rule or bar to separate the articles. The *Pentecostal Evangel*, which faces the situation often, uses a thin vertical rule at the left edge of every article, even when the article starts a left-hand page.

A two-page spread (the article starts on the previous spread) from Crown Zellerbach's first issue of Northwest. *It combines square-finish and silhouette halftones (all in duotone) with copy and blurbs. The blurbs, set off with thin horizontal rules, are really like subheads, picking up wording from the paragraphs immediately following. Notice how designer Peter Moore relates the silhouetted figure at the bottom with a photograph just across the gutter. Notice too the prominent display of a chain and hook (the article is about a logging boom). Except for identification of people (this is a magazine for employees) the photographs do not need captions. The text acts as one big caption.*

The main illustration develops right before the reader's eyes as he moves through each spread of this 10-page New York article. An accompanying boldface blurb changes position on each two pages as the illustration changes, adding to the feeling of movement. The original is in full color. Like many magazines, New York runs a small-size reproduction of its logo at the beginning of the main article in each issue. The reader has gone through a number of pages of distracting advertising and other front matter; the small logo refreshes his memory by reminding him what magazine he is reading. It also helps set aside editorial from advertising matter.

New York Faces Future Shock
By Alvin Toffler

"...Future shock may turn out to be the most devastating urban disease of tomorrow, and millions of New Yorkers are first in line, as usual. The challenge: how to control change..."

"...It is impossible to understand what is happening to human relationships in America unless we examine their duration..."

"...Instead of conversations, we send high-speed communiqués and search for all sorts of magic to accelerate friendship..."

When you have to display *more* than two articles, especially when they are illustrated, you almost have to use boxes or ruled lines.

Some magazines face the problem of presenting side-by-side columns of type in different languages. Unfortunately for the designer, type set in one language takes more space than type set in another. *Spargo,* published by Teleglobe Canada, Montreal, solves the problem by having the type in one language set wider than the type in the other. The columns in English come out in a 17-pica width; the columns in French in a 20-pica width.

The right-hand start

You get your most dramatic display when you use an entire spread—a left- and a right-hand page facing one another—to

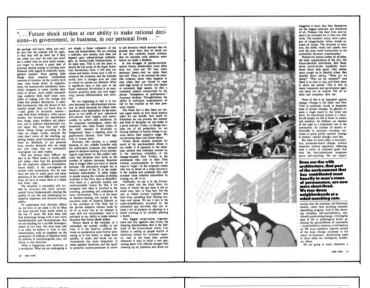

Annual Meeting

President
Raps Government
White Paper

Teller combines colorful art and typography for lead articles with a more subdued look for standing features. This news section makes use of horizontal lines, sans serif headline faces, roman body copy, and numbered pictures. Part of the magazine is printed on glossy white paper; this section, and several other news-oriented sections, are printed on dull-finish, blue-tinted stock.

open an article or story. Often you would use one piece of art so big it stretches across the gutter, uniting the two pages.

Sometimes it is necessary to start an article on a right-hand page. If the left-hand page is an ad, you will have an easy enough time of it making the opening look different from the advertisement so the two will not be read together. If the left-hand page is the ending of a previous article, you should keep art off that page so the page will not compete with the new opening page.

To get the reader to turn the page you should direct the thrust of the page to the right. You might want a slug saying "Continued" at the bottom of the page. But, please: no arrows.

Continuity

Designing facing pages so they go together is only part of the problem. You also have to arrange the spreads so *they* go together.

Some magazines like to have all pages related. Others are content to unify only those pages used for a specific article; the collection of article units making up a single issue can represent any number of design approaches.

As you unite your spreads, you may well think of yourself as performing a function similar to that of the *motion picture art director.* In fact a background in motion picture work would not be a bad background for a magazine art director. Asger Jerrild got his experience at Warner Brothers before he took over as art director of *The Saturday Evening Post.*

You can achieve a continuity for each spread by sticking with the same typefaces and the same kind of art and by positioning these consistently on the pages. You also can set up a series of horizontal visual axes and relate each spread to them.

Varying the approach

While you want the pages to work together, you also want to introduce some variety to keep the reader interested. If you can't get him to take in the whole article, at least you can get him to read the title, look at the art, and read the captions and blurbs. Many magazines now don't let a spread go by without at least offering one blurb. A few magazines have tried running subsidiary features as part of the main features. For instance, the January 1977 *Atlantic,* for an Arthur Hoppe article on tennis, shows a cartoon drawing on the spread following the opener. It is the first of a series of cartoons, one to a spread, until the article is over. The reader gets caught up in the cartoon story, which is related to the theme of the article. You see first a group of startled people at a tennis club. They have been drinking and relaxing. You see the same group on the next spread, still drinking but puzzled. And you see them again on the next spread. In the final cartoon a serious-minded player, now in the room, asks, "Tennis, anyone?" The people in the club are all dressed the part. They are even holding rackets (as well as drinks). But it is obvious they are there to socialize, not to play tennis. Now that the reader is into the spirit of the thing he will turn back and get into Hoppe's prose.

Some magazines running gag cartoons now are looking for gags that are appropriate to the subjects of the articles. These magazines are no longer content to simply plunk down cartoons as merely visual oases.

Raymond Dorn, manager of art and layout for American Medical Association magazines, has come up with something he calls the "Midwest style" of layout in which each 8 1/2 × 11

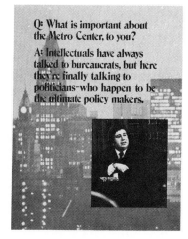

Anytime it runs a Q. and A. article, Johns Hopkins Magazine reproduces one question and one answer in large type as a title. This has the advantage of getting the reader right into the article. But it isn't always easy to arrange. As editor Elsie Hancock points out, "Grabby and central quotations seldom come in a manageable length, especially as you also have to have room for a fairly specific question and for the picture at some size. . . . It seems to be critical that the subject be actually talking in the picture, or you lose some effect of liveliness. If he's been cropped back to 20 picas or so, it also helps if he faces his words. . . ." Here you see two opening spreads using this approach. One utilizes a photograph that became only part of the opening page; the other utilizes a bleed photograph, with surprinted display type, and a smaller photograph mortised in.

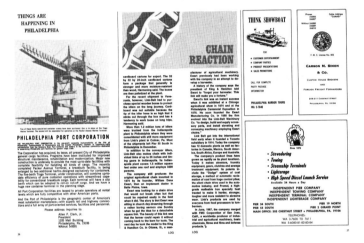

page of a magazine contains three columns of unequal width: one narrow, one wide, one regular. Copy might start in one width on the page and move over to the next column in a wider or narrower width. Photos would be cropped to fit any of the three widths or any combination of them. The typical page would contain two columns of copy and one column of art, although the art would not ordinarily occupy the full depth of the column. While such a style creates problems of copyfitting and marking, it does bring variety to magazines stuck with only routine photographs. As Dorn points out, "It creates its own pace and rhythm, even when only straight copy . . . [is available]. It also . . . forces the layout artist into using white space."[1]

1. Raymond Dorn, *How to Design & Improve Magazine Layouts,* Brookwood Publications, Oakbrook, Illinois, 1976, p. 98.

The editorial

We think of editorials as appearing only in newspapers. But magazines carry them, too. A magazine like *The New Republic* carries several of them at the beginning of the publication, before the articles. *U.S. News & World Report* carries an editorial at the end. The general-circulation weeklies used to carry editorial pages about a third of the way into the publication.

A trade journal is likely to give an early page up front to an editorial and let the editor sign it. (Newspaper editorials are almost always unsigned.) A company magazine often carries as its "editorial" a letter from the president, along with his picture.

The signing might better be done in type rather than in handwriting. A big handwritten signature issue after issue can be a design irritation.

But the editorial, because it represents pure opinion, should be made to look different from anything else in the magazine. One way to set it apart is to present it in one wide column, heavily leaded, with extra white space on either side. The format should allow for a different length each time. An editorial writer should not be made to write to fit.

There is no reason why a magazine can't dress up its editorial or editorial page with an editorial cartoon, either drawn especially for the magazine or picked up as a reprint from a newspaper or syndicate.

Products pages

Some magazines put together products pages, which are a sort of a hybrid: part editorial matter, part advertising. The editor and art director work from press releases and photos supplied by manufacturers. For each item you have a headline, some description, and usually some art. Or maybe you just have a photograph and caption. A tag line invites the reader to circle a number on a "Reader Service Card" and send it in for further information.

The designing of these sections—and the cards, which are bound into the magazine—can tax the art director, because the items are short and numerous and the art is uneven in quality.

Separating editorial matter from ads

Because advertisers don't like isolation, because they like to be up there with articles, stories, and editorials, magazines will continue their present practices of scattering advertisements throughout their pages.

Given the circumstances, Cortland Gray Smith, as editor of

In this single-page feature, Jordan, *the quarterly published by the Jordan Information Bureau, Washington, D.C., uses white space effectively to unify the title, art, and copy. The white space stays in two places, essentially: at the top and at the lower right. The reproduction does not show it, but the title and art are in maroon, the body copy in black. In another issue, the title and body copy appear in black, the art appears in blue. In still another, the title appears in reverse letters on a page of green; the art and body copy appear in black.*

"Nutritional Terms. Easily Digested." is a sometimes feature in The Body Forum, used, according to managing editor Ray Garrett, "when we feel that our readers need to be alerted to new or infrequently used terms to aid their understanding of certain articles." The art carrying the feature's title juts out from the box containing the definitions. As a visual pun and to dramatize the "Digested" in the title of the feature, an artist does a little retouching on an ordinary photograph of a book.

Metabolism — A number of separate processes are always taking place for different purposes within the human body. Protoplasm or cell material, for example, has to be built up and broken down, and energy must be provided within the body for the vital functions. The total, or sum of all the processes by which the body functions is called metabolism.

Behavior Modification — Although this is a psychological term, it relates directly to nutrition and diet through eating habits. Genetic structure, past learning experiences, and present situations combine to produce the behavior of a person. Behavior modification works on the theory that we learn and follow behaviors because they are of positive benefit to us. Overeating, for instance, gives some people more benefits than drawbacks even though they may detest being overweight. Behavior modification attempts to influence behavior by changing our learning patterns. We find that new behaviors have more rewards than the old behaviors, thus the behavior, buying two pounds of chocolate chip cookies, for instance, changes.

Chelate—This is a combination of a metal, such as zinc, for example, and an amino acid. Certain types of chelates may be absorbed very readily by the body, while others are so completely tied up by the chelating agent that no absorption is possible.

Carbohydrate — Carbohydrates, compounds of carbon, hydrogen and oxygen, are found in sugars, starches and celluloses. Carbohydrates are the nucleus of many current debates regarding proper diet.

Endocrinology — This is the science that studies how the endocrine glands (such as thyroid or pituitary) produce secretions that are carried throughout the body via the bloodstream.

Glucose — Produced mainly by carbohydrates consumed in a diet, glucose is a primary source of energy for humans and other animals. It is a syrupy liquid that travels through the bloodstream to all parts of the body in need of energy.

Glycogen — The principal type of carbohydrate that is stored in humans and converted to glucose as needed is glycogen. It is usually found in the liver—its primary place of origin—and to some degree in the muscles.

Hypoglycemia— One of the big questions marks in current dieting studies revolves around hypoglycemia, a disease characterized by an abnormally low amount of glucose in the blood. Among the numerous symptoms are tremulousness and headache. The degree of glucose insufficiency, and its effects on human feelings and behavior at various levels, is the center of the question.

Transfollicular Percutaneous Absorption—Refers to the process by which a substance applied to the skin passes down a hair follicle and into the bloodstream. By using the follicle as an entrance, and crossing into the bloodstream at the hair root, the substance can bypass the normal impenetrability of the skin. This is thought to be a possible route of access for Keratin protein into the body.

Better Editing, drew up a list of rules for separating editorial matter from advertising.[2] Among them:

1. Make editorial matter look "as different as possible from the usual advertising pattern." Editorial usually has a quieter look.

The art director usually does not know what the advertising will look like until he sees the Vandyke or page proofs. Sometimes he must make adjustments at that point. He may even convince the business side to move an ad.

If the advertiser has too successfully imitated editorial style, the magazine may run the line over the ad, "An Advertisement," to warn the reader.

2. Adopt an editorial look or pattern that is *consistent* in its use of type styles and spacing. What Smith is saying here, essen-

2. See Cortland Gray Smith, "Page Design for Flow-Through Makeup," *Better Editing*, Spring 1970, pp. 17-19.

tially, is that the formalized, highly ordered magazine has an easier time separating editorial from advertising than the more circuslike magazine.

3. Allow an extra measure of white space between editorial and advertising.

4. Concentrate ads *between* editorial features, not *within* them. He's asking here that the art director, representing the editorial department, work with the business and advertising department to establish a better lineup of page allocations.

Which brings us to one of the art director's most important jobs. Before each issue is put to bed, he should go over the Vandyke or page proofs as though he were one of the subscribers, this time not to check his design of editorial pages (he's already done this) but to see how the book looks as a unit—how the ads fit in with the articles and stories. Up until this point, he probably had no idea what each ad was to look like. Each was only a blank rectangle around which he had fit his own material. Advertising departments and editorial departments on magazines, for good reason, do not influence each other as an issue is put together.

This last-minute check can save much embarrassment. No tribute to a grand old lady will be juxtaposed with an ad for Playtex living bras. No article on the plight of the poor will start across the page from an ad for Cadillac. No antismoking article will be followed by an ad for Winston.

If you want a classic case, turn to pages 76 and 77 of the January 24, 1967, issue of *Look*. The left-hand page, all copy, features the title: "Who Will Control the GOP in 1968?" The right-hand page has a full-color, three-quarter-page bleed closeup of a young man yawning, presumably because he's comfortable on a United Air Lines flight, not because he's bored with the Republican Party.

Jerome Snyder, the late art director for *Scientific American*, said that whenever he skipped this last check, sure enough, every time, an ad fell into place next to editorial matter wholly inappropriate to it. Not that the magazine should consciously work out relationships between ads and stories. But it should keep items separated that are obviously incompatible.

Much has been written about how placement of an ad affects readership, and some advertisers pay premium rates for op-ed placement, "Campbell Soup" position, up-front placement, and so on. Recent studies tend to show that placement has less effect than was originally supposed. Ads do not necessarily have to be next to "reading matter." Editors have been moving away from the practice of continuing articles and stories in the back of the book so they will trail through ads. Perhaps eventually they will bunch the ads completely in one section of the book so that art directors can arrange editorial material into a unified whole.

NEWS NOTES

Any news? Send us a note.

One of the best-read sections of a company magazine is the section dealing with job changes and other personnel matters. Names appear frequently in bold face, so they will stand out, and mug shots decorate the page. It is a problem, sometimes, to gather the information. Some departments or plants cooperate with the editor, some don't. But is this the answer: running a special box that dominates the page? It makes those persons already named on the page appear to be publicity seekers.

The case for departmentalizing

Routine stories—of deaths, job changes, etc.—should be gathered under collective headings. This makes the design job much easier. It also makes related items easy for the reader to identify.

An obit column with a single heading makes unnecessary an editor's hunt for synonyms for death. The subheadings over each item can simply name the person. Appropriate black borders may be included with the column.

On the letters-to-the-editor column it is not necessary to start each letter with "Dear Editor" or "To the Editor." The salutation is understood. Letters should be grouped by subject. Nor does each letter need a subheading. A new subheading is necessary only when the subject changes.

Look added art—and interest—to its letters column by taking sample quotes from letters and playing them up in display type—one for each page or column of letters. The type for this display was simulated typewriter type. The letters themselves were set in sans serif type.

Look also ran a box at the end of the column giving the magazine's address and explaining the policy on letters.

At one or two spots inside the magazine you might want to run a smaller version of the cover logo: on the table of contents page and, if you have a number of advertising pages intervening before you get to your article section, at the head of the opening article. How well a cover logo will take reduction should be a consideration in its design.

You do researchers a favor when you keep the name of your magazine consistent. A number of magazines, unfortunately, use a term like "Weekly" or "Monthly" on the cover but drop it when the magazine is named inside on the table of contents page and in the masthead. You also do researchers—and readers—a favor when on each spread you name the magazine in a folio line and include the date and page number.

Interior logos

Editors tend to think of their material as falling into two categories: special departments or columns and articles or features. One of the jobs of the art director is to segregate the two. The special departments or columns appear either early or late in the publication, and standing heads mark them. Ideally, these heads share a design approach that ties them to the logo on the cover. We call them *interior logos.* Some magazines manage with type alone; others incorporate art. Like regular logos, interior logos work best with a flat, almost abstract look that over the months does not grow tiresome. And they must be kept

small—smaller, certainly, than the logo on the cover.

They often incorporate bylines and mug shots of the writers and a bit of art that tells what the writing deals with. But the real display, of course, is reserved for the major articles in the center of the book.

Coming up with column names

You give your imagination a brisk workout as you try to come up with names for your standing columns. What you settle for is important when you consider that you will be using the names for months, maybe years.

Some magazines use no-nonsense names, like "Letters" for the letters-to-the-editor column, and that may be the safer course. But other magazines are more inventive. *Trans-action*, before it changed its own name, came up with "Feedback from Our

Four of the many interior logos used by Boys' Life *to mark special sections or columns in the magazine. These go above whatever title or byline the features carry for that month. The depth changes a bit, but the width and basic format remains the same. In each case a bigger rounded rectangle with illustration sits atop a smaller rounded rectangle with type. The stencil type duplicates the stencil-type logo on the cover. Larry Ortino is the designer.* Boys' Life *is published by the Boy Scouts of America.*

This is the inside front cover for Teller, a 9 × 12 slick paper monthly published "in the interest of the staff" by the Royal Bank of Canada. Teller *reproduces its logo and (in a small size) its cover and combines them with a masthead and a table of contents printed in reverse letters on a black background. Note that the editor has really made a table out of the table of contents. The blackness of the page complements a black border around art on the cover.*

Readers," which was appropriate for its social scientist readers. *Essence,* the high-fashion magazine for black women, for a time called its letters column "Write On!" *Campus Life* at this writing was calling its letters column "Assault & Flattery." *Decision* magazine, another religious publication, breaks up its letters column occasionally with a reproduction of a letter as written. The letter chosen is from a youngster, and the handwriting or printing is awkward but charming and clear enough to reproduce well.

JAMA, the Journal of the American Medical Association, used "AMAgrams" for its column of short news items: "AMA" for the American Medical Association; "gram[s]" from a Greek word meaning "written." The art put each letter in a block, and the blocks were slightly scattered to represent blocks used in the game of anagrams. *Fitness for Living* headed its column of short news items on fitness with "All the News That's Fit," a takeoff on the slogan of the New York *Times. Tennis USA* at this writing was using "Net Results" for a column of match scores.

The title for a record column in *Senior Scholastic* was "DISCussions." The all-cap beginning was art enough. The title for a record column in *Harper's* was "Music in the Round." *Oak Leaves,* Oak Park, Illinois, called its birth announcement column "Hello World." (A good title, but it needed a comma after "Hello.")

National Review for years has put a "RIP" over its obit-editorials, and although the acronym is perfectly proper ("Rest in Peace"), it startles the reader somewhat because of a recent meaning "rip" has acquired.

Most magazines these days give as much attention to the design of a table-of-contents page as to other pages in the magazine. And for a 48-page magazine or better—a magazine like National Review—*a table of contents is likely to take up a whole page, especially when you add a partial masthead giving information on frequency of publication and other matters. The remainder of the masthead, containing editors' names, appears on another page. Photos of writers and pieces of art, reduced, from inside the book run across the top as a sort of abbreviated table of contents. The full table, boxed with a heavy rule at the top and lighter rules on sides and bottom, organizes material under several broad headings. James W. O'Bryan is art director.*

The table-of-contents page

For many years the table of contents was a no-man's land in American magazines. No longer. Now the table of contents—and the entire table-of-contents page—is a magazine showpiece.

Saul Bass made a high art of motion picture titles and credits. Today many motion pictures run an additional credit line at the beginnings or ends: "Titles by _____." Magazines haven't gone that far, but their art directors have given more thought to the table-of-contents page than ever before.

What goes on that page varies from magazine to magazine, but on most magazines, the page includes (1) the table of contents, (2) the listing of staff members, (3) the masthead, and (4) a caption for the cover picture along with a miniature version of the cover. There may also be some copy on the page, as, for example, an editorial, a preface to the issue, a statement from the publisher or editor, or an advertisement.

For some reason *The New Yorker,* alone among major

magazines, did not for many years run a table of contents. For that matter it did not—nor does it yet—run bylines, except at the ends of articles and stories. Nor do many of the opening spreads carry art. Perhaps the magazine expected readers to start at the beginning and read straight through. Perhaps it felt readers didn't have to be lured. Competition from *New York* and a general change in readers' attitudes changed *The New Yorker*, at least to the extent that in the late 1960s it began to carry a regular table of contents.

The table of contents for a magazine lists the titles of articles and stories, the names of the authors, and the page numbers where the articles and stories start. If the table is extensive, the editor divides it into sections, like "Articles," "Stories," and "Departments." *The New Yorker* and *Saturday Review* list the full names of cartoonists appearing in each issue—a worthwhile service when you consider the unreadability of most cartoonists' signatures.

For their tables of contents art directors increasingly are taking parts of illustrations inside the magazine and reproducing them with the table of contents. Raymond Dorn suggests bringing up a whole page or spread from inside the publication and reducing it way down to put on the title page.

The listing of staff members should feature the main members in the order of their rank and in parallel terminology. It should not, for instance, use "editor" for one staff member and "production" for another. Many magazines find it desirable to list principal staff members in one size type, lesser staff members in another. Editorial staff members are usually run separately from business staff members. On many magazines, the three top editorial staffers are the editor, the managing editor, and the art director. The listing need not be in the form of a table; it can be "run in" to save space.

In a democratic spirit, *Ms.* lists its staff members alphabetically under headings like "Editing," "Editorial Research," and "Design." No titles show. Patricia Carbine (who happens to be vice president of the corporation that publishes the magazine) appears third on the list, after the *Bs*, and Gloria Steinem (who happens to be president) appears near the bottom. "Design" lists three persons.

The masthead, usually in agate type, carries basic information about the magazine: date of issue, volume number, frequency of publication, name of publishing firm, editorial and business addresses, information on submitting manuscripts, information on circulation, price per copy, annual subscription rate, etc.

The masthead should make it easy for the contributor and subscriber to find the correct addresses (editorial offices often have addresses different from circulation offices). It might be a good idea to introduce each address with a boldface line: "If you

	Cover
	Contents
	Editorial
	Ads
	News
	Body Language
	Body Language
	Ads
	Entertainment
	Sports
	Sports
	Profiles

West Side Story, *a newsmagazine in tabloid form published by West High School, Iowa City, Iowa, for 1975 used huge numbers on each page. So, asked its editors, why not capture the flavor of the numbering by using part of the huge numbers in the table of contents run on page 2? This is a sample table, shown in a greatly reduced size.*

want to submit a manuscript" for one and "If you want to subscribe to the magazine" for the other. Maybe a third will be needed: "If you want to place an advertisement." Every editor should take time once each year to rethink his masthead and work with his designer to better organize the material it contains.

Every magazine has to run at least an abbreviated version of a masthead, but if the magazine is thin enough, say with sixteen pages or fewer, it can probably skip the table of contents and the listing of staff members. Or it can compress the table of contents and masthead into a single column.

For big magazines, the table of contents can go on one page, the masthead on another, the listing of staff members on still another.

Columns about people are a familiar feature in most company magazines edited for internal audiences, but often these columns suffer from poor design. Editors relegate them to the back of the book, treating them often as a necessary evil. The Illuminator, *a tabloid published by Appalachian Power Company and Kingsport Power Company, comes up with an effective way of laying out such a column. You see here one of several pages given over to short items about employees. When a mug shot is available, it runs just above the related copy. In one case (upper right corner) two mug shots are run together, so they, unlike the others, have short name-captions underneath. Typical of the other pages, this one uses heavy black bars under each of the headlines. Although the page offers six columns, other pages in this tabloid offer three, and they are of unequal widths. With columns so narrrow, copy can not be justified at the right. The reproduction here does not show that the vertical column rules are printed in color.*

Chapter 10

Newspaper makeup

In 1977 a total of 1,762 daily newspapers and 7,579 weekly newspapers were being published in the United States. The dailies also accounted for 650 Sunday papers. Almost all the weeklies and 1,200 of the dailies were printed by offset lithography.

The average daily newspaper carried close to 60 pages each day. The average Sunday carried 180 pages.[1]

The design of newspapers

The typical daily or weekly newspaper is not designed, really; its parts are merely fitted together. They are fitted together customarily in such a way as to fill in all the available space—to the top, the sides, the bottom of the page.

Sort of like a jigsaw puzzle.

Newspaper executives talk vaguely about upgrading the design of their publications, but usually they make only token efforts. These are word-oriented people, these executives—or business-oriented; and they take a hard-bitten attitude about newspaper format that, not seriously challenged in several centuries, will not quickly change now, even with late-twentieth-century technological revolutions. The late Bernard Kilgore, editor of *The Wall Street Journal*, said, "The market wraps fish in paper. We wrap news in paper. The content is what counts, not the wrapper." Forget what's going on in magazines. On TV. The newspaper executive lives by the book.

And the book says:

1. From an April 25, 1977 news release of the American Newspaper Publishers Association, Washington, D.C.

page five
news
shield
January 14, 1977

A page of news items from Shield, a monthly tabloid—a newsmagazine—published by A. N. McCallum High School, Austin, Texas. Shield also runs pages devoted to editorials and features, each page clearly labeled at the bottom, under the box. The publication usually confines ads to page blocks, alternating between a page of advertising and a page of editorial material. On this page, the editors arrange photos to form a single, irregular-shaped unit. A sophisticated design. Randy Stano is publications adviser.

1. The newspaper shall be broken up into narrow vertical columns, eight to the page, or, if you are in the avant-garde, six to the page.

2. The columns shall be separated by ruled lines.

3. Headlines shall be standardized.

4. At the top of the first page shall go the nameplate, in an Old English face, preferably in an inline or outline version.

5. Beginning on page 2, the ads; and they shall be arranged in half-pyramid form, with the greatest concentration on the right-hand side of the page.

6. With a border established uniformly for the pages, printed matter shall extend to all four sides and corners. No blank areas except in the ads, which the sponsors are free to do with as they wish.

Perhaps there is no better way to present the newspaper fare. So varied are the stories, and so numerous, they simply cannot be given the luxurious display treatment magazine articles and stories get. And the demands of daily if not hourly deadlines discourage the kind of design experimentation that goes on in the offices of more leisurely edited publications.

One man who has helped give newspapers a face-lifting is Edmund C. Arnold, former head of the graphic arts department of Syracuse University's School of Journalism now teaching at Virginia Commonwealth University. He has redesigned a number of major newspapers and served as consultant to the Mergenthaler Linotype Corporation. Carrying on the traditions established by John Allen and Albert Sutton in the 1930s and 1940s, Professor Arnold in his frequent lectures to conventions of newspapermen and in his numberless articles and books, first anesthetizes his audience with his wit, then pounds home his admirable dicta: wider columns, no column rules, more white space, all-lowercase headlines. But after several years he has succeeded only in substituting for some papers one set of rules, admittedly superior, for another.

Publisher Gardner Cowles put his finger on the problem at a meeting of the William Allen White Foundation at the University of Kansas. "A good newspaper needs a good art director. When I say this, most editors don't know what I am talking about."

He explained: Papers today are laid out or made up by editors or printers with no art background or training. Other media would not think of assigning so important a task to people not equipped for it.

On successful magazines, the art director ranks right below the top editor in importance and authority. He has a strong voice in helping decide how a story idea is to be developed. He suggests ways to give it maximum visual impact. He knows how to blend type and photographs so that each helps the other. His responsibility is to make each page come alive and intrigue the reader. Newspapers need this kind of talent. Too few have it.

Among papers that have employed art directors are the late Chicago *Daily News*, Providence *Journal* and *Bulletin*, Miami *Herald*, *Newsday* (Long Island), and *Today* (Cocoa, Fla.). *The Bulletin* of the American Society of Newspaper Editors for January 1971 ran a report on the duties of these art directors and concluded that any newspaper with a circulation of more than 50,000 needs the services of an art director. *The Bulletin* predicted that the idea of art directors for newspapers would spread.

When design help comes to newspapers it will come from outside the fraternity. It will come from graphic designers with magazine or advertising agency experience who are fast enough

A pleasantly and efficiently organized page of information about goings-on in Portland, Oregon, the area served by Willamette Week, an interpretive newspaper. The interior logo at the top echoes the style of the page 1 nameplate designed by Byron Ferris. The roman type for headlines remains constant, except for size changes. The combination of thick and thin rules nicely segregates the material. Outlined photographs combine with small line sketches to give the page some areas of visual relief.

In the new Winnipeg (Man.) Tribune, stories, at least those on the front page where ads do not interfere, form rectangles. This page could almost represent the blocked-in canvas for a Mondrian painting. The nameplate "floats" partially down on the page and takes a shape similar to what could be occupied by a news story. You see no "ears." The continued lines under three of the stories refer to the first words of headlines inside. (Reprinted by permission of the Winnipeg Tribune.)

Controls will end Oct. 14, says paper

TORONTO (CP) — The Star wage and price controls will start to be lifted Oct. 14 this year.

The newspaper says confidential documents, now being circulated by Ottawa to provincial finance ministers, set out a point-by-point argument for ending controls on Oct. 14, exactly two years after they were imposed.

Under current law, controls are not scheduled to come off until December, 1978.

The Star says Jean-Luc Pepin, chairman of the anti-inflation board, told provincial labor ministers this week that the October date is most likely.

It says the documents refer to "the equity among different groups of workers which would be obtained if the starting date for closing out the program was Oct. 14, 1977."

This date "implies that most workers would have been subject to control for two years," the newspaper quotes the documents as saying.

In general, those groups which were first in, would be first out," the documents continue.

Federal Labor Minister John Munro denied that Ottawa has decided to begin lifting anti-inflation board wage and price controls on Oct. 14, a year earlier than planned.

"I can state unequivocally that no discussions in that area have been made in cabinet," Munro told Montreal reporters asking him about a published report that Ottawa had plans for phased withdrawals from controls beginning on that date.

Speaking Saturday after attending a conference on multiculturalism, Munro said, "We have discussed various techniques for decontrol . . . what policies would be fair."

Amin warns against rescue try

NAIROBI, Kenya (AP) — President Idi Amin has moved his meeting with U.S. citizens in Uganda to Entebbe Airport, delayed it until Wednesday and warned the United States not to emulate its Israeli allies with an attempted commando rescue.

In Washington, President Carter said he "closely, trying not to upset President Amin, and trying to take advantage of his good wishes that he has expressed."

Radio Uganda reported on Sunday that Amin postponed the meeting to 8 a.m. Wednesday from 11 a.m. Monday at the request of the U.S. nationals in his East African country, who are estimated by the state department to number about 240.

Amin is apparently summoning fictions as well as U.S. citizens to a meeting with him Wednesday. British diplomats said they were checking reports that members of the 260-strong British community were ordered to attend.

Sunday's broadcast said the location of the meeting has been changed from the International Conference Centre in Kampala, the capital, because the main lounge at Entebbe is the only facility in the country large enough to accommodate the 2,000 persons who were to attend. However, there was no indication who would be present beside the Americans and Amin.

The official radio also warned Ugandans to be alert for signs of an invasion. It said after the Israeli raid on Entebbe last July,

the presence of U.S. naval vessels off the Kenyan coast "must be taken seriously."

Quoting a "military spokesman," believed to be Amin himself, the broadcast said: "In the event of an invasion, the invading force will be disintegrated by the Ugandan armed forces."

The United States and the nuclear-powered aircraft carrier Enterprise and its escorts are cruising in the Indian Ocean off East Africa following a goodwill visit to Kenya last week.

Police arrest 35 strikers

About 35 strikers were arrested this morning outside the Griffin Steel Foundries Ltd. plant in Transcona.

The strikers were attempting to prevent the plant, which has been closed since Sept. 18, from opening today with new employees.

The strikers warned last week that they would resist efforts by the company to hire strikebreakers and break the 22-week-old strike.

The strikers, who sat with arms linked in an effort to

block traffic to the plant, were removed forcible by police. They were taken in paddy wagons to the police station in the Transcona district.

Police said no charges had been laid late this morning, but that the attorney-general's office was being consulted.

No injuries were reported. Police said about 35 new employees and management personnel passed through the gates to the plant.

No. 49   Monday, February 28, 1977.   ★ ★   Final Edition

Separate Quebec viable, but disastrous: Trudeau

By Ben Tierney
Southam News Services

WASHINGTON — Prime Minister Trudeau conceded here Sunday that Quebec has all the "essential requirements" of nationhood, but insisted it would be both pointless and disastrous for the province to separate from the rest of Canada.

In a nationally televised interview with U.S. newsmen, taped at the completion of Trudeau's three-day visit to Washington last Wednesday, the prime minister said Quebec Premier Rene Levesque was right when he told a meeting of businessmen in New York last month that Quebec could be a viable nation.

"But," said Trudeau, "what I don't think he realizes is that his argument boomerangs so beautifully.

"So what? I mean Quebec has exist-

ed in this way for hundreds of years and it has progressed and it has matured freely under our federal form of government.

"It has had its language, it has had its civil laws, it has had its educational system, it has had its territory which was largely aggrandized at the beginning of the century courtesy of the federal government.

"And my answer to Mr. Levesque is, 'Well, a good point, but why separate?'"

Trudeau claimed separation would be disastrous for Quebec when asked why, during his three-day visit to the U.S. capital, he had emphasized the danger of a Quebec separation to the U.S. and left the impression that it would not be all that serious for Canada.

Trudeau replied: "Don't misunder-

stand me. I don't think it wouldn't be grave for Canada. I think it would be very grave. And as a French-Canadian myself, as a Quebecer, I think it would be disastrous for Quebec to separate.

"As a French-Canadian I think it would be terrible if we sort of ghettoized ourself rather than use the whole country as a sounding board for the French reality in Canada and so on.

At other points during the interview, which was 90 per cent taken up with Quebec, Trudeau:

• Argued that last November's Quebec election result was not a vote for separation, and that in the two previous Quebec elections, in which the Parti Quebecois campaigned openly as a separatist party, the voters of Quebec had overwhelmingly rejected it.

See QUEBEC, Page 5

The lost tread on the jetliner's tire is barely visible on the outside left wheel.

Tribune photo by Gregg Barrow

Retread forces jet landing

An airliner with 119 people aboard made an emergency landing at Winnipeg Saturday with landing gear problems.

The Transair jet, a Boeing 737, landed without incident at Winnipeg International Airport. A faulty tire was replaced and the charter flight to Mazatlan, Mexico, re-started three

hours after the touchdown.

Bob Scott, public relations director for Transair, said the plane, designated flight #83 from Winnipeg, lost the tread from a re-capped tire during its takeoff run.

The pilots noticed vibrations and, once aloft, looked out a viewing port and saw the missing cap, he said.

Departure time was 7 a.m. and the plane, which has no provision for fuel dumping, circled the region for three hours to burn off some tons of fuel and land at the proper weight.

Transport Canada's emergency plan went into operation during the wait. Hospitals were notified, ambulances

See TIRE, Page 5

Bill planned in Que.
Language limit eyed

QUEBEC (CP) — Legislation being prepared by the Parti Quebecois government will restrict freedom of choice in the language of education to citizens whose mother tongue is English.

Sources close to Cultural Development Minister Camille Laurin say there is general agreement in the cabinet on the new policy but many details have yet to be worked out before the proposed legislation is tabled in the Quebec national assembly in the session beginning March 8.

The sources said the criterion used to determine the language of education will be that recommended by the Superior Council of Education before the adoption of the Official Language Act, commonly known as Bill 22.

Under the proposal the language of education would be French for all children except those whose mother tongue is English. In doubtful cases checks would be made of

civil documents such as birth certificates to determine the mother tongue of a child.

However, the council, made up of representatives of both French and English-speaking communities, also recommended that children with brothers or sisters already in English schools be allowed into the English school system.

The sources said the government is divided on that recommendation because some ministers do not want to leave the doors of English schools open to brothers and sisters of children whose mother tongue is not English.

The PQ government wants to avoid at all costs regulations such as English proficiency tests required under Bill 22.

Premier Rene Levesque vowed overcame demands from within the party that English-language schools be abolished immediately and replaced by a unilingual French education system, sources said.

Why they go West

You've heard about the good life in British Columbia.

So have many Manitobans.

Each year, hundreds of Manitobans retire, decide they've had enough of Manitoba's ice and snow, and head west to B.C.

We thought you'd like to know how they're faring, so we sent Dave Cross, assistant managing editor, to Victoria, Penticton, Kelowna and Burnaby, to interview ex-Manitobans.

He tells about his visit in a five-part series entitled Westward-Ho, starting today on Page 18.

Ashtrays now replace sinks in school washrooms.

Students organize cleanup
Grim lesson learned

By Anne Marie Travers
Tribune Education Reporter

Students at Sisler High School don't eat their lunches in dirty washrooms anymore.

They don't fill sinks and toilets with gum and cigarette butts or strew their garbage on washroom floors like they used to.

They learned a grim lesson this month when one of their 15-year-old classmates died of hepatitis.

It was a lesson they are not likely to forget.

Up until the girl's death Feb. 15, some students were congregating in school washrooms for lunch.

While there is no evidence the girl contacted hepatitis this way, the school administration has since warned students against such habits, citing possible health hazards.

Medical officials say unsanitary practices like those at Sisler increase the risk of spreading disease.

In an interview Friday, Dr. John Waters, deputy provincial epidemiologist, said "you're talking about an increase in a small risk but it is increased, there's no question about that." The circumstances would be conducive to the transmission of all sorts of germs and viruses, he said, noting however, that hepatitis is most often spread through close and prolonged physical contact.

There is no evidence the girl contacted hepatitis by eating in the school washrooms. In fact, her friends said she never did. But the potential danger is real and other children admitted to eating there under filthy conditions.

The Tribune visited Sisler Friday in response to parents' charges that there was moss growing on the walls of the boys' shower stalls, girls smoking and eating in the washrooms; sinks full of butts and a dirty lunchroom.

Pop cans, wet socks, tissue paper and a jock strap were found scattered on the floor of the boys' change room. The blue-green shower stall walls were peeling and almost all shower heads were missing. There was no evidence of moss but rust-colored splotches gave the impression of growth.

All but one of the girls' washrooms were locked for the lunch hour. The girls described them as "condemned," implying they were off limits.

In the one open washroom, girls were smoking but there was no sign of food.

Hand-printed signs on the walls read: "Clean up operation now in progress"; "Welcome to the can . . . enjoy," and a third which urged students to flush cigarette butts

See STUDENTS, Page 5

Inside your Tribune

News summary	2
Local news	3, 4
World news	42
Editorials	6
Comics	27
Crossword	27
Entertainment	8-12
Sport	13-18
Lifestyle	20-41
Business	38-21
Deaths	7, 15
Movies	27
TV	28
Classified	15-25

Don't miss reading today's Trib Classified to catch such "best buy" items as

GOLF CLUBS: SPALDING TOP FLITE registered iron set, 4 woods, chippers putters, Ajay Reg. auto cart with 12 house, virtually no bag wear. $400.

It all starts on page 23 of today's Trib. To place your Free Private Party Want-Ad phone us today at 866-8790.

The weather: Sunny this morning, clouding over this afternoon with a high near -7. Low tonight near -18. Tuesday, clear with a high near -5.

Printed and published daily except Sunday by Southam Press Limited, at 257 Smith Street, Winnipeg, Manitoba.

Daily 15 cents, Friday, (with TV-Times) 20 cents Saturday (Weekend Edition) 20 cents

and flexible enough to deal with multiple daily deadlines and late-breaking news and, more important, who are capable of making editorial as well as art and design decisions. It will come from graphic designers who are verbally as well as visually literate.

Persons with these traits are hard to find, because, as Clive Irving, the British designer, points out, "tradition has separated the two."

One paper found such a person. What happened on that paper, from a design standpoint, may have been a first step in revolutionizing the newspaper look.

Portugal devalues currency

LISBON (Reuter) — Portuguese tightened their belts Saturday after the announcement of a 15-per-cent devaluation of their currency and the most wide-ranging package of economic measures since the 1974 military coup which ended almost a half-century of rightwing dictatorship.

The austerity drive—combined with incentives to investment and exports—is designed to rescue and revive the country's ailing economy and boost its chances of joining the European Common Market.

It is the first official devaluation of the escudo since the Bank of Portugal began fixing the rate in 1931, although its weakness on international markets has been evident for some years.

Other main measures contained in the package are:

- A price freeze for a year on basc foods
- Tighter control on non-essential imports and an extension of a 60-per-cent surcharge on such goods
- An increase in the bank rate from 6½ to eight per cent
- Tax concessions to boost Portuguese exports
- Higher postal charges and telephone rentals

Detective dusts for fingerprints on remains of bank safe

Burglars pulled boner, empty safe destroyed

RYAN, Okla. (AP) — Would-be robbers almost reduced the People's Bank of Ryan to a mass of rubble early Sunday in an attempt to steal a 5,000-pound safe that turned out to be empty.

"Just driving up here, you would have thought they used explosives," said Jefferson County Sheriff Don Allen. He said no damage estimate had been made.

Someone pried open the bank's front doors and ran a cable from a winch truck to the steel safe in a far corner of the bank, Allen said. The thieves then activated the winch and began pulling the safe toward the door.

"The safe tore and pushed through the door," he said. "About two feet of the front of the bank is brick veneer and the rest is glass. When it went through the door, it pulled frame, door and all out."

When police arrived, they found the safe in the middle of Main Street, about 60 feet from what used to be the front of the bank. The cable was still attached to the safe.

A winch truck was found abandoned near the Red River, a few miles south of here.

Allen said the truck probably was stolen and the bandits were strangers to the area./

"Everybody around here knew it wasn't used any more."

Having trouble keeping up with all the news? Don't miss The Tribune's News of the Week in Review every Saturday in the Focus section.

From Page One

Students clean up own mess

(Continued)

down the toilet instead of leaving them on the floor and in the sinks.

The girls claim they congregate there to smoke because there is nowhere else to go. (Smoking is not permitted in the school.)

They launched a clean-up campaign in early February when they became fed up with the filthy conditions.

"It was really bad in here," said one girl. "You name it and it was on the floor and in the sinks.

Students accepted full responsibility for the conditions. As one girl put it: "We all made the mess and we all cleaned it up."

Everyone pitched in one day and washed the walls, swept the floors and scoured the sinks and toilets, she said.

The timing of the campaign — just after their friend took sick — was merely coincidental, they said.

J. D. MacFarlane, the school principal, attributed the volunteer clean-up to "feelings of pride and shame on behalf of fellow students that the school they live in day to day was in that condition."

Shortly after the girl's death, he said, the student council proposed a student patrol to monitor behavior in the washrooms, lunchroom and corridors.

The patrol, which started Feb. 21, consists of 10 senior and 10 junior high school students who assume their duties through the lunch hour.

Student president Gary Dolski said the patrol can either warn a student or take him to the principal's office. He said four students have been reprimanded in the past week.

Mr. MacFarlane said the patrol idea came in direct response to the girl's death. "It shocked the kids and they figured it's time we corrected some of the things that need correcting. There was no feeling that picking up soft drink cans would stop someone from dying, but there was a feeling that there were some conditions in the school that weren't what they should be."

Asked why the administration had failed to take action about children eating in the washrooms, he called it repulsive and said he wasn't aware it was being done on such a large scale.

"There was no feeling there was any serious health hazard. If kids are going to smoke you can't stop them. Sometimes it takes something like this to bring it home to everyone.

"With high school kids you prevent them doing things that will be harmful to others but if they're going to do things that are harmful to themselves, what can you do? Smoking is a case in point," he said.

He said students receive instruction about good health practices and are especially warned about the dangers of smoking.

As for the dangers of eating in the washroom, he said he didn't think it was ever the subject of a health lesson. "It's one of those things where hindsight is better than foresight."

Boys' shower room at Sisler High.

He said school facilities for lunch are more than adequate and rarely full. Grade 12 students were provided with a separate lunchroom last year, he added, but it was closed because of vandalism.

As for the boys' shower room, Mr. MacFarlane said he asked the school board some time ago to tile it but no action was taken. However, he said, he has been promised it will be repainted, and equipped with shower heads and a ventilation system.

Dr. Waters said the condition of the shower room was more an aesthetic problem than a health hazard.

Mr. MacFarlane said a city health inspector gave the school a clean bill of health the day after the girl's death.

Sisler High school, with a student population of more than 1,300, is one of the city's largest schools.

Winnipeg school trustees discussed the unsanitary conditions at the school at an in-camera board meeting Feb. 22.

The discussion was not public because it touched on matters relating to personnel, a source said.

37 N.B. hockey fans hurt when arena roof collapsed

ST. BASILE, N.B. (CP) — Thirty-seven people were taken to hospital at nearby Edmundston, N.B., for treatment of injuries suffered when a portion of the roof of the arena here collapsed Sunday during a hockey game.

A hospital spokesman said early today that 10 of the 37 were being kept in hospital, one was under further observation, eight had been released and the remainder were awaiting examination or x-rays.

He said none of the injuries appeared to be critical although several people were suffering from broken bones.

Roger Auffrey of St. Basile, an off-duty RCMP constable who attended the hockey game with his wife, said about a quarter of the arena was covered with debris when the roof collapsed during an intermission in a game between St. Basile Aces and Riviere du Loup, Que., Three Ls of the Republican Hockey League.

About 800 people attended the game in the arena which can hold about 2,000.

Guy Lebel, a photographer who was attending the hockey game, said some people were badly cut by aluminum from the arena roof.

If the accident had happened when all the fans were in their seats "it would have been a massacre," he said.

Constable Auffrey said several people were trapped under the metal roofing, between large beams, making it difficult for rescuers to get to them. Others, including the constable's wife, were thrown out of the danger area when the seats collapsed.

Mrs. Auffrey had bruised her leg but, like many others, did not go to hospital for treatment.

Lebel said the arena is about 25 years old.

Mayor Edmund Theriault of St. Basile said he believed the weight of people in the stands—not the snow on the roof—caused the wall which supported the roof to give way.

He said the collapsed portion was about 120 feet square.

The crowd at Sunday's game was considered unusually large for this village of 3,500. An extra attraction was a presentation for Jean-Louis Lavoie, a long-time goaltender for the St. Basile Aces.

Lebel said attendance was double the number that usually attend Republican League games.

Tire forces jet landing

(Continued)

were on standby and crash trucks were stationed near the point of touchdown.

In the terminal building itself, there was no evidence of alarm; very few people were aware that airport officials were dealing with a critical situation. Up to the last few seconds before touchdown, flights departed normally and a pair of aged DC-3s continued their tedious touch-and-go landing practices.

The twin-engined 737, registered CF-TAQ and named "Fort Rouge," made a low, slow pass in front of the control tower to allow controllers a visual check of the tire, then went into its approach circuit.

The 60-ton aircraft eased down the glide path and touched gently on to the runway, slowing down gradually as the thrust reversers on its engines roared. The crash trucks, beacons flashing, sped after it, then stood by as the plane eased to a halt.

The jet was towed to the Transair ramp but neither the 113 passengers nor the six crew members were allowed to speak with reporters about the incident.

Mr. Scott said it was a "fairly routine" incident, but conceded it had only occurred about three times in Transair's last five years of operations.

Passengers were told about the problem just after take-off, and they remained calm throughout, he said.

Re-capped tires are common on company aircraft and comply with Transport Canada regulations, he said. Two of the four tires on the main landing gear were new and two were re-caps — one on each of the two main wheel assemblies.

Tires are inspected daily by Transair maintenance crews as part of the routine safety check. As well, aircrews do visual checks before each flight, said Mr. Scott.

Transport Canada is investigating the incident, a standard procedure for such occurrences, said a spokesman.

Quebec holiday could further relations: Clark

OTTAWA (CP) — Progressive Conservative Leader Joe Clark has suggested that more English Canadians vacation in Quebec to help improve mutual understanding with French Canadians.

Speaking on how individual English Canadians may help defeat Quebec separation, Mr. Clark said "it would not hurt" if "more English Canadians made it a point to, for example, take their holidays in the province of Quebec."

"It might sound minor—I think it isn't," he said in an interview for broadcast on CTV's Question Period on Sunday.

Commenting on Prime Minister Trudeau's Washington speech that "a small majority" of Quebecers support separation, Mr. Clark said it is a minority but "I don't know how small it is."

"It would be wise, prudent for us, for federalists, to assume" that the 40 per cent of the Quebec voters who elected the Parti Quebecois government "have at least taken a first step towards separatism," Mr. Clark said. And they have to be persuaded to choose one Canada.

Mr. Clark, who became leader of his party a year ago, called his first year as leader a period of "organization and identification."

"I think the second year is probably consolidation and definition. That's my political task as I look ahead."

Answering a question, Mr. Clark said that he doesn't intend to "get into the wholesale vending of specific policy matters because I really believe that's irresponsible."

"I expect to be taken seriously when I articulate a policy and so I'm only going to do it when I know we're able to say something we can act on later."

However, Mr. Clark said he expects that "over the next several months, we will be indicating, I hope, more clearly the areas in which we differ" with the Trudeau government.

Mr. Clark acknowledged that historically the Conservative party has not done as well as the Liberals in Quebec, but said his party's problems are much less severe in Quebec than the problems of the Liberal party are in other parts of the country."

Missing man's car found

Winnipeg police today were thoroughly examining a car owned by Henry David Elsasser, 70, who disappeared Jan. 28.

The car was found by a snowmobiler Sunday about 200 feet from the Red River near the end of Drury Road, half a mile south of the Perimeter Highway, a police spokesman said.

Mr. Elsasser failed to return a month ago to his home at 268 Minnehaha Ave. in West St. Paul, after seeing his son off at Winnipeg International Airport. His dog returned home two days later.

The police officer said the car was found off the end of the road, just over the river-bank incline, about 4:45 p.m.

"We're keeping an open mind on it and having a good look at it today," he said.

Quebec viable separate: PM

(Continued)

- Reiterated that he would accept separation if the people chose it democratically, and that he would not use force to keep Quebec within Confederation unless force was being used to take it out;
- Repeated his view that the November election in Quebec has forced English-Canada to face the reality of the French fact in Canada and confronted it with the choice of responding maturely to that reality or allowing Quebec to go;
- Restated his view that the break-up of Canada would present more of a threat to the U.S. than the Cuban missile crisis, suggesting, without specifically saying so, that Quebec could become another Cuba.

Dealing with his contention that last November's vote was not a vote for separatism, Trudeau said the Parti Quebecois "had two general elections in the province where it tried to get elected on a separatist plank . . . and it was very, very roundly defeated.

"This time they said, 'We are not going to campaign on separatism, we are going to campaign on good government. We want to provide an alternative to the third government.' And they insisted separatism was not the issue.

"Whenever separatism was put to them (the voters of Quebec) as a question, 'Do you want a separatist government?,'' they said no, and they said no very roundly . . . when given a choice they rejected it."

Commenting on the use of force to keep Quebec within Confederation, Trudeau noted that there is no provision in the Canadian constitution for the peaceful cecession of a province.

"But," he added, "my attitude is that a democratic country like Canada should only hold together because the people want to hold it together.

Coffee laced with acid

PHILADELPHIA (AP) — A 16-year-old student, reprimanded the previous day, served his photography teacher a cup of coffee laced with hydrochloric acid, school officials said.

Bailey Dean, 31, said he felt ill after taking only a sip of the coffee Friday. He reported to the school nurse, then was taken to hospital where he was treated and released.

"Being a teacher, you can take the obvious kind of assault," Dean said.

Police were called to the school and Dean, following procedures suggested earlier this year by city school Supt. Michael Marcase, pressed charges against the youth.

The boy, whose name was not released, was charged with reckless endangerment and two counts of assault.

Was top Nevada labor leader kidnapped?

LAS VEGAS, Nev. (AP) — Nevada labor leader Al Bramlet telephoned the Dunes Hotel shortly before he disappeared and asked a hotel executive to deliver $10,000 to a Las Vegas casino, said Bramlet's wife.

Bramlet, 60, has not been heard from since late last Thursday when he did not return home from a business trip to Reno. Authorities have no leads, and his union has posted a $25,000 reward for information leading to his whereabouts.

His wife of two months, Barbara, 27, said Bramlet made the telephone call to the Dunes on Thursday night and asked that the money be delivered immediately to a downtown casino.

The call was the last word from Bramlet, head of Local 226 of the Culinary Workers Union for the last 24 years and president of the state AFL-CIO for more than a decade.

"I hope we don't have a Hoffa case on our hands," said an investigator, referring to the disappearance of former Teamsters boss James Hoffa 18 months ago.

Mrs. Bramlet said the unidentified executive called the casino where the money was to have beeen delivered and found that officials there knew nothing of the planned delivery.

Mrs. Bramlet said the Dunes didn't deliver any money but the casino agreed to make $10,000 available to anyone who came in asking for it. No one did, she said.

Mrs. Bramlet said she still believes her husband is alive and is being held by kidnappers. "I'm just really hanging on to hope. Now as time goes on, the scales tip the other way, but I think it's still too early to give up hope."

Bramlet, who started his culinary career as a potwasher in Peoria, Ill., in the mid 1930s, rose to power in 1953 by taking over leadership of the local here when the strip was not much more than a two-lane highway. Since then he has guided the local to a membership of 22,000, giving him the power to meet and bargain with the state's top politicians and businessmen.

An inside page (page 5) receives the continued stories, and helps the reader find them with a "From Page One" box. Just to the left of that box is what would qualify as an "ear": a little ad for a feature in the paper later in the week. Like page 1, this page, without ads, divides into pleasantly proportioned rectangles, with rules defining the areas. Notice that inside the "From Page One" section the horizontal rules separating the three continuations are light; this helps keep the section together.

The look of the late Herald Trib

It would be nice to report that because it tried harder the Avis of New York newspapers was able to catch up with the stodgy New York *Times.* Unfortunately, the *Herald Tribune* not only failed to catch up; it failed to survive. And yet, in its last days, it was, by all odds, America's best-designed newspaper.

Once a near-equal to the *Times* in circulation in the New York morning field, the *Herald Tribune* by 1963 had fallen far behind. In desperation its management considered a number of editorial changes and—more important to the readers of this book—a

Here's your new Tribune!

If you are going to the trouble of redesigning your newspaper, promote the new look. Here is the wrap-around used by the Winnipeg Tribune to introduce the first issue after the redesign. Yellow and black were used. The inside of the four-page section pointed out that "The Trib's new design is the result of months of work to produce a newspaper with a modern look, and an arrangement of features and stories that will save your time and energy. . . . This new look isn't just cosmetics; it's designed for you, the reader, with sharper headline type and a reorganization of the paper to put things where our research said you wanted them. . . . And to make it easier to find what you want to read, just about every page in the new Tribune is labelled, so you'll know at a glance what you're getting."

number of design changes. Long a pacesetter in typographic excellence among newspapers, the *Herald Tribune* decided a *radical* change was in order.

The man management turned to was a stranger to newspapers: Peter Palazzo, an advertising and graphic designer. With no preconceived notions of what a newspaper should look like, Palazzo conducted a study and was surprised to find that newspapers—all newspapers—had scarcely changed at all in format over the years.

Convinced that in competition with magazines, newspapers, from the standpoint of quality, were running a poor second, Palazzo recommended changes for the *Herald Tribune* in both design and editorial content and treatment. To improve itself the paper would have to coordinate its editorial and design operations. And yet Palazzo asked for nothing revolutionary. He worried, rightly, about reader habit.

"One must be very careful about tampering with habits which have built up over a long period of time," he said. Perhaps he was thinking of the 1962 storm that followed the about-face made by *The Saturday Evening Post*.

What Palazzo asked for and got, essentially, was a magazine look for the paper. He concentrated on the Sunday issue, especially the Sunday magazine section and the front pages of the other sections.

He insisted that more thought be given to selection, editing, and placement of pictures. Cropping of pictures was often needed, he admitted, but he reminded his client that when you crop a picture you change what it says. Cropping does more than simply "move the reader in close."

For its headlines the *Herald Tribune* had been using Bodoni Bold, an "in" face among the better-designed newspapers in America. Palazzo requested Caslon, which, as far as management was concerned, was a face for advertising and book typography. Anyway, did it have the quality Palazzo ascribed to it? To convince the skeptics, Palazzo lettered a four-letter word, first in Bodoni, then in Caslon. And, by golly, in Caslon the word looked almost respectable!

Print, the prestigious magazine of graphic design, in its September/October 1964 issue, applauded the new *Trib* look, saying the change has been "widely hailed as a milestone in newspaper design." But other papers were not willing to emulate it because it was, essentially, a *magazine* look. Only in their locally produced magazine sections did the look take hold. Most editors of these sections recognized *New York*, the Sunday magazine of the *Herald Tribune*, as the most beautiful in the industry. Some of these editors, moved by what they saw, shortly after the appearance of the new *Trib* began to make greater use of white space, heavy and light horizontal rules, old-style roman headline faces in lighter-than-usual weights, and even italic swash capitals where appropriate. *West*, the Sunday magazine of the Los Angeles *Times*, took on the look of the *Herald Trib*.

By the end of 1966 the New York *Herald Tribune*, its design already compromised through merger with other papers earlier in the year, gave up altogether. Good design—and some fine writing, especially in the magazine section—could not save the paper.

Following his experience with the *Herald Tribune* Palazzo redesigned a number of other papers, including the Providence *Journal*. Among his later projects was the redesigning of the Winnipeg (Man.) *Tribune*, which appeared in its new dress

The nameplate for the redesigned Winnipeg (Man.) Tribune. In designing it, Peter Palazzo picked a size for the "The" and the "Winnipeg" that allowed him to fit the two words into areas left free from ascending strokes in the main word. To assure a better fit, he eliminated the right arm of the T in "The." The outline, shadowed letters and the rounded box surrounding them, with plenty of blank space around the letters, give the nameplate a strong, modern appearance. On the front page of the Tribune it appears in a size much bigger than this, of course, and with yellow ink filling in the space between the box and the outlines of the letters.

Some interior logos for the Winnipeg Tribune, shown smaller than they actually appear on the pages. Note the design relationship they bear to the paper's nameplate. But unlike the nameplate, these logos combine solid with outline letters. The nature of the boxes remains the same, although they are shallower than the box for the nameplate.

September 6, 1975. ". . . We regard Peter as not only an excellent graphics man," says Gerald Haslam, editor, "but equally important, as a designer who is able to relate his knowledge and proposals to the people in the newsroom who actually do the work."[2]

When the New York *Times* was making plans in 1975 to go from eight to six columns for page one, *New York* asked Peter Palazzo, as an exercise for that magazine, to redesign the *Times's* page one. You can see his solution in a two-page sequence in the

2. Letter to the author from Gerald Haslam, February 4, 1977.

A front page and an editorial page of the Minneapolis Tribune, redesigned in 1971 by British designer Frank Ariss. With its precise, clean, contemporary look, appropriate for computer-assisted production, the Tribune is one of the most attractive and readable newspapers in the United States. There are no column rules and no paragraph indentations. The most important front-page story appears at the top left rather than at the top right. The nameplate and headline face are in Helvetica. The symbol of the open newspaper (or of the sheet of paper on a web press; it depends upon how you look at it) appears on various pages.

April 1975 issue (pages 45 and 46).

One criticism Palazzo had for the eight-column paper was that it didn't clearly enough tell readers which stories were really important. "Why must page one be a do-it-yourself kit?" Another criticism centered on the use of pictures more to break up blocks of type than for the information pictures themselves carry.

Palazzo argued against the concept of bylines. They are great ego boosters for reporters, he said; but they are a design nuisance. He suggested "tag lines" at the ends of stories instead.

Palazzo also quarreled with the use of condensed, all-cap

---

8 A   Tuesday, April 13, 1971

Minneapolis

Established 1867

Bower Hawthorne Editor
Wallace Allen Managing Editor
Leonard Inskip Editorial Editor

Volume CIV Number 324

The new individualism isn't enough

By James Reston
New York Times Service

Public concern about the prisons

The fall of Jens Christensen

The Partnership for the Arts

Contradictory expectations

Ralph Ellison
in "Invisible Man"

"The original is in the British Museum."

Great leap forward

Letters from readers

Arneson responds to article

Oil and the war

Cigarette advertising

High earners productive

Flakne's charge of 'politics'

Nixon's 'half-satisfying' speech

By William F. Buckley
Washington Star
Syndicate

New York

Letters
from readers

Two versions of a heading for
the letters column of the Minneapolis Tribune, shown here
actual size. When the column
spreads over onto two pages,
the paper runs one of these on
the editorial page, the other on
the op-ed page.*

headlines, the overuse of decks for headlines (although he did
not advocate doing away with them altogether), and the arbitrary appearance of an occasional all-italics headline.

His redesigned page had more of a horizontal look, with
multi-column rather than single-column headlines; photographs
clustered rather than scattered; pictures and captions presented
as self-contained units; a summary column of news that, with
page numbers, served as general table of contents to what was
inside; better displayed stories but fewer of them; and consistent
typographic devices to segregate "hard" from "soft" news.

The look of the New York Times

While the New York *Times* does not yet have a front page that
rivals the clean look of some other papers, it has made great
strides in the redesign of its special sections, especially those carried in the Sunday issues. The crisp typography there, the

*Headings for regular columns
in the* Tribune *are look-alikes:
each carries a line-conversion
portrait, balanced at the right
by a heavy bar that forms a
near-box. Samples are shown
here in actual size. Note that
one heading only names the
columnist; the other does that
and carries a column title, too.
Still, the headings clearly are
related.*

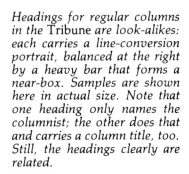

horizontal rules, the white space, and the imaginative art has inspired newspapers all over the country to reexamine their dress. The *Times* special-section look now is widely imitated.

And on its news pages the paper's use of photography has been outstanding. Only its poor quality letterpress reproduction keeps the paper from being mentioned more often as a showplace for good photojournalism. A writer in the *Columbia Journalism Review* notes that the "good, gray *Times*" publishes more pictures than the *Daily News* does; the *News*, he said, ought to drop its motto, "New York's Picture Newspaper."

Like many other newspapers, the *Times* has gone to a six-column format, not so much to improve the looks of the front page but to save money. In changing from eight narrow to six wider columns, the paper was able to chop off a modest three-quarters of an inch from the page and save itself $4,000,000 a year in newsprint costs.[3]

Observing the changes at the *Times* and other papers going for the six-column format, a writer in *Columbia Journalism Review* expressed some misgivings. The changes, he thought, would mean a shrinkage of news content. Wider columns meant an increase in type size.[4]

Even Clive Irving had misgivings about what was going on at the *Times*. That its front page had always looked a bit intimidating added to the paper's greatness, he thought. "I have learned to read its codes and to respect it as a basic American institution. At a moment when nothing else seems to hold together, why add to the confusion?"

Like others, he suspected that the changes would result in less material being presented. "And you won't know how good the old page one is until it's gone."[5]

Page three of The Paper, *a short-lived daily at Oshkosh, Wisconsin, was always a second "front" page, free of ads. Where page one devoted itself to national and international news, page three devoted itself to local news.*

The attempt to keep up with the times

Clive Irving observed in 1975 that "In the last decade cosmetic surgery has swept . . . U.S. newspapers, often as part of the revolution in printing technology. In places as disparate as Minneapolis, Louisville, and Providence, the message seems to be that the packaging of newspapers works like the packaging of almost anything else—improving it moves the merchandise."[6]

The concensus was that, by and large, newspapers still had a long way to go. Newspapers look as though they are appealing to readers 30 or 40 years ago, said Peter Palazzo. "We're living

3. Clive Irving, "Does God Care What the Times Does with Page One?" *New York,* April 14, 1975, p. 47.
4. Fred C. Shapiro, "Shrinking the News," *Columbia Journalism Review,* November/December 1976, p. 23.
5. Clive Irving, *op. cit.,* p. 47.
6. Clive Irving, *loc. cit.*

One of the nation's handsome small-city newspapers, The Dispatch *of Lexington, North Carolina, recently redesigned, uses traditionally narrow columns and caps-and-lowercase headlines and yet achieves a today look. "In designing our paper," editor Ralph Simpson reports, "we tried to become more interesting without becoming too folksy; we wanted to be dignified without being stodgy." Notice the "Good Afternoon" greeting at the top, accompanying the prominent dateline; the nicely-drawn modern-roman nameplate with its "A" jutting up higher than the other letters to compensate for its pointed shape; the heavy rules used in conjunction with lighter rules; and the unheadlined 3-unit table of contents at the lower right.*

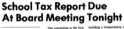

in an age of audio-visually educated readers, and competing with much brighter visual products," said Thomas Winship, editor of the Boston Globe. *"Too many papers look dull in comparison."*[7]

Those new sections

New York magazine started it all with its "survival kit" journalism showing readers how to cope in a city beset by crime but brimming with adventure and good buys. Other city magazines offered similar warnings and advice. Newspapers followed suit, some with special tabloid sections.

7. "The Great Paper Chase," *Newsweek,* May 31, 1976, p. 73.

And to gain or regain youthful readers—all the surveys showed that the TV-reared generation was ambivalent to print—newspapers made special efforts to appeal to the young. "Although our circulations are increasing," says Barry Bingham Jr., editor and publisher of the Louisville (Kentucky) *Courier-Journal* and *Times,* "our percentage of penetration is going down, especially among the young. If this continues, we will become a geriatrics medium of communication."

Young readers were the group advertisers wanted to reach. They were the group that spent money. Big-city newspapers launched tabloids and special sections that dealt with recreation, the outdoors, entertainment, lifestyles. Some of the added publications attempted to be hip. "Clearly, the newspaper

For its editorial page, The Dispatch *uses the nameplate type for "OPINION" with bold lines across the top, as on page 1. The neatly designed masthead (the box that names the top officers and gives other information) is centered in the area carrying the editorial (for this issue, an editorial from another paper), with the Oliphant editorial cartoon just below. Mug shots of columnists are cropped unusually close and made into horizontals instead of the usual verticals. Perhaps the design theme would be better served on this page if the double-ruled lines above the "Letters" column, the Jack Anderson column, and the Patrick Buchanan column and under the cartoon were filled in to make single lines as bold as the ones at the top of the page.*

OLD

NEW

'repackaging revolution' is speeding ahead . . . , in cities large
and small, and among suburban papers as well [as metropolitan
dailies]," wrote Fred Danzig in *Advertising Age* in 1977.

The proliferation of tab sections caused some critics to
wonder if newspapers were losing sight of their basic reason for
existence: to present the news so that the people can be informed
and make intelligent decisions on important matters.

Design under existing conditions

To suggest ways to revolutionize the standard format for
newspapers is too much of a job for a book dealing generally
with all aspects of publication design. All this volume can do is
point out that newspapers stand in *need* of change. That change
will come eventually seems certain.

In the meantime, readers of this chapter will want to know
how they can best operate under existing conditions. What
follows is a discussion of the best current techniques for laying
out the pages of a standard newspaper.

First, the editor—or makeup artist—will have to understand
newspaper production.

To illustrate a speech he was to make a group of newspaper executives, Dan Kelly, senior vice-president and creative director of the Chicago office of Foote, Cone & Belding, asked art directors at his agency to redesign some newspaper front pages, four of which are shown here. Original pages are shown at the left, redesigned pages at the right. Although the art directors admitted that their suggested formats might be impractical, they did feel that "newspapers can be more inviting, more interesting, and more relevant to their readers in the communications explosion of the '70's." The designers are Dave Hunter (Knoxville Journal), Pat Sindt (St. Louis Post-Dispatch), Jay Fisher (Tulsa Daily World), and Bert Hoddinott (Chicago Today). Chicago Today was a tabloid.

To see if there are "other ways to design newspapers so they'll be more exciting and interesting," the Louisville (Ky.) Times brought 30 editors and designers together for a seminar in 1974. Each designer redesigned the front page of the Times. This one, by Paul Back of Newsday, struck participants as the most promising. Back uses a device here of emphasizing the first word of each headline, helping the reader speedily choose those stories he wants to read.

Louisville Times

SATURDAY EVENING   JUNE 1, 1974 / 10¢

Secretary of State Henry Kissinger brought back good news from his 34-day Middle East peace mission. Yesterday he spoke with President Nixon in the White House Rose Garden about the talks.

Prisoners exchanged by Israel and Syria are greeted by joyous throngs

Associated Press

Joyous crowds in Damascus and Tel Aviv greeted the first returning prisoners of war today as Israel and Syria began the exchange of wounded POWs promised in their development pact.

The prisoners had been captured in last October's war.

Red Cross medical planes left the two cities midway apart this morning carrying a total of 38 repatriated prisoners, some legless or in casts.

An hour later 12 wounded Israeli soldiers stepped off the shattered Fokker Friendship plane at Ben Gurion airport near Tel Aviv. They were greeted with kisses, tears and flowers from moist-eyed women soldiers.

At about the same time 25 Syrians and one Moroccan arrived in a wildly emotional welcome in Damascus. Red-bereted military police formed a crowd of hundreds from the plane to enable the POWs to disembark.

Women wailed and men cheered in Damascus as the plane taxied to a halt. But a hush fell over the crowd as the first wounded man was carried out to stretchers. Legless, he sat rigidly upright, his right hand raised in a military salute.

Legs are nothing. We are ready to give our souls," he shouted. Cheers broke out drowning his words.

He then muscled up being lifted from his stretcher and placed on the ground as he could bend down to kiss the soil.

Prime Minister Golda Meir, Defense Minister Moshe Dayan and Chief of Staff Lt. Gen. Mordechai Gur were among the hundreds who greeted the returning Israelis.

"This is the first stage of the end of the war," said Dayan as the men, some on bandages and in casts boarded ambulances for a brief drive to Tel Hashomer hospital.

He pledged that Israeli troops would not budge from the Syrian front until all the prisoners are back.

The scenes of joy contrasted sharply with the earlier POW departures from the airports.

In Damascus, newsmen were barred from the airport as the Israelis were led away.

*See JOYOUS
Back page, col. 3, this section*

Trains that once flew now crawl along the tracks

By ROB KASPER
Louisville Times staff writer

When railroad monorails sang about today a Chicago-to-Louisville passenger train they aren't are likely words like "Cannonball," "Special" or "Zephyr." They'll choose slow, heavy, bluesy words.

For the most notable characteristic about this Amtrak train — known as The Floridian because one of its terminal points is Miami — is that when it rolls between Chicago and here, it is one of the slowest trains in the United States.

When it gets past Louisville it flies. But in Indiana it just shuffles, a Floridian passenger said recently.

Last Saturday, for instance, the train lumbered into Chicago at 10 a.m. exactly, 12 hours after it left Louisville. That is an average speed of 25 miles per hour for the 300-mile trip.

Tuesday morning it edged into Louisville's Union Station in slightly better time. On this journey the train averaged 26 m.p.h. and rolled to a stop at 7 a.m. 10 1-2 hours after leaving Chicago.

At 30 m.p.h. a car can travel from Louisville to Chicago in slightly less than 6 hours.

Buses make the trip in 7 hours and jets take less than an hour airport to airport.

"This train is a disgrace," complained a gray-haired woman as the train chugged through the Indiana dusk. "It is so slow and the rough ride ... I couldn't sleep last night."

"I agree," replied the porter receiving the brunt of the woman's anger.

It is those Penn Central tracks," the porter continued. "Our fixed time of the scene ones last week, but the Penn Central is bankrupt."

In a nutshell, that is the main problem with the train. From Chicago to Louisville The Floridian rides on Penn Central track. Since 1970, when the railroad petitioned for bankruptcy, its track

*See TRAINS
Page A6, col. 1*

It's a long, slow ride from Chicago to Louisville. Mrs. Etta Faber, of Chicago, and fellow Floridian passengers relied on reading and sleeping to help pass the time on a train that usually averages only 25-30 m.p.h.

Drinking on credit doesn't go down well with the state

By LES WHITELEY
Louisville Times staff writer

Walk into your neighborhood tavern, where you are a regular patron, ask the bartender to let you have a drink on credit and he starts to reply "Sorry, but I'm not allowed to sell liquor on credit. You've got to pay cash."

But walk into a hotel motel restaurant or large nightclub, where you've never been before, hand the waitress a credit card to cover your drinks and she probably won't bat an eyelash.

The latter, according to the state Alcoholic Beverage Control (ABC) Board, is as unlawful as the former.

State law (KRS 244.380) is very explicit on the subject, said Porter Collier,

field director for the ABC in Frankfort. The law prohibits any retailer from selling liquor on credit, he said.

The only exception to the on-credit rule, Collier said, is the extension of reasonable credit by private clubs to their members, and hotels to their registered guests.

Yet a large number of the liquor-by-the-drink establishments in Jefferson County, particularly restaurants, motels, hotels and large nightclubs — routinely accept credit cards as payment for drinks, either with meals or separately. In fact, some issue their own credit cards which may be used to purchase meals and or drinks.

Times reporters visited 12 establishments on a recent weekend and found only three that didn't accept credit cards. They were Mills Lounge, 2403 W. Broadway; the Pirates' Cove Lounge in Bon Air Manor shopping center, and Sahara Club, 3906 Bardstown Road.

Drinks were charged on major credit cards at Haumann's, 1028 Barret Ave.; Churchill Inn, 6444 Dixie Highway; the Tin Tiger Lounge, Goldsmith Lane and Bardstown Road; the Patio Lounge, The Mall; the D-Mate Lounge the Palm Lounge, 304 N. Fourth St.; the Ramada Inn,

*See DRINKING
Back page, col. 1, this section*

Bluegrass festival brings downhome music to downtown

By ROB KASPER
Louisville Times staff writer

Downhome" moved downtown yesterday as the Bluegrass Music Festival folding through its first day.

When people hear downhome it pulls them in a relaxed mood ... genuine sincere, kinda folksie" said Buck White, who together with his two daughters and Ruby and Cheryl, and son in-law Jack Hicks played some soft and some sassy tunes on the River City Mall.

Last night a crowd tapped its feet on the Riverfront Plaza concrete to tunes provided by Bill Monroe and other bluegrass groups.

The festival sponsored by Louisville Central Area Inc. and Philip Morris Inc. will be held today and tomorrow, rain or shine officials said.

"The festival in its second year continues through tomorrow night. The 11 a.m. performance today was to be held on the River City Mall. The 7 p.m. show today and the 2 p.m. and 7 p.m. shows tomorrow will be held on the Riverfront Plaza.

Yesterday's lunch-time performance drew about 1,000 listeners. But the foot-stompin' feeling that White and others say is characteristic of bluegrass music was slow starting.

For a while the people in the audience acted as though they were in an elevator — looking straight ahead, not talking to anyone around them, ignoring pleas of the highground Stringband to dance.

Then Charles B. Fort, a 51-year-old fork lift operator at Louisville's Anaconda Aluminum Co. jumped up to dance.

"I was just down there by the stage, my feet were agigglin'. Finally they couldn't stand it anymore," he said.

After Fort broke the ice a warm feeling swept through the crowd, dissolving the armor that sets folks wrap around their feelings, and limbering up stiff backbones.

Soon, about 15 people — an older woman in a bantoul college students, elementary school students, elementary school kids —

*See DOWNHOME
Back page, col. 2, this section*

Sunday may really be sun-day

If you were raised on country sunshine, tomorrow should remind you of Sundays at home.

The sun is supposed to end tonight and the sun is scheduled to be shining for tomorrow afternoon's bluegrass concert on the Riverfront Plaza.

Tonight's low temperature will be in the upper 50s and tomorrow's high will be in the middle 70s. Last night's low was 64.

Tonight will also feature a large bright moon known among bluegrass folk as the blue moon of Kentucky.

Full weather data on **Page A6.**

Where to look

VOL. CLXXIII—No. 26 36 PAGES
Copyright 1974 The Louisville Times
FINAL HOME

Kathleen Orndorff and her son Brennan, 4, snuggled down comfortably on the River City Mall pavement yesterday afternoon to hear the friendly sounds of bluegrass music. The Bluegrass Music Festival continues today and tomorrow on the River City Mall and the Riverfront Plaza.

The printing of newspapers

The newspaper format lends itself to letterpress. Only since World War II has offset lithography posed any real threat to letterpress as the preferred method of printing. But in that short time it has replaced letterpress on almost all of the weeklies and most of the dailies. Its advantages: better and cheaper picture reproduction on poor-quality paper, greater flexibility in design, less expensive typesetting, a more even laying on of solid color and black areas. Offset's advantages are particularly impressive on short press runs. They diminish as the runs get longer.

Letterpress in recent years has been able to adopt some of offset's advantages. Some letterpress papers no longer use heavy lead plates. They set their type in photocomposition and paste up their pages, as if they were offset publications; then they make plates from thin metal or photopolymer. The letterpress New York *Daily News,* the daily with the largest circulation, uses an electronic composition and makeup system that results in complete pages from which stereotypes are made and from which lithographic plates can be made if—when—the paper goes offset.

The newspapers sticking with letterpress tend to be those that recently purchased letterpress equipment. At any rate, both processes seem firmly established in the industry for the next few years.

Rotogravure, a third process, will continue to serve best the

Peter Palazzo at the Louisville Times *seminar offered several possibilities to consider. You see them here. Note especially his handling of the nameplate. Some of his pages make use of a three- rather than a six-column format. The* Times *is a full-size newspaper.*

216

Some examples of center spreads in The Christian Science Monitor. That both pages are on the same sheet encourages the use of across-the-gutter art and headlines. The Monitor makes dramatic use of this space, varying the approach from issue to issue. The spread almost always has a strong horizontal thrust. Note especially the handling of the "Halting the Desert" feature and the way the sifting sand partially covers the headline. For some of the photographs on these spreads the editors use a textured screen. (Reprinted by permission from The Christian Science Monitor. © 1977 The Christian Science Publishing Society. All rights reserved.)

producers of syndicated Sunday magazine sections and Preprint and SpectaColor advertising inserts.

The new technology

"To err is human; to really foul things up requires a computer," one reporter has been quoted as saying. Old-line reporters—some of them—watch uneasily as the computer takes its place in the newsroom. 'The computer is demanding—and making possible—precision never before known to newspapers," observes John H. McMillan, executive editor of the Huntington (West Virginia) *Advertiser* and the *Herald-Dispatch.* "And the full burden to be accurate will fall on editors and reporters.

"If the computer must be fed accurate data, it also must be given exact instructions on what to do with that data."[8]

Since 1960 the computer has had some use—in some newsrooms—in justifying right-hand margins. Now it becomes the key to all the new systems used by newspapers: video display terminals, optical character readers, and direct-input typewriters. The computer stores and processes the copy.

Occasionally, the system "crashes" (breaks down). "A backup system is needed to keep you from being helpless if your system crashes," observes Jack Trawick, state news editor of the Winston-Salem (North Carolina) *Journal.*[9]

Joseph M. Ungaro, executive editor of the Westchester-Rockland (New York) Newspapers, in 1977 saw the elimination eventually of all walls between the newsroom and the production department. The newsroom would take on more of the burden of producing type and putting pages together, he said. A number of papers would be put together by going directly from computer to plate, with laser beams used to create the plates.[10]

The dummy

In laying out the pages, some editors paste galley proofs onto full-size layout sheets. (The printer makes available simultaneously two sets of proofs: one to proofread, the other to clip and paste.) With a dark or bright-color pencil, the editor marks the number of the galley across the face of every story—perhaps every paragraph—then with scissors or razor blade cuts away excess paper, making a unit out of each story.

Other editors prefer to use half-size sheets, calibrated into in-

8. *A Primer for the Newsroom on the New Technology,* Associated Press Managing Editors Association, n.d., p. 6.
9. Jack Trawick, "SNPA Workshop Examines New Technology Impact," *Editor & Publisher,* November 13, 1976, p. 52.
10. "Copy Editors to Feel Automation Impact," *Editor & Publisher,* March 19, 1977, p. 16.

The tabloid-format Christian Science Monitor *always devotes its last page to editorials, making the page easy to turn to. Guernsey Le Pelley's editorial cartoon always occupies about a quarter of the space, giving it plenty of impact. Four columns is standard on this and most other pages in the paper. The logo across the top is the same as on page one, but smaller and without the familiar rounded-corner box. The Monitor went from a standard size newspaper to a tabloid, with Albert J. Forbes, a London-trained designer, establishing the new format. (Reprinted by permission from* The Christian Science Monitor. © 1977 *The Christian Science Publishing Society. All rights reserved.)*

ches and columns so that 1/2 inch on the sheet represents a full inch in the newspaper. To use such sheets, the editor takes measurements off the galleys and with boxes and lines marks story placement on his layout sheet. He can mark—rather than cut and paste—on full-size sheets, too, if he wishes.

The pasteups or drawn designs need not be 100 percent accurate. Lines need not be perfectly aligned. The dummy serves only as a *guide* to the printer; he squares things up and adjusts the fit as he handles the type and later pulls his page proofs.

The basic formats

The editor using a newspaper format has two basic choices: the full-size sheet, approximately 15 inches wide by 23 inches deep, usually with 6 or 8 columns to the page; and the tabloid sheet, approximately 11 inches by 15 inches, with 4 or 5 columns to the page. The tabloid, really a half-size paper, was developed to serve the strap-hangers on mass transit systems. It became less popular with the demise of mass transit systems and because it became associated with the discredited sensational press in some big cities. But it does have the advantages of giving better display to small ads and creating the impression of a "thick" paper. A number of newspapers publishing their own Sunday magazine sections choose the tabloid format because it provides greater layout flexibility. And *The Christian Science Monitor* chose it as its format when it went through a redesign program.

Kinds of makeup

"In theory, all front pages begin as blank paper," observes Clive Irving."In fact, they all have a preordained basic structure: the vertical division imposed by the columns, and less visible horizontal boundaries which determine the placing of stories—in descending order of importance."[11]

Authors dealing with newspaper makeup tend to categorize it under six headings:

1. *Symmetrical.* You'll be hard pressed to find examples of symmetrical newspaper pages today. Even the New York *Times* has pretty much abandoned them.

2. *Informal balance.* This is far more common and sensible; all the other kinds of makeup are really nothing but variations.

3. *Quadrant.* Informal balance is achieved on a page that is cut into imaginary quarters; each quarter has some art and some heavy typography.

4. *Brace.* Liberal use is made of stories that start out with multicolumn heads and leads, funneling down to single-column

11. Clive Irving, *op. cit.,* p. 44.

tails. One *L*-shaped story fits snugly into another; or a picture fits into the *L*. Stories look like braced wall shelves, hence the name.

5. *Circus.* Such makeup is loudly informal and gimmick-ridden. Otto Storch gave it magazine respectability on the pages of *McCall's* in the late 1950s.

6. *Horizontal.* This informal makeup has many multicolumn heads and pictures, with stories blocked off into horizontal rectangles several columns wide. Horizontal, but not vertical, column rules are used.

To these Edmund Arnold has added:

7. *Functional.* There is increased emphasis on readability. Crowding is out; white space is in. Furthermore, the nature of the news determines the look of the page.

Which is as it should be.

"All bad newspaper layout is bad because the process is performed backwards; somebody dreams up some pretty shapes and then the poor material is massaged to fit," says Clive Irving.

Prof. Roy Ockert of Arkansas State University, while admitting that newspapers need to be better designed, warns that design should not be a first consideration. "The news always should be, and therefore design must be functional. Art in the newspaper business must take a back seat to timeliness and practicality. It's easy for an artist (or good make-up man) to produce a more attractive page when he is not pressured by a deadline, as news editors on dailies always are."

Jumping the stories

A crucial decision that must be made—and there are strong arguments for both sides—is whether the editor should crowd as many stories as possible on the front page or limit the selection to just a few. A lot of stories increase the chance that every reader will find at least *something* of interest on the page. A page with only a few stories, on the other hand, makes for less clutter, allows for more white space, and makes possible full development of the stories on that page. Fewer jumps to inside pages would be needed.

Edgar T. Zelsmann, president of Carl J. Nelson Research Corp., Chicago, says surveys show that half the readers are lost when a story jumps from one page to another. Furthermore, when readers follow a story to another page they may not get back to the page where they started the story. For these reasons newspapers try to develop their stories as complete units on a page. They break a long story into two stories and put the second on an inside page.

Newspapers that do jump stories make finding the second half as easy as possible for readers. The Winnipeg (Manitoba)

This 7-Up ad is one of the earliest of the FlexForm ads, run just before Christmas, 1968, in the Peoria, Illinois, Journal Star, which originated FlexForm ads. When an advertiser buys a FlexForm page, he can design his ad in any shape he chooses, zig-zagging among the columns for up to 65 percent of the space, getting full-page dominance without full-page cost. His ad can appear in more than one piece, as in the ad above. When it first came out, FlexForm was hailed as "the first significant change in the use of regular newspaper pages in 50 years." The advertiser who uses FlexForm undoubtedly gets remarkable impact with the various shapes FlexForm allows, but because editorial matter has to be squeezed into the remaining holes, FlexForm makes even more difficult the display of editorial matter on the inside pages. That's news copy under "The Golden Crescent" headline and on either side of the deer.

Tribune runs its continued-from-front-page stories on one inside page that carries a large "From Page One" logo. The Huntington (West Virginia) *Herald-Dispatch* screens the headlines over continued sections of stories to a medium gray. Nearby headlines over stories that begin on those inside pages are in black, of course.

When stories jump they should jump to a page in the section they start in, ideally on the back page of that section. Then the reader can easily return to the front page. The jump headline can either restate the original headline or take up the subject being dealt with at the jump. (The original headline usually deals with the lead paragraphs of the story.) Logic suggests that the jump headline be smaller or at least no bigger than the main headline.

You signal the reader that a jump is ahead with a "Continued on" or "Please Turn to" line. But when a story simply carries over to another column you do not need such a line. In a magazine you don't need such a line when an article carries over to the next page or spread.

Inside the paper

Most redesign of newspapers concentrates on the front page. But, as Edmund Arnold told a seminar on newspaper design sponsored in 1974 by the Louisville (Kentucky) *Times*, "We have to make sure there isn't an immediate and dramatic letdown in quality when a reader turns to Page Two."

Good design of inside pages is not likely to come until the papers gather their ads into rectangular blocks that leave rectangular news holes. Unfortunately, most newspapers think they must arrange their ads into half pyramids in order to put each ad next to "reading matter." But you can't do much with design when your news hole zig-zags diagonally up one side.

Would advertisers sit still for such arrangements? Participants at the *Times* seminar who had tried it said they received few complaints.

Still another solution would be to arrange ads so that they are confined to their own pages, leaving full-page news holes inside the paper. Right now, only the tabloids seem able to do this.

Further complicating the problem of inside pages is the advertiser who, insisting that his advertising appear next to editorial matter, buys not a *full* but a *near*-full page. What do you do with an *L*-shaped news hole 1-column deep and then 7-columns × 1 inch across?

Making it easy for the reader

Readers appreciate a news digest on the front page, boxed or otherwise set aside, perhaps over the nameplate, with single paragraphs devoted to each of the major stories. The wise editor

During the lull just before Christmas, wire service operators fill the wires with art they compose at their keyboards. They use Xs for their basic designs, Ms and Ws for darker areas, periods and colons for lighter areas. The Library of Congress has recognized their efforts as an unusual art form and has accumulated a permanent file of designs. One of the most widely admired wire service artists is Charles Reeser of the Washington, D.C., Bureau of Associated Press. "Peace on Earth," at the right, was his contribution for 1970. Newspapers, which receive art like this with their regular wire service copy, sometimes reproduce it in their Christmas issues. Magazines can make use of this art form, too. An artist can produce such art using a typewriter.

is stingy with details here; he doesn't want to spoil his reader for the whole story. When page numbers follow each entry, the digest serves, too, as a special table of contents.

For large papers, there should be a general table of contents pointing the reader to regular features.

It is a good idea to establish regular placement for standing features and pages. Portland's *Oregonian* drives its readers mad by moving its editorial page around from issue to issue; but at least the paper always makes it a left-hand page. Because they take more time to read, editorial pages on most papers (including the *Oregonian*) go toward the back; the skimmers can drop off then without missing the important stories—and the advertisements.

The thoughtful editor runs standing features and pages in the same position, issue after issue. And the reader thanks him for it. *Time* magazine proved that "departmentalizing" the news pays off after all.

Obits should be gathered in one section of the paper under a standing heading or between symbolic black bars. Obits need no individualized heads. How many ways can you say—would you want to say—that a person has died, anyway? The full name by itself is headline enough. Besides, you avoid awkward part-present tense, part-past tense heads like this: JOE SMITH DIES TUESDAY. (Sounds as if poor Joe is set to face a firing squad.)

The Indianapolis *News* solves the problem of obit headlines by using subjects and predicates but putting them in past tense. The past tense, contrasting with the present tense elsewhere in the paper, says "death" by implication: "Joe Blank Ran Car Agency" or "Carol Cook Taught at Jefferson." The Denver *Post* bunches its obits under a column heading that includes an abstract drawing of a sunset.

So can engagements and weddings be gathered together under standing headings and run with label, name-only heads. And you can avoid hunting synonyms for "Wed."

Readers also appreciate an arrangement of material—possible only with large newspapers—that makes separate sections out of sports pages, financial pages, and other special pages. That way the whole family can enjoy the paper at the same time. Ideally, each section would be printed on its own tinted stock. That's not a very practical suggestion; but some papers have at least printed their sports sections on a green tinted stock.

The question of emphasis

Makeup is largely a matter of assigning proper emphasis to stories. Usually, one story gets bigger emphasis than any other. On some days, however, the page may have two stories of equal significance. Maybe three.

It is a good idea to think of stories as falling into three general categories of importance—major stories, important stories, and fillers—and assign emphasis accordingly.

You can emphasize through placement. You can also emphasize through size, unusual handling, blackness, color.

Until recently, the No. 1 spot on the front page was always the top of the eighth column, because that was where the banner headline ended. With decreased emphasis on newsstand sales, the banner is less important and not often used; there is no reason, then, why the No. 1 story can't go at the top left of the page, where the eye normally first settles.

At one time, all the emphasis was confined to the top half of the page. Now the entire page is considered; editors take specific steps to get some typographic display "below the fold." Edmund Arnold talks about "anchoring" all four corners of a page with something heavy. Run dark headlines, boxes, pictures, or other typographic weights to "define" each corner, he advises. This seems a bit arbitrary. One wonders: What's so important or mysterious about corners that they need defining?

Newspaper typography

The character of the publication, the kind of paper it's printed on, the amount of space available—these considerations affect the designer's choice of typefaces. That the typical newspaper is published for persons of varying backgrounds and ages suggests types should be simple and familiar. That the paper stock used is cheap, absorbent newsprint suggests types should be open and somewhat heavy. That space is at a premium suggests types should be somewhat condensed.

Chapter 6 describes body faces available and tells how these types are set for both letterpress and offset newspapers.

Headlines

For headline type, newspapers—offset and letterpress—use sans serif, slab or square serif, or modern roman in display sizes. A few use old style or transitional romans, provided they are on the heavy side, like the Cheltenham used by the Milwaukee *Journal*. Most editors prefer a condensed face so that they can get a better "count" for their headlines. Among the sans serifs, Spartan is popular; among the slab serifs, Stymie; among the moderns, Bodoni bold. For standing column heads, a paper is likely to turn to one of the decorative or miscellaneous (and, frankly, boorish) faces, like Kaufmann bold or Brush.

Letterpress papers rely on Ludlow for headline typography, offset papers on photographic headsetting machines.

All papers draw up a "head chart" or "head schedule," which reproduces sample heads in various sizes and arrangements, gives them numbers, and tells what the maximum count is per line. The count can only be approximate; it is based on a system which puts all letters, numbers, and punctuation marks into four width categories: 1/2, 1, 1 1/2, and 2. With some exceptions, punctuation marks are 1/2; lowercase letters, 1; numbers and capital letters, 1 1/2; lowercase letters *f, i, j, t,* and *l* usually count as 1/2, lowercase *m* and *w* as 1 1/2; caps *I* and *J* as 1. The space between words can be 1/2 or 1 unit, but it should be consistently one or the other.

The advantage of a head chart is this: Referring to it, the copyreader can pick quickly a "stock" style and size appropriate to the story, scribble the code number at the top of the sheet, shoot it over to the headline writer. The code tells the headline writer what style is wanted, how wide in columns the head is to be, how many decks are wanted, how many lines are wanted in each deck—and what the maximum count is. He can't exceed the maximum count, but he can stay under it. Some newspapers insist that each line take up at least two-thirds of the maximum count and that in a multi-line headline the longest lines be kept at the top.

It could be worse.

The few newspapers who remain faithful to the geometric-shaped heads of an earlier era—flush-left-and-right, cross-line, step-line, hanging indention, inverted pyramid—require an *on-the-button* count. Fortunately, the flush-left heads now so universally used do not so seriously restrict the headline writer. The heads are more readable. And they are better looking, too.

Edmund Arnold has recorded two important dates in newspaper design: September 1, 1908, and December 4, 1928. On the first date, the Minneapolis *Tribune* became what Arnold believes was the first newspaper to use caps-and-lowercase headlines. Until then, all newspaper headlines had been all-caps; and for years afterwards—on through most of the 1920s—most newspapers continued to use all-caps headlines. Unreadable though they are, they find favor on a few newspapers even today.

On that second date, the *Morning Telegraph,* a specialized newspaper in New York, became the first newspaper to use flush-left headlines. Until then, all newspaper headlines had been contorted into inverted pyramids, hanging indentions, and other stringent and crowded shapes. A few newspapers in the East today continue to use hard-to-read and hard-to-write heads. But only a few.

The argument now is over the adoption of all-lowercase heads. These are heads with only the first word and all proper nouns capitalized. Magazines have long since adopted such

Columns

	units per pica	1	2	3	4	5	6
14 R	1.794	24	50				
14 I	1.704	23	47½				
18 R	1.395	18½	39	59	79½		
18 I	1.326	18	37	56	75½		
24 R	1.046	13½	29	44	59½		
24 I	.9945	13	27½	42	56½		
30 R	.8372	11	23	35½	47½	60	72
30 I	.7856	10½	22	33	44½	56	67½
36 R	.6977	9½	19½	29½	39½	50	60
36 I	.663	9	18½	28	37½	47½	57
42 R	.5978	8	16½	25	34	42½	51½
42 I	.5755	7½	16	24	32	41	49½
48 R	.5233	7	14½	22	29½	37	45
48 I	.4973	6½	14	21	28	35½	42½
60 R	.4186	5½	11½	17½	24	30	36
60 I	.3978	5	11	17	22½	28½	34

The head chart worked out by Dave Emery for the Eugene (Oreg.) Register-Guard, an offset daily newspaper. The large numbers running down the side represent type sizes for upright letters (the "R" is for "roman") and italics. The uprights happen to be Cheltenham; the italics Goudy. The big numbers running across the top represent widths in columns (columns are 13 1/2 picas wide). Hence, for a two-column head set in 18-point Cheltenham, the count would be 39. The units-per-pica column takes care of odd-width headings. Emery has designed a lamp-shade-like box to hang down over the copy desk with the head chart reproduced on all four sides. The box is designed to be bigger at the top so that the chart slants at an angle for easy reading. No head chart works all the time because the count is based on average widths of letters, but this one works 95 percent of the time, Emery reports.

heads—or "titles," as they are called in that medium; newspapers gradually are coming around. A headline contains a subject and predicate. It is a sentence picked out from among the first few paragraphs and enlarged. It follows, then, that it should *look* like a sentence. That each word should be capitalized does not help.

The modern newspaper has dropped the idea, too, of the multiple-deck headline. Today, on most papers, a headline consists of one or, at the most, two decks of two or three lines each. Headlines are not so deep as they were; but they are wider. They spread across several columns, adding to the horizontal look.

Subheads

Sub-headlines within the bodies of stories provide necessary typographic relief when stories are long. Four styles are common:

1. Flush left.
2. Centered.
3. Lined up with the paragraph indentions.
4. Run-in.

These are almost always in boldface type and often in capital letters. The first three must be displayed with sufficient white space above and below, preferably with more white space above than below.

The run-in subhead needs only a little white space above. Usually it begins at the regular paragraph indention. It can be a line complete in itself. Or it can be simply the first three words or so, set in boldface. An advantage of such a subhead is that it comes from the reporter already "written."

Some papers use, instead of or in addition to subheads, occasional complete paragraphs set in boldface type, often in a narrower measure than regular body type. Such paragraphs cheapen the look of the page and give arbitrary emphasis to parts of stories.

The nameplate

From journalism's beginnings, editors felt names of their newspapers should stand out as copies were peddled and hawked on city streets. About the only dark type known or available was the blackletter, a face we know today as Old English. Even today, partly because of tradition, partly because of what editors consider the "dignity" of the face, many nameplates still appear in that same unlikely face.

It is time newspapers adopt a face for nameplates more in

When the weather takes an unusual turn, a newspaper may doctor its nameplate to make it appropriate. Here's a doctored nameplate and a front-page story you are not likely to see again coming out of Miami. Yes, Miami! The year was 1977. Note the snow-flakes and the snow-covered tree in and around "The Miami News." "Snow fell on Miami today for the first time in recorded history," the lead story begins.

keeping with the times and with their headline and body types. Plenty of boldface types are available; and we know today that even small faces can stand out provided they are displayed with a generous amount of white space.

If a paper can't bring itself to give up Old English for its nameplate, it can at least simplify the type. The New York *Times* did this recently, greatly improving the looks of the nameplate. Compare it to that of the Washington *Post,* also Old English, but in an *outline* version.

The typeface in a nameplate can be in strong contrast to the headline face, or it can be in the same face, say in all caps where headlines are caps and lowercase.

Actually, a newspaper's nameplate is almost always drawn and photoengraved—that's why it's called a name*plate.* The drawing often incorporates a line sketch of an insignia or some local scene. An effective nameplate can be made of reproduction proofs of type cut and repasted and retouched by an artist familiar with letterform.

Many newspapers use a single design in more than one size. The nameplate may "float" to any location from issue to issue. Steve Sohmer, creative director of the Bureau of Advertising of the American Newspaper Publishers Association, suggests that newspapers incorporate the day of the week into the nameplate. Instead of the *Daily News,* you would have the *Monday News,* the *Tuesday News,* etc.

Photographs

Newspaper practice puts photographs in a role secondary to copy. Editors use pictures to fill holes. The New York *Daily News*'s idea of great art, so Edwin Diamond reports in an article in *New York* (February 1971), is "a group color photo of the Mets."

Philip N. Douglis, photojournalism columnist for *IABC News,* called the daily press "a photographic disaster area." What bothered Douglis and what bothers other critics is the preponderance of staged shots and meeting pictures that can interest only those who pose for them.

J. C. Donahue, Jr., editor and publisher of *Suburban Trends,* Butler, New Jersey, complained about the photographs that followed up the call-in show put on by CBS radio for President Carter shortly after he took office. "In paper after paper," Donahue said, "there appeared photos of people with telephones, ostensibly elated at being one of the elect to reach the President.

"It doesn't take much to figure there was no way of knowing in advance who was going to get through, in order to assign a photographer to record the moment. Yet not one cutline among those I saw identified the photo as a posed, after-the-fact set-up, or reenactment. In fact, they seemed designed to mislead."[12]

The constant search for novelty or irony or humor in a photograph leads sometimes to embarrassments. A prestigeous small daily, to accompany a news story about the state senate's passing a bill to allow terminally ill persons to direct the withdrawal of life-support systems, uses a photograph of the bill's co-sponsor that happens to include an exit sign in the background. So the paper crops the photograph into a dramatic deep vertical that shows only the state senator and the sign. The cutlines say that the senator "co-sponsored the bill passed by the Senate Wednesday that would allow Oregonians to exit with dignity." Is such a visual pun appropriate to the story?

If art in newspapers is to improve, one place to start is with picture size.

If the case is strong for larger pictures in print media generally, the case is overwhelming for newspapers. The 65-line screen for reproducing photographs by letterpress on newsprint remains constant as the size increases. The larger the picture the

A swearing-in ceremony does not offer much chance for innovative photography. Nor would Eugene (Oreg.) Register-Guard photographer Paul Petersen place this shot among his best photographs. But compared to what an unimaginative photographer would do with an assignment like this, Petersen's photograph is a nicely designed piece of art.

12. In a letter to the editor of *Editor & Publisher*, March 19, 1977, p. 7.

finer, in proportion, will the dot pattern appear.

The photographer taking pictures for his paper now moves in close on his subject. If he doesn't, the picture editor crops the picture to emphasize what may be a small portion in the original. Even then, he runs the picture large. Most editors agree with their photographers that the paper is better off with fewer but larger pictures.

While in gallery photography the picture may speak for itself, in journalistic photography it must be explained in words. Under the halftone goes the caption (called by newspaper people "cutlines") in a width equal—or almost equal—to the picture width. Boldface or italic can be used, in a size that is a point or two smaller than body copy. For an unusually large picture, the caption may be set in two or more columns. Some newspapers use captions set considerably narrower than picture widths, with small multi-line headlines placed at the right side, flush left or flush right or centered. If a picture accompanies a story, it needs no headline; the story's headline is its umbrella.

Bill Kuykendall for the Worthington (Minn.) Daily Globe *captures the mood of "the celebrated secular monk" Ralph Nader in this memorable photograph. The story accompanying the photo describes Nader on the platform: "As he speaks, his eyes lift up to meet the crowd, his back arches up, his voice gains in volume and authority. He does things with his hands. He folds them into prayer position. . . ."*

A wash drawing is executed by the author in India ink. The ink was used in its original state for outlines and in a watered down state for tones. Such a drawing calls for highlight-halftone reproduction. The Eugene (Oreg.) Register-Guard ran the drawing to illustrate a feature on a local crackdown on fathers who had deserted their families. It had to be a drawing; the story didn't lend itself to photographic coverage.

Illustrations

Before the turn of the century the typical daily newspaper employed a stable of staff artists whose job it was to supply illustrations for feature stories, maps and charts for news stories, cartoons for columns, editorial cartoons, and other visual delights. Then along came photography, and along came the syndicates, and the need for staff artists dwindled.

A paper today might employ one or two illustrators for the news/editorial side and a few more for the advertising department; but the art factories that once existed on newspapers have closed down. Artists employed by newspapers now are more likely doing pasteups. And nobody spends a lot of time retouching photographs anymore.

Still, some 125 daily newspapers have their own editorial cartoonists. And as a change of pace many of these papers call on the services of a cartoonist or illustrator to illustrate an occasional letter to the editor or to dress up a feature that does not lend itself to photographic illustration.

Newspapers have a wealth of syndicated material to draw from. Syndicated editorial cartoonists, for instance, supply caricatures along with their regular features. Editors can drop these into their stories and columns about public figures.

There are also plenty of stock-art services, as chapter 7 points out. What editors must guard against is reaching over into the advertising mat services for editorial art. The art from there has an advertising look that any knowledgeable reader would be able to spot.

Editors also must guard against using illustrations or cartoons merely as filler material. The reader gets the impression when looking at the typical editorial page with its several syndicated editorial cartoons that the cartoons were picked not for what they say but for the space they can occupy. Some editors even bunch two or three editorial cartoons by the same editorial cartoonist, unwittingly making of them a sequence that the artist did not intend. And whenever you put two or more compelling pieces of display together, they have a tendency to cancel each other out.

Newspaper color

Despite valiant efforts by the newspaper industry to achieve magazine quality in color reproduction, newspapers remain hopelessly outclassed. No matter how much care is taken by the photographer and photoengraver in making separations for three-color process work, the inability to keep a fourth plate in register, the coarseness of the screens, and the inferiority of the paper stock make faithful reproduction of the original impossible. If the newspaper can't get its color through preprinted rolls of rotogravure material, it might well consider confining its color to solid or even-screened areas—to flat color, in other words.

Indiscriminate use of process color does nothing to improve the communication. In fact, color can hurt rather than help. Why hold out for a washed-out, too-purple color halftone when a less-costly-to-produce black-and-white halftone shows up clearer?

Nor does *flat* color necessarily improve the communication. Type in a too-light color becomes hard to read. Halftones in a too-light color lose their detail. Flat color is best when laid out in reasonably large areas in solid or screened tones to contrast with nearby type or art.

Newspapers printed by offset lithography get better results with color than newspapers printed by letterpress.

The horizontal look

Until recent years the vertical look predominated among newspapers. Single-column, multiple-deck headlines plunged deep into each page, while unbroken black lines fenced off each column from its neighbor. Today on an increasing percentage of papers, the horizontal look prevails.

The first break with the past came with the extension of

headlines across one column and into the next. Not only were multi-column heads better looking; they were also more readable. That the headline writer had more space to work with meant he could avoid some of the headline clichés—those miserable three-, four-, and five-letter words that only a deskman could love.

Another break came with the elimination of column rules. They had made pages monotonously vertical. But it was impossible to eliminate column rules without adding extra white space. Without rules, you needed as much as a full pica of space between columns. Otherwise, you sometimes had more space between words than you had between columns.

Where was the extra space to come from? Newspapers couldn't very well make their pages wider. Nor could they make their columns narrower. Columns were too narrow as it was. The standard column measured out at 11 or 12 picas, too narrow for good readability, even with copy set in small news type. Two Minnesota psychiatrists showed that columns set in 7- or 8-point types, common then, would be more readable if the columns were 15 or even 18 picas wide. Yet at the close of World War II, publishers, facing rising newsprint costs, trimmed another pica from their narrow columns. (It was a painless way to raise advertising rates; a column inch was still a column inch, even when it took up less space.) To compound the felony against readability, they increased body-type size to 9 points.

The logical step was to cut down on the number of columns—from nine or eight columns to seven or six. Edmund Arnold saw value in the "7 1/2" format, in which one column was slightly wider than the other six. The slightly wider column could be used for a feature column or a news roundup. Eventually publishers bought the idea of the wide column for newspapers. Today the six-column format is common.

The case for wider columns

It would be a mistake to write off the narrow column altogether. Under some circumstances, in limited doses, the narrow column serves the reader well, especially when it is set with an unjustified right edge.[13] But when columns stretch from top of page to bottom, row on row, page after page, narrow measure puts too much of a burden on readers.

It holds them back.

A study conducted by Jack Nuchols, Jr., working under the direction of J. K. Hvistendahl, associate professor of journalism

---

13. Cf. the 4-column-page design used in *Fell's Guide to Commercial Art* (Frederick Fell, Inc., New York, 1966), co-authored by this writer and Byron Ferris.

at South Dakota State University, showed that 9-point Imperial, a news face, could be read 4.1 percent faster in a 15-pica width than in an 11-pica width.

Moreover, narrow columns take longer to set. Albert Leicht, also working under the direction of Professor Hvistendahl, found that Linotype operators, using the same face, could set matter with 15-pica lines 35 percent faster than matter with 11-pica lines.

Wider columns mean fewer lines, less hyphenation at the ends of lines, and more consistent spacing between words.

Of all the suggestions for improvement of newspaper format made in recent years by Arnold, Hvistendahl, and others, the wide column stands the best chance for universal adoption. Despite what Arnold calls "the reluctance of the industry as a whole to break out of timeworn habit," newspapers one by one are adopting a six-column format for the regular eight-column-size sheet. *The Wall Street Journal* has long used the wide-column, six-column format. *The National Observer* chose the format when it started in 1961. The Louisville *Courier-Journal* and the Los Angeles *Times* were among the first dailies to make the conversion.[14]

By the mid-1970s papers everywhere were making the move to six columns, if not on all pages at least on their front pages. And those that did go to an all-six-column format for news/editorial material went in the opposite direction for advertising: from eight to nine columns. This meant some adjusting to line up six-column news/editorial formats with nine-column advertising formats on a page, but it was a way of painlessly raising advertising rates. In addition, some newspapers went from nine columns to ten columns for their classified advertising sections.

Meanwhile, national advertisers were troubled by too much format variety in newspapers, and the industry was forced to standardize somewhat in order to encourage agencies to buy space.

The case for unjustified lines

In his first few years of teaching, this writer worked a great deal with high school journalists and teachers, many from small-town schools that could afford to produce only mimeographed newspapers. The young editors attached to these publications felt cheated, somehow; oh how they envied their peers at larger institutions who directed more glamorous offset or letterpress operations! Grimly they did what they could to make the mimeographed product look "printed." For one thing they in-

---

14. J. Clark Samuel, editor of the Foxboro, Massachusetts, *Reporter,* a weekly, wrote to *The American Press,* January 1966 to point out that, so far as he knows, his paper has used the six-column format since its founding in 1884.

sisted on justified body copy for all their stories.

This meant typing each column twice. On the first round, the typist carried each line as close to the maximum width as possible, filling in the end of the line with x's. She counted the number of x's for each line, then, on the second round, put the required number of extra spaces between words. The copy for these papers was typed in the same narrow measure newspapers used.

It was a senseless procedure, of course. It took far too much time. And the finished product was the worse for it.

The young editors could not accept the fact that ordinary typewriters are not flexible enough to produce natural-looking justified lines. Nor could they see that the 10- or 12-point typewriter typefaces (elite or pica) were too large for their narrow columns. They made a mistake all too common in the graphic arts: they tried to make one medium fit the mold of another.[15]

Ironically, while the young editors were trying to emulate regular printed newspapers by justifying their columns, regular printed newspapers for their news columns were toying with the idea, already established in advertising, of ragged-right edges.

The advantages of unjustified lines appear to be these: complete consistency of spacing between words, less need for hyphenation at ends of lines, less chance of the reader's "losing his place" as he moves from line to line, less expense in setting copy and making corrections. Research has not confirmed all these advantages, but Professor Hvistendahl, one of few persons to do any work in this area, suggests that you can read unjustified lines "a little faster" than you can read justified lines. But when you call the lack of justification to the attention of readers, they are likely to say they prefer the lines justified.

How research helps

After the Rapid City (South Dakota) *Journal* discovered, through research, that its readers wanted more information they could use in their daily lives, the paper in 1976 became more consistent in its placement of items, making them easy to find, and more willing to put national and international news on inside pages, devoting the front part of the paper mainly to local news. A "Lifestyle" section each day concentrates on a single subject. For instance, on Monday the subject is "money."

15. The author was not above making the same mistake. As an artist for a letterpress high school newspaper in the days when linoleum blocks were used for line art (photoengraving was too expensive for some school-paper budgets), he did everything he could—including the heating of the linoleum to make cutting easier—to make the block look like a regular line engraving. He failed to realize that the inherent crude, strong, black look of a linoleum block could be the look of graphic art of a high order.

Research can be useful in helping designers make up their minds about which course to take. And if the newspaper itself can't conduct the research, plenty of studies exist that can be consulted.

The American Newspaper Publishers Association, Washington, D.C., in the 1970s sponsored a series of News Research Bulletins on newspaper design and typography. One, by J. W. Click and Guido H. Stemple III, showed that readers, young and old, prefer newspapers with "modern" front pages. By "modern" the authors meant six-column instead of eight-column pages with a horizontal rather than a vertical emphasis. David K. Weaver, L. E. Mullins, and Maxwell E. McCombs found that there was a tendency in competing situations for the second newspaper to adopt a more modern format: no column rules, six rather than eight columns to the page, fewer stories on the front page, larger photographs and color photographs, smaller headlines. J. K. Hvistendahl and Mary R. Kahl found that newspaper readers prefer roman to sans serif body types.

Edgar T. Zelsmann, president of Carl J. Nelson Research Corp., Chicago, reports that headlines four or more columns wide attract twice as many readers as one-column headlines do.

Coming up with the unexpected

Radio and television news programs present their stories with a sameness that makes it difficult for listeners and viewers to sort out the important from the unimportant. Newspapers allow readers to skip and choose, and when something is really important, newspapers can turn up the visual volume. Newspapers with a usually quiet, subdued front page especially serve their readers in times of crisis. When crisis comes, an across-the-page banner announces it, and the readers understand. An always screaming newspaper, on the other hand, has no typographic device to turn to.

Now and then a newspaper tries something unusual.

When fire destroyed Garden State Park, a racetrack at Cherry Hill, New Jersey, in 1977, the Camden (New Jersey) *Courier-Post* turned the front page on its side and, leaving the nameplate in its regular place, used the rest of the page for truly horizontal treatment. The banner ran down what would have been the right edge of the page, and stories and large photographs filled in the remainder of the space. It was fitting treatment, the editors felt, because the fire was the largest in South Jersey in years.

The look to come

Newspaper design will change as newspapering itself changes. TV will help. Most journalists admit now that the electronics

Newspapers, like magazines, get into subsidiary publications: publications for advertisers and for employees, for instance. Publications for employees or near-employees can become specialized, as this one for 13,000 carriers shows. It is a quarterly publication of the Detroit News. *Coming in a 12-inch square (roughly) format on newsprint, the 12-page publication presents its news of awards and circulation drives in lively fashion. The front cover serves as an illustrated table of contents. Frederick R. Peters is art director.*

media do a better job with spot news than the print media. The trend in newspapers will have to be away from the "what" to the "why." TV whets the appetite; newspapers deliver the details, the background. The interpretive newspaper will dispense with the hodgepodge and take on more and more the look of the magazine. Better design.

But change comes slowly.

Writes Clive Irving in the *Penrose Annual* 1967: ". . . Printing advances are being introduced whose potential is not even recognized [by newspapers] let alone exploited." Editors use offset and phototypesetting to produce papers that look just like the old standby letterpress papers. "Yet the mechanical restraints imposed by the use of hot metal and rotary presses are no longer there. The prison door has been opened but the prisoner refuses to leave the cell."

He adds: "Newspapers at the moment are a technically underdeveloped resource. Their place in life is so important that this neglect jeopardizes not only them, but the health of society."

It is easy to criticize the newspaper look of the 1970s. It is not so easy to come up with anything more than superficial advice on how to change that look.

Perhaps the following three suggestions are not wholly practical, but it seems to this observer that if they were adopted newspapers would, in the phrasing of Clive Irving, "move from the Stone Age to the Space Age."

First, *the package itself—the size—could change*. The standard broadside newspaper (roughly 15 × 23) is too big for consecutive page design.[16] The tabloid size (half the regular size) provides a much more workable format. Unfortunately, we associate the tabloid with the cheap and sensational New York journalism of the 1920s: the *Graphic*, the *Mirror*, the *Daily News*. But you can't eschew a good thing just because someone in the past has misused it. It would be like abandoning the word "freedom" to the John Birch Society.

Among the more respected newspapers to use the tabloid format are the Chicago *Sun-Times* and Long Island's *Newsday*. The latter, with a clean, crisp look and handsome typography (Century heads and Century Schoolbook body copy), is one of the nation's best-designed newspapers.

But in the late 1970s only 27 of the dailies were tabloid, down from 50 in 1970. This despite the fact that tabloids enjoy an advantage over their full-size competitors in that they need to display fewer items on each page. Fewer items mean better organization.

16. The oversize newspaper page was originally a tax dodge. Beginning in 1712 British papers were taxed by the page. Taxes eventually disappeared, but by then editors and readers had gotten used to the oversize page.

Where a full-size newspaper has from six to eight columns per page, a tabloid has four or five.

Some advertisers who like full pages have raised objections to the tabloid format. You don't get the impact of a broadside, they say. But the *Reader's Digest* has shown repeatedly that in magazine formats full pages draw as well in pocket size as in *Ebony*-size. A full page is a full page is a full page.

Second, *ads could be arranged in solid blocks.* No more stacking them in half pyramids to put each "next to reading matter." News holes could be kept as horizontal or vertical rectangles, so that the designer will have a better field in which to arrange the elements. Another advantage of the tabloid is that it allows fewer ads per page: there is less need then for pyramiding them.

Finally, *headline schedules as drawn up by most newspapers could be abandoned or made more flexible.* Headlines should not be written to fit a space; they should be written to be appropriate to the stories. Lines should not be separated according to count; they should be separated according to sense. If that means a one- or two-word line followed by a six-word line, so be it. Whenever possible, put the whole headline into a single line.

It should not be necessary to vary the weight of the headline according to the length of the story. A same-size headline face in several column widths is variety enough. Additional variety can be achieved through picture sizes and shapes, placement of white space, use of horizontal lines.

Nor should headlines be subject to arbitrary editorial rules that say they must always have a subject and a predicate, be written in present tense, be free of words like "and" or "the," and so on.

Suggested further reading

ALLEN, JOHN E., *Newspaper Designing*, Harper & Brothers, Publishers, New York, 1947.

ARNOLD, EDMUND C., *Modern Newspaper Design*, Harper & Row, Publishers, New York, 1969.

BASKETTE, FLOYD K., AND SISSORS, JACK Z., *The Art of Editing*, Macmillan Company, New York, 1977. (Second Edition.)

CLICK, J. W., AND STEMPEL III, GUIDO H., *Reader Response to Modern and Traditional Front Page Make-up*, American Newspaper Publishers Association, Washington, D.C., News Research Bulletin No. 4, June 4, 1974.

CROWELL, ALFRED A., *Creative News Editing*, Wm. C. Brown Company Publishers, Dubuque, Iowa, 1975. (Second Edition.)

GILMORE, GENE, AND ROOT, ROBERT, *Modern Newspaper Editing*, Bond & Fraser Publishing Company, San Francisco, 1976. (Second Edition.)

HULTENG, JOHN L., AND NELSON, ROY PAUL, *The Fourth Estate: An Informal Appraisal of the News and Opinion Media*, Harper & Row, Publishers, New York, 1971. (Chapters 2, 8, and 9.)

HUTT, ALLEN, *Newspaper Design*, Oxford University Press, New York, 1967. (Second Edition.)

HVISTENDAHL, J. K., ed., *Producing the Duplicated Newspaper*, Iowa State University Press, Ames, Iowa, 1966. (Second Edition.)

LOWN, EDWARD, *An Introduction to Technological Changes in Journalism*, University Microfilms International, 300 North Zeeb Road, Ann Arbor, Michigan, 48106, 1977. (By the world news editor, Newburgh [New York] *Evening News*.)

MacDOUGALL, CURTIS D., *News Pictures Fit to Print—Or Are They?* Oklahoma State University Press, Stillwater, Oklahoma, 1971.

WARD, WILLIAM G., *Student Journalist and Designing the Opinion Pages*, Richards Rosen Press, New York, 1969.

WESTLEY, BRUCE, *News Editing*, Houghton Mifflin, Boston, 1972.

How to Produce a Small Newspaper, The Harvard Common Press, Harvard, Massachusetts, 1977.

A Primer for the Newsroom on the New Technology, Associated Press Managing Editors Association, n.d.

Chapter 11

Miscellaneous publications

Regularly issued publications like magazines and newspapers account for only part of the money spent for printing and only part of the activities of editors, writers, designers, and artists. In this chapter we center our attention on a vast print medium sub-culture consisting of one-shots, infrequently issued publications, direct-mail pieces, and shoe-string operations. A final chapter will take up the subject of books.

The term "miscellaneous publications" hardly describes this array of printed pieces, but no other term works any better. Every conceivable format is involved; and few persons associated with print media escape producing the pieces. Nobody escapes reading them. Even regularly issued publications produce miscellaneous publications—to increase their audiences, to impress advertisers, to communicate with their employees, to comply with the law.

They range from elaborate printed pieces of cloth, leather, and materials other than paper to scruffy sheets of newsprint that are barely decipherable. They cost their sponsors anywhere from less than a penny to several dollars a unit. It is impossible to estimate the total funds going into these pieces, but the amount, if it could be calculated, would be staggering.

Every one of these pieces has to be designed.

Many of them are designed by people who don't know what they are doing.

Among them are some of the most beautiful and readable printed pieces ever produced. Some art directors would rather work with miscellaneous publications than with periodicals because each represents a brand new challenge.

With a magazine or newspaper your design becomes cumulative. You see your mistakes in one issue and began to

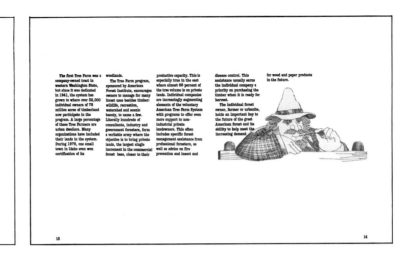

The cover and two non-consecutive spreads from a 24-page 8 1/2 × 11 booklet, Managing the Great American Forest, *published by American Forest Institute, Washington, D.C. The story starts on the cover. The 2 1/2-inch sink inside remains constant, with an occasional jutting up of a headline. To encourage reading, the booklet offers its copy in almost display-size boldface slab-serif letters, with columns unjustified. Each page features art in black and a second color: green. In the second spread, where a section of the story ends, the designer uses a portion of the illustration from the earlier spread, but enlarged and made into a silhouette.*

correct them in the next. Eventually you finely tune your design to a point where, at least for the moment, it really works for you. With miscellaneous publications you never know. You make your mistakes and create your triumphs, but they work only once. On the next assignment you start all over again.

Of course, some miscellaneous publications come out frequently enough that you can get a handle on the design, but then you probably have a budget so limited that you can't do what you want anyway.

Miscellaneous publications can take regular magazine and newspaper formats and, in addition, these:

1. leaflets (single sheets) or cards, loose or stapled;
2. folders (sheets folded one or more times);
3. broadsides (extra large sheets like maps that are folded down for easy reading or handling);
4. booklets (similar to saddle-stitched magazines, but usually smaller—small enough, say, to fit into a No. 10 business envelope);
5. brochures (extra fancy booklets with oversize covers, die cuts, pockets, etc.);
6. books (paperback or hardbound), catalogs, directories, and manuals.

Moving from one format to another

In corporate and industrial journalism you see plenty of switching back and forth among the formats. In the 1970s, a number of company magazines decided that the traditional magazine format did not lend itself very well to news items. Something closer

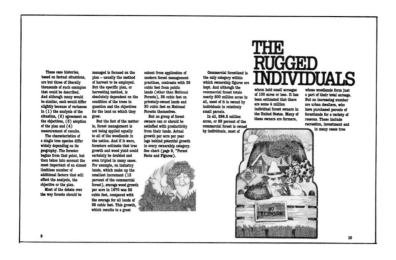

to a newspaper format would work better. If the magazine consisted primarily of news, it went to a newspaper format or, more commonly, to a tabloid format. Such a format represented savings not only in paper costs (the editor could use newsprint rather than book stock) but also in binding costs. To affect further savings, some editors went to a newsletter format.

If a magazine consisted of both feature material and news, editors—some of them—went to two formats: the magazine continued to carry feature material; the new tabloid or newsletter, perhaps issued more frequently, carried the news and chit-chat associated with the typical magazine for employees.

And for publications used as sales tools, you see much experimentation with format. Sometimes the job seems to call for a simple folded sheet, sometimes something bound. A department store, for instance, instead of settling for one of those numerous tabloids we see nowadays inserted in our daily newspapers, decides on something that looks like a cheaply bound paperback book to go through the mails. Anything to be different. Anything to get a jump on the competition.

Similarly, in public-service journalism, you see experimentation. The annual report may come in the form of a tabloid rather than in the more familiar form of an 8 1/2 × 11 booklet or magazine. The regularly issued publication may turn out to be a newsletter rather than a journal.

Corporate design programs

Industrial concerns and nonprofit organizations, too, put more emphasis than ever before on the design of their publications because they have bought the concept, put forth by the firms

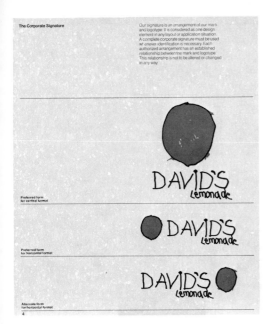

Our signature is an arrangement of our mark and logotype. It is considered as one design element in any layout or application situation. A complete corporate signature must be used wherever identification is necessary. Each authorized arrangement has an established relationship between the mark and logotype. This relationship is not to be altered or changed in any way.

Preferred form
for vertical format

Preferred form
for horizontal format

Alternate form
for horizontal format

4

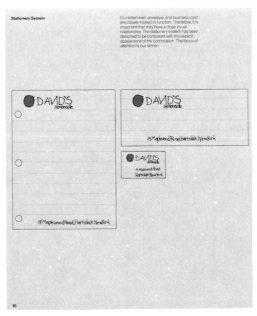

Our letterhead, envelope, and business card are closely related in function. Therefore, it is important that they have a close visual relationship. The stationery system has been designed to be consistent with the explicit appearance of the corporation. The focus of attention is our lemon.

10

Sanders Printing Corporation, New York, puts out Folio *booklets occasionally to demonstrate its expertise in printing.* Folio 15 *was a tongue-in-cheek "Corporate Identity Manual" for the mythical David's Lemonade stand. If you've ever seen a real corporate identity manual, solemnly laying out rules on exactly how symbols, special typefaces, and signs must be used, you will appreciate the satire here. This page, one of 24, deals with the company signature. We are told that three forms can be used: one for vertical ads, one for horizontal ads, and an alternative one for horizontal ads. The original page (this reproduction is greatly reduced) shows the lemon with a second color, yellow, crayoned in.*

This page from the manual shows how stationery must be designed. You see here the letterhead, envelope, and business card. The ruled lines on the original are in blue.

that specialize in corporate identity programs, including redesign of corporate symbols, that all printed and televised materials as well as signs on and in the company buildings should bear a family relationship and convey the impression that the firm is innovative and contemporary. It would not do, for instance, for a company to work out a beautifully designed and coordinated set of stationery and business forms and then allow the employee relations department to issue an internal magazine, newspaper, or newsletter that looks as though it were laid out by someone who couldn't make the art staff of a padded-cover yearbook put out by a rural high school.

When a company goes through a program of redesign, from trademark to company magazine, it often introduces the changes through ads and direct-mail pieces. To cite one example: When Republic Steel redesigned its logo it issued a booklet to all employees so that they could share "the sense of pride and excitement" management felt "at the introduction of our forceful, distinctive and wholly modern appearance which portrays Republic Steel as the dynamic, forward-looking, growth-minded company we all know it to be."

As the booklet explained, the new corporate identity program

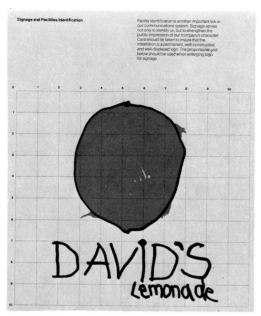

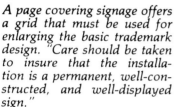

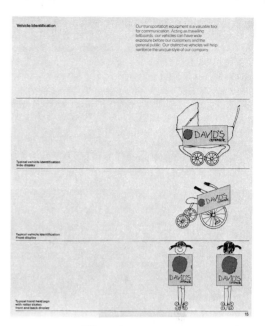

Facility identification is another important link in our communications system. Signage serves not only to identify us, but to strengthen the public impression of our company's character. Care should be taken to insure that the installation is a permanent, well-constructed, and well-displayed sign. The proportional grid below should be used when enlarging logo for signage.

Our transportation equipment is a valuable tool for communication. Acting as travelling billboards, our vehicles can have wide exposure before our customers and the general public. Our distinctive vehicles will help reinforce the unique style of our company.

Typical vehicle identification
Side display

Typical vehicle identification
Front display

Typical hand held sign
with roller skates
front and back display

15

A page covering signage offers a grid that must be used for enlarging the basic trademark design. "Care should be taken to insure that the installation is a permanent, well-constructed, and well-displayed sign."

There is even a page covering "Vehicle Identification." "Our transportation equipment is a valuable tool for communication." One illustration shows a "typical vehicle identification side display," another a "typical vehicle identification front display," and a third a "typical hand held sign with roller skates, front and back display." The concept and design of this delightful piece of promotion was by Fulton + Partners Inc. Earlier the design firm had done an "annual report" for David's Lemonade. Of the current booklet, the firm says, "Utilizing its extensive experience in graphic communications, Fulton + Partners has developed this timely Corporate Identity Manual to permit David's Lemonade to achieve a stature commensurate with its corporate capabilities."

revolved around the company name. It stayed the same, but "Republic" grew bigger in the design "Because there are many other steel companies, but only one Republic. . . ." The company also adopted a special color—"Republic Blue"—"for unique and dramatic expression. . . ." Of course, the blue was used as a second color throughout the booklet.

For management people and others involved in corporate communications, companies undergoing corporate identity redesign programs issue manuals telling exactly how to use the new symbols and signs. Placement must be just so, the manual cautions. Colors must be exact. Reading one of these manuals you feel as intimidated as when reading one of those mattress labels warning that "removing this label is punishable by. . . ."

Where pictorial symbols are involved in corporate design, the designer simplifies, settling for abstract shapes rather than realistic portrayals. Sometimes initials-only do the job.

With simplification, though, goes the risk of duplication. It is almost impossible sometimes to come up with a design someone else has not used, as NBC, to its embarrassment, discovered when it decided on its *N* logo in 1975. NBC had to settle out of court with the tiny Nebraska Educational Network, which had

242

The University of Maryland Student Handbook for 1975-76 won a Gold Quill Award of Excellence as the best example that year of a recruiting booklet. This spread, representing two of the 54 pages, shows the design used: three columns per 8 × 10 1/2 page with several pieces of funky art on each spread. The art varied in size, but all of it was in the same style. Note the use of both horizontal and vertical rules and the large page numbers. Main headings are in all caps, secondary headings are in caps and lowercase, but all in the same type. Two colors are used throughout, with an additional feeling of color achieved through screening. Roz Hiebert edited, Heidi Kingsley designed, and Russ Fleury compiled.

in use an *N* that was almost exactly the "N" Lippincott & Margulies invented for NBC.

Tom Wolfe does not share with many art directors an enthusiasm for purely abstract logos. They make no impact, he holds, except to create a feeling of vagueness or confusion. "Pictorial logos or written logos are a different story. Random House (the little house), Alfred Knopf (the borzoi dog), the old Socony-Vacuum flying red horse, or the written logos of Coca-Cola or Hertz—they stick in the mind and create the desired effect of instant recognition ('identity')."[1]

Deciding on a single function

An art museum official was showing off a quarterly published, she said, to bring news of shows and acquisitions to supporters and friends. The publication, an oversize two-fold (6-panel) folder printed on slick paper, carried a few photographs, but mostly it carried short items written in the reporter's traditional who-what-where-when-why-how style. Composition was hot type.

"Why a quarterly?" she was asked.

"We can't afford to come out more often."

"Couldn't you drop back to cheap paper, use strike-on composition, and come out monthly, maybe as a newsletter?"

"We want it to be a prestige publication."

And so the museum supporters and friends once every three months got their "news" in the form of a dressed-up direct-mail piece. In the process an image was polished.

Perhaps.

1. Quoted in "A Vanity Industry," *New York*, January 26, 1976, p. 48.

More probably the publication was trying to do too much, and as a result it was doing nothing. It could serve an example of what's wrong with many company and institutional publications today: fragmentation of purpose or, worse, no purpose at all. You get the impression looking at them that too many publications exist simply because some Higherup, noticing what the competition is doing, says: "We ought to have a publication." The editors are in the position of Robert Benchley, who, arriving in Venice, wired friends at home: "STREETS FLOODED. PLEASE ADVISE."

If the purpose of a publication is primarily to bring news to readers, it cannot afford long intervals between issues. Even coming out monthly may not be often enough. If the purpose is primarily to build an image, perhaps to boost the fund-raising program, the organization needs a less frequently issued publication, probably not in a folder format, and certainly not a publication that specializes in short—and old—news items. This is not to say that a simple, economical format can't help an organization's image. It certainly can. It can say to the reader, for instance: "This organization is not wasting its resources trying to impress me."

A format that has been growing in popularity in recent years is the two-fold folder with six 8 1/2 × 11 pages (three on each side of the sheet). It is ideal for organizations that want to come out often but with only a few pages. An economic advantage is that no binding is needed. And occasionally, when visual impact is desired, one whole side can be used as a sort of poster: you have a 25 1/2 × 11 sheet to work with. Some publications use the two-fold folder format for smaller than 8 1/2 × 11 pages and others use the format for tabloid-size pages.

One-shots

Sometimes a magazine of rather broad appeal gathers enough material on one of its areas of interest to put out a special issue apart from the regular issues. A shelter magazine, for instance, may put out a publication about furniture and distribute it to newsstands as the magazine itself is distributed. This special publication may gather together material that has already appeared in the magazine, or it may present all new material. We call the publication a one-shot, even though it may catch on and become, say, an annual publication.

Designing a one-shot could involve picking up the basic design of the magazine and applying it to the special issue; or it could involve a brand new design approach appropriate to the subject matter.

Of course, any publisher can bring out a one-shot. A publisher can specialize in producing one-shots. That publisher

The back page of a full-size, full-color newspaper (or magapaper), RF Illustrated, published by The Rockefeller Foundation. You see here an article, "The Years of Neglect," and a sidebar inside and another right below. At the bottom is a house ad about some Foundation "working papers." Notice the handling of initial letters in the article. They start out large and get progressively smaller as you read through the article. Each is an outline letter with full-color illustrations inside. The initials are of the kind that extend up from their paragraphs rather than down into them.

then acts much as a book publisher would act, but the product takes on the look of a magazine instead of the look of a book.

Direct-mail pieces

The term "one-shot" can be stretched to include direct-mail pieces. Direct-mail pieces are produced by every conceivable kind of company or organization to do a public relations or selling job, and they appear only once, then they are forgotten. Unlike other one-shots, they are meant mostly to be given away, not sold. The term "direct-mail" comes from their usual method of distribution; but many direct-mail pieces are handed out at doors or from counters. Another term for these pieces is "direct advertising." Still another term is "direct marketing."

In producing a direct-mail piece, the designer starts from scratch. Paper stock, format, type for body copy, even the printing process has to be selected. The designer in effect launches a new publication every time he designs and produces a direct-mail piece.

When you think of all the folders you see advertising and promoting products and causes and institutions, all the leaflets you see in packages, all the booklets you pick up at counters, and all the mailings you get urging you to subscribe to magazines, you begin to see how massive a medium this is. In dollars spent on advertising, direct-mail ranks right up there with newspapers. For years it has been the number 2 medium, ahead even of TV. Certainly in dollars spent it is ahead of magazines and radio. Magazines themselves—many of them—could not exist were it not for the direct-mail medium to gain and hold subscribers.

The trend in direct mail as used by magazine and book publishers is to overwhelm the potential purchaser with a vari-

An inside spread from McGraw-Hill's marketing guide to its many trade magazines. The large type, printed in a redish brown, indicates categories, as "Metal Producing," "Mining," "Trucking," and "Oil Marketing." Under "Mining," for instance, you see two magazines and information about them. You might want to compare the Fleet Owner cover under "Trucking" with the other Fleet Owner cover reproduced elsewhere in this book. The dark bands on either side of this spread represent the cover overhang. (Reproduced by permission from The Marketing Guide to McGraw-Hill Publications Company.)

ety of separate pieces crammed into one large envelope. Lately the full-color broadside has become popular to carry the main message. The typical mailing consists of the broadside, a letter, a return card and envelope, and an extra letter wondering how on earth you can afford to pass up this bargain. All must be designed to build up to a sale. Sometimes the pieces are unified in design; sometimes the designer purposely produces a hodgepodge to overwhelm the recipient.

The advantage of direct mail is that the recipient, theoretically, reads all this material without distraction from other printed material. It is a selective medium in that a direct-mail piece can be designed and sent to a specific class of persons. But most important to the designer, the medium is flexible; it can utilize any printing process, any paper, any format, any design style. And gimmickry is limited only by the designer's lack of ingenuity.

The folder is probably the most common form of direct mail. A single cut sheet, it can be folded once, twice, three times, or more after printing; and several different kinds of folds can be used. What results from the folding are panels; you would have six panels to design in a two-fold folder, three on each side of the sheet. You would have eight panels to design in a three-fold folder. The trick is to design the panels to take advantage of the sequence of the folding.

A folder is cheaper to produce than a booklet because no binding costs are involved. But the design of the two involves similar problems.

Some designers try to design folders so that each panel works separately. Other designers try to make spreads out of the panels.

Paper choice makes a big difference to the design. For instance, some papers fold well only with the grain. Size, quality, opacity, bulk, and durability desired all figure in the paper choice. So do mailing factors, printing process to be used, and the nature of the contents. An all-type piece may call for an antique (rough surface) stock, for instance, while a mostly-photography piece would call for a slick, coated stock. The size of the piece would be determined by how economically it cuts from the sheets or rolls available to the printer.

Even different inks in the same color can be a factor. For one of his direct mail jobs—it was a combination folder and poster—Jim Bodoh, a designer at the University of Oregon, used two different blacks, one a regular, one a matte finish. He printed a sheet of music in glossy black over a block of matte black and achieved an interesting and subtle pattern in which he reversed some type.

As a designer, you would do your rough layout or comprehensive to size, trimmed and folded as the piece is to appear

Llegando, a publication of Agencia Marti, Flores, Prieto Marguina & Cuchi, Inc., Puerto Rico, occasionally uses a fold-out format that results in three 8 1/2 × 11 pages printed on one side of a sheet, three on another. A six-page publication with no binding. You see here the first page, then the first page thrown back to reveal two new pages, then the right-hand page thrown back to show three pages. Rounded photographs and a double rule help unite the pages, printed in dark brown ink on a buff stock.

in print. That way the client can hold it in his hands, study it for design and color, and get the feel of how it folds before okaying its final printing.

Before picking a printer you would want to get some estimates of costs. For a big job, you would go to two or three printers. Be sure that each printer bases his bid on the same set of specifications and the same rough layout. Price alone would not necessarily determine the successful bidder. Sometimes a higher bid turns out to be more of a bargain.

Sometimes the designer presents camera-ready copy to the successful bidder, sometimes just the rough layout. If the printer is expected to furnish his own pasteup, his cost is likely to be higher.

The design of direct mail falls usually to the advertising department of the company producing it or to its advertising agency. In almost every city freelancers take on direct-mail designing assignments, too, making anywhere from $25 to several hundred dollars per item, depending upon whether or not they furnish camera-ready copy or just a rough. Freelancers can also work with printers or engravers or platemakers.

Company magazines

Company magazines have already gained considerable attention in this book, but because they come in so many varieties, some additional information seems appropriate here. *Gebbie House Magazine Directory* lists more than 4,000, but that figure doesn't begin to touch them all. Company magazines are omnipresent, and they appear in every format imaginable. The saddle-stitched 8 1/2 × 11 magazine is standard. Students looking forward to magazine careers no doubt will find most opportunities lie with company magazines. In most cases, the editor does it all: writes, edits, takes photographs, designs, lays out, and even pastes up. The bigger books leave the designing to an outside art director. In some cases the editing and art directing are done by the company's advertising agency.

Few company magazines carry ads. The publications are themselves advertisements—institutional advertisements—for the companies publishing them. In that respect, they fall under the heading of direct-mail advertising. Some company magazines communicate mostly with employees; some communicate mostly with customers, potential customers, dealers, and opinion leaders on the outside; some try to serve both internal and external audiences.

Just as general-circulation magazines have grown specialized, so have company magazines. The big companies publish a whole series of magazines, each narrowing in on one aspect of the business or addressing itself to one level of employees or customers.

Association publications

An estimated 40,000 associations exist in this country to promote the interests of industrial, professional, educational, charity, religious, social, and other groups, and 92 percent of them are involved in publishing activities. They produce magazines, newsletters, directories, manuals, annual reports, and direct-mail pieces of all descriptions. They spend an estimated $700,000,000 putting out these publications.[2]

Until recently these publications carried material of interest only to persons associated with or sympathetic to the associations. But they are broadening their appeal now and concerning themselves with the world outside. Most of the regularly issued publications exist to educate members and keep up the funding of the organizations.

The magazines issued by associations look like any other magazines, except that they try harder, usually, to keep costs down. About 1,000 association magazines accept advertising.[3] In that respect, they differ from company magazines.

Newsletters

Talking about the design of company publications, you tend to think only in terms of saddle-stitched 8 1/2 × 11 magazines or larger tabloid newspapers. You forget about a third important format, unless you happen to read or edit a publication that uses it. It is the newsletter.

And even among newsletters, you have a variety of sub-formats, ranging from pages inside regular magazines through loose sheets on up to folded and even bound sheets. The binding can take the form of a single staple in one corner or the saddle stitching used by magazines. The distinction between newsletters and magazines, especially when you get up to eight pages, becomes blurred.

There must be thousands of these publications, among them a publication called *The Newsletter on Newsletters* (44 West Market Street, Rhinebeck, New York 12572). There is also *The Newsletter Yearbook/Directory*, a Newsletter Clearinghouse, and a Newsletter Association of America.

Prof. Albert Walker of Northern Illinois University calls newsletters "the number one print medium among business com-

A house organ for editors of house organs (company magazines). A number of these are published in the United States and Canada by chapters of the International Association of Business Communicators. They take a newsletter format. This one is a four-pager, with a pre-set logo and body copy simply typed out on a typewriter, with no attempt made to justify the right-hand margin. Which is as it should be. Note that for headlines, the editor (Matt Miller) simply uses the all caps on his typewriter (or on the typewriter of his typist). Well-printed photographs on some of the pages add interest. This is an effective and inexpensive way to produce a publication of limited circulation. Miller is also editor of General Tire's World, *published at Akron, Ohio.*

2. Robert H. Kruhm, "Those Print-Hungry Associations," *DA*, vol. 63, no. 1, 1977, p. 2.
3. Elaine Jorpeland, "Another Vote for the Specialty Magazine," *DA*, vol. 63, no. 1, 1977, p. 17.

A spread just inside the cover of an eight-page saddle-stitched 9 × 11 newsletter, Alum News, published by Bristol-Myers for its retired and former employees. The front page—and all pages—look very much like these sample pages: all the stories carry headlines in a single typeface. This nicely unifies the publication. Occasionally the editor uses a smaller size headline, as the "Continued" headline at the top of the left page shows. Thin horizontal rules above and below the headlines give them added display. Lines of the headlines are centered. Boxes surround some of the stories, and the familiar small box appears at the end of the stories as a typographic device saying "The End." Alum News is one of several publications produced by Editorial Services, a division of Bristol-Myers, New York.

municators." He estimates that 50,000 organizations issue newsletters. The typical newsletter acts as a means of internal communication between management and members or employees of an organization, and it is distributed free; but 2,000 newsletters dealing with specialized information circulate to business and professional persons who are willing to pay a high price to subscribe, in some cases several hundred dollars a year.

"Readership surveys reveal that subscribers to newspapers and magazines are scanners and skimmers," reports Professor Walker. "In fact, one survey revealed that many subscribers to magazines may not get around to reading some issues of the magazine they pay for.

"On the other hand, subscribers to newsletters are likely to read every issue from cover-to-cover."[4]

He adds: "Increased reader confidence [in newsletters] may . . . be due to the newsletter's simplified format. . . ." There is much to be said for keeping it simple. Too often designers try to make of a format something that it is not. Perhaps they try to make a newsletter look like a newspaper or magazine. The very nature of a newsletter dictates that the copy not be cluttered with useless ornamentation. A single wide column of copy, typed on a typewriter, unjustified, with extra space between paragraphs and with typed, all-cap heads at the top or at the side should do the job. Keeping the items short and separating them with extra space or stars or something similar works well in most cases. A preprinted logo at the top of the first page starts things off.

The standard newsletter format works well enough to be copied by magazines that run "newsletters" as pages of late news in their regular issues. To duplicate the tinted-stock look that

4. Albert Walker, "Newsletters: Fastest Rising Print Medium," *Journal of Organizational Communication*, 1977/1, p. 22.

These three front pages show the design stages one newsletter (six to eight pages) has gone through in the past few years. In 1974, Hawaiian Electric Company's publication was called Current Events. The name carried over to the change the following year, when the logo went to an Avant Garde-kind of type. Then the name changed to Hawaiian Electric Currents, as the 1977 page shows, with the word "Currents" drawn to make it stand out prominently on the page. All logos involved a second color. The newest logo is drawn to take a heavy outline on the outside and a thin outline on the inside. "HAWAIIAN ELECTRIC" snuggles up to the C, and the date of the issue lines up with the n in "Currents." The three-column format remained during the design changes, but the body copy moved from a roman to a standard sans serif to, finally, a modern sans serif with a big x-height. In the last two design approaches, Candy Irvine decided not to justify the right hand margins, and in the final one she did not even worry about lining up the columns at the bottom of the page. As a result she achieved a more contemporary look.

many newsletters carry, the magazines often run the items over a tint block or a color.

The duplicated publication

It took printers long enough to admit that offset lithography deserved admittance to the ranks of printing processes, to take its place with letterpress and gravure. Printers are not likely to further open the gates to grant admittance to the various duplicating processes.

Duplicating, in contrast to printing, produces only a few hundred copies per master. And even though the quality is inferior to printing, the product of the duplicator may be just as important to readers, and it may command just as much respect.

Chief among the duplicating processes, so far as publications are concerned, are spirit duplicating and mimeographing. In spirit duplicating, also called fluid duplicating, the image is typed or drawn on a master backed by an aniline-dye carbon sheet. A deposit of dye is transferred to the back of the master, which is used to do the printing. In mimeographing, a stencil permits ink to pass from a cylinder to the paper. Although it is possible to make stencils electronically for a mimeograph machine, both spirit duplicators and mimeograph machines reproduce successfully only typewritten copy and simple line drawings.

The publication thus produced can be simple, clean, and easy to read. And that is design enough. Editors make a mistake when they try to dress duplicated publications to make them appear to be printed.

Here are some suggestions for duplicated publications:

1. Forget those electronically produced stencils with their imitation halftones. Such halftones can never be as good as halftones made by regular printing processes. Settle instead for

clean, crisp line drawings traced directly onto the masters.

2. Forget justification of the right-hand margins of body copy. An ordinary typewriter does not have the subtleties of spacing necessary; the copy ends up with large, uneven spaces between words. There is nothing wrong with an unjustified right-hand margin. If it is good enough for art directors with access to Linotype machines, it ought to be good enough for editors of duplicated publications. Besides, by not justifying the lines the editor saves the extra typing necessary to figure justification.

3. Decrease the number of columns per page. If you have three columns per 8 1/2 × 11 page, go to two. Typewriter type is too large, even in elite, for narrow columns. Such type looks better in a two- or even a one-column format. Besides, you can avoid considerable hyphenation.

4. Type the headlines in all caps rather than letter them by hand. Your page will look neater. And don't feel that you have to run the headlines all the way across the column. Leave plenty of white space above, below, and at the right.

5. Avoid newspaper layout practices. Avoid ruled lines, boxes, and other typographic dingbats and strive for a clean, simple page. It is better to give your publication the quiet, self-confidence of a newsletter than the awkward, self-conscious look of a publication out of its visual class.

There is a process that lies somewhere between duplicating and printing, but closer to printing, called Multilith. If yours is a duplicated publication, you should investigate its possibilities, for it can reproduce photographs and art and print in color just as its big brother—offset lithography—can.

Yearbooks

As a print medium, yearbooks fall somewhere in between magazines and books. Because they are permanently bound and because they serve both historical and reference purposes, they have many qualities of the book. But because they are issued periodically, they also fit the magazine category. Increasingly, they have taken on the look of the magazine.

Many kinds of organizations issue yearbooks, but schools and colleges make the most notable use of this medium. While interest in yearbooks may be only slowly coming back in the large state universities, it continues strong in the smaller colleges, and especially in high schools, where students identify more with each other and their institutions. Most junior high schools and many elementary schools publish yearbooks, too.

The yearbook's main offering is the photograph: the informal shot, the group shot, the mug shot. Over the years as visual sophistication has increased, editors have given more attention

The first issue of a four-page (one folded sheet) newsletter, printed in black on quality light brown paper. Each three-column page features art similar to what you see here on page 1. The art butts up against the horizontal rules and bars in some cases; in other cases it juts up over them. Media *is a publication for the staff and clients of Campbell-Ewald Advertising.*

to the informal shot, less to the group and mug shots. But they ignore the latter at the peril of decreased sales. Yearbooking these days turns out to be a constant battle between the editor's and designer's urge to be creative and the reader's desire to have an album of portraits to file away for later perusal. There is room for experimental typography and design in the front of each book, of course, but the real challenge to the designer is to work out a readable, orderly, and attractive display of the

High school yearbooks, once a repository of examples of what not to do in graphic design, have become much more design conscious. This is the title page spread and a spread from the introduction to the Eugenean, *1968, award-winning yearbook of South Eugene High School, Eugene, Oregon.*

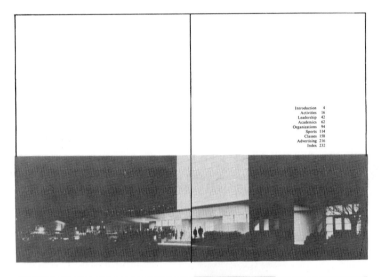

The Haliscope *for 1974, a yearbook published by Halifax County Senior High School, South Boston, Virginia, combines its table of contents with its title page. The section headings insert themselves between the lines that name the book and locate the school. The page comes in two colors: black and orange.*

routine lineup of same-size pictures in the back.

To arrange the large, dramatic, informal pictures in the front of the book, the typical yearbook designer draws inspiration from the national magazines. The look there is modular. The mood is one of excitement.

Settling on a theme proves to be a first hurdle for most editors and designers. *The Haliscope* published in 1974 by Halifax County Senior High School, South Boston, Virginia, started out with 80 themes, boiling them down, finally to six really promising ones. "But further reduction was impossible," the editors wrote in the back of their book. "There wasn't one major story of the year. The story was multiple. What seemed to be happening in student life wasn't happening in academics. Clubs had their own story; so did sports." So *The Haliscope* for that year presented six themes, each section getting its own. Each section had its own design style, too, with the unifying force in the book coming from standard caption and headline type styles. Publications adviser Richard J. Fitz, Jr., thinks the design may have been the best his editors have produced. And *The Haliscope* is a much-honored book.

The theme, singular or plural, should be appropriate to the school and to the year. It should not simply evolve from some special interest of the editor. It should not be a typographic and visual gimmick used as an excuse to bombard the reader with a lot of verbal or visual puns.

A theme too blatantly developed can do more harm than good in unifying a book. It takes over, calling attention to itself rather than to the book's real content. Some designers manage to put out yearbooks without themes or rather with themes that are only typographic: for instance, the type remains consistent throughout the book.

All publication designers have a tendency to imitate one another; yearbook designers carry imitation to an extreme. Because most of the designers are inexperienced and unsure of themselves, they gather all the yearbooks from other schools they can get their hands on and study and borrow liberally from them. It is a sort of blind-leading-the-halt operation. If not that, they engage in wild typographic experiments that succeed only in making the text difficult to read and the pictures hard to identify.

So the imitation of major magazines or books from commercial publishers, where design is more subtle, is encouraged by yearbook advisers and judges of organizations that rate yearbooks.

Uppermost in the designer's mind is—or should be—the use to be made of the book years after it has been purchased. There is a momentary excitement while the buyer hunts through the book to find himself and his friends, but soon the book goes on a shelf to be retrieved years later when the real enjoyment begins. To read the book then, the reader must be helped along by captions. All photos must be identified. There may be some validity to the argument that photographs should stand by themselves, without the crutch of captions, in other publications, but in memory or

gymnastics 60

The '75 Knight of A. N. Mc-Callum High School, Austin, Texas, uses double spreads for some of its features, holding left and right pages together with one box that transcends the gutter. You see a left page here. The art in the original is line-conversion in blue over a gray base. Note the oversize but thin-letter page number. An initial letter starts things off.

Instead of running solid pages of mug shots, '76 Knight, yearbook of A. N. McCallum High School, Austin, Texas, combines features about academics and activities with the mug shots. The features, which spread across the gutters, occupy about three-fourths of each spread. But what to use as illustrations for some of these features? For one on Field Biology, the book shows a page from a student-kept log, complete with taped-on snapshot. A tint area defines the edges of the page. Randy Stano is publications adviser.

Provided you don't do it too often in a yearbook, you can sometimes get dramatic effects by playing around with photographs. The Trojan Epic for 1975 puts together parts of two students—a female and a male—and adds extra legs to show the fashions for the year. "From overalls, to painter pants, to high waisted wool cuffs, to quilted patchwork jeans, to cotton cuffs or just plain levi's . . . all styles could be seen at West High," says the caption.

history books, surely captions are necessary except in those few places—division pages, for instance—where only mood is needed. Even so, a mood years later may have to be reestablished.

Some thought should be given to the durability of the binding. And if a yearbook has only a limited number of pages, the editor is not likely to make it look really bigger by giving it a padded cover. A padded cover only signals that the book is small.

Nor need the cover necessarily present some striking art or carry the school colors or symbol. The best covers sometimes are those that carry only the name in a good looking, well spaced and placed type.

If the school for that year has an eager and productive artist, he should have a chance to show his work, but he should not take over the book. He should be used sparingly. His work should get the same careful scrutiny the editor gives copy that comes in. And it is unlikely that a lettering expert will show up who can duplicate the beauty of typefaces already available. It is better to use real or press-on type.

Whether or not the yearbook includes special division pages, the editor and designer should organize the material into divisions or departments and include a table of contents to make things easy for the reader. An index at the back helps readers find people they want to see and read about. That means that all non-bleed pages should be numbered. On the title page or right near it should go a paragraph of information about the school, its location, and frequency of publication. Main staff members should be listed, too. The title of the book should remain constant on the cover, title page, and wherever else it is mentioned. If "The" or the year is part of the title, it should always appear in formal references to the book.

Dedications and even acknowledgments and colophons are only optional, and certainly preoccupation with the staff and its problems should be discouraged. Too often yearbooks end up with orgies of printed self-congratulations.

Advertisements should be kept in the back of the book. Whether or not advertisers appreciate all the effort made by some schools to (1) localize the ads with photographs of student "customers" and (2) insert editorial material into advertising sections is questionable. From a journalistic standpoint the practice deserves some rethinking. This is not to say that the ads themselves cannot be designed to do a selling job.

The most common ailments in yearbooks, from the standpoint of design, are these:

1. "Clutterphobia." This comes about when the designer is afraid to discard anything. "We used two pictures of the fall term dance; we better use two from the winter term dance, too." Or: "Here are fifteen pictures of the class play, and they're all so *good!*" This condition can be cleared up when the designer

A full-page high-contrast photograph used to set a mood for a feature section in the 1976 Round Table, *much-honored yearbook published by Northwest Classen High School, Oklahoma City, Oklahoma. The well-composed photograph nicely places its figures and brilliantly displays its textures. The caption appears in the upper-left corner, well away from the image area of the photograph. M. E. Burdette is adviser.*

For its index pages, The Trojan Epic *for 1976 uses double page bleeds of crowd scenes and superimposes the columns of names over the grayed photographs. The style of this book was to use giant page numbers throughout; you see how it works at the lower left corner. Section titles run up the side from the page numbers. The index bears the title "Who's Who." This is the yearbook for West High School, Iowa City, Iowa; Ben Van Zante, adviser.*

A page from the index of The Haliscope *for 1974, a 950-circulation publication of Halifax County Senior High School, South Boston, Virginia. Each page of the index features at least one photograph to provide visual relief from the list of names. The photos, like the boxes that surround each page, have rounded corners. Richard J. Fitz, Jr., is publications adviser.*

adopts a policy of no more than two or three pictures per page. Mug shots, of course, are an exception.

2. "Myriad fever." "The printer has thirty-four typefaces; let's use one of each."

3. "Differentitis." The designer desperately wants his book to look different from last year's, so he distorts type, cuts pictures into strange shapes, and otherwise creates chaos on his pages. "There! They didn't do *that* last year!"

Annual reports

For companies listed on the stock exchange, annual reports are a requirement; and what they must contain is spelled out by government regulation. Such minor matters as size of type are prescribed. But even companies not bound by such regulation, and nonprofit organizations, too, issue annual reports. Beginning in April of each year, which is about as early as anyone can get all the figures and features together and publish them, these booklets, some pretentious, some rather commonplace, go into the mails or over counters to people interested in what these organizations are doing.

Albany General Hospital, Albany, Oregon, gives citizens of the town an "Annual Review" as a tabloid supplement to the Albany *Democrat Herald*. Like any annual report it carries revenue and expense statements and various statistical information as well as feature material. It is generously illustrated.

While annual reports for profit-making organizations are designed primarily for stockholders, three-fourths of the nation's large manufacturing companies distribute annual-report information to employees, too. From some companies the employees get the same annual report stockholders get; from others, regular annual reports with special sections inserted; from others, specially prepared annual reports simplifying all those tables and financial reports. Sometimes the company magazine devotes one issue a year to the annual report.

Few companies or organizations are willing to resort to humor in annual reports—annual reports are serious business—but in recent years the reports have offered readers feature material and informal photography as well as the expected statistics and financial statements. A number of them revolve around themes, as yearbooks do. For instance, Time-Life, Inc., designed a recent annual report to look like a magazine.

Ford Motor Company took an unexpected turn in its 1976 annual report, running this headline in one part of the publication: "Not Everything Went Right." The copy that followed discussed recalls of cars, miscalculation of the small-car market, service dissatisfaction, sponsorship of violence on TV, and union problems. It was a year Ford could afford the admissions, for profits

An annual report does not have to take the usual booklet format. This one, published by the Lane Transit District, Eugene, Oregon, appears as an 11 × 5 3/4 flapless envelope. When you remove the report, it folds out into a broadside, with all the pertinent information on one 22 × 21 slick-stock broadside, printed in black and the colors used on the buses: blue and light green. That all the type is reversed hurts readability, of course, but the takes are short and the piece is colorful. And it could be argued that the job of an annual report is often more to impress than to inform. Advertising Services, Inc., designed and produced the piece. (The envelope is shown in a smaller scale.)

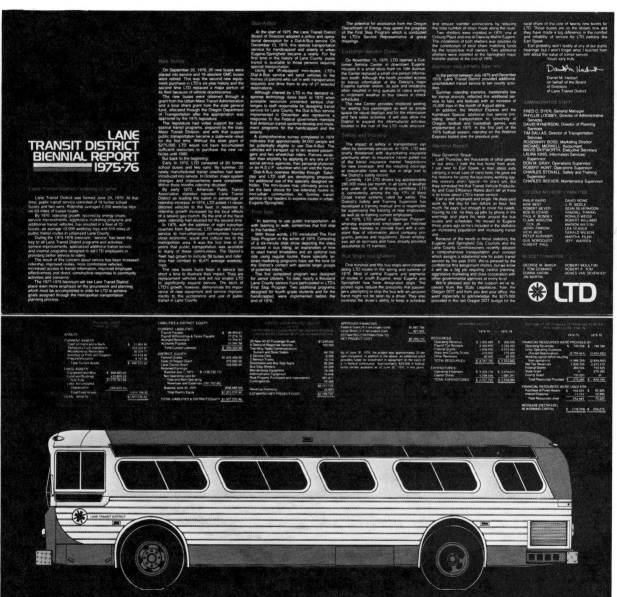

Safety Scoreboard

Beginning with this issue,
PAPER TIMES will list
the continuing safety performances
of Boise Cascade's
14 North American pulp
and paper mills.

PERIOD COVERED		JAN.-SEPT. 1976

LOCATION	NUMBER OF LOST TIME CASES	NUMBER OF WORK DAYS LOST	TOTAL OF REPORTED CASES
BRATTLEBORO	0	0	5
CALCASIEU	2	15	19
DeRIDDER	13	373	19
FORT FRANCES	18	316	173
INTERNATIONAL FALLS	16	89	64
KENORA	5	307	81
MIRAMICHI	20	202	26
RUMFORD	39	1897	49
ST. HELENS	2	47	47
SALEM	19	205	34
STEILACOOM	10	478	19
VANCOUVER	1	19	13
WALLULA	7	76	23
WEST DUDLEY	2	21	2

*"Lost-time Case" means all accidents resulting in lost work time.
"Number of Work Days Lost" indicates the total days lost due to accidents.
"Total Reported Cases" include all cases involving both lost-time and non-lost-time accidents.*

If you must use a table, give it some design and surround it with a little art. This from Paper Times, *a magazine for employees of Boise Cascade Paper Group. The original occupied a full 8 1/2 × 11 page.*

Paper Times *uses a pie chart, but gives it dimension and realism. The chart was an illustration for an article that establishes the fact that "The average American manufacturer earns a net profit of less than* five cents *on the sales dollar.* But the man on the street thinks profits are much higher."

were up. A public relations director for the company explained that not everyone in management was overjoyed at the inclusion but that chairman Henry Ford II felt "we should share with the stockholders the problems management has, sweep them up and put them on one page so no one will miss them."

Some organizations are getting away from the usual 8 1/2 × 11 saddle-stitched look. Their reports come in oversize or undersize formats or folders. These are fine, provided they can be filed conveniently by the recipient.

The cover can be a decisive factor in getting the reader into the annual report and even in setting the mood. The theme, if there is one, starts here. Special papers and inks can be chosen that are appropriate to the report and the organization. Often the cover comes from a heavier stock than what is used on inside pages. And the cover can come in the form of a gatefold or with an extra tissue-paper or acetate wrapper. Die cuts can also be used.

Like magazines, annual reports can carry bound-in signatures of different paper stock and even of different page sizes.

Nowhere in graphic design is white space more important. White space helps carry the concept of quality, a concept stockholders and members of an organization can appreciate.

Color is an important consideration. If used, it should be planned from the beginning. Color becomes especially useful in dramatizing charts and graphs. But Professor Bob Anservitz of the University of Georgia School of Journalism observes that in

Corporate profits: a pretty thin slice

PROFIT

Profit is not a four-letter word.
It's the ingredient that makes
our free-market system work.
Dinwiddy's Diner—and Boise-
Cascade—are part of that system.

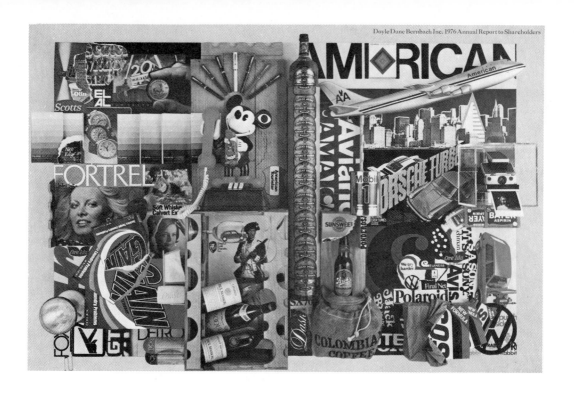

many charts and graphs color is used only decoratively when it could be used to key the information.

In recent years many companies have cut back on color, art, inserts, and other production niceties. Other companies continue to dazzle readers. "Research done by my students and me has shown that there is no direct relationship or predictability between the poshness or austerity level of the annual report and the p & l [profit and loss] statement," reports Professor Anservitz. ". . . In a poor year, a company may forego worrying about some shareholders grumbling about the gloss and heft of any obviously costly report and may issue a particularly Sybaritic report to satisfy the felt need to bolster the egos of another genre of shareholders and financial analysts."

The several big paper manufacturers make available booklets of advice on preparing and designing annual reports—and other publications—with the hope of improving the chances that the paper selected for these jobs will be theirs. One such booklet is *Annual Report Planner* from Potlatch Corporation, Northwest Paper Division, Cloquet, Minnesota 55720.

The front and back cover of the annual report issued in 1977 (for the year 1976) by Doyle Dane Bernbach, the advertising agency. The original is in full color. The montage represents the various products and companies that are the agency's clients.

Suggested further reading

ALEXANDER, SHIRLEY B., *An Inside Look at the Newsletter Field: Report on Survey of Newsletters*, Newsletter Clearinghouse, 44 W. Market Street, Rhinebeck, New York 12572, 1975.

ARNOLD, EDMUND C., *The Student Journalist and Editing the Yearbook*, Richards Rosen Press, New York, 1974.

BRANN, CHRISTIAN, *Direct Mail and Direct Response Promotion*, Halstead Press, John Wiley & Sons, Inc., New York, 1973.

DENTON, MARY RAYE, *A Blueprint for Yearbooks Today*, Crescendo Publications, Inc., P.O. Box 28218, Dallas, Texas 75228, 1976.

HODGSON, RICHARD S., *Direct Mail and Mail Order Handbook*, Dartnell, Chicago, 1976. (Second Edition.)

HUDSON, HOWARD PENN, ed., *The Newsletter Yearbook/Directory*, 44 W. Market Street, Rhinebeck, New York/ 12572.

JONES, GERRE, *How to Prepare Professional Design Brochures*, McGraw-Hill Book Company, New York, 1976.

KLIMENT, STEPHEN A., *Creative Communications for a Successful Design Practice*, The Whitney Library of Design, New York, 1977.

PATTERSON, N. S., *Yearbook Planning, Editing, and Production*, Iowa State University Press, Ames, Iowa, 1976.

PRITCHETT, ELAINE H., *The Student Journalist and the Newsmagazine Format*, Richards Rosen Press, New York, 1976.

RAINES, GAR, *How to Design, Produce, and Use Business Forms*, North American Publishing Company, Philadelphia, 1971.

STONE, BOB, *Successful Direct Marketing Methods*, Crain Books, Chicago, 1975.

WALES, LaRAE H., *A Practical Guide to Newsletter Editing & Design*, Iowa State University Press, Ames, Iowa, 1976.

The Compendium of Annual Reports, The Compendium of Annual Reports, Inc., New York.

Chapter 12

Book design

This final chapter will attempt to cover some of the fundamentals of book design, production, and illustration. The reader who wants to get into this subject in depth will find an abundance of literature, more by far than for magazine and newspaper design, for the bibliophile has perhaps commanded more attention than he deserves from the book publishing industry. A once-a-month column on "Bookmaking" in *Publishers Weekly* is especially instructive.

Understanding book publishing

To be effective the book designer should have some understanding of the book publishing industry and how it operates.

Think of a book publisher as essentially a middleman between the writer and his audience. It is the book publisher who arranges the details of publication and distribution of the manuscript and who finances the project. His job is to make money for both himself and the writer.

Under the standard contract between writer and publisher, the writer gets 10 percent of the retail price of every book sold, a little more if the book goes into high sales figures. The other 90 percent is used to pay for the editing, design, production, printing, promotion, and distribution of the book, and other business expenses, and to provide some profit to the publisher.

More disorganized, more hazardous than most businesses, book publishing is unique in that its product constantly changes. Each book published—some houses publish 600 or 700 titles a year—must be separately designed, produced, and promoted.

The book publishing industry tends to divide most of its output into two broad categories: tradebooks and textbooks. Textbooks are those volumes, mostly nonfiction, published to meet the specific needs of students at all levels. Sales depend upon adoptions by teachers, departments, and boards of education. Tradebooks include most other books, fiction as well as nonfiction. They do not serve a captive audience; sales must be made on an individual basis, and they often depend upon impulse buying. For this reason, tradebooks, unlike textbooks, require jackets as an aid in selling. Sales are made through retail stores, through mail order, through book clubs.

Textbooks and tradebooks use different pricing structures. The difference between the list price and the dealer's cost for a trade book is 40 percent. For textbooks, the difference is only half that, which explains why textbooks, like this one, are hard to get at regular bookstores. Textbooks for college students must be sold by college bookstores where large numbers are ordered for classes.

Reference books (dictionaries and encyclopedias) and children's books ("juveniles," as the trade calls them) are in categories of their own. They require different kinds of selling methods and different design and production approaches, too.

Some publishers specialize in one kind of book, some in another; and some publishers produce books in all categories. Several hundred book publishers in the United States produce among them close to 40,000 different titles each year.

With the publication of a book by Charles Colson and the election of Jimmy Carter to the presidency, the term "born again" came into prominence. So when Word Books in 1977 brought out Billy Graham's *How to Be Born Again*, it ordered a first printing of 800,000 copies and called the printing the "largest . . . in publishing history." Perhaps it was. Certainly it was larger than the typical first printing, which comes closer to 5,000 or 10,000. If a book sells well, the publisher may go back into a second printing, a third, and however more are needed.

This is not the same thing as putting a book out in a new *edition*. A new edition involves an updating and rewriting of all the chapters and probably a rearrangement of them. It involves dropping certain chapters and adding new ones. It involves new typesetting and design. In short, it means a brand new book but one that draws on the goodwill and promotional buildup of the first edition. The book you are reading is the second edition of a book that went through several printings before the publisher decided it was time to redo it.

In the early years of book publishing, the publisher, printer, and seller were one and the same. As the industry grew, each became a business by itself. Today few publishers do their own printing; and, except for mail order sales, the retailing of books is also a separate business.

Although good design was very much a part of early books, it was forgotten as books became more readily available to the masses. Mechanical typesetting equipment and a great variety of new—and mostly vulgar—typefaces in the nineteenth century were partly to blame. Near the turn of the century, one man in England, William Morris, fighting the trend, revived the earlier roman types and brought hand craftsmanship back into vogue. But only a few books were affected. W. A. Dwiggins in 1920 observed that "All books of the present day are badly made. . . . The book publishing industry has depraved the taste of the public."

But design was returning to books. In England, people like Eric Gill, and in America, people like Daniel Berkeley Updike, Bruce Rogers, Will Bradley, Merle Armitage, and Thomas Maitland Cleland restored bookmaking to the high art it once had been. Dwiggins himself became a design consultant to Alfred A. Knopf, a publisher who then and now produces some of America's finest books, from the standpoint both of content and design. Adrian Wilson calls Knopf "perhaps the greatest influence on the making of books in America after World War I." From 1926 to 1956 Dwiggins designed an average of ten books a year for the publisher. "His salty typography and ornament were additional hallmarks of the Knopf firm, the assurance of an inviting page and pleasurable reading."[1] Others who designed for Knopf were Warren Chappell, Herbert Bayer, Rudolf Ruzicka, and George Salter.

These designers combined classic roman faces with appropriate decorative borders. In the meanwhile in Germany the Bauhaus, before Hitler moved in and shut it down, developed a revolutionary concept in graphic design: "Form follows function." Gone were the flourishes. In their place: a stark, highly organized, geometric look. It was a look that, applied to books, had a beauty that seemed particularly appropriate to the times.

Still, to most publishers of popular books, design was not much of a consideration. In more expensive books, design played a role, but often it looked as if it were an afterthought, something tacked on just before the book went to press. For many books, no one designer took charge. "If the carpenter still determined our architecture, what would our buildings be like?" asked the book designer Ralph E. Eckerstrom in 1953.

With the coming of television, with increased competition from other media, with a growing appreciation of visual beauty even among the less sophisticated book buyers, this changed. Textbooks, especially, took on a more exciting look both out-

1. Adrian Wilson, *The Design of Books,* Reinhold Publishing Corporation, New York, 1967, p. 23.

side and in. One reason textbook publishers were willing to devote extra effort to design was that mass adoptions of these books were often dependent on their appearance. Furthermore, the average textbook enjoyed greater total sales than the average tradebook, so more could be spent in anticipation of sales.

Some of the best design was found in the product of the university presses. Feeling less pressure than commercial publishers felt to show a profit, they could afford to devote a larger percentage of their budgets to the design and printing of their books.

Does design spur the sale of a book? Probably not, admits Marshall Lee, a book design and production specialist. But poor design can hurt sales. "The general public's reaction to book design is, in most cases, subconscious," he writes. "Except where the visual aspect is spectacular, the nonprofessional browser is aware of only a general sense of pleasure or satisfaction in the presence of a well-designed book and a vague feeling of irritation when confronted by a badly designed one."[2]

Who does the design?

Only the large houses, those publishing more than 100 books a year, seem willing to employ full-time art directors and designers. Some houses don't even have production departments, turning that job over instead to independent shops and studios.

Some houses—Alfred A. Knopf is one—use the same designer or group of designers to develop a "house style," making books from that house easily recognizable.

The typical book designer, though, is a freelancer who works for a number of houses. He may design a book for as little as $100 or $200. For a jacket, a designer sometimes gets even less. Fleet Press Corporation, according to 1977 *Artist's & Photographer's Yearbook*, pays $150 for a book jacket design. Farrar, Straus & Giroux, Inc., typically pays $285 for 3-color finish. Clarkson N. Potter, Inc., pays $250 to $300 for jacket design "not including type costs." The book publishing industry is not noted for its lush commissions to freelancers. But there is a satisfaction in this work, designers tell themselves, that can't be had in the much higher paid area of advertising or even in the slightly higher paid field of magazine journalism.

The book designer's approach

There are two basic approaches to book design (and this is true, really, of all graphic design). One is the *transparent* approach

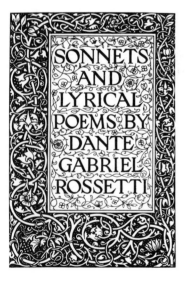

A title page designed by England's William Morris in 1894. Morris was influenced by the books of incunabula.

2. Marshall Lee, *Bookmaking: The Illustrated Guide to Design and Production,* R. R. Bowker Company, New York, 1965, p. 13.

(Marshall Lee's term), where the design does not intrude. The designer makes reading as effortless as possible.

The other is the *mood* approach, in which the designer sets a stage for the reader. His choice of typefaces and illustrations amplifies what is in the text. In some cases, they call attention to themselves. Obviously, this second approach is the more spectacular, perhaps even the more desirable. But it has to be good. The designer has to know what he's doing.

The first approach is safer. The second approach—more fun.

When dealing with mood, the designer takes into account not only the subject matter but also the nature of the audience. Certain typefaces, he knows, are more appropriate for children than for adults (although, ironically, it is the child, whose eyes see best, who gets the larger, bolder faces). The kind of picture used depends to a large extent on the kind of reader the book seeks to reach.

Some of the best design in publishing—certainly some of the best art—can be found in children's books. That children may not appreciate all this—may miss some of it—is beside the point. It is the adult, after all, who decides which children's book to buy.

The designer is particularly concerned about unity for his book. He achieves unity by sticking to the same typeface throughout, preferably for both titles and text; using the same "sink" for the beginning of each chapter; placing the page numbers and running heads at the same spot on each page; and establishing a standard copy area and sticking to it throughout the book. He should insist that the printer honor his placements and measurements. He asks for perfect backup. This means a reader (if he has nothing better to do) should be able to stick a pin through the printed book at either bottom corner of the copy block on an opening page and have the copy blocks on all other pages line up perfectly with the hole.

New designers hired by book publishers tend to overdesign the books assigned them. But most books cannot afford an avant-garde treatment. "Our design problem in the book industry today is not a lack of creativity—we have more creativity than we can use," reports Robert Scudellari, corporate art director for Random House. "Rather, we need quality in execution, and our problem is to discipline young designers to the proper execution of routine tasks on which their creativity must rest if it is to produce quality end results."

Textbooks, juveniles, and how-tos

Textbooks and juveniles present a special problem to the designer because they are picked or purchased not by the readers but by teachers or parents. The designer then must satisfy two

A Will Bradley-designed page of 1896. Bradley was one of the American book designers influenced by William Morris.

different audiences.

In both of these book areas, writers play an important role if not in design then in art selection. Art and copy must be integrated, and the author is in the best position to help along that integration. ". . . Ideally, there should be no separation of author, illustrator and designer," says Alexander J. Burke, Jr., president of McGraw-Hill Book Company. "Communication through word, picture and design is, or should be, a simultaneous act of creation. Where it is, we get better education and better bookmaking."[3]

With textbooks reaching new highs in cost to students, good design becomes even more important. This is especially true in the United States where, according to Ed McLarin, vice president of international sales for McGraw-Hill Book Company, college textbooks are the best designed and most attractively produced in the world.[4]

Color is almost mandatory for textbooks designed for high school audiences or for courses in college with large enrollments. The competition is fierce here.

How-to books also represent a special challenge to designers. Usually, there are several available on the same subject on the bookstore shelves. Potential readers have only a short time to make their decisions. The name of the author is not likely to be decisive. The appearance of the book may make all the difference. Obviously, a heavily illustrated how-to will look more inviting than one with only a few illustrations. And color may also be crucial.

Production and the book designer

On magazines the art director turns over the more routine chores to a production editor who follows through on fitting type, ordering halftones, and doing pasteups. In book publishing, the art director—let's call him the designer—plays a more subservient role. Often a production editor hires the designer and supervises his work.

The production editor, along with the editor, imposes upon the designer a number of limitations: a proposed number of pages for the printed book, some art that will have to be included, a budget. The designer goes to work from there.

If he's good, and if the editors have confidence in him, he can argue successfully for changes. Sometimes the designer is in on planning of the book. In a few cases, the book is designed first and the text then written to fit, or the design evolves as the book

3. Quoted in "New Research, Team Approach Needed in Textbook Design," *Publishers Weekly,* January 3, 1977, p. 54.
4. "Marketing Managers Tell AIGA Clinic How Design Influences Book Sales," *Publishers Weekly,* April 4, 1977, p. 74.

is written. A few books—juveniles and art books—are written, designed, and even illustrated by the same person. A few non-artist writers like to get in on the act, too. For instance: John Updike. "We don't always agree with him," says Robert Scudellari, "but usually his ideas are followed."

In the course of his work the designer soon becomes an expert in production, if he wasn't one to begin with. Especially he learns how to cut costs—without lowering the quality of the book. He finds, for instance, that he can produce clean, simple pages and in the process cut typesetting and composition costs. By confining color and art to certain signatures, by slightly altering page size, by omitting head and tailbands (they pretty a book a bit but add nothing to the strength of the binding), by having process color reproductions tipped on rather than printed on the signatures, by avoiding multiple widths of the text, by changing from letterpress to offset and from hot type to cold type—by doing many of these things he finds he can save his publisher money and still produce a handsome book.

Ernst Reichl of Ernst Reichl Associates has observed that a book designer more than pays for himself in that "the charge for design, measured against the plant cost (composition and plates) of a book, is extremely small; and a well-planned book costs so much less to produce than an unplanned one. . . . [The designer's] most obvious value is that of a safeguard against unpleasant surprises."

The time needed for putting a book through production varies from as little as three weeks, for "instant" paperbacks based on news or special events, to six months, for complicated picture books. Of course, for the author, the time lag is more; because before the production department gets the job, the manuscript has to be accepted, approved, and copyread—processes that can take more time than production takes.

The look of the book

So far as the designer is concerned, the book represents a problem with several possible solutions. Ideally he tries them all, then chooses the solution that seems to work best, bearing in mind the theme of the book, the nature of the book's audience, and the method by which the book will be sold.

If the book is to sell mainly in bookstores, it should have an attractive jacket, a thick or hefty appearance, and, if possible, lots of pictures. If it is a gift book, it should look large and expensive, even if it isn't. If it is a mail order book, it should be printed on lightweight paper, to save postage costs. If it is designed primarily for library sales, it should have a strong binding. If it is a textbook for elementary and high school use, it should have lots of color.

In choosing typefaces and illustrations the designer should avoid satisfying his own taste at the expense of what the author's approach calls for. The design should be appropriate to the book.

In every case, the designer reads the manuscript rather carefully before starting his design. He must stay within his budget, but at the early stages he can forget the budget and come up with the ideal solution even though it is beyond what the budget can support. He can then modify the design to fit the budget.

University presses often can experiment more than commercial publishers can. A small book Muriel Cooper designed for MIT Press, *File Under Architecture,* was set in various typewriter fonts, printed on kraft paper, and bound in covers made of corrugated boxboard. All of this was appropriate because the book challenged a lot of architecture principles.

As it has to other units of the print-medium industry, the computer has come to book publishing. Many book publishers use computer typography, and they buy it from outside, just as they buy their printing from outside. The type may be set in one part of the country; the printing may go on in another part of the country—or in some other country, for that matter. For less important books—say for instructors' manuals that accompany textbooks—the type may set "in house" with typewriter—or "strike on"—composition. Much "in house" typography is dreadful; and the computer has added some quirks in typography that old-line designers do not like. But Ernst Reichl,

A spread from Robert L. Tyler's Rebels of the Woods: The I.W.W. in the Pacific Northwest. *Designer Douglas Lynch chose a condensed sans serif type for his chapter headings to give them the feel of newspaper headlines. Note his use of a vertical axis and short, heavy horizontal rule. (Reproduced with the permission of University of Oregon Books.)*

a book designer for 50 years, says that ". . . it is possible to get a decent, attractive, even beautiful type page out of the computer if you insist on the standards you learned in using hot metal composition."

The lineup of book pages

Once in a while a designer gets a book like Stephen Schneck's *The Night Clerk* (Grove Press, 1965) to design. That book started right out on page 9, in the middle of a sentence. People who bought the book thought they had defective copies. The publisher had to send a notice around to booksellers assuring them the book was meant to be that way.

The usual book is a little more logically planned. In fact, the lineup of pages stays pretty much the same, book after book.

Here's the lineup of pages for a nonfiction book:

"Half" title (this page goes back to the time when books were sold without covers; the real title page was thus protected).

Advertising card (list of the author's previous works or of other books in the series).

Title.

Copyright notice and catalog number.

Dedication.

Acknowledgments (or they can follow the table of contents).

Preface or foreword (it's a preface if written by the author, a foreword if written by someone else).

Table of contents.

List of illustrations.

Introduction (or it can follow the second "half" title).

Second "half" title.

Chapter 1.

Additional chapters.

Appendix.

Footnotes (if not incorporated into the text).

Bibliography (or it can follow the glossary).

Glossary.

Index.

Colophon (a paragraph or two giving design and production details about the book).

This list does not take into account blank pages in the front and back of the book. Nor does it show whether these are left- or right-hand pages. Customarily, main pages, like the title pages, are given right-hand placement.

Up through the second "half" title page, the numbering system used is small roman. From chapter 1 (or from the introduction, if it follows the second "half" title page) the numbering is arabic.

How far to go

The designer does not design all the book's pages. That would be repetitious; most of the pages are essentially the same. He designs only the opening and strategic pages and sets basic standards for the others.

Among the pages he designs are the title, table of contents, a chapter opening, and two facing pages inside a chapter (to show how running heads, subheads, and page numbering will look).

The designer also provides the printer with a specification sheet on which he lists or describes the following:

1. trim size of pages,
2. size of margins,
3. size of copy area,
4. size and style of type and amount of leading,
5. amount of paragraph indentation,
6. handling of long quotes (set in different type or size? narrower width? centered or flush left or flush right?),
7. handling of footnotes,
8. size and placement of page numbers (folios),
9. handling of chapter titles, subheads, running heads, and initial letters,
10. amount of drop between chapter titles and beginnings of chapters,
11. handling of front matter, including title page and table of contents,
12. handling of back matter, including bibliography and index.

The printer goes ahead and sets some sample pages according to the designer's specifications to enable the designer to check them to make sure all instructions are understood, and that his design works. He can change his mind better at this point than after the entire book is set. The setting of the front matter of the book is deferred until last.

The necessary steps

The designer starts with a carbon copy of the manuscript. The first order of business is to "cast off"—count the number of words or, better, the number of characters in the manuscript and, using standard copyfitting techniques, determine how many pages of print the characters will occupy. The longer the manuscript, the more likely he is to choose a small typeface, but he does not go smaller than 10 point, unless he chooses to set the book in narrow columns. If the manuscript is short, he may use a larger face and more leading than usual, and he may choose a high-bulk paper to give extra thickness to the book. Whenever possible, he arranges the book so that the final number of pages, including front and back matter and blank pages, comes to a multiple of 32.

After the editor approves the designer's type selection and sample page layouts, the original manuscript, now copyread, goes to the printer or typographer for setting. When proofs are ready, the designer gets one set to use to prepare a dummy of the book. The extra number of pages remains somewhat flexible as he wrestles with fitting problems. He may have to increase or decrease some of his spacing in order to come out even on signatures. He may find it necessary to add or subtract a signature.

The designer prepares his dummy by cutting and pasting the proofs roughly into place, along with copy prints of the art. That's as far as he carries the pasteup, unless the book is to be printed offset or gravure; then he or someone in production does a camera-ready pasteup, using reproduction proofs rather than galley proofs. The dummy serves as a guide, then, either for the printer, if the book is letterpress, or for the pasteup artist, if it is offset or gravure.

What role does the author have in all this? It depends upon the publisher. Obviously, most publishers prefer that their writers stay out of the process once the manuscripts are copyread. But many send sample designs and trial pages to the author to get his okay before the book is finally put on the presses.

Book paper

As much as 25 percent of the retail price of a book goes to pay for production and printing. According to an estimate by Marshall Lee, one-fifth of that 25 percent goes for paper.

More so than other designers, the book designer must know the special qualities of papers. Where a magazine designer usually needs to make a choice only once, the book designer must make a choice for every job. These are the four basic kinds of paper used for book printing:

1. *antique stock.* There are many textures, finishes, and weights, but essentially these papers are soft, rough, and absorbent. They are especially good for books made up wholly of text matter; that they are nonglare makes them easy on the eyes. For quality books, the designer may choose an antique stock with deckle edges.

2. *plate or English-finish stock.* Essentially, these are antique papers that have been smoothed out, making possible sharper reproduction, especially for pictures. Paper used for the big magazines falls into this category.

3. *coated stock.* Simple polishing (calendering) may not suffice to give the paper a finish that is smooth and slick enough. The designer, then, can choose a coated stock, smooth to the

feel, rich looking, and highly desirable where maximum fidelity is desired in picture reproduction. But coated stock is expensive.

4. *offset stock.* The offset printing process needs special papers that will resist moisture. (Offset, you'll remember, makes use of plates that carry both moisture and ink.) Were the paper not treated, it would stretch, shrink, and curl. Offset papers come in a variety of textures and finishes, but the most common is the rather smooth, severely white stock used for so many company magazines and for books that carry numerous halftones.

In addition to these basic papers the designer should familiarize himself with the special papers, including kraft, available for end sheets.

Doubleday once brought out a book, *The Sleeping Partner,* in a great variety of papers, a different one for each 32-page signature, causing William Jovanovich, president of Harcourt, Brace & World (now Harcourt Brace Jovanovich), to remark: "This is, no doubt, a way to clear out one's inventory in the name of Art."

Book page sizes

These days books come in a greater variety of sizes than ever, but the most common trim sizes still are 5 3/8 × 8, 5 1/2 × 8 1/4, and 6 1/8 × 9 1/4. Mass paperbacks come usually in 4 1/8 × 6 3/8 or 4 1/8 × 7 sizes. As in magazine publishing, there is a trend toward the square format, especially for volumes dealing with the fine arts.

As for all printing, the designer should check with his printer on paper sizes available and choose a page size that can be cut with a minimum of waste.

Establishing the margins

It may not seem that way, but the nontype area of a book—the white space—accounts for close to 50 percent of the total area. For art books and highly designed books, white space may account for as much as 75 percent of the total area.

Where he puts this white space counts heavily in the designer's thinking. For his all-type pages, he concentrates white space on the outside edges of his spreads, but not in equal-width bands.

The idea is to arrange the copy on facing pages so that the pages will read as a unit. For the typical book the designer establishes margins that tend to push the copy area of the two pages together. Book margins are like magazine margins. The narrowest margin on each page is at the gutter (but the combined space at the gutter is usually wider than other margins). The margin increases at the top, increases more at the outside edge, and increases most at the bottom. The designer is careful to keep the margin at the gutter wide enough (never less than 5/8 for books in the 6 × 9 range) so that the type does not merge into the gutter when the book is bound. When he runs a headline or title across the gutter, he leaves a little extra space at the gutter to take care of space lost in the binding.

Book typography

Typesetting may be done by one firm, photoengraving by another, printing by another, binding by another. It is the job of the book designer, working with the publisher's production department, to combine the various parts of the book into a unified whole.

By far his most critical decisions will be made over matters of typography. Hot type or cold type? Which faces? Which sizes? How much leading? What about placement and spacing? His decisions on type hinge upon his decisions regarding other production matters.

His showplace pages are the title page and the pages with chapter openings.

The trend is toward a two-page title spread. Why should the left-hand page be blank and the right-hand page be crowded with all the information that makes up a title page? The title, or elements of the title page, cross the gutter to unify the two pages. The effect is dramatic. It seems to say: "This book is important."

Type for the chapter headings usually matches the type for the title pages. The headings seldom go over 18 or 24 points, and often they are smaller. Small-size type displayed with plenty of white space has just as much impact as large-size type that is crowded.

Text type in books ranges from 8 points to 12 points, depending upon the width of the column, the length of the book, the face used (some faces have larger x-heights than others), the amount of leading between lines, and the age level of the reader.

The usual practice is to begin the opening paragraph flush left. Paragraph indentation starts with the second paragraph. The first paragraph is not indented because (1) the flush-left arrangement looks more like a beginning and (2) the chapter title already serves as an arresting agent; an additional arresting agent—indentation—would be redundant. It is often the case that the paragraphs that follow subheads are not indented either.

At one time in book publishing it was popular—for some kinds of books it still is popular—to start first paragraphs of chapters with initial letters. Initial letters are usually larger than the type used for the chapter headings. The type style for the initials and for the headings should be the same.

For nonfiction books, and especially for textbooks, subheads are important. They help the reader organize the material as he reads. They also break up large areas of gray type into convenient takes.

Subheads are best when kept close to the size of the body type. Sometimes they are in bold face, sometimes in all caps, sometimes in italics. They should be accompanied by some extra white space (both above and below) to make them stand out.

The author of a book supplies subheads with his manuscript and usually establishes the level of importance for each. Subheads can occupy up to four levels of importance. The fewer the levels the better.

The designer determines the type size for each level. He often chooses to keep subheads all in the same size type, centering those of the first-level, running the second-level ones flush left, and indenting those of the third-level. The fourth-level ones could go in italics.

Sometimes the designer runs subheads at the side of rather than inside the text.

Book art

In the well-designed book the style of the art complements the style of typography. Boldface types; powerful art. Graceful types; fanciful art.

One style of art that made an impact on book design in the late 1800s and early 1900s was Art Nouveau. It was then as it is now in its revival a revolt against the classical style. Japanese in origin, it is traceable nevertheless to Aubrey Beardsley in England, its most notable exponent. More decorative than functional, Art Nouveau is a style marked more by pattern than outline, although its outline, too, is remarkable in its grace and precision.

An Art Nouveau painter who saw a close relationship between art and typography in books was Maurice Denis. He said: "A book ought to be a work of decoration and not a neutral vehicle for transmitting a text." He added: "For each emotion, each thought, there exists a plastic equivalent and corresponding beauty."[5]

Another art movement that influenced book design was German Expressionism with its rugged woodcut techniques. Such art when used in books invariably called for a heavy sans serif type face.

Impressionism, Surrealism, Pop Art—all the various art movements have had their influence on book illustration. And with today's printing techniques the designer is free to call in ar-

5. Quoted by John Lewis, *The Twentieth Century Book: Its Illustration and Design,* Reinhold Publishing Corporation, New York, 1967, p. 9.

tists who work in any technique or any medium. Still, the predominant art form for books seems to be the line drawing done in the manner of Frederic Remington, Charles Dana Gibson, Howard Pyle, A. B. Frost, E. W. Kemble, and Rockwell Kent. One reason is that such art is the easiest to reproduce under any printing conditions.

In works of nonfiction, the photographer seems to have preempted the assignments from the illustrator, but perhaps not to the same degree as in newspaper and magazine publishing.

To give photographs and illustrations the display they need, the designer either bleeds them or places them next to white space. He does not crowd them up against copy blocks.

Where art occupies all or most of a page, he leaves off the page number and the running heads, because these tend to detract from the art. If he feels the paper used is not opaque enough, he may decide to leave blank the sheet backing the printed art.

As he does in magazine design, the designer of a book usually sets the captions in a face different from the body copy. He lines the captions up with the edges of the pictures or with edges inside the pictures. The pictures and captions should look as if they belong together.

The binding

Books come in four kinds of bindings:

1. *Sewn binding.* For this kind of binding signatures are placed next to each other. They are not nested, as for saddle-stitched magazines. Open up a book and look at the binding from the top or bottom, and you can see how the signatures fit together.

Two kinds of sewing are available: (a) Smythe sewing, in which the sewing is done through the gutter of each signature and then across the back; and (b) side sewing (less common), in which the thread goes through the entire book about 1/8 from the back. A side-sewn book does not lie flat when opened. But the binding is sturdy. Libraries, when they find it necessary to rebind a book, frequently use side sewing.

2. *Stapled binding.* The staples can go in through the spine, if signatures are nested; or they can go in through the side. Such binding is reserved for low-budget books.

3. *Adhesive binding.* Sometimes called "perfect binding," this system brings together loose pages rather than signatures. The binding is accomplished by applying glue across the back. Cheap, mass audience paperbacks use this kind of binding. Unfortunately, the pages have a tendency to separate when subject to constant use.

4. *Mechanical binding.* The most common mechanical bind-

After the Civil War, Howard Pyle became one of America's most influential magazine illustrators. Pyle both wrote and illustrated books. His style was rich, his design carefully controlled. This illustration is from The Wonder Clock, *a book published in 1887.*

ing is *spiral binding,* in which loose pages are held together by a wire that spirals along a series of punched holes. The covers of such a book can be heavy paper, cardboard, or boards covered with paper. Pages can be torn out easily. With some mechanical bindings, new pages can be inserted. Mechanical binding is used for books with short press runs—books written for technical- or practical-minded audiences.

The first three binding processes—the main binding processes—can be used for paperback as well as hardbound books. Most hardbound books, however, come with sewn binding since it permits a book to lie flat when it is opened.

The cover

With the kind of binding decided, the designer of a hardbound book turns his attention to the cover.

The designer must decide whether he wants the boards of the cover to be wrapped fully in cloth, partially in cloth and partially in paper, or fully in paper. If the boards are to be wrapped in cloth, should the cloth be all of the same color and texture? Or should the designer seek a two-tone effect? And what color or colors should he use?

He must further decide whether the cover should be printed by offset or silk screen. Or should it be die stamped?

For many books the cover consists merely of wrapped boards with the name of the book, author, and publisher printed or stamped on the spine. But even that small amount of type should be coordinated with the other elements of the book.

The type used can be printed on the cover material before it is wrapped around the boards, or it can be stamped on afterwards.

For their cover material publishers once used animal skins— vellum or leather—but now they use cloth, vinyl, or paper. Cloth gained popularity as book cover material in the latter part of the nineteenth century. The cloth used today is often a cotton impregnated or coated with plastic. Paper became popular during World War II when cloth was scarce. The paper most commonly used is kraft.

The cloth, vinyl, or paper is wrapped around binder's board (found in most textbooks), chip board (found in cheaper books), pasted board (found in most trade books), or red board (found in limp books meant to be carried around in pockets).

To keep the top edges of the book's pages from soiling, the designer may decide to have them stained. He can choose a color that complements the endpapers.

Endpapers in hardbacks serve more of an aesthetic than structural purpose. Their main function is to hide folded cloth and stitching. Endpapers often are nothing more than tan kraft paper, but increasingly they have taken on color and even art.

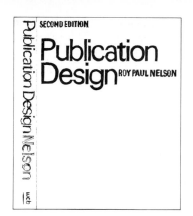
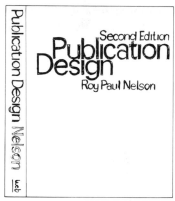
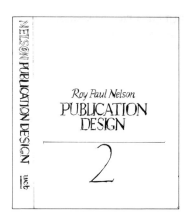

For *sets* of books, hardbound as well as paperback, publishers often supply *slipcases,* which unite and encase the books, leaving only their spines exposed.

The cover for a *paperback* book represents a special challenge to the designer in that it is both a jacket and a cover. Because paperback sales are so dependent on impulse buying, paperback cover art must be particularly compelling. Like the jacket for a hardbound book, the cover for a paperback is as much an exercise in advertising design as in book design. "After all, aren't book covers packages, and isn't packaging a function of advertising?" asks Ian Summers, executive art director of Ballantine Books.

As a book publisher art director, Summers works on 150 titles at a time (Ballantine publishes 400 titles a year). As an advertising art director, by way of contrast, he worked on 10 projects at a time. Summers looks upon book covers as similar to two-page advertising spreads in magazines. But the front cover is the most important part of each design. "We are in the business of making posters that are only four by seven inches tall," Summers says.

While Ballantine tries to be innovative with its covers, some covers never change. People who buy gothic novels, for instance, do not respond to anything but frightened women running from castles. The only way to upgrade such covers is to hire the very best illustrators. "My ability to put the right book together with the right illustrator is probably by most important contribution," Summers declares.

Science fiction offers some of the best possibilities for high-level illustration. You look for super-realism here. "The science fiction fans are probably the only category of readers who really care about the quality of art on their books. They know their artists and consider them heroes."[6]

Three rough layouts submitted by the author/designer to his publisher for consideration as the cover or jacket. The narrow panels at the left represent the spine of the book.

6. Ian Summers, "Selling a Book by its Cover," *Art Direction,* October 1976, pp. 59-62.

Designing the cover for a paperback is not unlike designing the jacket for a hard-cover book. Here are the front cover, back cover, and spine for The Tales of Rabbi Nachman *by Martin Buber (Discus Books, New York: Barbara Bertoli, art director). The publisher evidently feels that the name of the author, "one of the great thinkers of our time," is more important than the name of the book. Note that the designer has arranged his type and illustration on the front cover into a sort of an upside-down L, leaving one big area in white. The type and illustration form one unit. The original is in black, grayed red, and light olive.*

With their heavy-paper covers, paperback books have experimented with various devices to get casual browsers inside. They have used both real and fake embossing on their covers, xographs (three-dimensional pictures), and die-cuts that expose part of the title page. Still, covers are largely a matter of chance. "No scientific principles guide the decisions [at Bantam Books, world's largest paperback publisher]," writes Clarence Petersen in *The Bantam Story.* "Past experience helps, but mostly publishing executives call the shots by a sort of gut reaction. Bantam knows, for instance, that the color red sells books. It is the boldest of the primary colors, which in turn are the boldest of all."[7]

The trouble is, everybody knows this, so many publishers, including Bantam, go to other colors to make their books stand out from the sea of red. Soon all publishers seem to settle in on some other color. In many seasons, white becomes a favorite principal cover color.

Sometimes a publisher puts a book out with different covers to appeal to different buyers. Bantam's *Future Shock* by Alvin Toffler came out with six different covers. One advantage, Bantam discovered, was that some booksellers put all six versions on display, giving the book a big advantage over books from other publishers that had a single cover.

A single paperback book, if it enjoys a long life, may go through several different cover designs before it finally goes out of print.

7. Clarence Peterson, *The Bantam Story*, Bantam Books, New York, 1975, p. 65.

New American Library for its paperback release in 1977 of The Rockefellers *designed the book with two different covers so that two copies of the book put next to each other on display in bookstores would act as a sort of poster, with a book title looming large to catch the browser's attention. ". . . A revolutionary new cover treatment," claimed the publisher's promotion department. The book was written by Peter Collier and David Horowitz.*

The jacket

Jacket design probably is less important to hardcover books than cover design is to paperbacks. For a hardcover book, poorly designed jackets discourage buying but well designed jackets do not necessarily stimulate buying, says Alan Kellock, a sales manager at Harcourt Brace Jovanovich, the book publisher. Still, the jacket is where a book's design starts.

Once he knows for sure how many pages the book will take, the designer asks for a bound dummy, with pages blank, so he can get the feel of the book and so the jacket designer can properly fit the jacket.

Janet Halverson's jacket for Joan Didion's novel about "an emotional drifter" who has played her various roles "to the sound of one hand clapping." In black, magenta, orange, and yellow. (Reprinted by permission of Janet Halverson and Farrar, Straus & Giroux, Inc.)

Books didn't always come with jackets. The introduction of modern distribution methods required that books be protected, and the idea of the "dust" jacket was born. At first the jacket was nothing more than a plain wrapper. It did not become a display piece until after World War I. Then it helped sell the book as well as protect it.

Publishers run off more jackets than are needed to cover their books; they use the extra copies for promotion and as replacements for jackets worn and torn in shipping and handling.

The quality paperbacks of the 1950s with their well-designed covers upgraded the design of jackets for hardbound books. But in 1965 David Dempsey, writing in *Saturday Review,* said the dust jacket was "still a poor relation" in the book publishing industry. He observed that only a small group of design studios did jackets; Paul Bacon, Push Pin Studios, Chammayeff & Geismar, and Janet Halverson among them.

The best-designed jackets, he observed, were to be found on first novels. The jackets for best sellers were less imaginative because they had to carry in large type both the name of the author and the title. That didn't leave much room for experimentation.

The typical jacket features the name of the book and the name of the author on the front; a picture of the author on the back; and a description of the book and biographical information about the author on the inside flaps. The names of the book, author (often last name only), and publisher run from left to right at the top of the spine, if the book is thick enough; if the book is too thin, the names run in a single sideways line, from top to bottom for books published in America, from bottom to top for books published in Great Britain.

A jacket should emphasize a single idea, reflect the mood or character of the book, and lure the reader inside. Sometimes the name of the author is featured most prominently, sometimes the name of the book.

A question of ethics comes in when the designer gives undue play to a popular earlier work of the author, perhaps deceiving the reader into thinking that is the work he is buying. Ethics also become involved when the designer uses an illustration that promises other than what the book actually delivers.

What we are talking about here, really, is advertising. That is what a jacket is: a piece of advertising. For that reason the designer of the book itself often has nothing to do with the design of the jacket. In purpose, it is design of a different order.

For one of his zany books Alexander King once got his publisher to wrap each copy with two jackets, an inner one, staid and conservative, and an outer one featuring one of his somewhat vulgar paintings. Tongue-in-cheek, he invited any reader who was easily offended to dispose of the outside jacket.

Alfred A. Knopf brought out Edward Luttwak's *Coup d'Etat* with jackets in two different color combinations: half the copies had one jacket, half the other. Booksellers were encouraged to make what in effect was a two-tone display of the books to help sell them.

Grove Press, for a novel called *Commander Amanda*, produced three different jackets, all designed by Kuhlman Associates. Sets were sent to booksellers; they were invited to pick the one they wanted on copies they would be selling. This involved booksellers in the book's production and presumably made them more interested in the book.

The designer may find that, except for the author's portrait, he doesn't need art for the jacket. Type alone, artfully arranged, or calligraphy, along with some color bands, perhaps, could do the job.

Most jackets come in black plus a second color. The black is for the author's portrait on the back. To save costs, some publishers run their jackets in a single color on a colored stock.

The paper used is coated or varnished only on the side on which the printing is done. The side next to the book itself is rough-finished so the jacket will cling to the book.

First things first

All of these considerations add to the reader's enjoyment of a book, but they are as nothing compared to the Big Three contributions the designer can make.

1. Picking a paper that does not bounce the light back into the reader's eyes.

2. Picking a typeface big enough so he can read without squinting.

3. Printing the text of the book far enough in from the gutter so he does not have to fight the binding to keep the book open.

A summary

Readers do not buy publications—books, magazines, newspapers, whatever—to admire the versatility of their art directors. They buy publications so that they can be informed; they buy them for guidance; they buy them to relax with.

What they expect—what they must have—are headings and columns of type arranged for effortless assimilation, with large, clear pictures unencumbered by visual scars and typographic clutter.

What art directors must do, then, more than anything else, is make their publications useful to their readers. Design should help readers; it should not get in their way.

This is not to say that art directors should shy away from imaginative approaches. Far from it. It takes imagination—more of it—to truly organize the pages of a publication than merely to decorate them.

For this inside spread in a 16-page, two-color, 8 1/2 × 11 recruitment booklet, designer Jim Bodoh reuses a large photo he had used in an earlier spread. But this time he chops it into squares, and in some of the squares he inserts new, smaller pictures. The reader recognizes the original photo, though; it contains the three large faces and arms and shoulders that connect them. The eye travel starts with the heading at the left and ends with the heading at the right. The College of Education, University of Oregon, is the publisher.

BAILEY, HERBERT S., JR., *The Art and Science of Book Publishing*, Harper & Row, Publishers, New York, 1970.

BALKIN, RICHARD, *A Writer's Guide to Book Publishing*, Hawthorn Books, New York, 1977.

BLAND, DAVID, *A History of Book Illustration*, University of California Press, Berkeley, 1969. (Second Edition.)

DAL, ERIK, *Scandinavian Bookmaking in the Twentieth Century*, University of Illinois Press, Urbana, 1968.

DAY, KENNETH, ed., *Book Typography 1810-1965: In Europe and the United States of America*, University of Chicago Press, Chicago, 1966.

DESSAUER, JOHN P., *Book Publishing: What It Is, What It Does*, R. R. Bowker Co., New York, 1974.

GRANNIS, CHANDLER B., *What Happens in Book Publishing?* Columbia University Press, New York, 1967. (Second Edition.)

GREENFIELD, HOWARD, *Books: From Writer to Reader*, Crown Publishers, New York, 1976.

HANSON, GLENN, *The Now Look in the Yearbook*, National Scholastic Press Association, Minneapolis, Minnesota, 1971.

HARROP, DOROTHY, *Modern Book Production*, Archon Books & Clive Bingley, Hamden, Connecticut, 1968.

HENDERSON, BILL, ed., *The Publish-It-Yourself Handbook: Literary Tradition and How to*, Pushcart Book Press, Box 845, Yonkers, New York 10701, 1973.

JENNETT, SEAN, *The Making of Books*, Faber, London, 1973. (Fifth Edition.)

KLEMIN, DIANA, *The Art of Art for Children's Books*, Clarkson N. Potter, Inc., Publisher, New York, 1966.

———, *The Illustrated Book: Its Art and Craft*, Clarkson N. Potter, Inc., New York, 1970.

LEE, MARSHALL, *Bookmaking: The Illustrated Guide to Design and Production*, R. R. Bowker Company, New York, 1965.

LEE, MARSHALL, ed., *The Trial of 6 Designers: Designs for Kafka's The Trial by George Salter, P. J. Conkwright, Merle Armitage, Carle Zahn, Joseph Blumenthal, Marshall Lee*, Hammermill Paper Company, Lock Haven, Penn, 1968.

LEVARIE, NORMA, *The Art & History of Books*, James H. Heineman, Inc., New York 1968.

LEWIS, JOHN, *The Twentieth Century Book: Its Illustration and Design*, Reinhold Publishing Corporation, New York, 1967.

MADISON, CHARLES A., *Book Publishing in America*, McGraw-Hill Book Company, New York, 1966.

PETERS, JEAN, ed., *The Bookman's Glossary*, R. R. Bowker, New York, 1975. (Fifth Edition.)

SALTER, STEFAN, *From Cover to Cover: The Occasional Papers of a Book Designer*, Prentice-Hall, Englewood Cliffs, New Jersey, 1970.

SMITH, DATUS C., JR., *A Guide to Book-Publishing*, R. R. Bowker Company, New York, 1966.

VANIER, DINOO J., *Market Structure and the Business of Book Publishing*, Pitman Publishing Corp., New York, 1973.

WEIDEMANN, KURT, *Book Jackets & Record Covers: An International Survey*, Frederick A. Praeger, Inc., New York, 1969.

WILLIAMSON, HUGH, *Methods of Book Design*, Oxford University Press, New York, 1966. (Second Edition.)

WILSON, ADRIAN, *The Design of Books*, Reinhold Publishing Corporation, New York, 1967.

WONG, WUCIUS, *Principles of Three-Dimensional Design*, Van Nostrand Reinhold, New York, 1977.

The Business of Publishing, R. R. Bowker, New York, 1976. (An anthology of articles from *Publishers Weekly.)*

Glossary

Terminology in journalism and art varies from publication to publication and from region to region. This glossary gives meanings of terms as the author uses them in this book and in his other writings.

abstract art   simplified art; art reduced to fundamental parts; art that makes its point with great subtlety. Opposite of realistic or representational art.

agate type   5 1/2-point type.

airbrush   tool that uses compressed air to shoot a spray of watercolor pigment on photographs or artwork. Used for retouching.

all caps   all-capital letters.

antique paper   rough finish, high-quality paper.

art   all pictorial matter in a publication: photographs, illustrations, cartoons, charts and graphs, etc.

Art Deco   the look of the 1920s and 1930s: simple line forms, geometric shapes, pastel colors, rainbow motifs.

art director   person in charge of all visual aspects of a publication, including typography.

art editor   see *art director.*

axis   imaginary line used to align visual elements and relate them.

back of the book   section of a magazine following the main articles and stories and consisting of continuations of articles and stories, ads, and filler material.

balance   stability in design; condition in which the various elements on a page or spread are at rest.

bank   see *deck.*

banner   main headline running across the top of a newspaper page.

bar chart   art that shows statistics in bars of various lengths.

Bauhaus   school of design in Germany (1919-1933). It championed a highly ordered, functional style in architecture and applied arts.

Ben Day   process by which engraver or printer adds pattern or tone to a line reproduction.

Bible paper   thin but opaque paper.

binding   that part of a magazine or book that holds the pages together.

bird's-eye view   view from above.

blackletter   close-fitting, bold, angular type that originated in Germany. Also known as *Old English* and *text.*

bleed a picture printed to the edge of a sheet. Use also as a verb.

blind embossing embossing without printing.

blueline see *Vandyke.*

blurb follow-up title for a magazine article, longer than the main title and in smaller type. Also, a title displayed on the cover. Also, copy on a book jacket.

blowup enlargement. *Blow up* when used as a verb.

body copy column or page of type of a relatively small size.

body type type 12 points in size or smaller.

boldface type black type.

bond paper crisp paper used for business stationery, often with rag content.

book bound publication of 48 pages or more, usually with a stiff or heavy cover. Some magazine editors call their publications *books.*

book paper paper other than newsprint used in the printing of books and magazines. Includes many grades and finishes.

box design element composed usually of 4 rules, with type or art inside.

brownline see *Vandyke.*

byline the author's name set in type, usually over the story or article.

calender to polish, as in the making of paper.

calligraphy beautiful handwriting.

camera-ready copy a pasteup ready to be photographed by the platemaker.

Camp art so bad it's good.

caption legend accompanying a photograph; newspapers use *cutlines.*

caricature drawing of a person that exaggerates or distorts his features.

cartoon humorous drawing, done usually in pen or brush and ink, or in washes.

cast off estimate the amount of copy in a book. In magazines, it's *copyfit.*

center fold center spread that opens out for two more pages.

center spread two facing pages at the center of a magazine or newspaper.

character any letter, number, punctuation mark, or space in printed matter.

circulation number of copies sold or distributed.

cliché something used too often, hence boring and no longer effective.

clipbook pages of stock art usually on slick paper, ready for photographing by the platemaker.

clip sheet see *clipbook.*

cold type type composed by typewriter, paper pasteup, or photographic means.

collage piece of art made by pasting various elements together.

colophon paragraph or paragraphs of information about a book's design and typography, carried at the end of the book.

color separation negative made from full-color art for use in making one of the plates.

column section of a book's or magazine's text that runs from top to bottom of the page. Also, regular editorial feature in a newspaper or magazine, usually with a byline.

column inch area that is one column wide by one inch deep.

column rule thin line separating columns of type.

combination cut printing plate made from both a line and halftone negative.

comic strip comic drawing or cartoon that appears in a newspaper on a regular basis as a series of panels.

commercial art   art prepared for editorial or advertising purposes, for any of the media.

comp   short for *comprehensive layout.*

compositor   craftsman who sets type.

comprehensive layout   layout finished to look almost as the printed piece will look.

condensed type   type series with narrow characters.

continuous-tone art   photograph or painting or any piece of art in which tones merge gradually into one another. Requires halftone reproduction.

contrast   quality in design that permits one element to stand out clearly from others.

copy   article, story, or other written material either before or after it is set in type.

copy area   see *type page.*

copyedit   see *copyread.*

copyfit   estimate how much space copy will take when it is set in type.

copyread   check the manuscript to correct errors made by the writer or reporter.

copyright   protection available to the owner of a manuscript, piece of art, or publication, preventing others from making unfair use of it or profiting from it at the expense of the owner.

copywriting   writing copy for advertisements.

cover stock   heavy or thick paper used as covers for magazines or paperback books.

credit line   the photographer's name set in type, usually right next to the photograph.

crop   cut away unwanted areas in a piece of art, usually by putting marks in the margins.

CRT   cathode ray tube. Part of the typical VDT.

cut   art in plate form, ready to print. For the letterpress process.

cutlines   see *caption.*

deck   portion of a headline, consisting of lines set in the same size and style of type.

deckle edge   ragged, feathery edge available in some of the quality paper stocks.

design   organization; plan and arrangement of visual elements. A broader term than *layout.* Use also as a verb.

designer   person who designs pages or spreads.

die-cut   hole or other cutout punched into heavy paper.

direct-mail piece   folder, leaflet, booklet, or other printed item issued on a one-time basis.

display type   type larger than 12-point, used for titles and headlines.

double truck   newspaper terminology for *spread.*

downstyle   style characterized by the use of lowercase letters wherever possible.

drop   see *sink.*

dropout halftone   see *highlight halftone.*

drybrush   rendering in which partially inked brush is pulled across rough-textured paper.

dummy   the pages of a magazine in its planning stage, often unbound, with features and pictures crudely sketched or roughly pasted into place.

duotone   halftone printed in two inks, one dark (usually black), one lighter (any color).

duplicator   machine that reproduces a limited number of copies of a publication. Large press runs require regular printing presses.

dust jacket   see *jacket.*

ear   paragraph, line, or box on either side of a newspaper's nameplate.

edit   change, manage, or supervise for publication. Also, as a noun, short for *editorial.*

editing   the process by which manuscripts and art are procured and made ready for publication.

edition   part of the press run for a particular *issue* of a publication.

editorial   short essay, usually unsigned, stating the stand of the publication on some current event or issue. Also used to designate the non-business side of a publication.

editorial cartoon   single-panel cartoon of opinion found on the editorial page of a newspaper.

element   copy, title or headline, art, rule or box, border, spot of color— anything to be printed on a page or spread.

em   width of capital M in any typesize.

emboss   print an image on paper and stamp it, too, so that it rises above the surface of the paper.

en   width of capital N in any typesize.

endpapers   sheets that help connect the inside front and back covers to the book proper.

English finish   smooth finish. English-finish papers are widely used by magazines.

expanded type   type series with wider-than-normal characters.

face   style or variation of type.

family   subdivision of a type race.

feature   any story, article, editorial, column, or work of art in a publication. Also used as a verb: play up.

filler   short paragraph or story used to fill a hole at the bottom of a column of type.

fine art   art created primarily for aesthetic rather than commercial purposes.

fixative   clear solution sprayed onto a drawing to keep it from smearing.

flag   see *logo.*

flash forms   signatures of four, eight, or more pages held out by the editor until the last minute. Often they are printed on different paper stock from what is used in the remainder of the magazine.

flat color   see *spot color.*

FlexForm ad   newspaper ad in other than the usual square or rectangle shape.

flop   change the facing of a picture. If a subject faces left in the original, he will face right in the printed version. Not a synonym for *reverse.*

flow chart   art showing a manufacturing process.

flush-left   aligned at the left-hand margin.

flush-left- and-right   aligned at both the left- and right-hand margins.

flush-right   aligned at the right-hand margin.

folio   page number. Also, a sheet of paper folded once.

font   complete set of type of a particular face and size.

foreshorten   exaggerate the perspective.

format   size, shape, and appearance of a publication.

formula   editorial mix of a publication.

foundry type   hand-set metal type.

fourth cover   back cover of a magazine.

four-color   .red, yellow, blue, and black used to produce effect of full color.

freelancer   artist, photographer, designer, or writer called in to do an occasional job for a publication.

gag cartoon   humorous drawing, usually in a single panel, with caption, if there is one, set in type below.

galley   tray on which type is assembled and proofed.

galley proof   long sheet of paper containing a first printing from a tray of type.

gatefold   magazine cover that opens out to two additional pages.

gingerbread design   design with an overabundance of swirls and flourishes; cluttered design.

glossy print   photograph with shiny finish.

gothic   term applied in the past to various typefaces that have challenged the traditional. Currently, modern sans serifs.

graphic design   design of printed material.

graph   see *bar chart, line chart,* and *pie chart.* Also, short for *paragraph.*

gravure   method of printing from incised plate. For magazines, a rotary press is involved, hence *rotogravure.*

grid   carefully spaced vertical and horizontal lines that define areas in a layout; a plan for designing pages.

gutter   separation of two facing pages.

hairline   very thin rule or line.

halftone reproduction   process by which the printer gets the effect of continuous tone, as when he reproduces a photograph. It's done with dots.

hand lettering   lettering done with pen or brush.

head   short for *headline.*

headband   piece of rolled, striped cloth used at the top of the binding to give a finished look to the book.

heading   headline or title. Also, the standing title for a regular column or section in a publication.

headline   display type over a story, article, or editorial in a newspaper.

headline schedule   chart of different headline sizes and arrangements used by a newspaper.

hed   short for *head,* which is short for *heading* or *headline.* Mostly a newspaper term.

high Camp   see *Camp.*

highlight halftone   halftone in which some parts have been dropped out to show the white of the paper.

horizontal look   lines of type, rules, and art are arranged to make the page or spread look wide rather than deep.

hot type   type made from metal.

house ad   advertisement promoting the publication in which it appears.

house organ   publication of an organization or business released regularly for public relations reasons.

house style   style that is peculiar to a publisher or that remains the same from issue to issue or publication to publication.

illustration   drawing or painting.

illustration board   cardboard or heavy paperboard made for artists, available in various weights and finishes to take various art mediums.

incunabula   books printed before 1501.

index   alphabetical listing of important words and names in a book or magazine, accompanied by page numbers. Found in the back of the publication. The table of contents is found in the front.

India ink   drawing ink.

India paper   see *Bible paper.*

initial first letter of a word at the beginning of an article or paragraph, set in display size to make it stand out.

intaglio see *gravure.*

interabang combination exclamation mark and question mark.

Intertype linecasting machine similar to Linotype.

issue all copies of a publication for a particular date. An issue may consist of several *editions.*

italic type type that slants to the right.

jacket paper cover that wraps around a book.

jump continue on another page.

justify align the type so it forms an even line on the right and the left.

keyline drawing drawing done partly in outline to use in making plates for spot color printing.

kicker short headline run above main headline, often underscored.

kraft paper heavy, rough, tough paper, usually tan in color.

lay out put visual elements into a pleasing and readable arrangement.

layout noun form of *lay out.*

lead (pronounced *ledd*) put extra space between lines of type.

leading extra space between lines of type.

legibility quality in type that makes it easy for the reader to recognize individual letters.

letterpress method of printing from a raised surface. The original and still widely used printing process.

letterspace put extra space between letters.

letterspacing extra space between letters.

libel published defamatory statement or art that injures a person's reputation.

ligature two or more characters on a single piece of type that join or overlap.

line art in its original form, art without continuous tone, done in black ink on white paper. Also, such art after it is reproduced through *line reproduction.*

linecasting machine see *Linotype* and *Intertype.*

line chart art that shows trends in statistics through a line that rises or falls on a grid.

line conversion continuous-tone art that has been changed to line art.

line reproduction process by which printer reproduces black-and-white drawing.

Linotype linecasting machine that produces type for letterpress printing or type from which reproduction proofs can be pulled.

lithography process of making prints from grease drawing on stone. See also *offset lithography.*

logo short for *logotype.* The name of the publication as run on the cover and sometimes on the title or editorial page. On a newspaper it is called the *flag* or *nameplate.*

lowercase small letters (as opposed to capital letters).

Ludlow machine that casts lines of display-size letters from matrices that have been assembled by hand.

magapaper magazine with a newspaper format. Or newspaper with a magazine format.

magazine publication of eight pages or more, usually bound, that is issued at least twice a year. Also, storage unit for mats for linecasting machine.

mass media units of communication: newspapers, magazines, television and radio stations, books, etc.

masthead paragraph of information about the publication. It is run on an inside page, under the table of contents, for a magazine, and on the editorial page for a newspaper.

mat   short for *matrix*. Cardboard mold of plate, from which a copy can be made. Also, brass mold from which type can be cast.

matrix   see *mat*.

matte finish   dull finish.

measure   width of a line or column of type.

mechanical   see *camera-ready copy*.

mechanical spacing   non-adjusted spacing between letters; the opposite of *optical spacing*.

media   see *mass media*.

medium   singular for *media*. Also, paint, ink, or marking substance used in drawing or painting. In this context, the plural of medium is *mediums*.

modular design   highly ordered design, marked by regularity in spacing.

moire   undesirable wavy or checkered pattern resulting when a halftone print is photographed through another screen.

Monotype   composing machine that casts individual letters. Used for quality composition.

montage   combination of photographs or drawings into a single unit.

mortise   a cut made into a picture to make room for type or another picture. Use also as a verb.

mug shot   portrait.

Multilith   duplicating or printing process similar to offset lithography, but on a small scale.

nameplate   see *logo*.

"new journalism"   journalism characterized by a highly personal, subjective style.

news hole   non-advertising space in a newspaper.

newsprint   low-quality paper lacking permanence, used for printing newspapers.

OCR   optical character reader. It converts typewritten material to electronic impulses and transmits them to a tape punch or computer. It is also called a "scanner."

offset lithography   method of printing from flat surface, based on principle that grease and water don't mix. Commercial adaptation of *lithography*.

offset paper   book paper made especially for offset presses.

Old English   see *blackletter*.

one-shot   magazine-like publication issued only once. Deals with some area of special interest.

Op Art   geometric art that capitalizes on optical illusions.

op-ed   short for "opposite the editorial page." The page across from the editorial page.

optical center   a point slightly above and to the left of the geometric center.

optical spacing   spacing in typesetting that takes into account the peculiarities of the letters, resulting in a more even look.

optical weight   the visual impact a given element makes on the reader.

organization chart   art that shows how various people or departments relate to each other.

overlay   sheet of transparent plastic placed over a drawing. The overlay contains art or type of its own for a plate that will be coordinated with the original plate.

page   one side of a sheet of paper.

page proof   proof of a page to be printed letterpress.

paginate   to number pages.

painting illustration made with oil, acrylic, tempera, casein, or water color paints. Requires halftone reproduction; if color is to be retained, it requires process color plates.

paper stock paper.

pastel colors soft, weak colors.

pastel drawing drawing made with color chalks.

pasteup see *camera-ready copy.*

paste up verb form for *pasteup.*

pencil drawing drawing made with lead or graphite pencil. Usually requires halftone reproduction.

perspective quality in a photograph or illustration that creates the illusion of distance.

photo essay series of photographs that make a single point.

photocomposition composition produced by photographic means.

photoengraving cut or plate made for letterpress printing.

photojournalism photography used in the mass media to report news, express opinion, or entertain.

photolettering display type produced photographically.

pic short for *picture.*

pica 12 points, or one-sixth of an inch.

pictograph a chart or graph in picture form.

picture photograph, drawing, or painting.

pie chart art that shows statistics—usually percentages—as wedges in a pie or circle.

pix plural for *pic.*

plate piece of metal from which printing is done. See also *cut.*

PMT photo-mechanical transfer. Duplicate print of the original line art.

point unit of measurement for type; there are 72 points to an inch.

Pop Art fine art inspired by comic strips and packages. See also *Camp.*

Pre-print ad in a sort of wallpaper design printed in rotogravure in another plant for insertion in a letterpress newspaper.

press run total number of copies printed during one printing.

printer craftsman who makes up the forms or operates the presses.

printing the act of duplicating pages and arranging or binding them into copies of publications.

process color the effect of full color achieved through use of color separation plates; way to reproduce color photographs, paintings, and transparencies.

production process that readies manuscripts and art for the printer. Can also include the typesetting and printing.

proofread check galley and page proofs against the original copy to correct any mistakes the compositor made.

proportion size relationship of one part of the design to the other parts.

psychedelic art highly decorative art characterized by blobs of improbable colors, swirls, and contorted type and lettering.

publication product of the printing press.

publishing act of producing literature and journalism and making them available to the public.

race major category of typefaces.

ragged left aligned at the right but staggered at the left.

ragged right aligned at the left but staggered at the right.

readability quality in type that makes it easy for the reader to move easily from word to word and line to line. In a broader sense, it is the quality in writing and design that makes it easy for the reader to understand the journalist.

readership   number of readers of a publication. Larger than the *circulation*.

ream   500 sheets of printing paper.

register   condition in printing in which various printing plates, properly adjusted, print exactly where they are supposed to print. Use also as a verb.

relief   raised printing surface.

render   execute, as in making a drawing.

repro   short for *reproduction proof*.

reproduction   a copy.

reproduction proof   a carefully printed proof made from a galley, ready to paste down so it can be photographed.

retouch   strengthen or change a photograph or negative through use of art techniques.

reverse   white letters in a gray, black, or color area. Opposite of *surprint*. Mistakenly used for *flop*. Use also as a verb.

roman type   type designed with thick and thin strokes and serifs. Some printers refer to any type that is standing upright (as opposed to type that slants) as "roman."

rotogravure   see *gravure*.

rough   in cartooning, the first crude sketch presented to an editor to convey the gag or editorial idea.

rough layout   crude sketch, showing where type and art are to go.

rout   cut away.

rule   thin line used either horizontally or vertically to separate lines of display type or columns of copy.

run-in   let the words follow naturally, in paragraph form.

running head   heading that repeats itself, page after page.

saddle stitch   binding made through the spine of a collection of nested signatures.

sans serif type   typeface with strokes of equal or near-equal thicknesses and without serifs.

scale   quality in a photograph or illustration that shows size relationships.

schlock   vulgar, heavy, tasteless.

scratchboard drawing   drawing made by scratching knife across a previously inked surface.

script   type that looks like handwriting.

screen   the concentration of dots used in the halftone process. The more dots, the finer the screen.

second color   one color in addition to black or the basic color.

second cover   inside front cover.

sequence   series of related elements or pages arranged in logical order.

series   subdivision of a type family.

serif   small finishing stroke of a roman letter found at its terminals.

set solid   set type without leading.

shelter magazine   magazine that deals with the home and its surroundings.

sidebar   short story related to major story and run nearby.

side stitch   stitch through side of publication while it is in closed position.

signature   all the pages printed on both sides of a single sheet. The sheet is folded down to page size and trimmed. Signatures usually come in multiples of 16 pages. A magazine or book is usually made up of several signatures.

silhouette   art subject with background removed.

sink   distance from top of page to where chapter begins.

sinkage   see *sink*.

slab serif type   type designed with even-thickness strokes and heavy serifs. Sometimes called "square serif" type.

slick magazine   magazine printed on slick or glossy paper. Sometimes called simply "slick."

slug   line of type from linecasting machine. Also, 6-point spacing material.

slug line   significant word or phrase that identifies story. Found usually on galley proofs.

small caps   short for *small capitals*. Capital letters smaller than regular capital letters in that point size.

sort   what a printer calls a piece of type.

SpectaColor   ad printed in rotogravure in another plant for later insertion in a newspaper. Unlike a Pre-print ad, a SpectaColor ad has clearly defined margins.

spine   back cover of a book or magazine, where front and back covers join.

spot color   solid color used usually for accent. Less expensive, less involved than *process color.*

spot illustration   drawing that stands by itself, unrelated to the text, used as a filler or for decorative purposes.

spread   facing pages in a magazine.

stereotype   plate made from mat that in turn was made from photoengraving or type.

stock   paper or other material on which image is printed.

stock art   art created for general use and stored until ordered for a particular job.

straight matter   text that is uninterrupted by headings, tables, etc.

style   distinct and consistent approach to art or design.

subhead   short headline inside article or story. Also *subhed.*

surprint   black letters over gray area, as over a photograph. Opposite of *reverse.* Use also as verb.

swash caps   capital letters in some typefaces with extra flourishes in their strokes, usually in the italic versions.

swatch   color sample.

swipe file   artist's or designer's library of examples done by other artists, used for inspiration.

Swiss design   design characterized by clean, simple lines and shapes, highly ordered, with lots of white space; based on a grid system.

symmetric balance   balance achieved by equal weights and matching placement on either side of an imaginary center line.

table   list of names, titles, etc.

tabloid   newspaper with pages half the usual size.

tailband   piece of rolled, striped cloth used at the bottom of the binding to give a finished look to the book.

technique   way of achieving style or effect.

text   see *body copy.*

text type   see *blackletter.*

third cover   inside back cover.

thumbnail   very rough sketch in miniature.

tint   weaker version of tone or color.

tint block   panel of color or tone in which something else may be printed.

title   what goes over a story or article in a magazine. On a newspaper, the term is *headline.*

tombstone heads   same size and style headlines, side by side.

tone   the darkness of the art or type.

trade magazine   magazine published for persons in a trade, business, or profession.

transparency   in photography, a color positive on film rather than paper.

type   printed letters and characters. Also, the metal pieces from which the printing is done.

typeface   particular style or design of type.

type page   that part of the page in which type is printed, inside the margins. Sometimes called "copy area."

type specimens   samples of various typefaces available.

typo   typographic error made by the compositor.

typography   the type in a publication. Also, the art of designing and using type.

unity   design principle that holds that all elements should be related.

upper case   capital letters.

Vandyke   photographic proof from a negative of a page to be printed by the offset process. Sometimes called *brownline* or *blueline*.

VDT   video display terminal. It has a keyboard with a TV-like screen above. Stories can be set and corrected on VDTs.

Velox   photoprint with halftone dot pattern in place of continuous tone, ready for line reproduction.

vignette   oval-shaped halftone in which background fades away gradually all around.

visual   having to do with the eye.

visualization   the process by which an artist or designer changes an idea or concept into visual or pictorial form.

wash drawing   ink drawing shaded with black-and-white water color. Requires halftone reproduction.

white space   space on a page not occupied by type, pictures, or other elements.

widow   line of type less than the full width of the column.

woodcut   engraving cut in wood. Also, the impression made by such a plate.

worm's-eye view   view from low vantage point.

x-height   height of lowercase *x* in any typeface.

Zipatone   transparent sheet on which is printed a pattern of dots or lines. Fastened over part of line drawing, it gives the illusion of tone. See also *Ben Day*.

Index